Small Worlds

School for Advanced Research
Advanced Seminar Series

James F. Brooks
General Editor

Small Worlds

Contributors

Mary C. Beaudry
Department of Archaeology, Boston University

Kathleen Blee
Department of Sociology, University of Pittsburgh

James F. Brooks
School for Advanced Research on the Human Experience

Christopher R. N. DeCorse
Department of Anthropology, Syracuse University

Paul K. Eiss
Department of History, Carnegie Mellon University

Rebecca Jean Emigh
Department of Sociology, University of California, Los Angeles

Linda Gordon
Department of History, New York University

Michael Harkin
Department of Anthropology, University of Wyoming

Kent G. Lightfoot
Department of Anthropology, University of California, Berkeley

Richard Maddox
Department of History, Carnegie Mellon University

Dale Tomich
Departments of Sociology and History, Binghamton University

John Walton
Department of Sociology, University of California, Davis

Small Worlds

Method, Meaning, and Narrative in Microhistory

*Edited by James F. Brooks, Christopher R. N. DeCorse,
and John Walton*

School for Advanced Research Press
Santa Fe

School for Advanced Research Press
Post Office Box 2188
Santa Fe, New Mexico 87504-2188
www.sarpress.sarweb.org

Co-Director and Editor: Catherine Cocks
Manuscript Editor: Margaret J. Goldstein
Design and Production: Cynthia Dyer
Proofreader: Sarah Soliz
Indexer: Catherine Fox
Printer: Thomson Shore, Inc.

Library of Congress Cataloging-in-Publication Data

Small worlds : method, meaning, and narrative in microhistory / edited by James F. Brooks,
Christopher R. N. DeCorse, and John Walton. – 1st ed.
    p. cm. – (School for advanced research advanced seminar series)
  Includes bibliographical references and index.
  ISBN 978-1-930618-94-7 (pa : alk. paper)
  1. Anthropology—Miscellanea. 2. History—Miscellanea. 3. Methodology.
I. Brooks, James, 1955- II. DeCorse, Christopher R. III. Walton, John, 1937-

GN345.S565 2008
301–dc22

                            2007045247

 This book was printed on 30% PCR paper.

Cover illustration: Globe cluster © 2007 Giray, from Mondolibrary.

Contents

Figures

Tables

Small Worlds

1

Introduction

John Walton, James F. Brooks,
and Christopher R. N. DeCorse

> A species of hope resides in the possibility of seeing one thing, one
> phenomenon or essence, so clearly and fully that the light of its
> understanding illuminates the rest of life.
>
> —*William DeBuys*, The Walk, *2007*

The idea that intense reflection on a single event, place, or life might
yield insights across scales of space and time is hardly new. From William
Blake's notion that one might "see a world in a grain of sand" to Nabokov's
hapless Timofey Pnin's belief that a small history could be written of "customs, curiosities, literary anecdotes" so as "to reflect, in miniature, la Grande
Histoire," writers have sought to wed the richness of close detail to the comprehension of more distant significance.

In *War and Peace*, Leo Tolstoy argued that history is made not by the
deeds of great men and women but by the ensemble of collective actions
of all those involved in events. Speaking of the epic Battle of Borodino,
which turned the tide against the French army, Tolstoy observed that "it was
not Napoleon who ordained the course of the battle, for no part of his plan
was executed and during the engagement he did not know what was going
on before him. Therefore the way in which these men slaughtered one
another was not decided by Napoleon's will but occurred independently of
him, in accord with the will of the hundreds of thousands of individuals
who took part in the common action." Drawing a lesson from these events
of early-nineteenth-century Russia, Tolstoy concluded, "to elicit the laws
of history we must leave aside kings, ministers and generals, and select for

study the homogeneous, infinitesimal elements which influence the masses." Although the neglect of kings may appear to contradict the instruction to study all of history's actors, Tolstoy puts it as a matter of priority, given that previously historians had devoted only "one-millionth" of their attention to the actions of ordinary people. The story of Borodino, a turning point in the affairs of nations, links Napoleon, the head cold he suffered on the day of the great battle, the devastated Russian countryside, and the coming winter to the lives of the foot soldiers who fought the war. Customs, curiosities, and literary anecdotes—extraneous intimacies to most historians—found full and terrible convergence with the epic sweep of "big history" on September 7, 1812.

Tolstoy's reflections on the nature of history in the 1860s resonate with thinking now current in the historical social sciences. Growing dissatisfaction with global perspectives and meta-narratives has led to renewed interest in event, biography, and local vantage and the research genre known, somewhat ungracefully, as microhistory. Indeed, Carlo Ginzburg's exemplary book *The Cheese and the Worms* is a microhistorical study of the heresy trial of a sixteenth-century miller. It drew its impetus, Ginzburg says, "from *War and Peace*, from Tolstoy's conviction that a historical phenomenon can become comprehensible only by reconstructing the activities of all of the people who participated in it" (Ginzburg 1993:24).

The term *microhistory* appeared in European historical writing during the 1970s, although it had appeared as a self-defined term in varied contexts somewhat earlier (see Ginzburg 1993:10–13). As the term gained currency in the following decade, *microhistory* came to refer to a particular style of work rather than any codified method, a practice rather than a doctrine. Exponents of this new style shared disenchantment with grand theories of modernization, whether liberal or Marxist. Diverse practitioners of the emerging school urged a return to narrative, detailed analysis on a small scale, and the search for unforeseen meanings embedded in cases: "The unifying principle of all microhistorical research is the belief that microscopic observation will reveal factors previously unobserved" (Levi 2001: 101). In this sense, microhistory underscores the need for local perspective in understanding global patterns and wider narratives, as well as offering unique insights into phenomena and patterns that may lie outside of macrohistorical narratives or flatly contradict them.

Yet microhistory eludes formal definition. It is less a method than an orientation, sensibility, and aesthetic—an "exploratory stance" in the words of Richard Maddox (this volume). It finds adherents across the social sciences and humanities, including historians, sociologists, ethnographers, and archaeologists. Exemplary works best characterize microhistory deno-tatively. Emmanuel Le Roy Ladurie's *Carnival in Romans* (1979) describes the 1580 rebellion of a French village, whose hopes and sorrows fore-shadow revolutions still two hundred years away. E. P. Thompson's *Whigs and Hunters* (1975) interprets conflicts over poaching and common rights in England's royal game parks as key to understanding new practices of state-building. Natalie Zemon Davis's *The Return of Martin Guerre* (1983) builds from a family, a husband imposter, and a celebrated trial to ques-tions of identity, gender, and law in early modern France; her recent *Trickster Travels: A Sixteenth-Century Muslim between Worlds* (2006) extends its reach to a biography that illuminates the vast Mediterranean itself. Examples can be multiplied; microhistory is the strategy employed in stud-ies ranging from Junker estates of Brandenburg (Hagen 2002) and peasant villages in Mexico (González 1974) to biography written through the inter-disciplinary lens of the documentary record and archaeological past (Beaudry, this volume). The essential feature of this perspective is a search for meaning in the microcosm, the large lessons discovered in small worlds. Roger Chartier (1982:32) observes that "it is on the reduced scale, and probably only on this scale, that we can understand without deterministic reduction, the relationships between systems of belief, of values and of rep-resentations on one side and social affiliations on the other."

Appeals for grounded and eventful history risk descending into trivia or nostalgia. To confront this pitfall, microhistory claims, explicitly or implic-itly, to illuminate more general truths, wider patterns, or at least to draw some analogy to other cases. In the best of circumstances, microhistorical studies reveal in fine-grained detail how larger processes operate, how the case serves as a useful hypothesis for exploring other cases. The micro-historical place, event, or personage may function—to borrow Clifford Geertz's recent simile—"like a magnetic field passed through iron filings" to arrange and chart seemingly random scatters of historical debris (2006:23). We understand, for example, what the Hanoverian state in eighteenth-century England (and by extension the emergent modern state) was all about by discovering what its royal game parks were for and why village hunters and sod cutters where accused (but seldom convicted) of capital crimes for exercising their traditional common rights to the forest. The challenge lies in relating the microhistorical case to macrosocial factors, however the latter are conceived in a given inquiry (for example, as state-building, social movement, demographic change, environmental con-straint, or economic hegemony)—how to relate the local and the global. As Burke (2001:116–17) underscores, "If this question is not taken seriously, microhistory might become a kind of escapism, an acceptance of a fragmented world rather than an attempt to make sense of it."

Levi (2001:99) posits that "microhistory as a practice is essentially based on the reduction of the scale of observation, on a microscopic analysis and an intensive study of the documentary material." Yet this idea introduces an ambiguity of scale. *Small* and *large, micro* and *macro* are comparative terms that have meaning only in relation to one another. A village is micro if analyzed in relation to the state but macro if employed as the setting for a study of households. But the ambiguity can be turned to an advantage. Matti Peltonen (2001:348) argues that microhistory deals with levels and relations of social reality and especially the *intersection* of the micro and macro in a given case. Illustratively, the cultural knowledge that informs the small world of Ginzberg's miller intersects with the social control of the church and its Inquisition trials. Efforts to enforce (macro) church discipline reveal surprising (micro) levels of literacy and beliefs about the cosmos that flourish in peasant society. It is in these intersections that empirical discovery takes place. The link between micro and macro perspectives is not simply reduction or aggregation but rather qualitative and the source of new information (Peltonen 2001:357).

The preceding concerns frame this volume. These are twelve experiments in ways of using the detailed case to pursue fresh insights and innovative research maneuvers. The contributions are original interdisciplinary works that encourage interpretive stretch and comparative thinking about how social scientists and humanists of varied experience are engaged in writing history. The scholars represented are anthropologists, archaeologists, historians, and sociologists—although many of the contributors can be comfortably placed in more than one discipline. As the chapter titles suggest, their research examines a wide variety of subjects, time periods, and geographical settings. The authors share some temporal and geographic foci broadly framed by the era of the Atlantic world, concentrating on case studies from Europe and the Americas, although ranging in focus from fifteenth-century West Africa to twenty-first-century Yucatán. They are united through perspectives that examine wider patterns, through case studies that are local and particularistic: events, lives, and locations. A recurring theme is the construction of social history from below, the small ways in which ordinary people affect the world. The authors are scrupulous about detail, the interpretive significance of small clues otherwise overlooked, and, through them, discoveries with broader implications.

From that point on, however, the contributions diverge in many ways, as our subtitle is intended to suggest. They differ in method, language, epistemology, and disciplinary vantage. These differences are sometimes pragmatic and negotiable. At other times, they are firmly held convictions that are a source of deep epistemological division. The tensions, as well as the complementarities, that run through these contributions and emerge through their comparison are instructive. We draw out both for the reader to evaluate.

The collection is divided into two parts. Part 1 introduces varied perspectives of microhistory, including different approaches to methodology, data, and vantage, as well as the disciplinary tensions represented. These chapters are not disciplinary overviews or theoretical reflections but are case studies that serve to illustrate the seminar's diversity. They range from biography to social history, from essays on conventions of time and space to archaeological perspectives on European expansion. The case studies in part 2 further explore these issues, illustrating lenses of changing scales, progressing from event and biography to settlement and landscape. Their differing orientations are not solely about scale but also involve explorations of method, data, and epistemology.

Richard Maddox opens the discussion in part 1 with the uses of biography to take "microsteps toward a counterhistory" of Spain since the 1930s, tacking between macro- and microhistorical perspectives to investigate counterhistories and hegemonic processes. Much is written in Spain and elsewhere about the grand transition from dictatorship to democracy, with the implication that such changes are hegemonic in scope and reflected in individual lives. Maddox's story of one man, ordinary in some respects and extraordinary in others, not only belies this understanding of macrohistory but also compels reconsideration of distinctions between great and small events—much as Tolstoy proposed. Maddox comes at biography from below, from the vantage of a man who lived through the Spanish Civil War and Franco's dictatorship. Juan Vargas became a key informant in Maddox's ethnography of Aracena, a small town in Andalusia. Juan's career reveals shifting motives for his initial support for and later opposition to Franco, as well as to subsequent hegemonies of church and state. Maddox's examination of the tensions between macro and micro perspectives usefully frames the issues confronted in the following chapters.

Kathleen Blee examines similar tensions in a contemporary setting by studying the microhistory of collective action in its formative stages: how ordinary people and contingent acts shape—and reshape—the course of events often seen in retrospect as structurally determined social movements. Her study of an incipient social movement in Pittsburgh reveals how, in the case of a group battling neighborhood drug use, social movements emerge and transform their aims and constituents. Methodologically, Blee draws on observational data over twenty-four months, documentary sources, and oral histories of principal participants. This approach affords a way to scrutinize the "dynamics of social life," to understand their genesis in terms of earlier actions, and to understand the constraints and margins of possibility through which they emerge. Microhistory is modified and extended as a way of understanding context, recovering lived experience, and restoring it to a central place in historical explanation.

Paul Eiss offers a different kind of microhistory, in which the writing itself is part of a historical process connecting the author and events of the past as they continue to unfold. He examines a 1913 peasant uprising in Yucatán that was ultimately suppressed, but not before rebels left their message of liberation carved on a piece of wood, its text transmitted in successive later writings up to this volume. Like Maddox, Eiss tells a piquant story of resistance to domination—a story in which, ironically, the voice of the rebels outlives what once appeared to be one of history's great victories. In his telling, Eiss questions the positionality of the researcher and the potential for opening a space of encounter between historical actors and historians, as well as between historians of radically different backgrounds. Microhistory can be a political act.

Part 1 closes with a contribution by Christopher DeCorse that examines the tensions between interpretations drawn from documentary sources, oral traditions, and the archaeological record, each frame emerging through the examination of small and fragmentary pieces of evidence to build an interpretation that relates to broader histories and processes. DeCorse's excavations in coastal Ghana and the African trade entrepôt of Elmina is his entrée into examination of African–European interactions between the fifteenth and nineteenth centuries. DeCorse examines how the inconsistencies between material culture and the documentary record reveal a more complete historical account of the African settlement and the emergence of Elmina as a sociopolitical entity.

Part 2 opens with works that are seemingly narrow in scale, beginning with the event and individual and moving on to place, setting, and landscape. Ultimately, however, these case studies illustrate that whether the lens is an event, individual, or landscape, it can open onto much wider vistas. While playing off differences in scale, the papers also play off each other, intersecting in varied ways in the uses of data, method, and interpretation. John Walton's study of arson in two nineteenth-century California frontier communities builds on the social history of rural revolt in England but goes on to argue that comparative microhistory reveals new and contrasting phenomena. In one case, arson took the form of social protest against racism, but in another instance, it served the ends of popular justice, a form of social control on a lawless frontier. Walton shows how acts of arson expressed a style of popular justice in frontier communities, sometimes as a method of social control in the absence of law and sometimes as protest.

Michael Harkin's study of the lost colony at Roanoke Island urges a bold move for microhistory, previously confined by narrow conceptions of the "unities" of time and space. He argues for wide-ranging, imaginative, indeed playful comparisons across conventional boundaries—"shifting frames" that move from the Western Apache landscape to prewar Paris, from 9/11 to sixteenth-century Virginia. These varied contexts open new interpretations, a means of searching for multiple endings.

Linda Gordon's chapter on Great Depression–era photographer Dorothea Lange employs "biography as microhistory" in a demonstration of how one woman's life and art afford insight into New Deal political culture. Dorothea Lange and her husband, economist Paul Taylor, are legendary figures in the farmworkers' struggle, and their lives connect many threads in U.S. culture and society. Gordon's biography depends upon the technique and detail of Lange's images. Her study of Lange opens a window on the popular-front movement in the arts, the relationship between government (Lange's Farm Security Administration employer) and the arts, technical developments in photography, the industrialization of agriculture, and gender politics of the prewar era.

Like DeCorse and Lightfoot (see below), Mary Beaudry works at the intersection of written texts and the archaeological record as a means of examining the past. However, Beaudry's entrée into history is through anthropological biography. Her study of the homesite of two New England merchants uses artifacts and documentary sources to trace family lifestyles and changing fortunes across the late eighteenth century and the early republic; these are "archaeological biographies" derived from colonial history and material culture. Neither of these men were "famous" Americans, yet study of their lives emerges as more than particularistic narrative. Like Maddox, Beaudry views individual lives not as "small" elements of history but as the ultimate measure of history's consequences. Beaudry uses her study to examine the varied nature of historical and archaeological research and to revisit the constraints and opportunities afforded by reliance on different categories of data.

Emphasis on the view from below and individual agency animates Rebecca Jean Emigh's study of fifteenth-century Tuscan peasants and how their tax records illuminate local economy and society. Emigh argues that fifteenth-century Italian peasants developed an acute sense of working with figures—numeracy skills, if not conventional literacy, that made possible the creation of tax and accounting systems developed by emerging states. By aggregating microhistorical analyses of different forms of taxation, Emigh reveals the coherence of peasant economies.

In his contribution, Dale Tomich illustrates how microhistory finds fresh application in the study of Cuban sugar plantations and how intellectuals greeted the dramatic nineteenth-century industrialization of Cuba's countryside. Like Gordon, Tomich gleans insight into sweeping economic and cultural changes through examination of visual and textual records, in this case lithographs of sugar plantations created by French artist and lithographer Eduardo Laplante, superbly reproduced in *Los Ingenios* (1857), with text by Justo Cantero. *Los Ingenios* was a testimonial to the technological achievements of the Cuban sugar industry and the march of progress. Tomich interrogates Laplante's depictions and Cantero's descriptions of the mills to uncover clues to cultural attitudes toward nature, landscape, and industrialization. Although Cantero's use of the term *picturesque* in describing the mills seems at variance with Laplante's industrialized landscapes, Tomich's examination reveals a view of an idealized if transformed nature, and through it clues to locally configured Cuban identity.

James F. Brooks shares Harkin's relish for provocative comparison in his study of the nineteenth-century Argentine frontier and the hybrid Indian and creole societies whose intersection shaped the modern state. A sensitive reading of the contingencies affecting intergroup conflict suggests that history could have taken a very different course and that these suppressed historical alternatives remain as lessons for the present. Brooks examines indigenous opposition and adjustment to the subsequent domination of Argentine nationalism and, like Paul Eiss, hints at alternative futures that were once possible.

Examining another colonial world, Kent Lightfoot's study of the nineteenth-century Russian Colony Ross in northern California constructs the history of place from fragments of archaeology, written documents, and oral traditions. The study of Fort Ross juxtaposes archaeological evidence from the site with colonial documents, pictorial representations of the old fort, and Native American oral histories of life in the fort's environs, with particular attention to women's lives. Recollections of Native people are privileged in a reexamination and critique of colonial accounts. Each case suggests important reformulations of standard interpretations of colonial encounters and grand theories of capitalist development.

Collectively, the volume papers demonstrate varied perspectives of and on microhistory, some of which abruptly depart from the traditions fashioned over the past three decades. All these studies urge a rethinking of what we presume to be the great and small events of history, of who really rules, of the complex webs of collective action, and of what might have been. In the end, the studies elicit questions about the objectives of microhistory and the broader aims of writing history in the social sciences and humanities. Although some authors draw on microhistorical works such as Ginzburg (Blee, DeCorse, Harkin, Tomich), Thompson (Walton), and Levi (Eiss, Emigh), they find new applications. Others find conceptual parallels between microhistory and other disciplines, such as methods of biography (Beaudry, Gordon, Maddox), archaeology (Beaudry, DeCorse, Lightfoot), and historical ethnology (Brooks), even as the conceptual utility of the term is cast into doubt and disciplinary boundaries are explored.

Some contributors revisit the concern that microhistory may drift into the study of particularities and, consequently, become irrelevant. Emigh argues that microhistory on a too-small scale may prove a liability; she recommends instead aggregate and comparative microhistories in her own study drawing on three different data sources on how Tuscan peasants accounted their tax liabilities. Walton develops comparative microhistory to show how the social meaning of a given act (here arson) varies with historical context. Blee uses microhistory to understand the contexts in which social movements develop or fail. Other contributors question the theoretical and conceptual frameworks employed in microhistory. Eiss challenges the "positivism" he sees in some microhistory, its reliance on "optical metaphors," and the defense of scientific method against relativism raised by at least one of its exponents, Giovanni Levi. Eiss does not reject the methodological language of lens, scale, and scope but argues that microhistory must be opened up to include "the hermeneutics and politics of writing." In a related vein, Harkin argues that microhistory "attempts to maintain unities by circumscribing the frame of reference to a particular time and place" rather than by exploring the possibilities of unbounded comparison, analogy, and contrast. These are provocative challenges, new avenues that the authors pursue with profit in their contributions. Conversely, enthusiasts of microhistory find nothing positivistic in its tradition (quite the reverse, Levi notwithstanding), no restriction on the politics and hermeneutics of writing (for example, Natalie Davis's subject in *Martin Guerre*), and a positive relish for extending the range of time and space comparisons (for example, Ladurie's carnival rebels in *Romans* as "forerunners of equality").

The question is not whether these critical ideas are constructive—they are—but whether they diverge from or more fully express the potential of microhistory. Disputing these matters is a good thing. It is a starting point that may inspire researchers to move on in their own work with new analytical insight. This collection is about how twelve authors have done that in their own disciplinary, methodological, and theoretical ways. Microhistory never was one thing, never a codified procedure that one could embrace or reject. Rather, it is a loose, unrestricted label for a variety of works—many, but not all, European and produced in response to global meta-narratives—that discounted or undervalued the importance of the local, individual, or event in historical interpretation. In *Local Knowledge*, Clifford Geertz (1983:233) writes:

> We need, in the end, something rather more than local knowledge. We need a way of turning its varieties into commentaries one upon another, the one lighting what the other darkens. There is no ready method for this, and for myself I rather doubt there ever will be. But there is by now some accumulated cunning. We are learning...something about bringing incommensurable perspectives on things, dissimilar ways of registering experiences and phrasing lives, into conceptual proximity such that, though our sense of their distinctiveness is not reduced (normally, it is deepened), they seem somehow less enigmatical than they do when they are looked at apart...it is through comparison, and of incomparables, that whatever heart we can actually get to is to be reached.

The papers in this volume, individually and collectively, pose the challenge of comparing incomparables. We urge that potential commonalities of archaeology and history, sociology and anthropology, be recognized, and that historical interpretation move freely across disciplines. Historical study should be held up to the present and individual lives understood as the intersection of biography and history. Our authors develop these themes in a kaleidoscope of places and periods, small worlds that are the only worlds we experience, study, and sequentially fit together in bigger pictures. Although Geertz (1996:262) observed a decade ago that "no one lives in the world in general," these essays suggest that we all dwell in worlds larger than "some confined and limited stretch of it—'the world around here.'" We hope that this volume polishes a lens capable of the deeper depth of field necessary to bring worlds at once small and grand into full relief.

Part I

Microhistory
*Interdisciplinary Perspectives
and Concerns*

2

Lived Hegemonies and Biographical Fragments

Microsteps toward a Counterhistory
of the Spanish Transition from Dictatorship
to Democracy

Richard Maddox

A chronicler who recites events without distinguishing between major and minor ones acts in accordance with the following truth: nothing that has ever happened should be regarded as lost for history.

—*Walter Benjamin, "Theses on the Philosophy of History" (1978)*

IN THE NEWS: NEARING THE END OF THE END OF THE TRANSITION?

Early 2005 witnessed two milestones suggesting that the transition from dictatorship to democracy is not quite over in Spain. In March, nearly thirty years after the death of Francisco Franco, statues of "El Caudillo" and of José Antonio Primo de Rivera, the martyred youthful founder of the fascist Falange, were finally removed from parks and plazas in Madrid, Guadalajara, and Santander. In Guadalajara, the removal occurred late at night to reduce chances of conflict.[1] A month later, Santiago Carrillo, the former head of the Communist Party of Spain and a key figure in the transition to democracy, was assaulted by about forty ultrarightists outside a Madrid bookstore. Although quickly thwarted, the attack was evidently in response to a dinner held in honor of Carrillo's ninetieth birthday, which had been attended by the prime minister and other luminaries.[2]

These events might lead people to think that the bitter divisions of the past are still alive in Spain, but there is much evidence to the contrary. Younger generations of Spaniards are mostly uninterested in what happened during the Civil War and dictatorship and are even less engaged by the history of the transition to democracy. Moreover, outside of the Basque country, contemporary Spain almost entirely lacks radical political movements. Indeed, the events described above may have attracted disproportionate attention precisely because they appear anachronistic in a political climate marked by widespread passivity and the blurring of center-right and center-left liberalisms. Still, the legacies of the past linger on at least in attenuated and intermittent form. At election times, political name-calling often employs the old formulas of "fascists" versus "Reds," and social issues concerning abortion, divorce, and education generally follow the lines of old ideological cleavages.

So is the transition finally over or not? And what is it or was it about anyway? Most scholars of contemporary Spain would likely greet these questions with incomprehension and possibly scorn.

MACROHISTORY

According to some scholars, the transition ended with the adoption of the constitution in 1978. According to others, it ended with the failure of the Tejero coup in 1981, with the sweeping electoral victory of the socialists in 1982, or with Spain's entry into the North Atlantic Treaty Organization and the European Community in 1986 and 1987. Although opinions differ somewhat, there is general consensus that during the period 1975 to 1985, liberal democratic institutions were firmly enough established that the country could turn decisively toward building the future and away from its preoccupation with overcoming the past.

In greatly abridged form, the standard narrative goes like this: The modernization of Spanish economy, society, and culture in the 1960s prepared the ground for regime change. The death of Franco in 1975 created an opening that enabled the young king, Juan Carlos, and his prime minister, Adolfo Suárez, to engineer the self-destruction of Francoist institutions and begin a process of negotiation with socialists, communists, liberals, and other prodemocratic forces that led, via a series of pacts, legislation, compromises, referenda, and elections, to a new institutional and political order. This process was not easy. Political parties were formed and dissolved. Moderate elements of the old regime as well as the democratic opposition and Catalan and Basque regionalists struggled for recognition, influence, and advantage. Most of all, there was widespread anxiety about right-wing conspiracies and a pervasive fear that the conflicts of the period of the Second Republic and the Civil War would reemerge.

To counter these threats, the leaders of the transition joined together in a massive campaign of political persuasion. The key slogans and symbols they promulgated were those of "democracy," a "new beginning," "toler-ance," "pluralism," "reconciliation," "nonviolence," and "dialogue" (see Edles 1998:41–62). Political leaders also strove to meet the challenge of authori-tarian reaction by specific means. Much-needed military reform was intro-duced at a snail's pace. The Francoist civil service was left intact. Most critically, the Amnesty Law of 1977 forbade prosecutions for past political crimes and corruption. The cumulative effect of the reiterated calls to look to the future and forgo retribution was to repress public discussion of the evils of the Civil War and the dictatorship (Aguilar 2001). As a result, mem-bers of the former regime found it relatively easy to declare loyalty to the new liberal order.

All of this is broadly accepted conventional wisdom. However, there continues to be debate about the transition. The issue that has attracted most attention concerns the roles that political elites and the masses played in the process. Some scholars maintain that the transition is the purest example of liberalization and democratization through the action of elites, whereas others argue that popular social movements in favor of compro-mise exerted considerable or perhaps even decisive influence. Formulated in these simplistic terms of a sharp distinction between elites and masses, this debate is probably irresolvable. But what is hardly disputed is that the "Spanish model" of democratic transformation is exemplary and that many of its elements have been emulated in Latin America and eastern Europe (see Gunther, Montero, and Botella 2004). Thus, despite the lack of reso-lution of problems in the Basque country and elsewhere, conventional his-tories of the transition often have the triumphalist overtones of an almost unqualified success story of contemporary liberalism, a story in which huge obstacles and fearful dangers were peacefully overcome.

COUNTERHISTORY, HEGEMONIC PROCESSES, AND MICROHISTORY

Recently, signs of unease with this narrative have been accumulating. According to Josep Colomer (1998:117), "the virtues of the transition" have become "the vices of democracy." Thus the willingness to avoid conflict through compromise during the transition has allowed tolerance of crony-ism, corruption, and other antidemocratic practices to persist. Questions have also been raised in conjunction with efforts to recover memories of the Civil War and its aftermath (see, for example, Elordi 2002; Rodrigo 2003). Few people who held positions of authority during the period are still alive, and it has not escaped notice that the long-delayed need to con-front the past has occurred at such a late date that it is unlikely to produce revelations that will disrupt present social and political arrangements. This realization has led some scholars to question the character of the transition itself (Aguilar 2002; Bermeo 1997; Julía 2003). Nevertheless, ideas about what a counterhistory of the transition might be remain foggy.

No doubt there are many ways of creating such a history. However, since what is most obviously at stake in investigating the transition is a better understanding of the complexities of the movement from one dominant political and cultural formation to another, a sharper analysis of hegemonic processes seems a good place to begin. As Gavin Smith (1999) has stressed, hegemonic processes are Janus-faced. One dimension of hegemony centers on the direct political and ideological struggles of specific groups, parties, classes, and alliances to win and maintain leadership and control over the general direction of social life. Almost all the existing literature on the transition focuses on this aspect. However, far less attention has been given to the second dimension of hegemonic processes. This dimension consists of the more diffuse, indirect, and illusive cultural politics that permeate the conduct of everyday life and shape commonsense understandings of what is valuable, desirable, and practical in particular circumstances (Williams 1977).

Ultimately, the task of a counterhistory of the transition should be to render a comprehensive account of the ways in which the directly political and the broadly diffused cultural dimensions of hegemonic processes were variously "articulated" (see S. Hall 1988) during the period. However, to do so depends on having a better sense of how people experienced the possibilities, struggles, and threats of these years. What needs to be better understood is how hegemony was actually lived, and what is missing is detailed knowledge of the micropolitics and microhistory of the transition—that is, knowledge of the broad domain of "interpersonal negotiations" (Smith 1999) that were shaped by the interaction of deeply embedded social and cultural forces and by more immediate and transitory political pressures and constraints. This essay represents a small step in this direction, and it shares with other essays in this volume (especially those of Beaudry, Eiss, and Gordon) a desire to create alternative narratives of the lives of complex subjects in ways that help us rethink the politics of representation involved in conventional historical periodizations.

MY FRIEND (THE FASCIST?)

Over a period of several months in 1982, whenever I met Juan Vargas (a pseudonym), he patted my shoulder and greeted me in this way: "Ricardo ...Reagan—un actor y malo" (Reagan—an actor and a bad one). I always responded: "Señor Juan…Franco—un guionista y peor" (Franco—a script-writer and worse).[3] This was not exactly sparkling wit, but these exchanges served to establish a jocular, politically edged intimacy between us.

Juan was one of the first people I met in Aracena, a hill town and regional center of about seven thousand people in the Sierra Morena of southwestern Spain, where I began to do fieldwork in the early 1980s (see Maddox 1993, 2004:273–81). At the time, Juan was in his early sixties. Usually garrulous and animated, he was sometimes subject to dark moods that seemed to come and go without apparent reason and that oscillated between touchy irritability and silent, sullen indifference. Ordinarily, though, Juan took pride in presenting himself as an openhearted, *auténtico hombre andaluz* (real Andalusian man), and he liked to instruct me at length about matters that interested him—especially bulls and the *corrida* (bull-fighting). He was widely recognized as an expert on the corrida and possessed an uncanny ability to predict what was going to happen in the ring.

Juan also enjoyed talking about the way of life of the sierra and the virtues and vices of fellow townspeople. Yet I doubt that he would fit anyone's notion of an ideal collaborator. Although articulate and knowledgeable, he seldom stayed on any topic for long. He almost never answered questions directly, and he often responded by changing the subject with an irrelevant story or joke. Then, after two or three days or even two or three weeks had passed, Juan would return suddenly to whatever it was that I had wanted to know. But even his delayed responses were usually evasive.

Nevertheless, Juan did not hesitate to freely offer his opinions on contemporary political matters. Indeed, unlike many townspeople who professed to be uninterested in politics and were quite cautious about making pointed statements, Juan fearlessly, frequently, and openly proclaimed his radicalism. Although he was not a member of the Partido Comunista de España (PCE), he identified himself as a communist and sometimes argued forcefully, if with a twinkle in his eye, for such extreme positions as the abolition of private property. He also regarded Santiago Carrillo, the moderate head of the party, as an ideal political leader, and he had a number of favorite stories to tell concerning Carrillo's long years of courageous clandestine opposition to the Franco regime.

Even so, I soon began to suspect that Juan was not as straightforward as he seemed about politics. Although he proclaimed himself to be radical and progressive, almost as often he posed as a conservative defender of cultural traditions and railed against many aspects of modern life. I found it puzzling, for example, that for weeks after Manuel Fraga, a former Francoist minister and the leader of the most conservative major political party in Spain, visited Aracena and made a whistle-stop election speech that was replete with far-right rhetoric conveyed in a stentorian oratorical voice, Juan could scarcely contain his expressions of admiration for Fraga's personal charisma.

Moreover, most townspeople were clearly less impressed by Juan's political candor than I was. On several occasions when Juan's name was mentioned, someone would look at me, ruefully shake his head, and observe something to the effect that "these days it doesn't mean anything to change your shirt from blue to red" (that is, from fascist to communist). The repeated, apparently knowing references to Juan's past were unsettling because I was fairly certain that Juan's detestation of the Franco regime was deep-seated and heartfelt.

By the end of nearly two years of fieldwork, during which I saw Juan most days, I still did not believe that I was close to taking his measure. I regarded him as a friend but also as a protean shape-shifter, prone to contradictions and half-truths. To be sure, Juan had gradually revealed a great deal about his life to me, usually in the form of brief anecdotes and revelations dropped as offhand remarks, and I quoted him at length in two publications that followed my first period of fieldwork in Aracena (see Maddox 1993:254–56, 1997:275–90). Nevertheless, I discarded a life history that I was writing about him in the late 1980s because it seemed pointless and full of gaps, and I was unable to convince myself that a better use of scholarly methods of forging contexts and connections would ever help me pull the biographical fragments together. Although my view of the limits of conventional methods has not changed, what has changed is how I imagine my personal and historical relationship with Juan.

In part, my shift in perspective came about because I realized that in his own oblique way, Juan had always been primarily concerned with letting me know the kind of man that he believed he was. Equally important, though, I think that I now better understand Juan and his circumstances. As I approach the age Juan was when I knew him, I see the present period of political stasis and uncertainty in much of Europe and the neoimperialist adventurism of the United States in ways that resonate deeply with some of Juan's hopes, fears, and convictions about the politics of the transition in Spain. Time, distance, and the successive crises of contemporary liberalisms have not created an ever-widening historical chasm between Juan and me but have instead, at least momentarily, provided a fragile bridge between us.[4] Given this fleeting opportunity, I am using some of what Juan chose to reveal about himself as the experiential sources of a memoir or character sketch designed to cast a narrow but illuminating beam on some of the deficiencies of conventional accounts of the transition from dictatorship to democracy and of contemporary political culture in Spain.

Rustic Youth

Juan was born in 1918 in one of the *aldeas* (rural hamlets) that surround Aracena. The aldea had a population of about three hundred, and most of the adults scratched out a living as day laborers on the large estates of Aracena's landowners. Many residents were unemployed, and their families were undernourished for several months each year. Juan was better off than most because his family owned a house and some small plots of land, including an irrigated garden. This land enabled them to grow fruits and vegetables and to maintain a few goats and pigs, although the family's income still had to be supplemented by wage work. As Juan put it, the family was "poor but not hungry."

Juan was the middle child of three. In an old photo, Juan and his siblings and parents all look remarkably alike. This image of family solidarity and identity is poignant because Juan's parents did not survive the hardships of the Civil War period, Juan's older brother had to flee the region and returned for only a few short visits decades later, and Juan's relations with his younger sister became strained after she married a man whom Juan did not respect.

When Juan was about eleven, his father fell ill and the children were forced to go to work in the fields. Juan always praised his parents as honest and good-hearted people, but the most influential person in his boyhood was his paternal uncle, who had become a priest, a most unusual calling for someone of his background. The uncle had made it possible for Juan to attend school for a few years and had tried to instill him with respect for *el patrón, el cura, y el maestro* (the patron, the priest, and the teacher). Moreover, his uncle's accomplishments had given Juan hope that he might make a different kind of life for himself in the future. Nevertheless, by the time Juan became a teenager in the tumultuous years of the Second Republic, he, like his brother and all the youths of his village, had become radicalized. He hated the agrarian gentry as oppressors of the poor, rejected the church as a bulwark of class domination, and embraced the blend of socialist and anarchist ideologies of the workers of the sierra.

Juan's early experiences of the world had thus been shaped by two contradictory influences—those of his uncle, who acted as Juan's guardian and represented conservative values, and those of the people of the aldea, who adhered to a radical communitarian egalitarianism and sought to overthrow everything that his uncle defended. At the time, Juan's choice was clear: he sided with the people of the aldea. Soon, however, he had little choice but to strive for reconciliation between these different sources of value and meaning.

Conscripted and Seduced?

By the summer of 1936, political conflict in Aracena had become so intense that the news that General Franco's North African troops had risen against the Second Republic on July 18 instantly sparked a social revolution. Leaders of the radical left seized effective control of the town, initiated a redistribution of land, organized a popular militia, and jailed prominent members of the local gentry. Many rural workers argued for the summary execution of these men, while their leaders urged restraint and established a revolutionary tribunal of justice. On August 10, a crowd pillaged and burned Aracena's churches and expelled the town's nuns from their cloisters.

Shortly thereafter, news spread that Nationalist forces had achieved a series of easy victories around Seville. A few days later, local revolutionaries fought a short but fierce battle with Nationalist troops and irregulars in a neighboring town. The untrained workers were no match for regular troops and were quickly routed. Realizing the futility of engaging in another open battle, the revolutionaries decided to flee. Thus, when the Nationalist column arrived in Aracena on August 18, there was no resistance. After the occupation of Aracena, the military commander of the district appointed a new municipal administration, which one townsperson described as "extremely active in hunting Reds." For several weeks, troops and local volunteers scoured the sierra in search of leftists. At night in Aracena, soldiers went from house to house, taking suspects into custody.

Juan admitted to being an eyewitness to most events of the revolutionary period but usually denied directly participating in them. Nevertheless, when the revolutionaries fled, Juan went with them. Some men, Juan's brother among them, decided to travel northwest with the aim of joining Republican forces elsewhere. Others, including Juan, later retreated into the countryside, where they hoped that after a period in hiding they would be able to return to their homes. Most of these men were eventually arrested, brutally interrogated, and sometimes imprisoned. Scores were shot. Some, however, were conscripted into the Nationalist army, and a few workers and youths under surveillance volunteered for military service in the hopes of avoiding a worse fate. Whether Juan was a "volunteer" or a forced conscript, I do not know. On one occasion, Juan told me that a Nationalist patrol had discovered him at the side of a road and forced him into uniform. On other occasions, he told the same story about "a friend." In any case, Juan was soon in the Nationalist army.

Juan was lucky and never saw serious action. He spent part of the war in Extremadura and part in Aragon on garrison duty as a valet of a company commander. He tried to make the best of his situation by doing all he could to gain his superior's favor, and he soon succeeded. The officer began to treat him almost as a son and took delight in calling Juan on the carpet and accusing him of various petty offenses and derelictions. When Juan protested his innocence, the officer would laugh, relent, and extend him small favors. Juan was evidently soon captivated by this behavior and came almost completely under his commander's sway. This situation was fateful, because his commander, unlike most senior army officers, was a radical Falangist who frequently criticized the monarchy, the church, and the established order of class privilege and who maintained that it was possible to be both a defender of the popular masses and an ardent supporter of Spanish nationalism. After serving four years in the army under the tutelage and protection of this officer, Juan returned to Aracena in 1940. At the age of twenty-two, he was now a convert to the authoritarian hypernationalistic populism of the most radical wing of the Falange.

Blue-Shirted Veteran

The 1940s and early 1950s were hard times in Aracena. The war had devastated the agrarian economy of the sierra. Juan recalled the period as the "time of hunger," when "people thought of nothing but their stomachs." Political repression was also intense. Once again firmly in control, the agrarian gentry, although now considerably poorer, did not hesitate to use their power to pay off personal grudges and to deny work to suspected leftists. Petty vindictiveness in daily life reached absurd levels that older townspeople angrily recalled decades later.

The hallmark of this period of reaction was the reimposition of religion as a dominant ideological force in Spain. In Aracena, the emergence of "National Catholicism" as the primary ideology of the Franco regime was compatible with a local tradition of highly politicized religious activism among the gentry. Thus, throughout the 1940s, one campaign after another to "re-Christianize the masses" was launched in the region. At first Juan and other local radical Falangists criticized these efforts. However, as the fortunes of the Axis powers waned in the 1940s, the Franco regime took a conservative turn. The most radical elements of the Falange were effectively purged, and the new domesticated and bureaucratized version of the organization became, along with the church and the army, one of the "three pillars" of the "National Movement." Juan bitterly resented this change as a betrayal of the Falangist cause and the Spanish people. He began to hate Franco and to withdraw from direct involvement in politics.

Juan's disengagement was possible because as a Nationalist veteran with a good war record, he was not called on to demonstrate more than token loyalty to the regime. Indeed, he was favored by local authorities and was soon granted a job as a kind of gofer in the town hall. The job was menial and poorly paid, but it put Juan into daily contact with people in power. Because of the dire economic circumstances, this job gave him a considerable advantage over his neighbors. As long as he kowtowed to his superiors, Juan could participate in black market activities—a crucial element of local subsistence—with virtual impunity. Moreover, with his brother gone, he controlled the small but for the moment especially useful plots of land that represented his parents' legacy. In short, while most townspeople were desperate in these years, Juan soon had enough money from various sources to live in relative security.

By the mid-1940s, Juan's prosperity and connections had made him a good marriage prospect. He began a long courtship with María Pilar, a woman whose parents were pious and respectable members of Aracena's small commercial middle class. The Pilar family had an interest in a local hotel and ran a small building supply business, but the war had dealt a severe blow to their fortunes. Juan's position, growing ambitions, and capacity for hard work were appealing to them. So María's family, although hesitant, put no insuperable obstacles in the way of their union. Shortly after their marriage in 1950, and probably partly because of it, Juan received a promotion to a better-paying clerical position in the town hall.

"Din sin Don"

By the mid-1950s, agriculture seemed to be reviving in the sierra, but this revival soon proved illusory. The traditional agrarian system offered little scope for mechanization, and local landowners were unable to meet new government-mandated wage levels for agrarian workers and still make a profit. By the early 1960s, many members of the sierra's agrarian gentry were responding to these changes by seeking professional credentials and moving to the cities. Many of those who remained behind became known as *dons sin din* ("gentlemen without money"—that is, without *dinero*, or "din") and were reduced to scratching out modest livings from their landholdings. There was also a massive migration of rural workers in search of brighter futures. The exodus of both the richest and poorest sectors of the population transformed local society. Local authorities adopted a populist rhetoric and sought to generate jobs by promoting government services and new commercial enterprises. Class resentments were slowly mitigated by the effects of economic leveling and embryonic forms of consumerism. The integrist Catholic ideology of the 1940s increasingly became a hollow shell and was supplanted by a modernizing although still authoritarian civic boosterism.

These changes worked to Juan's advantage. Convinced that the Falangist hope of "patriotic socialism" was dead, Juan dedicated himself to making money. In addition to his municipal job, he helped his brother-in-law in his expanding building supply business and also became an insurance agent. His ties to local officials and his knowledge of the building trades put him in an ideal position to participate in a local housing and remodeling boom, and he reaped large rewards as an independent contractor for subsidized projects. By modest local standards, he became wealthy and was one of the leading figures of the new class of *dins sin don* (men with money but without family ties to the old elite).

By the late 1960s, Juan could afford to work less and began to devote more time to cultural pursuits. He accumulated a library on bullfighting and traveled to corridas throughout southwestern Andalusia. He also developed an interest in regional customs and literature. Indeed, he tried his hand at short prose pieces that recounted folktales and praised the natural beauty of the sierra. At first, these efforts met with gratifying success. Some of his essays appeared in town publications, and a local lay religious brotherhood once invited him to read an inspirational essay. Encouraged by this situation, Juan may have begun to take on the airs of a patron of culture in emulation of many *hijos del pueblo* (honored natives of the town). Unfortunately, his literary efforts led to public humiliation when he entered one of his essays in a contest sponsored by the town council. Juan lost the contest to the teenage son of a local politician, but this was not the worst of it. In the weeks before the awards ceremony, his work was openly denigrated, criticized, and mocked by a clique of Aracena's fading gentry, who favored the eventual winner. This was one of the bitterest experiences of Juan's life, and it rekindled his hatred of upper-class privilege and arrogance. He never wrote again, and when he told me the story years later, his eyes filled with tears of anger.

Juan had achieved a lot, but he was not particularly happy. He and his wife had never had children. When his wife died suddenly in 1970, Juan was left alone. He tried to act as the paterfamilias for his sister's children in the absence of their father, who was working in Barcelona, but he ultimately found this role more frustrating than rewarding. While constantly asked to help his nieces and nephews financially, he felt that they neither respected him nor heeded his advice. In some respects, his position in the wider community paralleled that within his family. Although he knew hundreds of people and was a member of many clubs and organizations, he was also somewhat socially isolated. Aracena's old elite viewed him as a useful member of the community but also as a somewhat vulgar *hombre del pueblo* (man of the people), while Aracena's working class viewed him as a hardnosed boss. Nevertheless, Juan had a small but close circle of friends on whom he relied for company. Like Juan, these friends were dins sin don who had grown prosperous through a combination of wit, luck, and hard work.

A Favorite Story

In Aracena's principal plaza, there is a statue that was erected in 1876 and depicts Julian Romero de la Osa as a man in clerical robes. Juan often recounted the story of this man, who single-handedly captured a French military payroll, buried the treasure, lived a modest life for decades, and eventually began to use his wealth for public projects, such as improving the town's water supply. Juan saw Romero de la Osa as a heroic figure because he had risen above his origins to become a patron of the pueblo and a paragon of traditional virtue.

Political Death in the Afternoon

During the last five years of the Franco regime, at a time when national political life was in tumult, local political life in Aracena was in a state of suspended animation. What remained of the old elite still exercised indirect control over the town, but most municipal offices were held by unambitious men of humbler backgrounds. The mayor was a bank clerk who approached his political responsibilities more as a loyal caretaker than an active leader. His governing style did not permit popular initiatives, but it did allow for fairly open political discussion.

Juan and his friends were highly critical of the existing state of immobility. What they desired was a revitalization of populism, a political order that would be well led but egalitarian in spirit and would end the influence of the old gentry class. If that meant liberal democratic reforms, then they were reformists. And as seasoned, still energetic, self-made men who were entering the late afternoon of their lives, they did not doubt that it was time for their cohort to assume an important role in this transformation.

For most people in Aracena, however, the initial response to the rapid disintegration of the Franco regime in 1976 was optimistic but far from populist or militant in spirit. Because many feared that the venomous class conflicts of the Civil War period would reemerge, they wished to proceed with reforms slowly. This desire was in sharp contrast with other Andalusian towns, where socialists and communists rapidly mobilized large working-class majorities, who demanded rapid democratization. Aracena was more evenly divided between conservatives and progressives and had few radical voices urging a sharp break with the past. Thus townspeople were particularly open to the appeals of national politicians who urged compromise and orderly change. And as local political groups coalesced, the majority of them sounded similar reassuring notes of restraint.

Many of the old elite and many established professionals in Aracena backed the national center-right coalition of the Unión Centro Democrático (UCD). The left was represented by a local branch of the Partido Socialista Obrero Español (PSOE), led by young men in their thirties. Some conservative Catholic businessmen formed a small independent group to compete for local office. There were also some regionalists of the Partido Socialista Andaluz (PSA). However, across the political spectrum, what characterized the politics of the transition in Aracena was the reluctance of politicians to directly broach divisive, ideologically charged issues. Virtually all the politicians rushed to define themselves as moderates in favor of rapid social and economic development.

In the run-up to and aftermath of the first democratic municipal elections in 1979, an intense and constraining politics of personal reputation and gossip substituted for explicit debate about policies and platforms. In this arena, political style and personal history counted most. Indeed, an uncomplimentary nickname or a good joke at the expense of people with aspirations to office was sometimes enough to undermine their political prospects. Even a politician's stance on the apparently trivial question of where the public and private pavilions for the town's annual fair should be located became a critical symbolic issue, because it indicated whether the politician was inclined to maintain or overturn old patterns of class discrimination.

The personalist dynamics of local politics presented Juan and his friends with insuperable difficulties. They were not at ease with the UCD, since it appeared to be a continuation of the old regime of elite domination in new garb. Nor were they at ease with the anxiety-ridden, pious conservatism of the independent group. On the other hand, the young socialist activists were unwelcoming to dins sin don, because they saw these older men as complicit with the day-to-day workings if not necessarily the ideologies of Francoism. Moreover, because of the anomalous class position and exceptional personal trajectories of Juan and his friends, they were unusually vulnerable to gossip, especially to the charge that their political postures were more opportunistic and hypocritical than sincere. The obstacles facing them proved so formidable that, despite their initial ambitions, most of Juan's friends had once again become politically disillusioned and disengaged by the late 1970s.

Juan certainly did not regard himself as a hypocritical opportunist. Rather, in his more reflective moments, he seemed amazed that he had ever believed in Falangism. And though susceptible to the seductions of political charisma, as a genuine hombre del pueblo who valued his own autonomy above everything else, he was fundamentally skeptical of all authority. Thus, although momentarily swayed by the personal magnetism of Manuel Fraga, he remained unconvinced and finally unmoved by Fraga's right-wing rhetoric. Ultimately, Juan respected the tough but rarely histrionic and much more convincingly democratic stance of the head of the Communist Party, Santiago Carrillo. However, it was not simply charismatic political leadership that led him to embrace a sometimes radical communist position. His reasons were more complex, and most important among them were his direct experience with and hatred of class privilege and his deep-seated egalitarian sentiments.

Even so, Juan was well aware that many of his neighbors were inclined to dismiss him as a former "blue shirt" or a social climber with pretensions to a culture and status that he could not rightfully claim. He was injured by this dismissal, and his protean evasiveness represented not so much an established character trait as the main tactical defense he used to deal with gossip and his dubious public reputation. But he was also genuinely angered and frustrated by what he considered his neighbors' self-righteousness, pettiness, timidity, and lack of political vision. In defiance, he frequently adopted a radical political persona that was reminiscent of the provocative, heroic, and overdramatized poses of *tremendista* bullfighters. Unfortunately, this was among the worst possible forms of political self-representation to embrace at the time. What townspeople had come to admire in politics was a more measured *torería del arte* that embodied flexibility, smoothness, confidence, and meticulous self-control. Juan knew this and sometimes tried to act the part of a calm and experienced wise man, but repeatedly in response to real or imagined criticism, he would suddenly jump to the far left and launch political tirades. And every time he aggressively pronounced his radical sympathies, he confirmed to his listeners that he remained a fascist at heart.

Retaliation

By the time I first met Juan in 1981, he had all but given up hope of playing an active role in local affairs. But he was far from being silenced. Indeed, he seemed determined to be a thorn in the side of local politicians. The municipal elections of 1979 had left no party with a clear mandate. Even though a large majority of townspeople clearly sympathized with the left, many had cautiously voted for conservatives. Nevertheless, the socialist parties used their one-vote advantage on the new town council to elect a mayor from the PSOE. The PSOE then quickly set about the task of winning a decisive majority in the next election that would relegate conservatives to the status of bystanders and enable the PSOE to govern without the need for a coalition with the regionalists of the PSA. As they pursued this goal, the PSOE socialists established the hegemonic political style that prevailed in the town for the next decade and more.

The hallmark of this style was the cultivation of an informal and youthful egalitarian posture that was ever optimistic and forward looking but modest, nonideological, and realistic in its ambitions. It was most clearly embodied by the new mayor, who was in his mid-thirties and until his election had worked as a ticket seller in the bus station. Among the mayor's virtues were friendliness, apparent humility, and a willingness to admit his own mistakes. Especially when under attack, he had the habit of proclaiming that he was just an ordinary, fallible human being who was trying hard to do his best. The mayor and his comrades almost never referred in public to the specific repressions and crimes of the Franco regime. Rather, they spoke vaguely of past "mistakes" and "injustices" and insinuated that their present political opponents were the arrogant and self-interested heirs of this legacy and not to be trusted. In contrast, they represented themselves as fair-minded friends of the pueblo who treated everyone equally and with respect. Although locally rooted, this strategy was in near perfect harmony with the public persona projected by Felipe González, a fellow Andalusian, the national leader of the PSOE, and the most charismatic politician in Spain.

Juan believed that he had been denigrated by the mayor and other members of the PSOE, and he despised them. He seldom let an opportunity to criticize and mock the PSOE pass. Once, for example, when the mayor was making an embarrassingly apologetic speech, trying to explain away long delays and cost overruns in a municipal project that had been undertaken by outside contractors with ties to the PSOE, Juan disrupted his adversary's usual ramblings about human frailties by loudly wondering which particular frailty had led the mayor to buy a big expensive new car "worthy of a bishop or a *jefe del Movimiento* [Francoist official]." Since the mayor had no known financial resources beyond his modest salary, Juan's wisecrack was tantamount to a charge of corruption.

On another occasion (see Maddox 1997), Juan railed for weeks against the PSOE's attempt to promote a "modern and truly popular" town fair by sponsoring the performance of a nationally famous glitter rock band. The concert had left most adult townspeople sleepless, mystified, and annoyed. Juan, however, tirelessly and gleefully maintained that the band and the PSOE were part of a vast conspiracy that was in its own way as deplorable and reactionary as "National Catholicism" because it amounted to a scheme to quiet political discontent by offering a new form of opiate to the masses. Silly as this seemed, Juan's diatribe was in keeping with his more general and quite serious effort to convince people that what was being accepted as democracy and freedom in Aracena and Spain was in reality a new market-driven and softer form of class domination and political dictatorship.

In a similar vein, Juan also liked to suggest that there was little practical difference between the wrongs involved in the old forms of gentry patronage and the *amiguismo* (friendship) and favoritism that the socialists were showing to their supporters. These sorts of claims were generally greeted with amusement and skepticism by his neighbors. But Juan was among the first to recognize that in spite of the apparent successes of the transition period, too many compromises had been made in the rush to get the institutional and political vehicles of advanced liberalism up and running, and he deplored the advent of what the mass media had taken to calling *el desencanto* (the disenchantment), which was leading to increasing political apathy in Aracena and the rest of Spain.

Clara and the Unknown Saint

One afternoon toward the end of my fieldwork in 1983, I met Juan as he was stepping out of his house. He said he was going to visit Clara. "And who is Clara?" I inquired. He grinned and replied, "She is the most beautiful creature in the world. Do you want to meet her?" Intrigued, I agreed to come along, and we were soon on the highway to Seville. A few miles out of town, Juan turned onto a dirt road and stopped the car alongside a stone wall. A young calf quickly approached with her mother, a cow of enormous proportions. Juan took some sugar cubes out of his pocket for the calf and said, "This is Clara." Juan began fretting and fawning over Clara and praising her mother's extraordinary fecundity in an affectionate and playful way that I had not seen before. We then spent the next couple of hours herding cows from one pasture to another, raising buckets of water from an old well, collecting bushels of figs to prevent the animals from gorging themselves, and finally chatting as the sun set and we rested on the crumbling walls of an old country house. This turn toward pastoral idyll was, as far as I knew, something new for Juan and quite a surprise to me. It seemed to represent both a retirement from his ordinary work in the public life of the town and a return to his childhood experiences in the aldea.

Over the next couple of months, I accompanied Juan to his finca several times. On almost the last visit I made there before leaving Aracena, in the midst of a long talk, Juan suddenly assumed a serious demeanor and said, "Let me tell you a story about another Juan." He proceeded to say that this Juan was a modestly well-off peasant proprietor from a town in Extremadura. For years, this Juan labored diligently in his fields, and his neighbors believed he had accumulated a lot of money. However, he was neither well respected nor liked because he was believed to be a mean-spirited and cruel miser who was hard on his wife and everyone else. After his wife died, this Juan became a virtual hermit and was rarely seen. When he died old and alone, his cousin came to town to oversee a simple funeral. Yet to his cousin's and neighbors' surprise, dozens of people showed up at the church on the morning of Juan's burial. One after another, these strangers revealed acts of charity and kindness that the man had performed. Thus it was revealed that over the course of his long life, this Juan, this "unknown saint," had given away all his money to the poor, the sick, and the desperate. Those who had misjudged him and treated him badly were suitably shamed by these graveside revelations and vowed to be less quick to judge others in the future.

After finishing his story, Juan looked at me with a self-satisfied smile and asked what I thought. Not knowing what to say, I expressed some doubts about the plausibility of this tale, and Juan indignantly insisted that it was true in every detail. Later, I wondered whether Juan's story of the secret patron of the poor was anything other than a crude attempt at self-validation that was designed to let me know that he thought his own situation and virtues were analogous. This was transparently the case to some extent, but Juan had recounted the story in partly ironic tones, and I guessed that more had to be involved than simply this. I could hardly believe that Juan really wanted me to make any definitive moral judgments about his life.

Pondering the story for a long time, I finally realized that Juan's seeming apologia had been more of a heterodox confession of faith. For in his stories and even (although more obliquely) in his life, Juan had always affirmed that moral and spiritual patrons can and do exist. His convictions about this belief were rooted in popular Spanish Catholic traditions of saint worship and notions of honor and thus expressed a profound cultural conservatism. But Juan saw no fundamental contradiction between this conservatism and his left-wing politics. He believed that people are born equal, that they have the freedom to pursue virtue through acts of self-sacrifice and compassion, and that the greater or lesser will with which different people do so creates a spiritual and moral hierarchy. The pursuit of virtue may be limited by circumstances and opportunity, it may go unrecognized, and it may be subverted by lies, ignorance, and hypocrisy. But even if true virtue is hidden, it is real and it always has the possibility of being revealed.

It may be that Juan also believed he had sometimes lost sight of this view of virtue, for under the sway of hegemonic constraints and pressures and in the face of direct ideological and political repression, Juan had intermittently been susceptible to the influence of charismatic figures, such as his uncle, his commanding officer, Fraga, and even Carrillo. And in Juan's efforts to emulate these figures in word and deed, his own sense of himself was partly displaced and possibly distorted by power and ideology.[5] However, it also seems that the stories he told about such figures as Romero de la Osa and the unrecognized saint provided him with a moral compass and means of self-correction. If sometimes his desire to search out patrons and to become a patron led to his practical compliance with existing relations of domination and inequality, this desire was at least as often expressed in his struggles to maintain a degree of personal autonomy and in his resistance to and criticism of much that he believed to be unjust.

FATALITIES, HOPE, AND COUNTERHISTORY

In conventional accounts of the transition from dictatorship to liberal democracy, people like Juan are marginalized, ignored, and forgotten. Nevertheless, Juan's life and his struggles to transform and revitalize himself without surrendering his most deeply held convictions are testimony to the will to endure and even to thrive in the face of repeated threats of social and political death. But there is one battle that everyone finally loses, and to my sorrow, Juan succumbed to a sudden heart attack in 1986 before I saw him again. Yet we can still ask what can be learned from his life and how it is pertinent to constructing a counterhistory of the period of transition in Spain.

For one thing, the kind of bedrock cultural and moral traditionalism that Juan embraced was not his alone. Certainly in many parts of rural

Spain and presumably in some urban areas as well, it was still a strong force at the time of the transition and influenced people's understanding of their own and their country's political and cultural possibilities. But thus far, efforts to understand how this diffuse but fundamental dimension of cultural politics influenced people's conceptions of justice, democracy, equality, and freedom have had almost no place in accounts of the time. Juan's personal political vicissitudes are also highly emblematic of the politics of the transition. His inclination to advocate and combine conservative and radical elements in various ways was more common than not in Aracena and probably elsewhere and calls into question the tendency of conventional histories to represent political dynamics primarily in terms of emergent party politics and disputes over platforms, policies, and programs. Moreover, while conventional accounts sometimes recognize the personalist dimension of Spanish political culture and its preoccupations with insider relations of patronage and friendship as a negative limiting condition of political development, very little attention is paid to personalism as an active, constitutive force in political life. But as Juan would no doubt be among the first to attest, the politics of reputation, favoritism, and faction were often central and decisive in determining how power was distributed and events unfolded.

Indeed, Juan's story indicates that one of the most critical, although largely unexamined aspects of the politics of personalism during the transition was the ability to represent one's opponents as fatally contaminated figures of the past. This strategy affected not just Juan and his circle of friends but also the entire generation of politicians who were middle-aged at the time of the transition and whose political identities had been firmly established under the dictatorship. Hundreds of members of this generation, ranging from monarchists and Christian democrats to socialists who refused to abandon Marxism, were subjected to a gradual but effective purge that prematurely relegated them to the sidelines of political life. Their places were taken by a younger generation of men and women in their thirties and forties.

Even exceptional figures were not immune to this strategy. Thus Santiago Carrillo, whose commitment to democracy was impeccable, was accused of being a "little red Franco" because of his supposedly authoritarian style of internal Communist Party leadership and was eventually forced into retirement. Similarly, Manuel Fraga finally recognized that his record as a minister of the dictatorship made him unelectable as prime minister. Therefore, after overseeing the rebirth of the Alianza Popular as the more liberal center-right Partido Popular, he retreated to his conservative home region of Galicia. Even Felipe González, the socialist head of government for over a decade and the veritable embodiment of the forces of change in the 1980s, was accused in the 1990s of being arrogant, secretive, and criminally tolerant of illegal activities, such as the underhanded work of the security forces to violently suppress Basque separatists. But rather than attributing such failures to democratic shortcomings and fundamental flaws in a well-established liberal national security state, many of González's adversaries claimed that the failures could be traced to González's first and formative experiences of no-holds-barred political warfare during the declining years of the dictatorship. Thus the clearest reason why many aspects of the politics of the transition lingered on in ghostly form long after the period of regime change ended is that the capacity to identify one's opponents with the sins of the past and to identify oneself with the values of the present and future is such a durable and effective weapon.

Ultimately, however, correcting the lapses in conventional accounts of the culture and politics of the transition is not the most important contribution that counterhistories of the period and microhistorical perspectives have to offer. Rather, the most important contribution is that these perspectives allow us to envision new horizons of historical possibility in ways that restore life to the past. Top-down, generalizing historical accounts are deadening because they suppress the complexities, uncertainties, and open-endedness of all that has already happened but is never quite determinable or concluded.

By approaching the cultural politics of the transition narrowly in terms of a tightly bounded periodization of successful regime change, conventional histories ordain a closure that converts the partial, contested, and rough-hewn establishment of a flawed liberal polity into a signed, sealed, and delivered historical destiny. They lead us to conclude that the great majority of Spaniards were nothing other than budding modern individualists and consumers, eager to pursue their political and economic self-interest, yearning to be liberalized, and frightened of everything that threatened their immediate security. Yet Juan and countless others hoped for far more from the early years of the transition than what they gained. Among many other things, they hoped for a revitalization of traditional virtues and values. They also wanted a radical rupture from the immediate past, a rupture that would enable them to achieve a new advance in human freedom and justice. Insofar as conventional histories homogenize and mute these differences or represent them as marginal and unrealistic, they diminish the hopes, cultural resources, and practical possibilities for fundamental social transformation by denying that there is a continuous and continuing history of multiple struggles, gains, missteps, defeats, rededications, and reawakenings.

As Walter Benjamin (1978) suggested, what we need for more hopeful and less scripted kinds of histories are accounts that are not so eager to distinguish between major and minor events and between major and minor political actors. What we need are accounts that are better able to bring to light the many ways in which what appear to be among history's greatest victories and decisive triumphs remain as transitory, as vital, and as open to reconsideration as the lives of its subjects.

Notes

1. *El Mundo*, March 28, 2005, 12.

2. *El Mundo*, April 16, 2005, 3.

3. In the early 1940s, Franco tried his hand at scriptwriting and the novel. His attempts are recounted in different versions of *La Raza*, a text probably best described as fictionalized autohagiography. See Preston 1994:219.

4. For a discussion of the importance of a sense of copresence and coevality with other historical subjects, see Eiss, this volume. For a defense of the kind of history that seizes "hold of a memory as it flashes up at a moment of danger," see Benjamin 1978. And for a discussion of the fleeting resemblances and odd continuities that link the lives of people living in different times and circumstances, see Maddox 1998.

5. For a broader discussion of mimetic displacement and the formation of historical subjects, see Maddox 1998.

3

The Hidden Weight of the Past

A Microhistory of a Failed Social Movement Group

Kathleen Blee

One hundred and fifty people—mostly white, about thirty African American—gather in a Catholic church basement on a late summer night in 2003 in the Readville[1] neighborhood of Pittsburgh. The church is an important institution in this largely Catholic and white working-class place, its school an alternative to public schools that residents regard as chaotic and scary. A walk on nearby streets gives clues to the nature of Readville, past and present. Most homes are old, small but solid, and brick, but many show signs of neglect, with crumbling steps, peeling paint, and sagging gutters. Nail salons, check-cashing bureaus, saloons, and furniture rental stores are plentiful, yet a closer glance shows that these storefronts were earlier occupied by businesses that catered to a more prosperous community: grocers, small manufacturing companies, and restaurants.

The history of Readville is evident in its storefronts and houses. Jobs in steel and manufacturing that supported an economically vibrant working class for a century left the area in the 1980s, as did young people with options elsewhere. Wages declined; new jobs appeared mostly in retail and service, paying little more than minimum wage. As its tax base eroded, Readville lost the city services that had sustained its public life in an earlier era. Its neighborhood center closed. As the number of elderly people, unemployed youths, single-parent families, drug- and alcohol-dependent persons, and the mentally ill increased, the availability of services for these groups plummeted. Residents don't see a way out. Readville is hemmed in on one side by an upper-middle-class white neighborhood with high property values and on the other by a poor African American neighborhood with a reputation for crime and violence.

Against the pervasive sense of despair that circulates in Readville, the church gathering is remarkable. Readville's residents have come together to try to change their fate, at least in one small way. In the church basement are a handful of men, mostly wearing T-shirts with the names of local baseball teams on the front and sponsoring businesses on the back. There are many more women, some dressed casually in jeans or shorts and others in dresses with carefully applied makeup. Most are adults, but there are some teenagers and younger children. Many greet people they know, directing them into parking spots and moving in groups downstairs, where they make small talk about schools and athletic teams or share news about deaths and illnesses. A few people—some of the whites and most of the African Americans—ask for directions to the hall, noting that they are "not from here." When I ask, they say they have come in response to flyers declaring "Heroin Kills" that are posted in hair salons and grocery stores and on telephone poles along the local business district, the same notices that brought me here. The African Americans are from the Readville neighborhood, but not from "here," this particular block. An outsider might regard Readville as fairly homogenous in its history and class character, but its residents perceive much finer gradations of geography defined by race, kinship, church affiliation, and a myriad of other factors.

At the church, one woman circulates through the crowd, pointing people to the cookies and punch and tables covered with literature about the dangers of drug addiction. Some people she greets by name. She directs everyone to Nancy, a middle-aged white woman, as the one who initiated the meeting when she "lost a son to heroin and just started to talk to people." The meeting opens, with no announcement of a plan or agenda, no introduction to the group or its founders. A series of speakers, clearly arranged in advance, takes the stage. Some give informational talks: police and community workers relate statistics on skyrocketing rates of heroin deaths and arrests in Readville. Others describe themselves as ordinary citizens and give personal accounts of being addicted to drugs or seeing family members addicted. Few of these stories are purely personal vignettes. Most move from a family story to larger community problems of drugs, crime, economic decline, and powerlessness. These are riveting stories and many end in tragedy: jail, homelessness, divorce, death.

There is a wide space of possibility at this first meeting, as speakers suggest numerous potential targets for action. One speaker chastises parents who "go to bars and set a bad example" for their children. Another decries the city's decision to close the local senior center, causing problems for the Narcotics Anonymous group that had met there. Others point to a lack of police enforcement that allows open-air drug sales in the grocery parking lot and in front of the high school. Still others want to educate parents about the drug problem or drive drug dealers out of the neighborhood. Although there is little formal effort to direct the meeting, there are hints that a direction might eventually emerge, that the group might develop a unified strategy. When one speaker talks of the neighborhood as "under siege" by drug dealers (a likely reference to the adjacent African American neighborhood), he is corrected by the next speaker, who notes that plenty of drug users and drug sellers come from this neighborhood. All neighborhoods, he continues, need to stand together, because "heroin isn't a ghetto drug anymore."

The evening's emotional peak comes when Nancy takes the stage to tell the story of her son's death of a heroin overdose two years before. She is introduced as the force behind this gathering, and, befitting this position, her story is powerful and told with the coherence of a story often repeated. As Nancy details her journey from denial through despair, the crowd is swept up in her emotional trajectory. Many are crying when she finishes. Nancy makes pointed personal references to individuals in the crowd—"as you remember, Joe" or "wasn't it like that, Norma?"—making it clear that many came here at her behest or through networks she activated. As she tells her story, Nancy skillfully brings together the ideas that have been evoked by others this evening. She relates her son's death as a tale of individual pain, as an exemplar of what is happening to Readville and similar neighborhoods, and as requiring immediate collective action. Somewhat surprisingly, she ends without specifying what actions should be taken. Although she acknowledges that she began the momentum seen here tonight, she insists that what happens now should be decided by "all of you." She circulates a sign-up sheet for anyone interested in becoming involved. The crowd disperses, some lingering to chat, but most heading for home.

It is more than a year later: fall 2004. What began as a gathering of worried, frustrated residents now has officers, a bank account, and a name, Readville Against Drugs (RAD). But at this meeting there are only sixteen people, and all are whites and adults. The meeting is held in a tiny Veterans of Foreign Wars hall, behind a gas station, difficult to find for anyone not familiar with Readville. The sole entrance is through a private tavern, into a room still set up for a funeral held earlier in the day. Everyone here knows each other; they refer to events and people they have in common. The group's officers, including Nancy, sit together behind a table. Others pull chairs haphazardly around them. In contrast to a year earlier, there is no discussion tonight about what problem they should work on or how they should work. All that is now settled.

Curiously, since no one here is new to RAD and would need instruction in its mission, there is still frequent repetition that the group is "working to save people from the tragedy of heroin and other drugs in their family." How they go about doing so, though, is narrowly circumscribed. RAD is now defined by its monthly reenactments of a teenager's struggle with drugs. In a "Reality Tour," an audience of adults and their children are recruited to watch a staged drama about a teenager who is pressured by peers to take drugs, arrested, convicted, jailed, and finally killed by a drug overdose. The performance ends with a funeral, the teen in a casket surrounded by his sobbing parents and friends.

Tonight, RAD's agenda is to assess its progress in recruiting teens and parents for the upcoming Reality Tour and to finalize plans for each scene. The group has had trouble securing convincing and reliable volunteers to act the parts of nurses, so considerable time in the meeting is spent discussing how this might be arranged. The officers go through a checklist, making sure that all actors and authentic props will be available. At the end of the meeting, there is time set aside to evaluate the group's progress. Nancy reads excerpts from evaluations written by participants in earlier Reality Tours, all very positive. Many of them mention feeling sad or fearful during the tour. Nancy reports that each tour has been filled to the maximum and declares their work a success. Whether the Reality Tour combats drugs and whether Readville's drug problem has abated are not discussed. There is no talk about the effects of drugs, only about preparing for the next performance. Earlier possibilities for identifying and changing Readville's drug problem are now decidedly off the table. Sprinkled throughout the meetings are expressions of individual desire to prevent kids from taking illegal drugs, but no personal stories about drugs are told and no emotions expressed. There is no need to do so; there are no new people in this group. Everyone here has heard the stories and responded to the emotions already. New members are not being sought—only people to play roles in the pre-scripted Reality Tour.

MICROHISTORY OF RAD

In this chapter, I use microhistory as a framework through which to understand both the specific case of RAD—how it so quickly lost its energy and potential to tackle issues of broad social change—and the nature of social movements more generally. Microhistorical accounts generally focus on events in the past. In this article, however, I use microhistorical analysis in a sociological study of a present-day social phenomenon. I have two goals. First, I examine the extent to which microhistorical understandings of context and social scale might permit a more robust social scientific understanding of the trajectory of the RAD group than would be otherwise possible. Second, I explore the possibility of combining a microhistorical analysis of context with new geographic and organizational theories of path dependency as a means of understanding more fully the emerging dynamics of contemporary social groups.

Context and Scale

Few scholars would disagree with the importance of social context for understanding particular social events or processes. Yet, as Jacques Revel (1995) notes, scholarship generally makes only "lazy" use of social context. Social science studies, in particular, tend to invoke a sense of context to generate a "reality effect" for descriptions of social life or to analyze social context alongside but not as explanatory of the social phenomena under investigation. For this reason, microhistorical analysis may provide an especially important analytic means by which social science studies can engage a deeper contextual understanding of social life.

One principle of microhistorical analysis that is particularly useful in creating a robust sense of context is the assumption of unity of individual cases and their contexts. As the microhistorian Giovanni Levi (1991:95) observed, "even the apparently minutest action of, say, somebody going to buy a loaf of bread, actually encompasses the far wider system of the whole world's grain markets." Traces of the wider (or macro-level) context can be discovered by close attention to smaller (or micro) levels of social life; the dynamics of the social whole can be identified in particular cases. This idea suggests that a focus on RAD may unlock more general features of social life.

A second principle of microhistory that is particularly useful for social science scholarship is the emphasis on tacking analytically among different scales of social life. Microhistorians accrue significant explanatory power by moving between attention to the particular and the wider context, between the small details of social life and the large context, between the micro level and the macro levels of society, and between time periods. These analytic shifts allow scholars to describe "vast complex social structures without losing sight of the scale of each individual's social space and hence, of people and their situation in life" (Levi 1991:95). In addition to understanding context by attention to particularities, we can grasp the specificities of the small by paying attention to a larger scale of social life (Eckert and Jones 2002; Lepore 2001; Magnússon 2003; Peltonen 2001; Revel 1995). Not only might a close analysis of RAD widen our understanding of social movements more generally, but a rich analysis of its social context will permit more robust explanations of the trajectory of a group such as RAD.

Tacking between past and present can bolster an understanding of causality in social processes. To take an example from my earlier research, it is clear that people who belong to extremist racist groups such as the Ku Klux Klan are fairly homogenous. They tend to have low-status or unstable jobs, minimal contact with their extended families, few friends outside the Klan, and highly conspiratorial political beliefs. Such characteristics are commonly regarded not only as descriptive but also as explanatory. It is widely believed that people are attracted to a group like the Klan precisely because they are economically marginal, socially isolated, and ideologically extreme. However, my studies of contemporary and early-twentieth-century racist groups cast doubt on such suppositions. People who join racist groups often differ very little—in background or even racial ideology— from those around them. They tend to have rather average jobs, family connections, and ideas. Once they enter a racist group, however, their lives change. As they begin to profess overtly racist ideas or wear Klan insignia, they lose their jobs and are rejected by family members and friends. They find it easier to be around those who do not challenge their ideas, becoming increasingly marginal and more susceptible to the extreme ideas of racist groups. Over time, they develop the characteristics that are presumed to have motivated their decision to join the Klan (Blee 1991, 2002). In this case, what *is* (its attributes) creates a misleading sense of *how it came to be* (the cause).

A similar process is evident in studies of RAD in that attention to its later stages would obscure the extent of its earlier possibilities. An observer who began to study the group in 2004 would likely regard it as a civic improvement project, absorbed with details of organizational continuity and practicality. There would be no sense of the earlier potential in the group, of moments at which it could have developed into a movement for broader changes in drug policy, laws, treatment, or prevention or, more sweepingly, alterations in the economic, political, and social disparities that are generating the declining fortunes of neighborhoods like Readville.

More importantly, an observer who began to follow RAD in 2004 would have little opportunity to understand the actions and choices that shaped its structure, self-understanding, tactics, and outcomes. By 2004, these aspects of group life were largely settled, rarely brought into conversation, and almost never explicitly contested. Observers of RAD at this point would find it difficult to understand the assumptions and parameters within which it operated, since these were now implicit. These were the hidden weight of its past, shaping RAD's present and future in an invisible, unacknowledged fashion (Becker 1995).

Indeed, without tacking between past and present, scholars of social movements are unlikely to study groups like RAD at all. When it began, RAD was too new to merit attention; most studies of social movements begin with groups that have proven themselves to be viable. At a later time, RAD's lack of interest in broad social change would exclude it from most studies of social movement groups. Yet crucial information about how social movements emerge (or fail to do so) is lost by bypassing such groups and by considering only those successful ones that survive over time. It is difficult to understand how and why people mobilize to change society if we study only groups that are established.

Geographic and Organizational Theory

Microhistorical work usefully suggests the value of attention to context in social life. Using recent theories of path dependency from geographic and organizational studies, it is possible to extend this insight further and consider how attention to context may reveal otherwise invisible features of social life. The basic argument of path dependency is that the weight of past action shapes future action, largely by creating structures that enable and/or constrain future possibilities (Pred 1981, 1984; also Levi 1991). The geographer Allan Pred (1985) notes that once a person has decided to do something at a certain time and place, it becomes impossible to do something else at the same time in another place, to do something that begins earlier and overlaps in time, or to do something that is impossible to reach in time or space. Thus actions at one time limit what is possible at a later time, or, in the terminology of path dependency, "residues of action at a given time constrain subsequent action" (Tilly 1988; also Billings and Blee 2000; Mahoney 2000).

Path dependency helps illuminate the cascading nature of many social processes in which a particular option, once selected, is progressively more likely to continue. In social movements, for example, as Francesca Polletta (2002:21) argues, "a tactical option or an organizational form may be appealing because it is similar to what we are used to." Moreover, path-dependent processes are self-reinforcing: if groups recruit new members who are similar to older members, the groups will become exponentially more homogeneous over time. Yet not all sequences are self-reinforcing; ruptures can transform paths (Mahoney 2000; Rhomberg 2004). For example, the departure of a founding member may create significant turning points by forcing groups to talk more directly about patterns that are otherwise assumed. With sensitivity to the "rolling inertia [that] allows for continuous flux within a stable mode of operation" (Molotch, Freudenburg, and Paulsen 2000:819), path-dependent theories make it possible to scrutinize social action in a deeply historical way.

In the sections below, I examine the short history of RAD, drawing on a microhistorical sense of context and social scale and a path-dependent sense of historical trajectory. These observations are from a larger longitudinal and comparative ethnographic study of groups in Pittsburgh that, between 2003 and 2006, organized protests or other challenges to existing state or nonstate authorities, using means other than those of conventional politics (Blee and Currier 2005). (I excluded groups that are accountable to another organization, focused on self-help, or largely challenge cultural norms.) RAD and other groups were identified through a wide-ranging and systematic survey of local newspapers and other media or public venues and repeated contacts with a network of key informants. For each group, I collected observational data on all meetings, public events, social gatherings, press conferences, and other events, using a semistructured template on a variety of group dynamics, including alliances and frictions (interpersonal), what is recognized as expertise (ideological), and incidents where rules are evoked or broken (organizational). Observational data record the trajectory of group life as it unfolds, capturing the fits and starts—the messiness—of social interaction that are often lost in accounts that rely only on a group's documents or the memories of its participants, and permitting consideration of both action and inaction (Jasper 2004), an analysis not possible in studies that use events (such as protests) rather than groups as the unit of analysis.[2]

MAKING RAD

An observer at the 2004 RAD meeting would see a white, adult, working-class group focused on a single issue, oriented toward providing services rather than confronting authorities, limited to a narrow vision of what it could accomplish, with intergroup dynamics that were task oriented rather than emotional. In short, an observer would see a fairly unimaginative, conformist, and conservative group of similarly situated people pursuing a pedantic agenda that was unlikely to change much over time. What happened to its emotional urgency, its desire for social change, and its racial diversity?

RAD's characteristics—its whiteness, single-issue focus, unemotional style, and so on—are not simply attributes of the group. They are outcomes of earlier actions. How RAD *came to be* racially homogenous is the product of choices about whether to recruit members, how to use social networks, what interpersonal dynamics were acceptable, and other factors. RAD's racial composition—like its projects, goals, and manner of working—is the sedimentation of earlier actions now obscured.

In one year, the group underwent a substantial transformation, one seemingly unnoticed—and unremarked upon—by its members. It began as a gathering of citizens united by a common concern about illegal drug sales but with many differences of age, race, social class, and position in the community. The core of a social network around Nancy was obvious at the beginning, yet efforts to draw in other people—from other neighborhoods and other races—were visible in the extensive public advertising for the initial gathering and in repeated affirmations that "everyone" in all parts of the city is affected by drugs. After the first meeting, however, the dynamics of recruitment changed substantially. Subsequent gatherings were increasingly smaller and more homogenous, consisting mostly of Nancy's white friends and neighbors, a change never discussed in the group despite its initial emphasis on the need for a large and broad-based membership. In addition, the group's sense of needing more members—a central theme in initial meetings—disappeared over time. Within a year, members were sought only for their potential as actors or suppliers of props for the Reality Tour. There was no effort to locate those whose personal connection to drugs might make them passionate about this cause.

As the composition of the group changed, so did the way it worked. At the initial gathering and for a time afterward, there was a concerted effort to diminish the need for specific leaders in the group. Nancy and others insisted on a "universal group," without hierarchy of position or power, in which members would be "equal in their level of passion and interest." Questions to Nancy about what *they* planned to do were consistently met with the retort, "Do you mean, what are *we* going to do?" Despite this verbal commitment, the positions of leaders and members became more distinct over time. Increasingly, Nancy made decisions and completed logistical work outside meetings, although she continued to disavow that she was "in charge." Moreover, what made someone a member changed from an

45

amorphous sense that whoever showed up at meetings should have input into the group to an implicit understanding that members were those who did work for RAD and were connected personally to Nancy or other leaders, as evidenced by the repeated references to specific "missing members" who did not attend meetings but were nonetheless "part of us."

As RAD's organizational structure tightened, its ideological vision narrowed. Confrontational talk about changing the culture of silence that allowed drugs to flourish and bringing the issue to the attention of politicians was dropped. Instead, participants now insisted that "we aren't political, just a bunch of people getting together." Complaints about police enforcement, the city's neglect of the neighborhood, and the broader problems of family and society through which drug addiction might be explained dropped away. By 2004, mentions of drugs in RAD meetings were almost always framed as a problem of individual failings, with disastrous results for family and community. The locus of the problem was firmly established as the troubled individual, not a troubled neighborhood, city, or society.

Paths and Contexts

Why did RAD change over the course of a year? Why did it become so homogeneous in membership and narrow in its vision and goals? It is tempting to rely on standard narratives that might attribute its increasing homogeneity and narrowing ideological vision to the difficulty of sustaining civic engagement. But are these explanations sufficient? Might a closer examination of RAD suggest more subtle processes and more important lessons?

Some microhistorians begin by investigating what seems puzzling, odd, or unexpected, what Matti Peltonen (2001) terms the "method of clues." I examine RAD's paths of action by starting with a puzzling observation: contrary to what might be expected in a group initially mobilized in the aftermath of the death of Nancy's son, her story and others like it gradually disappeared from RAD's meetings and literature. Why? Finding an explanation requires a closer look at the trajectory of emotional dynamics within RAD (see Goodwin, Jasper and Polletta 2001; Polletta and Amenta 2001).

By any measure, RAD's first gathering was emotionally charged and passionate. Nancy and others narrated in great detail the anguish of watching a loved one struggle with drug addiction and ultimately lose. They provided graphic accounts of disastrous outcomes, both for the addicts and for those around them. The audience was told that these stories could well be theirs, that their children might be—at this very moment—secretly in the grip of a deadly addiction. Everyone should be afraid, the speakers reiterated. Rather than retreating from this knowledge, however, Readville's citizens were instructed to acknowledge their vulnerability and channel their fears into an effort to end drugs in their community.

Within a few months of RAD's inception, its emotional tenor began to change. Emotional displays and talk of passion and fear were displaced in favor of a more dispassionate rhythm of assigning and reporting on tasks. Nancy's story, initially told or mentioned at every meeting, withered away over time to become nothing more than an occasional point of collective reference, reminding the group of its origin and importance. From a distance, such declining emotionality might seem simply a shift from passion to task orientation. But this categorization is belied by a closer look at the dynamics by which RAD originally came together and how these shaped its decreasing emotionality.

The official story of RAD, one repeated by Nancy and others at the first meeting and used consistently in media interviews, is that Nancy called together her friends and neighbors to post flyers that would attract notice by ordinary citizens touched by or fearing the onslaught of drugs. But when I probed for additional specifics, Nancy related a somewhat different story of the group's inception:

> A couple months after [my son] had passed away, I was down at [my doctor's] office....He was very sympathetic to what happened and just asked me how I felt, and did I feel that I had the courage to—or did I want to—help other people as far as the knowledge of drugs in this area and how to help other people not become involved as we did. And I said, "Yes, I would really like to do that." I really didn't know how we were going to get started, [but] a couple months later he contacted me and...said, "Are you still interested in trying to make a difference in the community?" and I said, "Absolutely, I think that's what my son would have wanted because he really was very devastated with his drug addiction and he really didn't want other people to suffer." So we just kind of just got together and he said, "okay, who in the community could help us out? Who would make a difference?"

This later version of the RAD origin story situates a local doctor, not Nancy, as the primary instigator of the group. Moreover, in this version Nancy relates that the discussion of forming RAD did not revolve around who might be personally touched by the issue of drugs, but who might be in an official position to help stop drugs from infecting the community.

The competing narratives of RAD's beginning help make sense of who was brought to the first meeting. Nancy enlisted not only her friends and others who worried about losing children to drugs but also antidrug workers, police, school principals, and civic leaders. These people represented competing ideas about the kinds of people who could "make a difference" in ending drugs in Readville. Their presence in RAD also presented different paths of action. RAD might become a venue by which people's painful experiences and raw emotions could be channeled into a collective demand for social change. Or it could move in a more dispassionate direction, supporting existing antidrug policies and strategies.

Why and how RAD moved away from emotionality and toward dispassionate action were conditioned, although not determined, by the wider social context in which RAD was organized. The seeds for this path can be seen in details of RAD's first meeting, during which testimonials by Nancy and others stirred the crowd's emotions but left the group floundering, without a clear direction for action. In white and working-class Readville, the question of how to channel emotion into action against drugs was problematic, because it was difficult to find an acceptable target for the neighborhood's anger. The police, who might be the logical locus of hostility in a neighborhood faced with lawless behavior, were off-limits in Readville. Many police officers lived in the neighborhood and had ties of kinship or friendship with organizers of RAD. In my conversations with residents of Readville, it was clear that residents were particularly protective of the police because of recent charges that white police officers had brutalized and even murdered a number of African American men. Drug dealers might be another logical aim for the neighborhood's anger. However, media-fueled stereotypes of Readville as an enclave of white racism made RAD wary of being labeled racist if it blamed neighborhood drug dealing on outsiders, generally understood to be those from nearby African American neighborhoods. At the same time, Readville's dense network of social ties made it difficult to blame indigenous drug dealers, who might well be connected to one's neighbors or friends. Even local government, a common target of neighborhood organizers in other areas, was a difficult focus for RAD, since Readville's economically strained residents feared that any demands made on the city would cause an increase in their taxes that they could ill afford.

Although the emotionality of RAD's initial meeting did not find a clear goal, it established a sense that the group needed to accomplish something in a short time lest Readville become the city's center of drug sales and violence. This sense of urgency—in the absence of a clear sense of how to proceed—is what, she later recalled, propelled Nancy to search the Internet for a plan of action that could be adopted locally. On the website of a Butler, Pennsylvania, antidrug group, Nancy found the Reality Tour and proposed that it be adopted. Lacking any alternatives—no leadership structure making anyone else responsible for generating ideas had been put in place—RAD adopted the Reality Tour as its strategy.

The decision to use the Reality Tour set RAD on a path of both increasing visibility and narrowing possibilities. From that point onward, RAD became focused on producing staged events that brought considerable publicity and funding but also undermined its original intent to create a diverse movement of citizens against drugs. Large numbers of members not only were unnecessary to produce the Reality Tour but could be counterproductive if they diverted the group from producing its tour. What mattered now was attracting specific kinds of attention—from those in a position to donate money and media coverage—and specific kinds of members: those who could act in or coordinate the staged productions. RAD members increasingly turned for help to people in their personal networks, those whose jobs and talents they knew and whose reliability could be assured. As a result, the group quickly lost its racial diversity and became, like Readville itself, virtually all white.

After the Reality Tour was in place, emotional displays were more likely to hinder than help RAD's work. Nancy's story and the stories of others were increasingly sidelined, brought to the surface only in new venues and with new audiences, such as interviews in the media. The personal stories through which RAD had been born gave way to the composite story of the Reality Tour. Emotions were evoked, but only in a form easily staged.

That the route from emotionality to task orientation is not inevitable in social groups can be seen more clearly by looking at another organizing effort in Pittsburgh at the same time. Eliminating Police Violence Together (EPVT) emerged as a group of poor African Americans who wanted to end police killings of African American men, the same situation that made RAD uneasy about attacking the effectiveness of the police. As with RAD, the initial meetings of EPVT were structured around the personal tragedy of one woman, Marilyn, who blamed the police for ineptly investigating the shooting of her son. The story of Marilyn's son—like that of Nancy's son—was the impetus for EPVT's initial organizing, and it commanded a central emotional position in the group's meetings. However, despite these initial similarities, RAD and EPVT developed very different emotional styles and paths of action over time.

The differing emotional paths of RAD and EPVT in part reflected differing styles of narrativity. Francesca Polletta (2002) argues that group narratives are more powerful when they are incomplete and thus require retelling. Stories of family drug tragedy in RAD were complete, needing no questioning, speculation, or elaboration, since deaths from drug overdose needed little interpretation. They fit into a widespread understanding of illegal narcotics as destructive of life and social relationships. In contrast, stories of abuse by the police in EPVT were open to interpretation. Such stories made sense—that is, became stories of police *abuse* rather than stories of necessary police *action*—only when juxtaposed against other stories of mistreatment of African Americans by police and white authorities. The power of Nancy's story was largely exhausted in RAD's initial mobilization, while the power of Marilyn's story grew over time in EPVT, eliciting additional stories of the problematic experiences of African Americans.

The differing emotional paths of RAD and EPVT also reflected the different contexts of each group's intended audiences. In RAD, personal stories of drug abuse and addiction remained at the level of individual disasters. Because of Readville's ties to the police and economic constraints, stories of individual tragedy were not able to shape in RAD a sense of larger possibilities for collective action and social change. The context for EPVT was different. Stories of abuse at the hands of white police did not challenge existing social relations in the economically struggling African American neighborhood in which EPVT was based. Indeed, its residents commonly spoke of abuses, large and small, that they endured from a wide range of white authorities and officials. Thus, while the context of life in Readville pushed RAD to become increasingly narrow over time, life in poor African American communities in Pittsburgh allowed EPVT's views to expand beyond the initial focus on the police to include an ever-widening range of issues, from health care to globalization and the US-sponsored war in Iraq. The spiral of ever-expanding stories of violence against African Americans moved the group increasingly toward a commitment to social change and collective action on issues far beyond its initial focus on white police officers in Pittsburgh.

The process by which Nancy's story became sidelined as the group's focus developed—while Marilyn's story was built on and expanded—hints at the complex and contingent ways in which collective action emerges over time. From an analytic distance, the story of RAD's transformation might be seen as just another example of the difficulty of sustaining movements for social change in the individualistic culture of the contemporary United States. A closer and more finely grained look, however, suggests that RAD's story is more complicated and more open-ended. RAD's changes over time were *possible* because of the conditions of its specific time and location. But micro-level factors, including how emotions were displayed and understood in the group, the idiosyncrasies of personalities, and the structure of social ties in RAD and Readville, shaped the particular path that RAD followed from incipient social movement group to civic improvement society. Standard narratives of social change pay insufficient attention to the ways in which small-scale aspects of social life shape the possibilities for large-scale social transformation.

CONCLUSION

What can be learned about the possibilities for collective movements for change by taking a close-grained look at one particular group, especially one that did not sustain its initial interest in broader social change? Or, as Edward Muir (1991:xiv) asks, "what can the few tell about the many, especially when the process of selection is neither random nor statistically rigorous?"

One lesson is methodological. From a macro-level perspective, social movements can seem to be a way in which people organize to make demands. Yet since studies at more micro scales of observation find that what people decide to demand is constructed in the process of collective action (Auyero 2004; Blee 2002; Larson and Sigal 2001), it is tautological to regard social movements as simple outgrowths of preexisting political ideas. As Doug McAdam (2001:223) argues, movements "are not, in any simple sense, born at the macro level." The microhistorical emphasis on interplay of scales of observation and the path-dependent emphasis on evolving action make it possible to understand the trajectory of a group like RAD without resorting to tautological explanations.

A second lesson is conceptual. Robert Goldman and Ann Tickamyer (1984) point out the homology between how humans are valued under capitalism and how humans are analyzed in much of social science. Capitalism emphasizes the quantitative value of things and people, neglecting that which is individual, personal, and specific. So do studies in which individuals are made into equivalent units. Such equivalency is achieved through commodification—abstracting away from particularistic contexts and social relations, restricting analysis to characteristics that are comparable across units, and developing reified categories that obscure underlying social relations, dynamics, contestations, and struggles. Such analyses obscure important variations in experiences, strategies of actions, and constraints on the lives of people so categorized (Doumanis and Pappas 1997;

Revel 1995; Rhomberg 2004; Walton 2001). Combining the insights of microhistory and ideas of path dependency offers a way to move beyond commodification and preserve the complexity of social life. It allows scrutiny of the dynamics of social life in a historical and contextualized fashion that attends to both the constraints and the margins of possibility for action in particular times and places.

A final lesson is analytical. The predominance of social scientific work on what Charles Tilly (1984, 1978) terms "big structures, large processes, huge comparisons" has tended to marginalize the study of micro-level processes and the interplay between scales of the large and the small. Yet this study may fill significant gaps in social scientific knowledge, even about macro-level phenomena. For example, studies of nation-states, global social change, and comparisons of collective violence across the world have made great strides in identifying the conditions under which warfare and violence are likely to erupt. But such research has provided little insight into why neighbors can turn suddenly and violently against neighbors, as happened in Rwanda, the former Yugoslavia, the border states in the U.S. Civil War, and many other places. The lessons of microhistory and path-dependency theory thus may prove most useful where macro studies are weakest: in examining emergent processes, uncovering mechanisms that underlie causal connections, and delineating sequencing of actions, events, and understandings over time.

Acknowledgments

This material is based on work supported by the National Science Foundation under Grants 0316436 and 0416500, which were awarded to the author. The author thanks Ashley Currier and Emily Long for assistance in data collection.

Notes

1. This name, as are all group and individual names, is a pseudonym.

2. Data were analyzed with the qualitative data-management software N6. Analysis is both longitudinal (within groups over time) and comparative (across groups). Details of methodology and analysis are available from the author.

4

To Write Liberation

Time, History, and Hope in Yucatán

Paul K. Eiss

"Mayo 4, 1913. an fabricado el gran mauser de Yucatán y su gran espada de acero. Por motivo de la libertad que viva la libertad muchachos que viva que viva los balientes que viva. Juramos que no rendimos. Juramos hasta que no la libertad."

Let me put that into English, leaving idiosyncrasies of grammar and spelling uncorrected: "May 4, 1913. They have made Yucatán's great Mauser and its great iron sword. For liberty, long live liberty, boys, *que viva*, long live the valient ones, *que viva*. We swear we will not give up. We swear, as long as there is no liberty."

There it is—the smallest meaningful "micro" unit. Zoom in any closer and you bring up isolated words or letters. But twist the lens in the other direction, and the field widens. A rifle comes into view, or rather a piece of wood carved to look like a rifle. The words are inscribed on its surface. Continue pulling back, slowly. There is trampled earth, the "gun" lying next to a "sword" fashioned out of an old barrel hoop, and a few spent cartridges. A little further out are walls, a yard, the arched facade of a building. There are some blotches of red   bloodstains—a trail leading from the house to a large water tank. Are those bloody handprints on its surface?

Men in uniform are walking around—soldiers or police. Cartridges are scattered everywhere. Let's pull back one last time, still using the micro lens. There is a complex of buildings, a large smokestack, stone walls, roads, cultivated fields, and columns of smoke rising somewhere in the distance. As we watch, a man in civilian dress walks out of the house, looks at one of the men in uniform, and speaks: "Está muerto—bien muerto" (He is dead—quite dead). The man continues on his way, inspecting bullet holes in the walls and scribbling in a notebook. He walks toward the "sword" and the "gun," kneels to stare at them for a moment, and transcribes the inscription in his book. Then he gets up and waves at a police officer, who comes over to collect the items and carries them off.

I offer this example of how the scene of microhistory, from the micro event setting to the crafting of microhistorical narrative, may be a scene of writing. At the center of the event, and at the tightest focus of historical meaning, we find an inscription. Widening the field slightly, but still very much within the most extreme parameters of the micro, we witness the act of writing itself, as a man reads the signs of his surroundings and finally transcribes the inscription in his notebook. To these two moments of inscription, I must add a third, indicating my own presence as a writer. Before finding the case file where the episode is documented, I read and transcribed many others relating to episodes of violence on Yucatecan haciendas. Here, at last, was one where the attackers had left behind a written inscription, as if to caption the scene, and where an investigator had taken the trouble to transcribe the inscription. Thank you. I hereby choose to make this fortuitous finding the central episode of this essay. Finally, let me footnote this discussion to signal that I too was "there"—not there on the hacienda, but there in the archive, the scene of my own transcription of a transcription, the penultimate scene of reading and writing prior to this writing of a microhistory.[1]

The methodological concerns of microhistory are often posed through the use of optical metaphors, by analogy with the operations of a microscope, telescope, or camera, or by comparison to cinematography or oil paintings. Microhistory's fundamental problems, we are told, are those of the "metric" or "scale" of analysis, of defining the relation between micro and macro processes and perspectives. Some deploy the language of positivistic social science to describe microhistory's purpose, as a project that promises the revision of comparative macro analyses through the discovery of "errors of aggregation," or the "generation of new theory" through the discovery of new points of linkage between macro and micro processes. According to the admonitions of one recent survey of the field (Levi 2001), one of microhistory's core missions is a defense of scientific method against the threats posed by "relativism," "neo-idealism," "irrationality," "postmodernism," and "autobiographical relativism." We are not to stray into interpretive, Geertzian, or hermeneutical approaches to microhistory (Ginzburg 1993; Levi 2001), all of which, according to Levi, tend toward the "reduction of the historian's work to a purely rhetorical activity which interprets texts and not events themselves."[2]

I do not mean to reject such optical, scalar, and metrical metaphors, which are varied, suggestive, and useful devices through which questions of microhistorical method may be broached. I do mean to suggest, however, that those metaphors are limited, failing to capture the complexities of interpretation and attention to textuality that have always been hallmarks of microhistory, from the now classic works of Carlo Ginzburg (1980a, 1983) to more recent studies (for example, Sullivan 2004). Practitioners of microhistory must remain open to diverse ways of understanding its epistemological status, and specifically to an understanding of the hermeneutics and politics of writing itself. Here, I shall take a reading of the inscription left at Chicché as an occasion for reflection on what attention to multilevel processes of writing and reading (see Clifford 1990; Geertz 1988; Ricoeur 1979) might offer microhistorians. I do not intend, through such a "graphocentric" approach (Clifford 1990), to consider "writing" generically but rather to consider processes of inscription, transcription, and description as they are manifested in the makings of event, document, archive, and microhistory. As suggestive as questions of scale might be in illuminating microhistory's method, I would like to suggest that it is in writing that we may find its ethics, politics, and poetics.

EVENT

Let's start with a tight focus and then slowly twist the lens, widening the field. We see a complex of fields, buildings, and processing machinery, which was called Hacienda Chicché—a plantation largely cultivated in henequen, a tall, spiky relative of aloe, whose fiber was used for the elaboration of rope and twine. Pulling back further we see that Chicché lay a few miles to the west of Tetiz, a pueblo whose inhabitants were about one thousand in number in 1913. Chicché was one among many henequen haciendas ringing towns and pueblos of the vicinity, an area called the Hunucmá District—after its head town—which we see on pulling back further, about five miles away. Receding yet further, we can place the Hunucmá region in the northwestern corner of a group of districts that made up the "henequen zone," a wide, densely populated swath of northwestern Yucatán, whose inhabitants resided in roughly equal numbers in the pueblos and on henequen haciendas.

While Hunucmá's towns and pueblos were already places of indigenous habitation before the Spanish conquest, by 1913 the region's social geography had been altered profoundly by a more recent history. Yucatán's mid-nineteenth-century Caste War, a decades-long conflict with Mayan rebels, resulted in the death of a large proportion of the state's population and the ruination of most of its sugar plantations. From 1876 onward, however, Yucatán, like the rest of Mexico, experienced swift changes attendant on a decades-long period of export-driven modernization, engineered and instituted by Mexican president Porfirio Díaz. Díaz enforced the new era of "order and progress" through authoritarian rule and the intermittent repression of resistance from peasants, workers, and political opponents. Yucatán's export economy was reborn as henequen haciendas, which produced fiber for the elaboration of rope and cordage in the United States, expanded throughout the northwest of the peninsula. Frustrated by a shortage of available wage labor, Yucatecan *hacendados* and government officials collaborated in the establishment of indigenous indebted servitude, by which Maya-speaking rural populations were compelled by means legal and extralegal to move their residences to the haciendas (Wells 1985; Wells and Joseph 1996).

Díaz's rule came to an end amid a deepening economic and political crisis and in the wake of several insurgencies that swept much of Mexico from 1909 forward, most notably those led by Emiliano Zapata, Pancho Villa, and Francisco Madero, the latter rising to the presidency in November 1911. In Yucatán, factional political violence spread as various political parties competed over the spoils of power at the state level and armed their supporters in the countryside, most of them indigenous workers and pueblo residents. While those parties differed somewhat by politics and ideology, their leaders shared a rhetorical commitment to the abolition of indigenous "slavery" on the henequen haciendas. They also shared a belief in the need to do so cautiously and gradually to avoid disruption of the lucrative henequen trade. In any event, in 1913, in the wake of a conservative military coup in Mexico City and the temporary restoration of Yucatán's old guard to power, the various factions agreed to lay down their arms and demobilize their rural supporters in the interest of restoring order on the haciendas and maintaining the flow of henequen money to Yucatecan oligarchs.

Considered in its regional context, the Hunucmá area stands out as diverse, even somewhat anomalous. The region was a core area of the henequen zone; it was immediately adjacent to Mérida, Yucatán's capital, and included both large and important towns such as Hunucmá and Umán and some of the state's largest, most populous, and most productive haciendas. In much of the region, like the rest of the henequen zone, haciendas ringed all towns and pueblos, henequen fields stretched into the area's dwindling woodlands, and indigenous populations were forced into debt servitude as resident peons on the fincas. But in contrast with most of the rest of the zone, the Hunucmá region was a geographic periphery, bordering on extensive and sparsely inhabited or uninhabited areas of woodlands, swamps, savanna, salt pools, and gulf coastline to the north and west. While some of these lands were attached to the haciendas for future planting, fuel wood for machinery, or the harvesting of salt or dyewood, much of the area remained an open frontier of woodlands and swamp intermittently occupied by subsistence agriculturalists and hunters.

Hunucmá's divided geography made for a somewhat different history from that of the rest of northwestern Yucatán. From the 1870s forward, even as many indigenous pueblo residents were forced out of the pueblos to become peons on the haciendas, others took to the woods. Large groups of men, sometimes numbering in the hundreds, blacked their faces, sneaked out of the pueblos, and, under cover of darkness, targeted haciendas established on old common lands and forests. They shot cattle, burned and slashed henequen fields, toppled walls enclosing fields, and shot or macheted hacienda employees—even, on occasion, hacendados or public officials. Then they slipped back into the woods, eluding their pursuers in the woodlands and trackless swamps that bordered the haciendas.

From the 1880s forward, these attacks increased in frequency and scale, reaching their peak under the leadership of an enigmatic Robin Hood–like figure known as the King of the Forest (El Rey de los Bosques). In 1892, after one particularly violent attack by "the King," the state government instituted an extended military crackdown—involving house searches, patrols, mass arrests, interrogations, detentions, and lengthy terms of imprisonment—to restore conditions conducive to "order and progress." But even as the haciendas renewed their expansion in the aftermath, simmering discontent and occasional outbreaks of violence on the haciendas and in the woods continued. In the wake of the political collapse of the Díaz regime in 1911, violence once again broke out in the Hunucmá region, quickly overshadowing factional violence elsewhere in the state in severity. The movement reached the scale of an insurgency under the leadership of Hunucmá resident Feliciano Canul Reyes and his second in command, José Pío Chuc. Henequen haciendas were deserted, as indebted residents fled for the pueblos or the woods, joining bands of attackers based in the forests, who periodically emerged to burn and bomb their way through the fincas.[3]

This brings us back to Chicché. That hacienda did not rank among the largest in the region in size or population but was a midsized operation. What distinguished Chicché (which in Yucatec Maya means "thicket") was its location—directly west of the pueblo of Tetiz and directly between it and a sizable area of unoccupied woodlands, savanna, and coastal swamps. Like other haciendas in the area, Chicché had expanded at an impressive pace from the 1880s forward, largely due to the annexation of communal woodlands. The owner of the hacienda was Don Diego María Solís, a powerful member of the local gentry. While serving as Tetiz's mayor in 1899, he ordered pueblo residents to build a road to provide access to the north-western woodlands—and, quite conveniently, to Chicché. Then, once out of office a few years later, he built a gate across the road, closing it to all traffic. Henceforth, all who sought to use the road would have to obtain his permission and pay a toll for the privilege. Directly adjoining the road, Solís built the main house of Chicché—an arched structure that he called, on one occasion, "a kind of fortress, since it has two floors." Indeed, the structure served that purpose, as gunmen posted on the upper level of the building scrutinized those who came and went on the road. For indigenous residents of the area, the house stood as both a material barrier between them and their livelihood and a symbolic monument to Don Diego's power.[4] It is thus unsurprising that Chicché became a flashpoint with the onset of the revolution. There were several bombing and arson attacks against the hacienda in 1911 and 1912, and old Diego was ambushed by gunmen on at least three occasions while traveling the road between Chicché and Tetiz. The hacendado came into frequent conflicts with pueblo residents over the woodlands adjoining Chicché, which they claimed as common lands of *el pueblo*. Solís filed criminal charges against them in 1913 and had two dozen men arrested for wood poaching.[5]

Notwithstanding such ferment, the attack of May 4, 1913, was unprecedented in scale and drama. Amid rumors of an impending attack on the finca, Don Diego and his principal overseer decided to stay on the finca to defend it, along with five trusted employees whom they armed for that purpose and posted on the second floor of the house. Shortly before midnight, the overseer heard a sound in the darkness and shouted, "Who are you? Answer, you bastard!" Someone shouted in response, "We are not bastards!" Then dozens of men, with faces blacked, emerged from the darkness and fired in unison on Solís and his men. After an intense firefight, the attackers withdrew without being able to take the main house, leaving one of Solís's retainers in his death throes. For the rest of the night, Don Diego and the other men looked out into the darkness from the top floor of the house, watching the glow of fires and listening to the sounds of explosions on the nearby fincas San Rafael and San Luis.

We now may consider the significance of the event at Chicché at several levels or scales, from micro to medial to macro. At the micro level, the attack on Chicché appears to be the culmination of previous conflicts over "poaching" of wood, between Don Diego, who claimed the land where the wood was cut belonged to his finca, and pueblo residents, who claimed those woodlands as common lands. At the medial level, however, we might reconsider the event at Chicché in terms of the social geography of the area—that is, in terms of the place of the hacienda at a strategic location blocking access to woodlands that were a vital resource for subsistence agriculturalists and hunters. This interpretation would help explain the targeting of San Rafael and San Luis, which, like Chicché, were henequen haciendas located near Tetiz and were composed largely of common woodlands recently annexed by their owners. The organization and scale of the attack, as a self-declared war of "liberation," might be considered indicative of a local insurgency aimed at destroying the haciendas and restoring the commons in the Hunucmá region.

But it is through the reconsideration of the event in light of its macro contexts that what might be the fullest significance of the attack on Chicché might be found. In the regional historiography of Yucatán, it has been argued that rural insurgencies, while involving elite and subaltern actors, emerged when political parties sparred but were suppressed by elite partisan leaders in the wake of the overthrow of Francisco Madero and the restoration of planter rule in the state. The events at Chicché, which occurred considerably after the demobilization and more than one year before the promulgation of an official liberation decree in August 1914, would seem to suggest that there was greater autonomy in the insurgencies than has been argued. The uprisings near Tetiz, it would seem, had less to do with partisan conflicts in the early 1910s and more to do with a much longer history of struggles of forest, field, and community in the region, which began more than one century before and would continue for decades into the future. In its broadest macro implications, therefore, the close study of this micro event might lead us to move beyond regional or national historiographical paradigms that tend to periodize history according to developments in the formal political realm and tend to identify the content of historical movements, revolutionary or otherwise, with the concerns and ideology of political leaders, whether government officials or partisan agitators.

Yet none of these interpretations take into account the significance of the inscription and the insurgents' decision to leave behind the inscribed gun and sword at the site of the attack. That was what distinguished the May 5 attack on Chicché from so many other attacks. Previous insurgent actions may well have been intended and perceived as acts of "liberation" by participants, but it was the written inscription left behind on this one occasion that gave this "event" its particular character. Why were those words inscribed on the gun, and why were sword and gun abandoned at the scene of the attack by those who had carried them? To explore this question is to embark upon a microhistory of practices of writing: from event to document, and from archive to history.

DOCUMENT

Writing was critically important to Maya populations, both before the Spanish conquest and afterward. Mayan scribes, and the archives of Yucatec Maya and Spanish documentation they kept and often transcribed, played fundamental roles in the survival of indigenous republics, or *cahs*, under colonial rule (Restall 1997). While much of the documentation kept by the cahs related to their territorial sovereignty, officials of the cahs also periodically produced petitions or letters meant to give voice to the concerns of local Mayan elites or commoners before Spanish officials and courts (see Emigh, this volume). Following independence in 1821, the indigenous republics continued a beleaguered existence and, until their abolition in 1868, continued to guard and produce documents largely intended to defend communal lands from the encroachments of haciendas. Subsequently, however, Hispanic residents, typically landowning gentry, assumed control over all institutions of local governance. As a result, indigenous working populations in the area of Hunucmá were left without access to a means of politically effective representation in written form—a situation reflected in Yucatecan elites' common usage of the euphemistic term *analfabeta* (illiterate) as a racial slur against those of indigenous heritage.

At the same time, however, representations—or, to be more precise, transcriptions—of the words of indigenous rural populations in the area of Hunucmá increased exponentially in quantity. From the 1870s onward, uprisings in the area led to campaigns of judicial inquiry into the nature and causes of events of violence and into the identities and potential motivations of those thought responsible. Along with mass arrests and interrogations, the translation and transcription of the testimony of workers and pueblo inhabitants was a principal responsibility of justices of the peace and other investigators, who produced case files that sometimes ran to hundreds of pages in length. Such investigations involved the collection of abundant micro-level testimony and evidence and the exploration of competing hypotheses about the nature of the violence (that is, whether it constituted acts of organized insurgency, incidents of banditry, or acts of personal vengeance). Despite the copious production of judicial case files, the investigations resulted only rarely in the conviction of those accused, and never in convincing or conclusive explanations or descriptions of the character of violent events. Nonetheless, the drawn-out nature of the legal process meant that those suspected of involvement could be subjected to lengthy interrogations, physical and psychological abuse, and imprisonment for months or even years under the presumption of guilt while trials proceeded. Transcription and related processes of documentation and investigation thus may have had their greatest effect neither in establishing individual guilt nor corroborating the nature of events, but rather as a means of collective punishment and intimidation.

A similar politics of investigation, transcription, and description was very much evident in the years leading up to Chicché, as police and courts responded to the violence in Hunucmá with a wave of mass arrests, imprisonments, and interrogations. But through decades of repression, indigenous residents of pueblos such as Tetiz, although largely illiterate and denied the collective avenues of written representation earlier offered by the scribes of the cahs, had gained direct experience with the connection between writing and power and had developed a set of tactics in response: systematically refusing to supply information and swearing their ignorance; refusing to betray others; taking off into the woods for lengthy periods while investigators were at work; joining forces with others to hide incriminating objects such as guns; and, later, taking revenge against those thought to have collaborated with interrogators. Their familiarity with tactics of interrogation is clear from a close reading of the Chicché case files, which show detainees—with the exception of one or two informers—frustrating their interlocutors and subverting cases through various strategies, including systematic denials and refusals to provide information.[6]

The decision to fabricate, inscribe, and then leave behind "sword" and "gun" thus bore special significance as an instance of writing directed at multiple audiences. Both items were symbols of proper military conflict rather than rural uprising. The sword, unlike the machetes typically carried by rural insurgents, was not a work tool but rather a military weapon. So was the Mauser, which made a sharp contrast with the shotguns that

Yucatecans employed for hunting deer, turkeys, and wild pigs. Moreover, the weapons were identified as the "great Mauser" and the "great sword" *of Yucatán*. Thus the facsimile weapons and their inscription seem to have been intended to make clear that more than an act of partisan violence, this was a military engagement by an army in a war embracing the entire peninsula (de Yucatán) rather than simply Hunucmá. Finally, the inscription was formulated as an oath—"We swear we will not give up. We swear, as long as there is no liberty"—one that was sanctified in violence and that claimed power through writing.

But most important of all was the timing of the attack on Chicché and the inscribed date on the gun itself: midnight of May 4, the inaugural moment of May 5, Cinco de Mayo. By coordinating their action with a national holiday, specifically one commemorating the victory of Mexican forces over French invaders in 1862, the insurgents were making a dramatic public claim that theirs was a war not only for the liberation of the commons or even Yucatán but for the liberation of the *patria*. By inscribing sword and gun, they drew an equivalence between hacendados like Don Diego and foreign imperialists, making the insurgency a war to liberate both the commons and *la nación*. The inscription of the date on gun and sword, in effect, was meant to make sword and gun stand as documents, and signifiers of history—that is, as links between past, present, and future, monumentalizing the attack on Chicché as the opening salvo of a liberation war yet to come.

Above all, the sword and gun were inscribed in order that their messages be read not only by participants but also by a wider audience, beginning with the police investigators and judges who found them at Chicché. By stating that "they" had made the weapons of war (*han fabricado*) rather than "we," the men clearly were placing themselves in the position of others, with regard to a potential audience that might write them into history rather than into a case file. That is, the inscription was directed as much to observers as to participants, and as much toward the future as it was to present and past. As historical "documents," sword and gun were meant to call forth an audience of future readers to transcribe their message and interpret its meaning.

ARCHIVE

In the days immediately following the May 5 attacks, as many as two hundred soldiers and police swept into the Hunucmá area. They engaged in firefights with large groups of men, first on the road between Chicché and Tetiz and then near other haciendas outside Tetiz. Police investigators and local judges scoured the area, detaining and interrogating dozens of suspects and taking and transcribing their testimony. At the same time, even as shootouts continued, newspaper reporters went into action. They interviewed officials and investigators, collected information and rumors, and began drafting narrative accounts of the events in Hunucmá. Thus courts and press collaborated in complementary processes of archival production—the former through the creation of a closed judicial case file to be consulted by criminal justices, the other through the creation of a public record for reading and consultation by a literate (and hence privileged) Yucatecan public. Both kinds of archiving, and the emergent descriptions of the events at Chicché that they provided, were to be intimately implicated in the wave of repression to follow.[7]

That the process of description, narration, and archiving worked in this way was not a new development in the Hunucmá region. From the 1870s and 1880s, local gentry and state officials boosted the region in the press as a place of progress and civilization, one appropriate for investment in haciendas and public works. But the 1892 attack of the "King of the Forest" changed that. From a region associated with uninterrupted order and progress, in a matter of days, Hunucmá was transformed in press reports into a place whose inhabitants had regressed due to lives spent in the "immense and dark forests [where] they base themselves...organiz[ing] their depredations, taking part in an uninterrupted series of evil deeds, and living a life of true savagery." From a gateway of progress, Hunucmá became an unstable frontier, where a new chapter in Yucatán's Caste War was to be waged by the forces of "civilization" against "Indian savages" who were "incarnations of evil and vice." Such descriptions of events provided the context for impassioned calls in all newspapers for an extended military campaign in the area, which was not long in coming, and incited the production of ever larger reams of testimony on events in Hunucmá.[8]

Two decades later, with the renewed outbreak of violence in Hunucmá in 1911, journalists once again took note of the upheavals there, but typically attributed them to banditry, Indian "drunkenness," or manipulation by outside political agitators. In several cases, documents authored by insurgent leader Feliciano Canul Reyes, and riddled with orthographic and grammatical errors, were recovered and published in newspapers verbatim. They were accompanied by sardonic commentaries on the "picturesque" and "expressive" style of Hunucmá's "famous literato," as well as caustic references to him and others as "'leaders' of illiterate Indians"—comments clearly meant to belittle the political importance of the movement in Hunucmá. But in 1913, as in 1892, the attack on Chicché triggered a dramatic change in the extent and tenor of the coverage. Like previous documents captured from the rebels, the inscription left behind by the insurgents made its way onto the front page of the most important Yucatecan newspaper, the *Revista de Yucatán*—but this time, with grammar and spelling corrected. It was as if ridicule of the rebels as a bunch of "illiterates" and the dismissal of the political threat that they represented were no longer options. Journalists, government officials, and the Yucatecan reading public scrutinized the facsimile weapons and their words both as echoes of a disturbing past and as ominous harbingers of the future. Reporters of the *Revista de Yucatán* ran the headline "The Horrors of *Zapatismo* in Hunucmá" and recounted to readers how Yucatán's Indian "Zapatistas" now stood, as had Mayan Caste War rebels of the previous century, at the very "gates of the beautiful city of Mérida," as a "stain on our civilization." Commentators made no note of the obvious intended reference to the Cinco de Mayo holiday but rather declared that Hunucmá's "Zapatistas" aimed at the destruction of the patria. *Revista* editor Carlos Menéndez called upon the Yucatecan government to "save the *patria*" by "crushing [Hunucmá's] arsonists, thieves, bombers and assassins...once and for all."[9]

The words carved on the wooden weapons thus did not have a single meaning but rather took on significance in the context of multiple transcriptions and descriptions, and readings by multiple audiences. Those who attacked Chicché left the inscriptions as a demand that their actions be recognized as political, liberatory, patriotic, and historic. The words were meant as an oath but also as a commemorative marker, indexing the future liberation with regard to which their action would be seen and eventually perhaps described as heroic and foundational. As a written inscription, however, those words took on meanings that could not be controlled by those who had authored them. In transcription, the inscribed message provided material for a radically different description of and reading on events—those of hacendados and government officials. For them, the message of sword and gun was that the violence in Hunucmá represented the outbreak of a class and race war that might sweep the peninsula. The inscription was publicly transcribed in the press not as a manifesto for liberation but rather as a charter for a state of exception in which civil rights would cease to exist and social and political "order" would be restored at any cost.

Thus government officials, police, courts, and local hacendados and authorities joined forces, egged on by jeremiads in the regional press, in what would become a truly massive wave of repression throughout the

Hunucmá district. Large groups of soldiers were sent to occupy the pueblos and towns of the region. They engaged in occasional firefights (with men typically identified only as "the enemy"), beat and harassed political organizers, ransacked stores and houses, and kidnapped, harassed, and sexually assaulted relatives of suspected rebels. They assisted hacendados in reestablishing control over the haciendas by tracking down and returning escaped peons, supervising laborers in the henequen fields, patrolling woodlands, and arresting men thought to be wood poachers. They arbitrarily detained and imprisoned large numbers of men in the pueblos, forcing them to build roads or labor in the henequen fields, or conscripting them for military service.[10]

Such measures seem to have only intensified the liberation war in Hunucmá. Growing numbers of men left their homes in the pueblos, and indebted peons fled the haciendas to join Canul Reyes's insurgents in their secret camps in the northwestern woods. Uprisings and violence continued on the haciendas, henequen fields were put to the torch, houses were set afire and bombed, and policemen and soldiers were attacked.[11] By August events at the national level presented an opening for the Yucatecan insurgents, as Venustiano Carranza's Constitutionalist revolutionary forces overthrew dictator Victoriano Huerta and occupied Mexico City. On August 18, Canul Reyes led Hunucmá's insurgents—who had joined with rebels from the port city of Progreso and declared their allegiance to Carranza, making them "official" allies of the federal government—in an attack on Progreso. While Canul died during an intense forty-minute battle with soldiers of the military garrison, the attackers were victorious. News of the fall of Progreso coincided with the overthrow of Mexico's military government, and Carranza immediately sent a new governor, Eleuterio Avila, to Yucatán, with orders to issue a decree ending indigenous debt servitude.[12]

Shortly after his arrival in Mérida, as if to fulfill the *Revista*'s terrified prophecies in the wake of the Cinco de Mayo attacks, Avila invited the insurgents from Hunucmá to pass through the gates of Mérida. They did so not as the "macabre hoards" of invaders conjured by the *Revista* but rather as allies of the new government, invited to witness the liberation and thus, it might have seemed to them, discharge the oath taken at Chicché. On September 11, the surviving insurgents assembled in Mérida's central plaza, where they were saluted by a government official as "true soldiers of order" who had "collaborated in the great works of the Constitutionalist Revolution." More than just praise, the official's words were speech acts meant to expunge events like the attack on Chicché from the archives of official memory: "You have not robbed, you have not committed arson, you have not attacked any homes, you have not violated the inviolable rights of civilized society." Then Governor Avila appeared with the liberation decree he had just signed and read it to the crowds assembled in the plaza, proclaiming the "redemption" of indigenous "pariahs," who would now be "restored to the embrace of our citizenry." Immediately following the ceremony, the forces from Hunucmá joined a group of two thousand people and traveled to the cemetery at Progreso. There, they visited the grave of Feliciano Canul Reyes, saluting him as a "martyr," "patriot," and "citizen." The events in both Progreso and Mérida had refigured them all publicly—from savages to citizens, from murderers to martyrs—and seemed to refigure the meaning of Chicché inscriptions as auguries of the conclusive liberation of September 11.[13]

Subsequent events, however, would change the terms of history and memory in ways that effaced the uprising of May 5, 1913, and even the dramatic liberation of the following year. The 1914 decree only abolished debt peonage, leaving the issue of lands, so critical in the Hunucmá region, untouched. Moreover, the Avila government immediately qualified and curtailed even the decree's limited provisions, applying it only in the narrowest of ways to a relatively small number of haciendas. Avila's successor as governor, General Salvador Alvarado, claimed for himself the title of "liberator" by enforcing the liberation decree, along with a more sweeping set of reforms. But while Hunucmá's erstwhile insurgents initially saw Alvarado as a potential ally, the revolutionary government remained cautious and conservative on the question of land distribution. Hostilities once again broke out in the region, as groups of armed residents of Hunucmá, now under the leadership of Canul's second in command, José Pío Chuc, occupied lands of the haciendas and intimidated or attacked government agents sent to mediate disputes. In response, Alvarado, who along with other government officials now referred to Chuc's men as "counterrevolutionary germs," authorized a new campaign of mass arrests and detentions, forced labor on public works, military occupation, and public executions. The official history of the revolution, as chronicled by historians and propagandists linked to the Alvarado government, would now credit Alvarado, rather than Avila, with securing the end of indigenous servitude. The insurgent conquest of Progreso, the inaugural strike on Chicché, and Hunucmá's long struggle for liberation would have no place in the official history of the revolution as it would be authored in the years to come (see Trouillot 1995).

But the effacement of the inscription and the transformation of May 5, 1913, into a nonevent were not simply the products of official silencing. In the wake of Alvarado's arrival in the peninsula and political conflict related to the rise of socialism in the region in the ensuing years, Hunucmá was riven by factional violence, which led, in the late 1910s and early 1920s, to a state of terror in the region. Mass killings became commonplace, as former insurgents—notable among them José Pío Chuc—were targeted by government officials and police, and targeted their own political rivals in turn. Various factions killed dozens of town and pueblo residents, many of them not political activists. In the most extreme case, Pío Chuc's men executed some thirty-six men and boys, throwing their bodies into wells in the woodlands outside Hunucmá; Pío Chuc's dismembered body would be discovered in the same location several months later. It is thus unsurprising, given official silencing and the legacies of terror, that contemporary residents of the area do not recall the events of the time as a war of liberation but rather as a concatenation of episodes of bodily harm, disfigurement, murder, and terror. The Chicché inscription, and the aspirations it signified, found their final destination in neither official history nor popular historical memory but rather in the old case files from Hunucmá, which were sealed and stored away in the darkness of Yucatán's penal archives.

HISTORY

"Mayo 4, 1913. an fabricado el gran mauser de Yucatán y su gran espada de acero. Por motivo de la libertad que viva la libertad muchachos que viva que viva los balientes que viva. Juramos que no rendimos. Juramos hasta que no la libertad."

There they are: words on paper. Twist the lens, and the field widens. The words are written on the middle of an old, yellowed sheet of ledger paper and are located at the center of an account scrawled by Tetiz's justice of the peace, Cristino Concha. The sheet is sewn with hundreds of others into a thick file, itself heaped with dozens of other old dusty files in a cardboard box. Continue pulling back, slowly. There are other boxes—row upon row and stack upon stack, hundreds of them standing in the darkness of a storage room. As we watch, a door opens, and a woman in a blue lab coat enters, flicks on a florescent light, and picks up the box. She turns around and walks back out the door, down a flight of stairs, through an antechamber, and then into a room with desks, tables, and books—a reading room? She carries the box to one of the tables, leaving it by a man (me) who sits there. "*Aquí está.* Box 928." I open the box and remove the files one by one before settling on one of them. I inspect it for a moment and then begin typing on a laptop computer, transcribing the words on those fragile pages: "Mayo 4, 1913…"

More than eighty years after the attack at Chicché, I found myself in Yucatán's state archives doing some of the same things Concha had done in the immediate aftermath of events: scrutinizing an inscription, puzzling at its meaning, transcribing the words, and carrying them off for future analysis, description, and citation. But even though the reading room, like Chicché, was a scene of writing, and even if some of my textual methods as a microhistorian might have been compared with those of a judge or inquisitor, the motivations were of course quite different. Mine were those of a graduate student at the University of Michigan in the early 1990s. I had come to microhistory through my acquaintance with slavery, emancipation, and post-emancipation studies. That field largely consisted of scholarship that aimed to recover the history of slaves and freedpeople as they struggled—in ways often autonomous from those of elite social reformers—to articulate what "freedom" might mean, as a horizon for mobilization under or against slavery or in diverse struggles in the aftermath of emancipation.

Such issues were then, as now, by no means only academic or intellectual in nature. The backdrop to my archival and ethnographic research in Yucatán in the mid-1990s was daily news of Zapatista resistance in Chiapas and of the Mexican army's campaign of repression in response. At the time, the Zapatista movement provided a critical political, cultural, and historical point of reference for me, as for many others. It dramatized the power of a coalition of indigenous groups to set in motion what was effectively a global struggle for "liberation," a term that embraced multiple domains, ranging from land to education, access to medical care, gender and racial equality, issues of cultural autonomy, and democratic politics. It was in this context that I "discovered" Hunucmá. In seeming defiance of Yucatán's renown for contemporary political and social quiescence, Hunucmá seemed to have had a vocation for rebellion, from the nineteenth century forward, in ways that resonated with both the historical experience of emancipation and the contemporary Zapatista movement. While complex, and differing in content at different historical moments, Hunucmá's struggles seemed to me to demonstrate a far-ranging penchant for and advocacy of "liberation." More often than not, however, my ascription of a self-conscious emancipatory project to Hunucmá's arsonists and bandits was based not on direct evidence but on "heroic inferences" (Walton, this volume) from suggestive but terse documents, typically authored by those charged with or sympathetic to the movement's repression.

This was the intellectual and political context of my initial encounter with the inscription on sword and gun. These were the words I had been seeking—a subaltern inscription, quite literally, and one that seemed a perfect confirmation of my microhistorical "discovery" of Hunucmá's epochal struggles for liberation. The insurgent struggles of the nineteenth and early twentieth centuries had been expunged from official history and had been largely forgotten or ignored by contemporary inhabitants of the region—or so I thought. Through the Chicché inscription, and my transcription of that inscription into the history I one day would write, I imagined that the inspiring and long-lost tale might at last be recovered, and might even be made available to contemporary inhabitants of the region.

I was thus surprised and momentarily disconcerted when a man I was interviewing in Tetiz showed me a book recently published by a friend of his from the town of Hunucmá. The 1996 book—a work by Anacleto Cetina Aguilar entitled *Breves datos históricos y culturales del municipio de Hunucmá* (Brief Historical and Cultural Notes on the Municipality of Hunucmá)— included an account of Hunucmá's revolutionary years. Cetina, whom I first met in August 2001 and interviewed on multiple occasions over the course of the years to follow, was born in 1941 into a working-class, Maya-speaking family in Hunucmá. With adulthood, he began a long exile from town as a rural teacher in indigenous communities in various locations throughout the state. His second vocation at that time was not that of a historian but rather that of a poet, whose work consisted largely of odes denouncing the poverty and marginalization of Latin America's rural poor and celebrating uprisings of leftist guerrillas and revolutionaries in response. After returning to Hunucmá in 1979 to take a lesser post as a primary schoolteacher, Cetina regrounded himself in town through poetry and politics. The focus of his poetic work shifted; he dedicated himself to authoring a series of idealized and romantic paeans to Hunucmá. At the same time, he joined the only credible opposition movement in the region, the right-wing Partido de Acción Nacional (PAN), rising to become its mayoral candidate in the 1993 elections.

But in 1994, even as he continued to work in PAN in Hunucmá, Cetina's imagination was captured by the Zapatista movement. Along with other activists from Yucatán and the rest of Mexico, he traveled to Chiapas in 1995 to take part in a large meeting with the Zapatistas in their jungle stronghold, La Realidad. There, he met and exchanged poems with Subcomandante Marcos. He even sheltered several Zapatistas in his home in Hunucmá when they were traveling through Yucatán the next year. Finally, even as he pursued pedagogy, poetry, and diverse political causes, Cetina Aguilar began to move in a new direction that would occupy him for several years—the writing of a cultural and historical survey of Hunucmá, entitled *Breves datos.*

Most of *Breves datos* consists of a compendium of historical and cultural data, assembled under broad rubrics ("History," "Culture," "Principal Residents," and so on). While some readers might detect a kinship of spirit between *Breves datos* and Luis González's classic study of pueblo history in Mexico (González 1974), Anacleto Cetina Aguilar makes no claim to be writing "microhistory," or even "history" per se. Rather, Cetina collects the apocrypha of local geography, architecture, history, and customs and presents them to the reader as holding intrinsic interest merely by virtue of relating to Hunucmá. The general tone of *Breves datos* is quite familiar, as if assuming that the reading audience is itself from Hunucmá, and rather than making a contribution to scholarship, the text clearly is meant to provide a substantial and intimate knowledge of the town's features and history to its current residents.

Yet at the heart of the historical chapter of *Breves datos* are several sections dedicated to the revolutionary years in Hunucmá. In substance and tone, they break sharply with the apocrypha of town history that precedes them and the details regarding town notables and edifices that follow. Cetina's reconstruction of Hunucmá in the times of revolution presents information he collected from interviews with older townspeople and his research into period newspapers, but whose significance he recasts via a reading of centuries-old Mayan prophetic texts. In ways that converged topically with my own interests in Hunucmá's revolutionary history but sharply diverged from my interpretations of that history, Cetina represents the revolutionary history of Hunucmá, as well as its contemporary condition and future, according to a narrative of martyrdom that is equally Christian and Mayan in spirit, millennial and revolutionary in tone (Cetina 1996:61). Cetina presents Feliciano Canul Reyes and José Pío Chuc as both social revolutionaries and Mayan heroes, redeemers of an outraged pueblo and martyrs in the cause of liberation. Referring to Feliciano Canul's flight to the woods near Hunucmá in 1913 to escape reprisals by authorities (in the wake of the May 5 attacks, of which Cetina makes no mention), Cetina directly relates Canul's experiences to the prophecies of the ancient Chilam Balam manuscripts. Canul, he writes, "had to flee to the countryside to fulfill the prophecy of Nahua Pech"—a prophetic figure who, Cetina relates, foretold an indigenous war to overthrow white rule.[14]

Similarly, Cetina's discussion of José Pío Chuc is intended to contest what Cetina saw as a biased image of Chuc as a savage killer. Cetina describes Chuc as also fulfilling the Chilam Balam prophecies, suffering "the same persecution, the same attacks, and the same necessity of the campesino, to flee like a game animal, hunted by predators, to seek refuge in the woods—the only place that offers him protection, and lovingly opens its thick arms to protect him with its green fronds." The result was that Chuc rose as a Mayan leader on a par with Jacinto Canek and other leaders of colonial resistance movements and the Caste War, a struggle against "more than three hundred years of slavery" that had earned him, like other Mayan rebels, only the infamy of "savages and butchers." In the *Breves datos*, the deaths of Canul and Chuc—the latter a martyr Cetina places on a par with "Spartacus, Gandhi, Hidalgo, Marti and Che Guevara"—set the stage for the later betrayal of their followers by government leaders, who once in power ignored the legitimate demands and grievances of the revolution's foot soldiers, turning their attentions instead to lining their own pockets through institutionalized graft and nepotism. Cetina holds up the contemporary Zapatista movement in Chiapas as the contemporary inheritor of the struggle for liberation. Cetina describes that movement as the "first step toward [a new] campesino uprising" and the "only road that bad governments and the executioners of the pueblo have left to el pueblo" (Cetina 1996:59, 151).

In some respects, the differences between me and Don Anacleto, as historians, could not have been greater. I spent most of my efforts in time-intensive work in the state archives and thus had the opportunity to find the Chicché file and read the inscription within. Cetina, however, was limited by his teaching responsibilities to the very strategic use of newspapers on weekends and days off (looking at issues for dates he knew were important, like the August 1914 battle in Progreso). Since he had never heard of the Cinco de Mayo attacks, he had no cause to search out information on them in newspaper collections and thus had not encountered the inscription as transcribed in the press either. But Cetina had access to stories he had heard from the 1940s forward, as well as more recently, in the context of speaking with old friends and family members—stories that I could never hope to find, except through him, given that most of those who had told them were no longer alive by the time I began my research. Those very differences, however, sustained our conversations. We had much to learn from each other and established something of a trading relationship: I handed him photocopies of archival documents relating to the insurgents, and he shared stories he had heard about the same men, even taking me to speak with several elderly town residents with whom he had previously spoken about Hunucmá's revolutionary years.

For both of us as well, the contemporary world—initially the Zapatistas but later the attacks of September 2001 and events in their wake—was an ever-present subject, interrupting our discussions and changing our respective understandings of history. These events affected us, and our approaches to history, in different ways. Cetina Aguilar's formerly romantic vision of Pío Chuc became ambivalent, or tragic, as he alternated between celebrating Chuc's liberation struggle and criticizing his "terrorist" methods. Cetina's critical stance on the contemporary conflict of terrorism and imperialism—"neither one nor the other!" he once told me—informed his new reading of history as a tragic and cautionary tale (see D. Scott 2004) of how "Pío Chuc's struggle became corrupted" and how the conception of liberty among Hunucmá's rebels was "too narrow" because it was focused on the question of land rather than embracing democratic and ethical conduct as well. While Cetina drew new conclusions on the lessons of Hunucmá for world politics and *panista* political strategy, I found myself turning back to the Chicché inscription—although informed by a renewed interest in exploring the possibilities of insurgent conceptions of "liberation" at a time when that word seemed to be heard only as a rhetorical supplement to bombardment and occupation.

But over the course of our conversations, despite our differences and despite the differences that set both of us apart from the insurgents of May 5, 1913, it became clear to me that Cetina's conception of history offered the possibility of identifying one important commonality among us all. In *Breves datos*, Cetina had presented the story of the martyrdom of el pueblo, from the Spanish conquest to the present, and concluded that Hunucmá, like the rest of rural Mexico, continued to suffer the burden of a past that, for him, has prevented the pueblo from having, or completing, its own "history" (Cetina 1996:68). When I asked Don Anacleto what he meant, he answered in a way that demonstrated that his concept of history depended as much on a future redemption of el pueblo as it did on a vision or interpretation of the past:

> EISS: In your book you wrote, "History is written by the winners, and the history that we know is what serves the present system. The definitive history of the campesinos and workers has not yet been written." What did you mean by that?
>
> CETINA: The reason I wrote that the definitive history has not been written is because the future of the peasant [campesino] is uncertain. Nobody has known where he can go, what he can do, how he can react, faced with the situation that he has had to endure, and still endures.
>
> EISS: You mean that the true history cannot be written because...
>
> CETINA: Because much remains to be done.

FIGURE 4.1

Ruins of Hacienda Chicché.

"True history" could be said to exist only when true liberation had been achieved. In its absence, only social and political activism could help establish the conditions under which a prophetic vision of liberation, and hence a writing of its "history," might become conceivable—even if some of the martyrs had strayed from the path along the way.

Despite the obvious differences that separated the insurgents of 1913 from the two of us, and that distinguished Anacleto Cetina Aguilar from me, it is this hope for a future writing of a "true" history of liberation—and a refusal of the closure of that history in the meantime (see Maddox, this volume)—that might unite us in a cast of mind and spirit that might be called critical romanticism. In some sense, all of us were after the same thing—the insurgents in carving a gun with an inscription calling for both a future event of liberation and its inscription in history; Cetina in writing a history calling for an end to political corruption, social disempowerment, and cultural alienation; and I, in a somewhat more attenuated way, in writing a microhistory of "liberation" in a time of seemingly never-ending terror and counterterror. All of us, each in our own ways, were seeking to read history, and to write it, for signs of hope.

Several years ago, I walked with a friend who lives on a large ex-hacienda near Tetiz to find the place where Chicché once stood. Like many haciendas in the Hunucmá region and throughout the state, the place is now abandoned and overgrown. The place where indebted peons once had their huts is now a field of scrubby trees and grass, the only visible vestige of those homes the stone circles of old wells. The machine house is a pile of rubble, broken walls, a fallen roof, and an old stone chimney. The main house is in the same condition. Look through the old windows, and you will see not the interior of a house but rather sunlight, and bushes and trees growing inside the structure, whose roof and floors have fallen away in chunks. The walls are pocked—are those bullet holes?—but Chicché still stands, as Don Diego Solís once said, as a "kind of fortress," although now a ruined one.

It is easy, when visiting a place like this, to gauge the distance of the past from ourselves in the material and visible symptoms of time's passage: fallen walls, trees growing inside old houses, rust. It seems natural to assume that the same distance separates us from those who attacked Chicché, San Luis, and San Vicente, leaving a facsimile gun behind for their pursuers to read and contemplate. Yet the inscription on that object was left as a claim on the future. It was a demand to be read not only by contemporaries but perhaps by others who might one day understand the events of that day as the beginning of a history that was yet to take place. Was I—or Don Anacleto—in some way present that day, if only as a possibility? Are the men who attacked Chicché in some way present in this moment, as I read the inscription and transcribe it once again?

In his "Theses on the Philosophy of History," Walter Benjamin explored the possibility of a redemptive relationship between past, present, and future, mediated by the writing of a materialist history against the trivialities of "once upon a time." In what Benjamin called a "secret agreement" between past and present, "our coming was expected on earth," thus endowing us with a "weak Messianic power" to redeem the unfulfilled struggles and utopian desires of previous generations. Against the "historicism" that contents itself with "telling the sequence of events like the beads of rosary," framed in a homogenous time moving from distant past toward the present, Benjamin charges the historian with grasping the "constellation which his own era has formed with a definite earlier one." In so doing, the historian might radically juxtapose and transform past and present, situating both in a "conception of the present as the 'time of the now' which is shot through with chips of Messianic time" (Benjamin 1969:262).

I take the inscription of May 5, 1913, like Benjamin's reflections, as a challenge to overcome the distance that appears to separate us, as objects and subjects of the microhistorical gaze. Whether or not we accept Benjamin's conception of the messianic and revolutionary vocation of the historian, we may find in it a suggestive way to think of the microhistory of liberation, or perhaps even to reconceive microhistory more generally. The metaphors of optics and scale that are so helpful in the exploration of methodological questions raised by microhistory may foster the illusion that we are merely scrutinizing "small worlds" rather than ourselves inhabiting them, or even cohabiting them, with our subjects and interlocutors. It is perhaps not so much scale but closeness that defines the spirit and possibility of microhistory—a closeness that might bring eras into constellation, for even a moment, in the "time of the now." If microhistory has an ethics and a politics, then both might begin here—with a recognition of the coevality (Fabian 2002), or shared time, that may, however briefly, unite past with present and historians with others.

Notes

I am grateful to Albrecht Funk, Alf Luedtke, Paul Sullivan, two anonymous reviewers, and participants in the SAR microhistory seminar for their reactions to earlier versions of this essay.

1. "1913. Causa seguida á Fabian Caamal y socios. Homicidio y asonada." Archivo General del Estado de Yucatán, Ramo de Justicia, Sección Penal (hereafter cited as AGEY JUS PEN), 928.

2. A full discussion of these topics is beyond the scope of this essay. For such visual analogies, see Revel 1995, 1996; Levi 2001; and Ginzburg 1993. For a thoughtful discussion of microhistory by analogy with cinematography, see Kracauer 1969.

3. For a few examples of the attacks of the 1870s and 1880s, see "1889. Diligencias muerte de Ricardo Aguilar Brito," AGEY JUS PEN, 170-C, reel 244, and especially "Los crímenes de Hunucmá: Luz y sombra," May 17, 1892, *Revista de Mérida* (hereafter *RdM*). On "the King" and his arrest, see April 26 and May 21, 1892, *Eco de Comercio* (hereafter *EC*); April 1, 3, 5, 24, and 28 and May 7, 1892, *RdM*; May 11 and 27, 1892, *Razón del Pueblo* (hereafter *RdP*); and May 22, 1892, *Sombra de Cepeda* (hereafter *SC*). See also "1893. Causa seguida a Florentino Poot por incendio y homicidio," AGEY JUS PEN, 13, 23.

4. See Jose M. Rosado Almeida, to Governor, June 27, 1914, AGEY, Poder Ejecutivo, Milicia (hereafter cited as PE MI), 465; and *Revista de Yucatán* (hereafter cited as *RdY*), May 7, 1913, and July 12, 1914.

5. See June 2, 1912 and May 7, 1913, *RdY*; and "Causa seguida á Fabian Caamal y socios."

6. See "Causa seguida á Fabian Caamal y socios" and "1913. Diligencias practicadas en averiguación de los sucesos ocurridos en Hunucmá el cinco del actual," AGEY JUS PEN, 929.

7. See June 2, 1912, and May 7, 10, 11, 13, and 15, 1913, *RdY*; and "Causa seguida á Fabian Caamal y socios."

8. See May 3, 11, and 27, 1892, *RdP*; May 7 and 21, 1892, *EC*; and May 17, 1892, *RdM*.

9. For previous citations of rebel documents see August 23 and 27, 1911, *RdM*. For initial reporting on Chicché, see May 6, 1913, *RdY*. The inscriptions as corrected and transcribed in the newspaper coverage were "¡Que viva la libertad, muchachos! ¡Que viva! Que viva los valientes, que vivan! Juramos que no nos rendimos! Juramos que hasta que no haya libertad!" and "Mayo 4 de 1913. Han fabricado el gran mauser de Yucatán y su gran espada de acero. Por motivos de la libertad."

10. See, for instance, "1913. Diligencias practicadas en averiguación de unas descargas hechas en Hunucmá," AGEY JUS PEN, 928; April 26, 1913, *RdY*; Juan de Dios Ché to Juez del distrito, July 1, 1913, AGEY JUS PEN, 721; "Relación de los individuos del Partido de Mérida...durante los meses de abril a julio de 1913, para cubrir las bajas del ejército, según expedientes," AGEY PE, Guerra, 719; and Tomás Pérez Ponce to Juez de Distrito, May 9, 1913, AGEY JUS PEN, 721.

11. See Felipe Molina Villamil, JP Hunucmá, to Governor, February 14, 1914, AGEY PE MI, 454 (and other correspondence, April–June 1914); assorted correspondence, AGEY PE MI, 468; April 29–May 1, 1914, *RdY*; "1914. Denuncia del señor Manuel Rios (destrucción de propiedad ajena)," AGEY JUS PEN, 947; and "1914. Lesiones a Cirilo Méndez y socios," AGEY JUS PEN, 936. Details on the rebel camps in Kaxek were provided in an interview with Doña Tomasa, Hda. Nohuayum, March 2, 2003.

12. Carranza intended the measure as a way of advancing cautiously toward a limited reform platform that could help build a wider base of popular support for the Constitutionalist cause while preventing a costly civil war from spreading to Yucatán, where it might have threatened henequen revenues that financed the Constitutionalist army. See August 19, 1914, *RdY*; and Wells and Joseph 1996:267.

13. See September 10–12, 1914, *RdY*.

14. The Chilam Balam manuscripts are compilations of texts dating from before the conquest to several centuries afterward (Restall 1998). The actual name of the author was Na Hau Pech.

5

Varied Pasts

History, Oral Tradition,
and Archaeology on the Mina Coast

Christopher R. N. DeCorse

[W]e opened fire all round the town which set it on fire....I had the King's quarter of the town set on fire, and mean to complete its destruction by blowing the houses down as soon as it can be properly arranged.

—*Lieutenant Colonel F. W. Festing, St. George's Castle, June 15, 1873*[1]

The commander of the British forces at St. George's Castle was describing the end of one of the major trade entrepôts on the African coast. The town that was bombarded and razed to the ground was the African settlement of Elmina, located in the Central Region of modern Ghana, what was then known as the Gold Coast. The town, with a population of perhaps twenty thousand people, was leveled for a parade ground. Better than any other place, Elmina's history and affluence, as well as its destruction, underscore the dramatic changes and consequences of African–European interactions between the fifteenth and nineteenth centuries. The barracoons of Elmina Castle symbolize the horror of the Atlantic slave trade and today remain a focal point for Africans in the diaspora. Yet the history of the town began long before the emergence of a plantation system dependent on enslaved Africans and extends beyond abolition and the antislavery squadrons of the nineteenth century. The town's destruction is emblematic of the tensions in objectives and worldviews that Africans and Europeans brought to their encounter. These cannot be understood outside of the wider historical, political, economic, and cultural contexts of which they were part. Elmina's story also leads us through the different

FIGURE 5.1

Castelo São Jorge da Mina as it appears today. Following the bombardment of the old town by the British in 1873, the ruins were leveled to make the parade ground seen in the foreground. Photograph by C. DeCorse.

coigns of vantage of the encounter provided by the documentary record, oral traditions, and archaeology.

The African town now known as Elmina was the site of Castelo São Jorge da Mina (later called St. George's Castle by the British), founded by the Portuguese in 1482 and the first and largest European trade post in sub-Saharan Africa. The settlement predated the European arrival on the African coast; the town's comparatively large size of perhaps one or two hundred people was one of the things that attracted European trade.[2] With the founding of São Jorge, the associated African settlement became a nexus of African–European interactions. The castle was captured by the Dutch in 1637 and remained the Dutch headquarters in West Africa until 1872, when it was ceded to the British. Tensions over the recognition of British authority culminated with the town's destruction in 1873.

The preceding can be considered "historical facts," insofar as the founding of São Jorge in 1482, Elmina's capture by the Dutch in 1637, and the cession of the castle to the British in 1872 are documented in European written sources. But much of the rest of Elmina's past—particularly its early history and the nature of the African settlement—is anything but clear. Documents, oral sources, and the archaeological record afford contrasting views of the fifteenth-century town, the nature of African–European interactions, and subsequent changes in African sociopolitical organization. These sources have played varying roles in narratives of Elmina's history and that of coastal Ghana. Elmina's past has been invented and reinvented; contrasting histories presented, accepted, and sometimes discarded. As Lightfoot (this volume) laments, these entrées into the past are palimpsests—blurred perspectives of events and inconsistent images. Perspectives on how these different sources are utilized rest on the researcher's disciplinary grounding, the scholar's ability to move across different categories of source material, and personal penchant. Beaudry's call for "playfulness" and her characterization of historical archaeology as "storytelling" are not a plea for artistic license, the production of fictional narrative. They are, rather, recognition of the methodological tension the researcher negotiates in bringing together varied sources in interpretation. Indeed, archaeological *productions*, like those of historians, sociologists, and anthropologists, are not transcriptions of the past but rather negotiations of meanings (see Beaudry, this volume).

To a greater extent, the narratives of Europe's intersection with Africa in the fifteenth century have been written through eyes of Europeans, some of whom visited the coast and, in some cases, played key roles in the events described. Others were minor functionaries. Like modern scholars, early European writers of Elmina's history drew from varied sources, although often with little or no attribution.[3] Coastal Ghana is one of the best-documented and best-illustrated parts of Africa. The documentary sources available, mostly written by European travelers, traders, and administrators, concentrate on the small European coastal enclaves, focus on bureaucratic details, and generally provide little insight into the customs, traditions, sociopolitical organization—and complexity—of the surrounding African societies. European illustrations of Elmina echo these contrasting views and ambiguities. Relatively detailed plans of Elmina Castle survive from early in the Dutch period. But images of the town are lacking in scale and perspective, and they concentrate on the European presence.[4]

The documentary sources on the opening decade of European trade, the establishment of São Jorge, and the interpretations of these events are illustrative of the varied ways in which historical productions may be written. Preeminent in the encounter between the Portuguese and the Europeans in coastal Ghana is the founding of Castelo São Jorge da Mina. The event is referred to in most histories of the coast and also referenced in Elmina oral traditions. This was, after all, the Costa da Mina: the coast of the mine, a reference to the amount of gold traded there. Yet no primary sources for the castle's founding exist—no letters, correspondence, or cargo lists, or even directions given to the expedition leader sent to the coast. While Portuguese sources for the early decades of African–European interactions do exist, these are frustratingly limited given the extent of the contacts (Hair 1994).

Although the dramatic founding of Castelo São Jorge da Mina over-shadowed previous encounters, by the time construction of the fortress began, more than seventy European ships had already visited the coast (Blake 1942, 1971; Hair 1994:4). By the late 1470s, the Portuguese were rel-atively well known to the Africans, at least in terms of trade. Prior to the founding of the castle in 1482, the African settlement at Elmina was known by the Portuguese as Aldea das Duas Partes, or the Village of the Two Parts (Hair 1994:54 n. 35; Vogt 1979:22). The most detailed account of the town is provided by Eustache de la Fosse, a young Flemish merchant captured by the Portuguese and imprisoned at Elmina in 1479. He describes a walk through the Village of the Two Parts, so called because the settlement con-sisted of "two villages, a bow shot one from the other" (Hair 1994:129). Later sources that recount the founding of Castelo São Jorge da Mina refer to the Village of the Two Parts, but the term is not used after that.[5] While the documents suggest that one portion of the original settlement was located near the castle, there is no indication where the other part was.[6] Fosse also recorded a list of words spoken on the coast, which is useful in establishing that the inhabitants were Akan.[7]

With the foundation of Castelo São Jorge da Mina, the name of the town became Mina and eventually Elmina.[8] A number of sixteenth-century sources give descriptions of the castle's founding, the principal accounts being provided by Rui de Pina and João de Barros (Hair 1994). Pina and Barros describe the decision by King João II of Portugal to establish a fort, against the advice of his counselors. An expedition was planned, and in late 1481 a fleet of ships under the command of Diego de Azambuja sailed for Guinea, arriving at Elmina in January 1482.[9] We are told that Azambuja sailed with an expedition of ten caravels, five hundred soldiers and ser-vants, and one hundred masons, carpenters, and craftsmen, although these numbers may be exaggerated.[10] The ships also carried precut stone for the castle's doorways, arches, and windows. At the Aldea das Duas Partes, Azambuja met the African ruler Caramansa and sought his permis-sion to establish the castle. Pina's and Barros's accounts of Caramansa's arrival closely correspond. Pina's account, which is slightly less elaborate, states: "Hither the king came, and before him a great noise of trumpets, bells and horns, which are their instruments, and he was accompanied by an endless number of blacks, some with bows and arrows, and others with assegais and shields; and the principal persons were attended behind by naked page-boys, with seats of wood, like chairs (*cadeiras*), to sit upon" (Hair 1994:20). After negotiations, Caramansa gave his permission. Although some conflict occurred when construction began, the Europeans appeased the Africans with gifts, and the castle was built.

Pina's and Barros's accounts of the founding of the Castelo São Jorge da Mina are not static presentations. Rather, as Paul Hair demonstrates, they are interpretations contingent on a variety of cultural and historical concerns of the sixteenth century (Hair 1994:6). There is some similarity between the two accounts, almost certainly because Barros was familiar with Pina's work. Both writers describe the same period of initial African–European interactions, although with somewhat differing perspectives. Pina may have collected information in the 1490s—shortly after the founding of the castle—and written his account in the early 1500s, revising it in the 1510s, before the import of Vasco de Gama's voyage to India. Barros also served in West Africa, and he probably had firsthand knowledge of São Jorge da Mina. On the other hand, he wrote during the 1520s, 1530s, and 1540s, when much of the focus of Portuguese expansion had moved from West Africa to Asia.[11] His vantage was beyond Elmina and West Africa. It is not surprising that the earlier account by Pina places São Jorge in the foreground, while for Barros West Africa was a precursor to Portuguese expansion in Asia.

Pina's and Barros's descriptions of the events of the founding of São Jorge have framed the historical discussions of encounter between Africans and Europeans in coastal Ghana. The Village of the Two Parts, Caramansa, and São Jorge have been used for historical syntheses—interpretive extrapolations—of Elmina's sociopolitical structure and the fifteenth-century African polities of coastal Ghana. The name Aldea das Duas Partes has been interpreted in various ways, including where the two parts may have been located and what they may have signified. Two suggestions have been made for the placement of the two parts—one idea being that both parts were located on the Elmina peninsula, the other being that one part was on the peninsula and one on the opposite side of the Benya Lagoon. The *duas partes* alluded to have further been seen as evidence of sociopolitical divisions, possibly reflecting the division of the town between the polities of Eguafo in the west and Fetu in the east. Historian Albert Van Dantzig (1980:9) states, "As the town straddled the Benya, which formed the border between the Eguafo and the Fetu states, there was no strong leadership."[12]

It has further been suggested that the two parts of early Elmina referred to ethnic quarters within the settlement: an indigenous Akan village and a section occupied by Mande traders from the north. The Mande are a wide-ranging ethnolinguistic group found in northern Ghana and the West African Sahel. A number of scholars have raised the possibility of Mande traders in southern Ghana. In his discussion of the trade on the Costa da Mina in the fifteenth and sixteenth centuries, historian Ivor Wilks (1962:339, 1982:336–39, 1993:4–8) discusses the presence of Mande traders (specifically the Wangara) at Elmina, while Van Dantzig (1990:207) further suggests that Elmina's two parts consisted of "a largely Mande trading town situated on the rocky tip of the Elmina peninsula and an Akan fishing and salt-making village farther to the west, where fisherman could safely land their canoes on the beach." Elmina is thus portrayed as well integrated into wider West African trade networks prior to European arrival on the coast.

Elmina oral traditions also refer to early Elmina, Caramansa, and fifteenth-century sociopolitical relations. These references coincide with some aspects of European historical narratives, but they also diverge in a number of important features. Because of their local vantage and their potential to extend documentary source material, they are potentially an important resource for reconstructing the past. A number of oral traditions are recounted in nineteenth- and twentieth-century written accounts, most notably by the Elmina historian J. Sylvanus Wartemberg. He interprets Caramansa of the Portuguese accounts as a reference to Kwaamina Ansa, king of Elmina during the founding of the castle and the sixth *oman-hen*, or king, of Elmina (Wartemberg 1951:18). Wartemberg further notes: "Credence may be attached to the tradition that El Mina [*sic*][13] was a fairly organized community prior to the European adventure on the coast and that the earliest adventurers found the town in a degree of civilization contrary to their most sanguine expectations" (14). He traces the founding of Elmina around AD 1300 to Kwaa Amankwaa, who was of "Asante royal stock" (16). Wartemberg also traces the extent of the Edina State, of which modern Elmina is the capital, largely following the boundaries of the present polity. Hence the tradition firmly establishes the Edina State and Elmina kingship centuries before European contact.

Some of Wartemberg's material, particularly the oral traditions reported and the history of early Elmina, were extensively criticized at the time of publication (Meyerowitz 1952a), and the interpretative problems faced in assessing Elmina oral traditions have also been noted (Henige 1973, 1974). Like Pina's and Barros's accounts of the founding of São Jorge, oral traditions are not frozen messages of past events but are open

to interpretation within the sociocultural contexts in which they were produced and in which they are currently embedded. They may be informative of otherwise hidden social relationships of the contexts that produced
them, distinct from other sources of information on the past and not necessarily intersecting with them.[14] In terms of the early history of Elmina,
oral traditions for coastal Ghana are particularly problematic. They provide
tenuous, uncertain links to fifteenth-century events, serving contemporary
purposes in which they are embedded. In some instances they have been
influenced by European historiography and conflate present practices, personal knowledge, and fictional narratives with historical material received
thirdhand from documentary sources.[15]

The histories of Elmina, both written and oral, are ambiguous, culturally ordered productions. The more recent histories of coastal Ghana are
informed by more detailed documentary records, more recent historical
memory, and the ethnographic present (for example, Feinberg 1989; Yarak
1990). But what was the nature of the early settlement of Elmina? Was
Caramansa, in fact, Kwaamina Ansa, and was Elmina the boundary between
the states of Fetu and Eguafo? The castle was built, and African–European
trade flourished. Beyond this, contemporary sources tell us nothing of
the location of the village's two parts, their ethnic composition, or the
sociopolitical organization of the coast or the wider hinterland of which
Elmina was part. Elmina's Mande quarter, long-distance trade in salt and
smoked fish, and fifteenth-century Elmina kingship are creations, interpretive productions that project aspects of Elmina's more recent past back
to the fifteenth century. To a large extent, this imagery is unsupported by
documentary sources, oral historical data, or the archaeological record.

Was Caramansa king of a fifteenth-century Edina State? While the organization of the modern Edina State may appear clear, its origins and structure are complex and have clearly evolved over time. Primary documentary
sources and oral traditions collected prior to the late nineteenth century
provide no evidence of the existence of the Edina State until after the
arrival of the Europeans, and there is no evidence for a single ruler (oman-
hen) of Elmina until the eighteenth century.[16] Caramansa is unmentioned
after São Jorge is founded, never to be mentioned in Portuguese records
again. Although some writers have referred to him as the "King of Elmina,"
on the basis of limited contemporary documentation, Caramansa can be
described only as a ruler, possibly from—or subservient to—a neighboring polity. Whatever his position, it likely did not conform to any contemporary European notions of status and power. Portuguese accounts of the
castle's founding clearly describe negotiations with a *single* African ruler,

something that presumably would not have been the case if approval of two different states was required (Hair 1994:55–56; compare Feinberg 1989:14). Caramansa, who alone negotiated with Ajambuja, can logically be seen as either ruler of an independent Elmina or leader of a neighboring polity. Given the limited evidence for kingship at Elmina prior to the eighteenth century, the latter inference is more likely.

While neighboring polities' claims to Elmina are documented beginning in the early seventeenth century, evidence for a jointly controlled, divided Elmina settlement at the time of European contact is tenuous. The earliest references to a division of the Elmina settlement between Fetu and Eguafo date to the early seventeenth century, almost 150 years after the founding of the castle. More recent writers have subsequently linked Fetu–Eguafo claims with fifteenth-century references to the Village of the Two Parts, further accepting that these parts were divided by the Benya Lagoon. Whatever the political relations between early Elmina and the neighboring African polities at the time of European contact, the town became increasingly independent. By the first decades of the sixteenth century, the settlement was already asserting its independence from neighboring polities, and the interdependent relations that would characterize African–European interactions for the next 350 years were emerging.[17]

The players in these political machinations were likely indigenous Akan, not Mande traders. There is no question that southern Ghana was incorporated into northern trade networks that included Mande people, yet evidence for a quarter of Mande traders at Elmina in the fifteenth century is tenuous.[18] The Portuguese were certainly familiar with the kingdom of Mali, and Portuguese missions were dispatched to Mali in 1487, 1488, and 1534, but these were from the Gambia River, not Elmina (see comments by Hair in Jobson [1623] 1999:7). The Portuguese also sent an emissary to Mali in the 1490s; this mission was likely also dispatched from the Gambia (Teixeira da Mota, cited in Hair 1994:51 n. 28). The primary evidence for the Mande at Elmina is linguistic, particularly the use the suffix *mansa* (as in Caramansa).[19] A Mande settlement at Elmina is not consistent with other linguistic evidence that indicates an entirely Akan orthography of local languages from the fifteenth century onward. Apart from the earliest descriptions, *mansa* does not appear in European accounts.

Elmina undoubtedly became a focal point of trade following the establishment of São Jorge, but its position in pre-sixteenth-century trade routes and an interior trade in salt and smoked fish are extrapolations of later sources that do not necessarily reflect the situation in preceding centuries. Ocean fishing using canoes, possibly including sails, long predates European

FIGURE 5.2

Salt pans in the Benya Lagoon west of Elmina. The thick mangroves in the lagoon were cleared in the twentieth century to make the salt pans.

contact.[20] The *Regimento* of 1529 states, "I [the king] am informed that the blacks of the village [Elmina] have many canoes in which they go fishing and spend much time at sea."[21] Yet the same sources indicate that fishing methods relied on smaller nets, iron hooks, and spears rather than the large nets that characterize modern practices (DeCorse 2001:104–9). In the seventeenth century, marine fishing was said to have been done with hooks, both on drop lines and in barbed lines that were dragged through the water.[22] While large nets (up to sixty feet long) were used, the technique was distinct from modern methods.[23] The canoes also seem to have been somewhat smaller than those used for fishing today (De Marees 1987:118). The techniques were likely more characteristic of pre-nineteenth-century subsistence strategies than the seine net fishing used in the nineteenth and twentieth centuries.

Elmina's role as a major producer of salt for trade is also recent (DeCorse 2001:140–42). The large Benya salt pans behind the town date to the late nineteenth and twentieth centuries; the Benya Lagoon was covered by brush until after 1873. Prior to this time, manufacture would have been dependent on boiling. Specialized "salt-making" villages are shown to the east between Elmina and the Sweet River on seventeenth-century Dutch maps.[24] A *sout dorp*, or "salt town," is located on the Baelarus plan of 1647, and a village where salt was produced by boiling seawater is discussed in

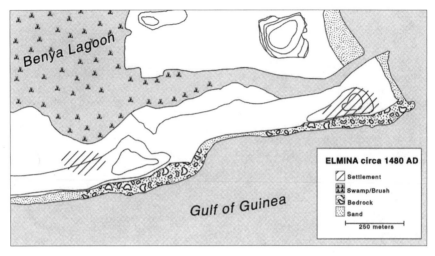

FIGURE 5.3

Map of the Aldea das Duas Partes, circa 1480. The plan shows two discrete settlement areas on the Elmina peninsula. The area to the east was later the site of Castelo São Jorge da Mina.

eighteenth- and nineteenth-century descriptions of the area (Feinberg 1989:81). Notably, however, the Dutch apparently did not rely on salt from Elmina but obtained it from Accra (Feinberg 1989). Salt production in early Elmina may have been limited, and much of the salt traded was produced in neighboring communities.

The archaeological record provides its own distinctive vantage, its own mode of historical production. The principal actors in oral historical and documentary narratives of fifteenth-century Elmina are invisible archaeologically. The meeting of Caramansa and Ajambuja, the town's capture by the Dutch in 1637, and even the settlement's destruction in 1873 are unrecognized or poorly viewed: individuals and events lie beyond the bits of broken ceramics, metal, and glass that are the archaeological record. Study of this residue of the past allows temporal insight into locally produced, more poorly dated industries, tracing the development of artistic and technological traditions, as well as settlement histories. These are valuable contributions, if somewhat lacking in relevance to wider interpretive synthesis. Yet the archaeological record provides clues to the nature of early Elmina and the wider socioeconomic transformations of which it was part. These features are manifest archaeologically in artifact inventories, settlement organization, and settlement patterns, which are to a large extent absent or inaccessible in documentary and oral sources.

Archaeological data indicate that the Village of the Two Parts was located on the Elmina peninsula, not on either side of the Benya Lagoon. At the time of Portuguese contact, the settlement likely extended all the way to the eastern tip of the peninsula (the later location of the castle), with a second occupation area located farther west. Concentrations of diagnostic local ceramics are located in these areas.[25] Two such sections or quarters located even a short distance from each other on the narrow Elmina peninsula could have been clearly discerned from ships in the Gulf of Guinea. Such a division would not be so striking in other topographical settings. It was Elmina's distinctive topographic character, rather than unique sociopolitical or historical factors, that lent its name to the site. After the construction of São Jorge da Mina, the castle became the settlement's defining characteristic. This would have been especially true if the easternmost "quarter" at the end of the peninsula had been destroyed or relocated during the castle's construction.

What the two parts may have meant in terms of cultural, ethnic, or social divisions is much more difficult to assess on the basis of archaeological data. Archaeological data is notoriously ambiguous as an indicator of ethnicity, at least with regard to West African ceramics (Atherton 1983; DeCorse 1989b; Graves-Brown, Jones, and Gamble 1996; S. Jones 1997; Shennan 1989). However, what is known is that fifteenth-century ceramic traditions in coastal Ghana are distinct from those found in the interior forest and northern hinterland. The ceramic types recovered in excavations at Elmina are consistent with those from other fifteenth-century coastal Akan sites. If Mande traders were present in Elmina at the time of initial European contact, they left no distinctive material traces of their presence. The specific sociocultural implications of the village's two sections can only be guessed at. Many African villages and towns have discrete clusters of houses or quarters that reflect ethnic or religious differences, areas occupied by craft specialists, or clan and phratry groupings (Agorsah 1983; Posnansky 1987:17–20). Any of these divisions might account for early Elmina having "two parts." Given the available information, division of early Elmina along the Eguafo–Fetu boundary or into Mande–Akan quarters remains speculative. Neither idea is stronger than the possibility that any division implied by the village's presumed "two parts" was based on clan or ethnic divisions. In fact, this explanation may be more likely.

Archaeological data also attest to sociopolitical change only poorly documented in written sources. At the time of European contact in the late fifteenth century, small villages, many located near lagoonal resources, dotted the coast (DeCorse 2001). Prior to the seventeenth century, the majority of the coastal population were fishermen and subsistence farmers. Based on the archaeological materials recovered, the exploitation of marine resources focused on shellfish and lagoonal species. Shellfish and fish bone make up a principal component of the archaeological bone. Notably, however, it is only in the seventeenth century and later that archaeological contexts include shark centra (DeCorse 2001:104–9). Their presence is significant, as sharks sink when they die and typically do not wash up on shore. Hence their presence in seventeenth- and post-seventeenth-century contexts is a good indication of marine—as opposed to lagoon—fishing. Some shark centra also have clear butchering marks (Bourque 1997).

With the advent of European maritime trade, the political economy of African coastal society was transformed. Archaeological data indicate that the smaller farming and fishing villages along the coast disappeared in favor of larger settlements adjacent to European forts and castles. These became centers of commercial activity and the conduits through which European goods flowed to the interior, as well as points from which enslaved Africans were transported to the Americas. In some cases, coastal towns emerged as independent states and focal points of trade, craft production, and specialization. A series of historically documented polities emerged; these subsequently dominated the coastal trade between the seventeenth and twentieth centuries. Elmina epitomizes these developments. A small lagoonal settlement that had likely been subservient to a neighboring polity in the fifteenth century emerged as the independent Edina State.

With urbanization came traders, as well as a variety of craft specialists. We can point to the documentary records of the succeeding centuries for reference to increasing specialization and evidence of production within the coastal communities, including salt production and fishing. Similarly, surveying the archaeological record, we can perceive an increasingly diverse material inventory, the elaboration of art forms, and transformations in earlier areas of production. Sites such as Elmina, which emerged as urban centers during the post-European-contact period, produce increasing evidence of specialized industries, including pottery manufacture, metalworking, bead production and modification, ivory carving, and salt making, a pattern that dramatically contrasts with the absence of such evidence on the coast during the preceding centuries.[26] The archaeological record provides specificity on these developments not found in documentary sources.

The late Paul Hair (1994:1) observed that when Castelo São Jorge da Mina was founded in 1482, it was the first military base established three thousand sea miles from the home country. Its presence secured Portuguese control of trade on the Ghanaian coast for the next century and set the stage for similar outposts. In the following three hundred years, Europeans would establish some sixty forts, trading lodges, and castles along this 150-mile stretch of the African coast. Among the Europeans who visited Elmina during its founding were Christopher Columbus, Pedro de Cintra, and Bartolomeu Dias. São Jorge thus also frames the cross-cultural contacts, conflicts, and intersections that have characterized the last five centuries.

When my work in coastal Ghana began in 1985, it was framed by an archaeological site.[27] My interest in Elmina was as a means of understanding the emergence of the Atlantic economy, particularly with regard to change and transformation at the local level. Given its primacy in documentary accounts and oral traditions, Elmina seemed uniquely suited to help me evaluate these developments. My initial work focused on the Elmina town: delineating the site, determining chronology, and describing the material culture represented. While this work was useful in demonstrating some aspects of the coastal Ghanaian past, ultimately it was unsatisfying. I was left with an incomplete picture of Elmina as a part of a whole, a view of cultural developments and economic transformations cut from an image without reference to the wider context of which it was part.

Elmina is unique, both in terms of its role in the history of African–European interactions and with regard to the unique opportunity it presents for archaeological investigation. It cannot be evaluated without a fuller understanding of the wider developments on the coast, the settlement patterns represented, the changes in subsistence that occurred, and the innovations in technology represented. Although work had been done on the history and archaeology of the coast, much of this information was similarly site specific, or in need of evaluation on the basis of additional archaeological data. My work subsequently became increasingly reoriented to the evaluation of regional patterns and developments. The archaeological record, documentary past, and oral historical data relevant to our understanding of the past five hundred years allow us to both contextualize Elmina's uniqueness and evaluate its significance in the broader history of the coast. The richness of the documentary and ethnographic records illustrates the grand historical themes of which Elmina was part and the complex, multivalent nature of the changes that occurred. Data from Elmina and the surrounding hinterland are equally essential to the interpretation of the historical and archaeological reconstruction of the consequences of African–European interaction, and they have immediate relevance to our interpretations. An understanding of the intersection between Europe and the non-Western world cannot be rooted in individual scales of analyses.

The need for varied vantage is, I hope, illustrated by the methodological and theoretical perceptions called for in some of the approaches articulated in our seminar. The contributions are an amazingly disparate group; finding commonalities was stimulating and frustrating in equal measure. Although the term *microhistory*—retained as a frame for this volume—implies a narrow frame of reference, studies viewed by their authors and others as "microhistorical" (for example, Davis 1983; Ginzburg 1993; Lüdtke 1995; Muir 1991; Muir and Ruggiero 1991; Revel 1995; Zunz 1985) are highly varied in terms of the temporal, spatial, and subject foci examined. Methodologically, the most significant point to be underscored lies in the advantage of moving through multiple scales of analyses.[28] This multilayered perspective, moving from the local to the inference of underlying structures, has a necessary role to play in both archaeology and history, which are inherently particularistic disciplines.

The preceding discussion of coastal Ghana during the era of the Atlantic world underscores aspects of analyses that call for methodological rigor, the articulation of macro and micro perspectives, and interpretive synthesis. In particular, study of the era of the Atlantic world benefits from an interdisciplinary, multiscalar perspective. Studies of European–indigene interaction at Elmina and the impacts of European expansion are made clearer by the *combination* of analyses that focus, on one hand, on regional patterns and transformations and, on the other, specific features, artifacts, and details that reveal local responses and behaviors. These interdisciplinary methodological and conceptual junctures are not simply useful but are necessary for the fullest possible reconstruction of the past.

Notes

Portions of this paper were initially presented in "The Mouse That Roared: Historical Archaeology as Microhistory" for the symposium Villes anciennes en Afrique histoire et archéologie: La complémentarité imparfaite, University of Paris, December 18, 2004. I am grateful to the late Paul Hair for providing comments on aspects of the documentary sources used. I thank Dale Tomich for reading earlier versions of this paper.

1. British Parliamentary Papers 1970.

2. There are only crude estimates of the settlement's size prior to the late nineteenth century. However, it is unlikely that Elmina had a population larger than one or two hundred people in the late fifteenth century (see DeCorse 2001:31–37, 52–55, 202–3 n. 79).

3. See Adam Jones (1987, 1994) for critiques of sources.

4. A sixteenth-century illustration of Elmina shows some of its natural features and the relative positions of the fort and town (see DeCorse 2001:8). The Benya Lagoon and St. Jago Hill are shown. The castle lies at the end of the Elmina peninsula; the town is located to the west, separated from the castle by a wall. However, for the most part, more specific features presented are fanciful.

5. Both Barros and Pina use the name Aldea das Duas Partes. The latter states: "[Azambuja] arrived near the village, which was called das Duas Partes" (translated in Blake 1942:72; compare Hair 1994:16).

6. This is inferred by a reference in Rui de Pina's description of the founding of Castelo São Jorge da Mina. It notes the destruction of some of the African settlement during the castle's construction. Pina states, "[T]he surround of the castle was forthwith begun, for which it was necessary to demolish some houses of the negroes, and this they and their women consented easily and without taking offense in return for large reparations and the gifts which were given to them" (translated in Blake 1942:77). A version of the same event by João de Barros and a slightly different translation of Pina are given in Hair (1994:33–34).

7. Akan languages are to a large extent mutually intelligible. They include Fante, which is the language currently spoken in Elmina.

8. For convenience, the name Elmina is used to refer to the African settlement. However, this name emerged in Dutch and German sources only in the mid-seventeenth century, becoming the most commonly used variant by the end of the seventeenth century (Hair 1994:44 n. 4; A. Jones 1985:14; Vogt 1979:192). Hair (1994:44 n. 4) suggests that the name likely resulted from confusion over references to "Mina" in Portuguese, Italian, and Spanish sources, the possible sequence being da Mina, de la Mina, della or dela Mina, del Mina, del Mina, d'el Mina, d'Elmina. French and English sources do not use the name Elmina until well into the eighteenth century. Occasional references are made to the local name Dondou, Dana, or ddena (Blake 1942:45, 47) and to Anomee (Wartemberg 1951:15). Elmina and Edina are the names used locally today.

9. These accounts are translated and analyzed in depth by Hair (1994).

10. Hair (1994:15) comments, "Whether the total complement was in fact 600 is, however, open to some doubt. Exact statistics were not expected from writers in this period and rounding of numbers in an exaggerated direction was common."

11. Hair 1994:6. Documentary evidence for Barros's service in Guinea has not

been traced, but Hair suggests that he may have served at São Jorge as a factor in the 1520s (Hair 1994:8).

12. Also see Burton (1863:63), Crone (1937:109), Blake (1942:44), Ward (1958:70), Ballong-Wen-Mewuda (1993), and Van Dantzig (1990:207).

13. It is unclear why Wartemberg uses "El Mina" in referring to the settlement, as this spelling conforms to neither the local etymology he suggests nor historical references (see note 8, above; Hair 1994).

14. See Schmidt 2006:26–27. Oral traditions are here considered to be stories or descriptions of events passed on from generation to generation. They are different from oral history, which is information received from an individual who participated in or viewed the events or features described. In analyzing oral sources, Africanists often make a distinction between oral histories and oral traditions, as these sources necessitate different methodological concerns in their interpretation.

15. Many inhabitants of Elmina are familiar with published written sources dealing with Elmina's past. Oral accounts of Elmina's past are often derived from these sources (see DeCorse 2001:2–4). For an overview of oral sources with regard to Elmina's history, see DeCorse (2001:2–4). Also see comments in Feinberg 1989:xiii; Hair 1994:45 n. 7; and Henige 1973, 1974.

16. The evolution of Elmina's sociopolitical institutions, as interpreted through oral histories and documentary sources, is succinctly reviewed by Henige (1974). As noted, Wartemberg provides a king list that extends back before the founding of Castelo São Jorge da Mina and identifies Caramansa (Kwaamina Ansa) as the omanhen ruling at the time of the castle's foundation (compare Meyerowitz 1952b:73; Wartemberg 1951:87). These oral traditions, however, seem to have been heavily influenced by late-nineteenth- and early-twentieth-century European historiography. In fact, Henige (1974:504) suggests that Caramansa can be considered no more than "a prominent personage in the Elmina area." However, as Hair (1994:55–56 n. 37) points out, he is referred to as a "king" or "prince" in Portuguese sources and was clearly "*the* most prominent personage locally." Hair also provides a useful discussion of the references to Caramansa, as well as the possible etymology of the name. Also see Hair 1966:18; compare Ballong-Wen-Mewuda 1984:95, 462, 465.

17. Hair 1994:38–41; Ballong-Wen-Mewuda 1993; Vogt 1979:85–86, 124–25, 155–57, 180–82. As early as 1514, the Elmina people were acting together with the Portuguese in military engagements.

18. The documentary data are critically appraised by Hair (1994:53–54 n. 33, 55–56 n. 37).

19. Garrard (1980:25) and Hair (1994:55) suggest that the term *mansa* was brought by African interpreters who accompanied the Portuguese. This word means

"ruler" in many Mande languages, but usage by the people of Elmina during the fifteenth century remains ambiguous. It is possible that the term was actually introduced by the Portuguese or their African interpreters, who brought it with them from Mande areas in the Upper Guinea coast that they had long familiarity with.

20. In the early seventeenth century, De Marees (1987:116–19) described canoes and fishing practices in some detail. He attributes the introduction of sailing technology to the Portuguese, and his illustration depicts a canoe with a European configuration of stays supporting a mast with sails made from mats of straw. However, as Greg Cook (personal communication) observes, the use of bark sails does not appear to have parallels in Iberian or Basque sailing technology, and the depiction of European-style rigging may have been artistic license.

21. Hair 1994:78 n. 130; compare Hair 1994:71 n. 97; Pereira 1967:121.

22. The earliest reference to fish hooks on the central Gold Coast may be in an English account of the 1550s: "yron worke they can make very fine, of all such things as they doe occupy, as darts, fishookes, hooking yrons, yron heades, and great daggers" (Hakluyt 1589, cited in Hair 1994:52 n. 29).

23. The nets seem to have been gill nets or special nets with hooks (De Marees 1987:120, 123–24).

24. The 1629 map shows several salt-making villages on the coast between Axim and Accra (Daaku and Van Dantzig 1966). I am grateful to Adam Jones for drawing my attention to the Baelarus plan. Also see the discussion in Hair (1994:53, 79).

25. These data accord with the limited documentary sources that do exist. The limitations of the source material for the early Portuguese period have been noted. Later documentary evidence indicates that settlement north of the Benya was limited until the nineteenth century. The oldest standing buildings in the present town, north of the Benya, are from the nineteenth century (Bech and Hyland 1978; Hyland 1970).

26. DeCorse 2001. Kea (1982), who examines transformations in specialization and the division of labor within coastal Ghana, observes that there is some evidence that individual coastal towns increasingly specialized in different types of production. Also note observations by Daaku (1970).

27. My initial archaeological work focused on the Elmina site (1985 to 1987 and 1990) included the survey of some two hundred acres and the excavation of almost forty structures (DeCorse 1987a, 1987b, 1989a, 1992a, 1992b, 2001). Archaeological work since 1993 has now extended to encompass the entire area between the Pra River in the west and the Kakum or Sweet River in the east.

28. See Lightfoot 1995:209–10 for multiscale approaches in archaeological investigation; also see Crumley and Marquardt 1987, Kristiansen and Rowlands 1998.

Part II

Shifting Lenses, Embedded Scales
Event, Biography, and Landscape

6

Arson, Social Control, and Popular Justice in the American West

The Uses of Microhistory

John Walton

In June 1996, President Bill Clinton delivered a televised message to the country, warning of "a recent and disturbing rash of crimes that harkens back to a dark era in our nation's history." A wave of arson, aimed at black churches and portending a new conspiracy of racial terror, was sweeping the country. Evidence indicated ninety-eight church burnings over the previous eighteen months—fifty-two affecting predominantly black congregations, thirty of those in the South. The purported crisis activated a variety of interests. Clinton seized the occasion to rise above election-year politics with a Lincolnesque appeal for racial tolerance. Congress, laboring under the obstructionist Contract with America, welcomed the opportunity to demonstrate cost-free compassion. National media revived the familiar civil rights narrative to organize and signify the assorted facts instead of interrogating them. The story had something for everyone.

But was it true? Writing in the *New Yorker*, the late Michael Kelly took another look. Although churches, black and white, are common targets of people's rage, national data actually show a sharp decline in arson since 1980. When culprits in church burnings are caught, their motives run a gamut from wage disputes to theological passions. In the fire that prompted

97

Clinton's news conference, the culprit turned out to be a disturbed teenage girl. Racial motives figure in some cases but usually as one among many precipitants, including insanity, fires concealing other crimes, random hooliganism, disputes over money, and so on. Some fires are set in black churches by disgruntled black parishioners. Evidence of an actual increase in black church burnings in the Southeast points to teenage vandalism (with schools also victimized) but no coordinated campaign or ideological message.

In short, detailed analysis shows there was no wave of church burning, no organized conspiracy, no return to the dark days of the civil rights struggle. There was, however, an opportunistic narrative fashioned from stylized facts and susceptible to its own explanation. Arson takes many forms: ubiquitous, multiform, polysemic, fungible. It appears in diverse historical settings that invite closer attention to their meanings and varieties.

At the outset, I distinguish between acts of arson that stem from pyromania and associated pathologies, and purposeful acts of what might be termed "social burning," however fuzzy the distinction may become in particular instances. "Arson is a crime that has always been with us and has been interpreted in a number of ways," writes a French historian (Abbiateci 1978:157). In the Middle Ages, incendiaries were considered possessed by the devil; later as simply possessed or mad; and lately as sexually conflicted. But arson is also a social fact that varies by time, place, and circumstance. Arson has a long provenance in European history. Peasant risings burned manor houses, crops, warehouses, and tax records from the sixteenth to the nineteenth centuries (Hobsbawn and Rudé 1968; Ladurie 1979). Cottage spinners and handloom weavers displaced by the factory system joined E. P. Thompson's (1966) "army of redressers" in arson attacks on new mills and machines. Spanish townspeople burned churches and their icons of elite domination (Maddox 1993).

Yet arsonists were not only, perhaps not even mainly, rebels and redressers. Court records from Germany and France document crimes by malcontents, beggars, thieves, extortionists, and the insane (Abbiateci 1978; Sabean 1984; Schulte 1994). Beyond Europe, arson was part of the resistance repertoire developed by slaves on plantations in the Caribbean and the American South (Genovese 1972; Naipaul 1969). Is there a common denominator for these diverse instances? Are there patterns, types, meanings?

Across the American West in the late nineteenth century, fire was a constant menace. Prairie fires, lightening fires, spontaneous combustion, and accidental fires all threatened rustic settlements that seldom afforded fire protection. Yet fires from natural causes were known and anticipated hazards of western living. Far more ominous was the surprisingly pervasive incendiary. Newspapers and other local history sources of the period document frequent instances of known and suspected arson, with targets including barns, fields, stables, stores, mines, trains, and hotels. Why was the practice so common? What did it mean?

Drawing on diverse cases, historians offer several interpretations of arson as a social phenomenon. For the moment, it is useful to consider explanations of arson per se rather than broader theories of collective action and protest that include incendiary acts in association with assorted other means of expressing grievance. Two general interpretations—arson as class action and arson as individual initiative—embrace most particulars.

Abbiateci subscribes to the claim of a nineteenth-century jurist that arson was "the favorite crime of the lower classes" (1978:158). His research in France identifies three major categories of arsonists: (1) madmen; (2) beggars and day laborers who threatened to set fires unless they were given bread; and (3) tenant farmers who refused to vacate farms. But each type fitted a more general interpretation. The threat of fire was "a means of applying economic pressure...the weapon par excellence of the poorest categories within rural society [calculated] to obtain minimum subsistence or to improve their daily fare" (163). Similarly, evidence from East Anglia suggests that incendiarism "was a traditional form of rural protest, together with poaching, maiming, the stealing of farm animals, machine-breaking, the sending of threatening letters, and organized opposition to low wages, high prices and unpopular aspects of the Poor Law" (D. Jones 1976:5). Arson outbreaks came in waves marked particularly by unemployment, and the firebugs were typically agricultural laborers and tenants. "[T]he business was more organized than contemporaries liked to admit...considerable planning was involved...it was customary for those concerned to meet in a public house beforehand and then to journey out at the appropriate time [in gangs]" (14).

Other researchers find little evidence of collective action or class awareness. Hobsbawm and Rudé (1968:205), focusing on some of the same counties in southeastern England studied by Jones, reached a different conclusion: "Arson and the writing of threatening letters were, then, individual acts and, even if related to the general labourer's movement, were rarely part of any organised plan." Genovese's study of American slaves (1972:614–15) agrees: "The arsonists' courageous display of militancy did not always win support and encouragement in the quarters. Arsonists usually worked alone or at most in groups of two or three; their action usually represented retaliation for some private offense or injustice." American slaves might disapprove of arsonists in their ranks because their vengeance typically targeted property (food stores, cotton), the destruction of which threatened the welfare of the community (economic losses led to slave sales and family breakups). The suggestive point here is that logics of collective action and their explanations depend very much on context.

This paper examines the meaning of arson using microhistorical methods. Microhistory is a research *strategy* rather than a singular method, an "exploratory stance" in the words of Richard Maddox (this volume). Microhistory focuses on the detailed case study and endeavors to use the particular for understanding broader processes (Levi 2001). The strategy rests on the proposition that case-study detail is an essential foundation for drawing inferences about other, more general processes and interpretations.

I shall analyze in detail two cases drawn from nineteenth-century California. First, Owens Valley is an agrarian community set alongside the eastern Sierra in relative isolation from the rest of the state. The valley was home to a pioneer settlement of homesteaders, as well as Native Americans who were dispossessed of their tribal lands and reabsorbed as wage workers in the frontier economy. Averaging ten miles wide and stretching one hundred miles north to south, by the turn of the last century, the valley embraced four small towns and a number of hamlets, railroad depots, polling places, and school districts, and some five thousand souls. During these years, Owens Valley farms and towns experienced a wave of incendiarism that fitted no obvious pattern. All manner of targets suffered unexplained fires. Culprits were sometimes known but never named, charged, or prosecuted. Residents seemed to understand the meaning of these events, although little was said of them publicly beyond routine reporting. Outside the precincts of local culture, they were a mystery.

The second case deals with a single act of arson at the elegant Hotel Del Monte, owned by the Southern Pacific Railroad and operated by its subsidiary Pacific Improvement Company in Monterey, California. On April 1, 1887, an overnight fire destroyed "America's most luxurious seaside resort." Like the Owens Valley arson wave, the Del Monte fire was never solved. Hotel owners accused a manager who had been discharged, but his public trial presented evidence that exonerated him. The fire was clearly arson, probably an inside job, but questions about who and why persisted. The large hotel staff included working-class whites, who faced the public as waiters and chambermaids, as well as a good many Chinese, who worked backstage in the kitchens and gardens. No one volunteered an explanation for the fire. Another mystery.

The two cases reveal at close range different worlds that lend different contextual meanings to arson. The key is in the details and their configuration. Two stories emerge—stories conveniently silenced in the past (Trouillot 1995; Walton 2001). In the end, we return to competing theories of arson and show how microhistorical analysis supports new and contrasting interpretations.

FRONTIER JUSTICE

On March 18, 1876, the *Inyo* (County) *Independent* published a routine news story, entitled simply "Fire," in its section on local affairs in the town of Bishop:

> A little after 12 o'clock on Tuesday night there was a cry of "fire!" which put a sudden stop to the festivities then in full blast at the reception ball in the Masonic Hall, and aroused all others in town from their beds. The cause of the alarm was soon ascertained to be a pile of bailed hay in Bennett's hay yard, situated between his law office and Rowley's store, in which is the post office. For a while it looked pretty much as if friend Rowley was to be a victim the second time within the year to the "fire fiend."…No doubt is entertained but this fire was the result of deliberate incendiarism, but whether in the hope of burning the town or certain of the hay only is more of a question.

Four months later, in the neighboring town of Big Pine, McMurray and Moore's store was set ablaze. The *Inyo Independent* (July 1, 1876) called the fire a

> deliberate attempt by a sneaking coward to destroy property, and take life, too, maybe, since two men were sleeping in the building, one in the store, and the other in the saloon adjoining …very little, if any, doubt exists among those on the ground as to who the guilty party is.

Subsequent weekly editions make no mention of efforts to apprehend or punish the sneaking coward.

Fire visited towns and homesteads with equal frequency. On August 4, 1877, the *Independent* reported,

> Last night parties here observed a bright light as if of an extensive fire down about George's Creek. This morning we learn that Mr. C. M. Joslyn was unfortunate enough to lose his haystack containing some forty or fifty tons, by fire, accounting for the

light. As the flames were observed long after nightfall, and as no one slept near the stack, the possibilities are that this was the work of an incendiary.

From settlement in the 1850s until its connection by road and aqueduct to Los Angeles in 1913, Owens Valley lived the full western experience. Paiute Indians confronted, resisted, and eventually accommodated a diverse breed of pioneer settlers. Archaeological evidence demonstrates that these Indians practiced horticulture based on irrigation systems that belie characterizations of their primitive hunter-gatherer subsistence (Lawton et al. 1976). By the authority of the U.S. Army and the Land Office, new arrivals took up government-gifted 160-acre plots under pre-emption and homestead acts. But abundant land and water were insufficient to raise agricultural production much above subsistence levels in this isolated region given to long winters. A network of small towns stretched like worry beads from mercurial silver mines in the south to a short-lived railroad link running north to Virginia City, Nevada. For many years, government was rudimentary; civil authority was exercised mainly through vigilance committees and cooperative irrigation societies, or "ditch companies," built on the original Paiute design. Conflict suffused local society: conflict over wages in the mines and fields (where harvests depended on Indian labor), over property boundaries and grazing rights, over prices, credit, barter, and fair play in the stores and saloons. Austerity and alcohol bred short tempers. Contrary to western lore, gunplay was rare in retributive quarrels, but arson served its purposes in more flexible ways.

Yet order prevailed too. A rustic civil society took root in the ditch companies, fraternal lodges, women's auxiliaries, business clubs (for women and men), and churches. A citizenry sprinkled lightly over the vastness from Sierra Nevada peaks to Death Valley supported only such necessities as a county seat and a contracted home for the infirm. Law enforcement was minimal, but in its stead, civil society developed with an inclination for "popular justice."

Incendiarism played a revealing role in local society. Arson was common, varied in application, simultaneously condemned and casually acknowledged—in a word, patterned. Table 6.1 lists all incidents of known and probable arson identified in a fairly exhaustive review of the local press over the forty-year period 1870–1910 (Walton 1992). Newspaper items, similar in tone to those quoted above, were coded for information on arson, including date, time, target, victim, surmised explanation, and ensuing action, if any. Evidence drawn from the local press is bound to be selective, understated, and filtered. Yet it is the only surviving record of these events as they were known to contemporaries. Without these reports, we would know little of the conflicts permeating frontier life. As E. P. Thompson (1975a:257) describes anonymous, threatening letters appearing in the *London Gazette*, they "lie, like so many bi-weekly lobster traps on the sea bottom…catching many curious literary creatures which never, in normal circumstances, break the bland surface of the waters [of] historiography."

Arson visited every social relationship and realm of local society. Indians fired the haystacks and buildings of their farm employers, miners burned machinery, disgruntled customers victimized businesses, farmers took revenge on one another over property and water disputes. The violence took place within and between classes. Table 6.1 identifies several large landowner victims (such as Stoutenborough and Shaw, who purchased and consolidated original homesteads), but it also lists smallholders locked in feuds with neighbors (Walter; Joslyn). By the end of the period, the targets and the local meaning of arson shift with the arrival of the Los Angeles Aqueduct. The fifty-two instances in table 6.1 reveal three critical social relationships in conflict: labor, market, and property.

Table 6.2 summarizes descriptive features of the instances. Like its European predecessor, frontier arson is a crime of anonymity and stealth. The incendiary's calling card takes the form of the deed. Fires typically occur in the middle of the night, targeting property rather than person. Summer, when agrarian labor and commerce are at their peak, is fire season, although it is a year-round sport. Favorite targets are haystacks, farm buildings, fields. Haystacks have special significance—they burn quickly, limit collateral damage, and send a message: "This could have been worse. Be advised!" Equally common targets are commercial establishments in town: stores, stables, saloons. Sometimes a place of business is attacked directly. Other times, moderation opts for an adjoining yard or outbuilding. Although knowledge of the arsonist's identity is frequently claimed, actual names are seldom given in the reports; when categorical identities are provided, they usually refer to outsiders. Unnamed Indians, tramps, and laborers are mentioned and only rarely an anonymous neighbor. This seeming paradox carries its own significance.

In some cases, of course, the arsonist's identity was unknown or merely suspected. In rare instances, the guilty party was identified and punished. John T. Dely, an unemployed Irish immigrant, torched a public bridge on the road between Lone Pine and the Cerro Gordo mine. The bridge, one of three costing the county $27,000, was a collective good; its loss inconvenienced everyone. Dely, moreover, was the quintessential outsider.

TABLE 6.1
Proven and Suspected Arson Incidents, 1870–1910

Date	Time	Target	Victim	Explanation	Action
Aug. 12, 1871	—	Lumber pile	—	Insane act	None
July 13, 1872	—	Haystack	Van Dyke farm	Indian malice	None
Sept. 21, 1872	—	Building	—	Indian malice	None
July 19, 1873	—	Stable	Hightower and Co.	Unknown arsonist	None
Oct. 2, 1875	3 a.m.	New house	Gerrish	Vagabond arsonist	None
Nov. 13, 1875	Night	Stable, haystacks	Plumley farm	Suspected arson	Arrest, Dismissal
Mar. 18, 1876	Midnight	Hay yard, law office, store	Bennett, Rowley	Suspected arson, second time	None
July 1, 1876	Midnight	Store	McMurray and Moore	Arson	None
July 8, 1876	Morning	Haystack	Stage company	Suspected arson	None
July 22, 1876	Midnight	Brewery	Walter	Arson threats by known person	None
Sept. 23, 1876	1 a.m.	Haystacks, farm building, house	Watson farm	Followed quarrel with neighbor	None
Nov. 11, 1876	10 p.m.	Polling place	—	Prank	None
Nov. 25, 1876	—	Mexican shanty	—	Suspected Indian arsonist	Suspect fatally shot
July 21, 1877	—	Coal pile	Cerro Gordo mine	Suspected arson, labor troubles	None
Aug. 4, 1877	Night	Haystacks	Joslyn farm	Suspected arson	None
Aug. 18, 1877	—	Mine machinery	Union Consolidated	Arson	Arrest
May 12, 1878	—	Mexican hall	—	Arson	Warrant issued
June 15, 1878	9 p.m.	Barn	Bond farm	Tramps suspected of malice/carelessness	None
July 20, 1878	—	Stable	Bennett	Indian malice, second or third incident	None
Aug. 17, 1878	10–11 p.m.	Mine building and machinery	Beaudry Co.	Arson during labor troubles	None
Aug. 17, 1878	11:30 p.m.	General store	Stoutenborough	Arson by known person	None
Apr. 5, 1879	7 p.m.	Bridge	Inyo County	Arson	Miner arrested
May 3, 1879	2 a.m.	Mining town hotel, buildings	—	Suspected arson during labor trouble	None
July 19, 1879	2 p.m.	Haystacks, machinery	Shepherd farm	Indian carelessness	None
Mar. 25, 1882	—	House	Harrell	Suspected arson	None

Date	Time	Property	Owner	Description	Conviction
Aug. 23, 1882	4 a.m.	Store, house, brewery	Stoutenborough	Arson threats by Indians, second incident	None
Apr. 28, 1883	—	Haystack	Shaw ranch	Possible arson	None
May 19, 1883	—	House	Williams farm	Suspected arson	None
Dec. 5, 1883	Night	Fields	Lewis farm	Possible arson	None
Dec. 5, 1883	—	Haystack	Briggs farm	Possible arson (the previous owner was also a victim)	None
Mar. 7, 1885	—	Fields	Robinson ranch	Indian mischief	None
Jan. 27, 1887	—	Haystack	Horton farm	Arson	None
July 20, 1889	—	Barn	John Dodge farm	Possible arson	None
Apr. 4, 1890	9 a.m.	Livery stable	J. G. Dodge	Possible second arson	None
July 23, 1890	3 a.m.	Commercial block	Ben and Michael Lasky	Possible arson, multiple instances	None
June 27, 1892	7 a.m.	Yard of general store	Ben Lasky	Arson	None
June 2, 1893	2 a.m.	Commercial building	Boland's building housing Lasky's general store	Possible arson, repeated instance	None
Sept. 8, 1893	3 a.m.	Home and office	Dr. Woodin	Possible arson	None
Mar. 2, 1894	10 p.m.	Home	Densmore	Arson	Chinese arrested and dismissed
July 20, 1894	Night	Shack	Goodale	Arson, homicide	Neighbors tried, found not guilty
Sept. 21, 1894	4 a.m.	County-contracted hospital	Mrs. Lewis	Possible arson, second incident	None
Dec. 20, 1895	9:30 p.m.	General store	Rhine	Arson	None
Dec. 27, 1895	Night	Livery stable, haystack	Julian's	Arson	None
May 19, 1899	2 p.m.	Haystack and buildings	Mairs ranch	Possible arson, vandalism at family store	None
Jan. 5, 1900	10 p.m.	Haystack	Walter farm	Suspected arson, second incident; quarrels with neighbor	None
July 26, 1901	10 a.m.	Haystack	Hessions farm	Possible arson	None
June 6, 1902	Early a.m.	General store, doctor's office	Rhine, Woodin	Possible arson, second incident for both	None
July 24, 1903	Midnight	Store, corral	Eibeshutz	Suspected arson	None
Jan. 4, 1907	—	Town building	Gollober	Arson, malice	None
Jan. 4, 1907	Early a.m.	Saloon	Johnson	Suspected arson	None
Feb. 13, 1909	Night	Aqueduct camp	Los Angeles City	Arson	None
Feb. 14, 1909	Night	Aqueduct camp	Los Angeles City	Arson	None

Table 6.2

Characteristics of Arson Incidents

Time of Day		Target	
6 a.m.–noon	4	Haystack, field, farm building	19
Noon–6 p.m.	2	Store, stable, business	17
6 p.m.–midnight	15	Home	6
Midnight–6 a.m.	14	Mine	3
		Public facility	4
Total	35	Other	3
		Total	52
Month			
January	4	**Suspect by Social Category**	
February	2		
March	4	Indian	7
April	3	Mexican	1
May	4	Tramp	2
June	4	Laborer	5
July	13	Neighbor	5
August	6		
September	4	Total	20
October	1		
November	3		
December	4		
Total	52		

Dismissed from a job in the mines, he had previously threatened revenge and had earned a reputation for insanity by claiming that the county had conspired to ruin his life. According to the *Inyo Independent* of April 5, 1879, the only question posed by his arrest was whether he would be treated as a criminal or a madman.

Compare Dely's case to the more common circumstance of the allegedly known but unnamed perpetrator. On August 17, 1878, the *Independent* reported:

> A dastardly attempt was made by some incendiary to destroy the store of J. H. Stoutenborough in Bishop....In [a shed built onto the rear of the building] coal oil boxes had been piled up against the house and a match applied to the bottom. The flames were running high up in the air when discovered by Wm. B. Hutchings,

FIGURE 6.1

Midsummer haying in Owens Valley was also the peak season for arson incidents stemming from labor disputes and quarrels between farmers.

at the saloon on the opposite side of the street. Pistol shots were fired as an alarm; a crowd soon collected and the blaze was extinguished without damage. In this case the perpetrator is known and doubtless proof will be found to send him [to jail].

Yet that was the last heard of the dastardly attempt. Reasons for its silencing are suggested by the details of the case. Stoutenborough was a prosperous merchant and farmer in an economy that relied heavily on personal relations of credit and barter among neighbors. The attempt on his store seems to have been intended for discovery. The outside wall of the shed selected as the point of origin minimized damage, and the initial flames, visible from a nearby saloon, promised quick detection. Moderation of the deed was vividly illustrated in another fire at Julian's yard in Lone Pine. The targeted haystack was first divided in half, and only one side was burned. Two empty coal oil cans were left at the scene, perhaps to discount any conclusion that the fire was accidental. Arson sent a message, a warning that victims very likely understood from its context. But frontier etiquette dictated that real agents and actual grievances were not discussed publicly. Local quarrels were private affairs.

A public story was constructed to fill in the interpretive gap between common crimes and their official neglect. Here, the venerable scapegoat proved to be outside agitators in ethnic costume. In August 1882, the Stoutenborough store, along with several adjacent town businesses, was badly damaged by an arson fire that also ignited explosives stored in a warehouse. On August 26, the *Independent* made no mention of the previous arson at the same location but proposed a new theory:

> The current opinion as to the cause of the fire is that it was started by drunken Indians—doubtless the correct one. A "noble red" was heard to say last evening that he would burn Stoutenborough....A calamity of this kind has been staring us in the face for many years, and still the Indian in all his drunken glory has been afforded to parade our streets, knife in hand, seeking whom or what he might devour. Worse than all, the miserable wretch who, in the teeth of the law, will persist in selling whiskey to every Indian who asks for it, has been permitted to live right in our midst and carry on the lucrative traffic with perfect impunity. Those who sell whiskey to Indians should be compelled forcibly to leave the place.... The Chinese quarters of town should be besieged and everyone compelled to evacuate. The Piute [*sic*] element should not be allowed to remain within the town limits after sunset.

The story reveals in several steps how the morality of arson was constructed. Outsiders in the form of Indians, Chinese, and tramps are the primary culprits. Merchants who sell liquor to Indians are perhaps more contemptible, but only Chinese vendors are identified. There is a determined effort to separate both the motives and the perpetrators of arson from the white settler community. In rare instances, the evidence provides clues to how quarrels developed within the community. In this case, Stoutenborough was victimized previously at the store, in which he also ran a brewery. Some combination of alcohol and commercial disagreement may explain the frequency of store and saloon fires. In truth, the abuse of alcohol by Indians and whites was a problem for public order, just as its production and sale were a profitable business in which the Chinese market share was small. The public story advanced to explain frequent incendiary fires intentionally obscured knotty quarrels among neighbors, silenced tensions underpinning the social order, and conveniently projected responsibility on outsiders. Like plantation slaves, Indians were deemed childish or mischievous rather than reasonably vengeful.

A critical case illustrates both the process in which disputes developed and the imaginative ways in which conflict was externalized in scapegoats. A late-night intruder attempted to burn the Independence residence of S. A. Densmore in 1894. The culprit entered a back pantry of the house as the family slept, splashed kerosene on the walls, struck a match, and escaped as the flames brought down cans from shelves, which served as an alarm. According to the March 2 *Independent*:

> The deed must have been perpetrated by some person familiar with the premises as no noise was made either entering or leaving the place, and a spaniel always left in the house made no alarm and was outside in the morning. A chinaman now in county jail is suspected of the crime. A few days ago he was discharged from the employ of Mr. Densmore....Near the back gate are the imprints of a China shoe followed by toe-footed tracks to the brush north of town. The accused party has had a bad reputation, having served a term in state prison at Carson. Should there not be sufficient evidence to connect him with this crime an effort will be made to get him out of the county under the law requiring deportation of Chinese felons.

The explanation is shaky. One doubts that a "China shoe" leaves a distinctive imprint, and the "toe-footed tracks" smack of Orientalist imagination. And in spite of this evidence fixing guilt for the "dastardly attempt," plans to run the suspect out of town without a trial, as indeed occurred within a few days, appear already in motion.

Was this an effort to silence a deeper conflict? Some intriguing processual details were omitted from the official story. Densmore had been engaged in a running feud with his rural neighbor C. A. Walter, a tempestuous farmer who had also been a victim of arson. Recently, Walter had published a public notice demanding that Densmore repair an irrigation ditch that crossed Walter's property and was damaging his pasture. Public notices of this sort appeared occasionally in local papers and signified intense enmities that defied informal means of conflict resolution. Bad blood existed between Densmore and Walter, but that fact was not mentioned among the circumstances leading to this arson attack or, more generally, as the kind of problem that doubtless motivated many quarrels in

TABLE 6.3

Incidents of Arson in Owens Valley, 1887–1910, by Population.

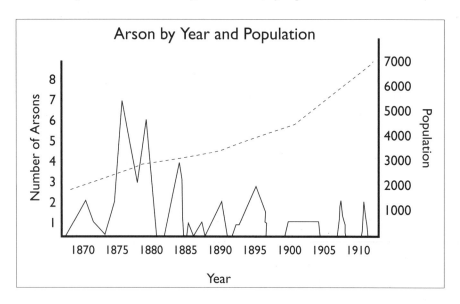

Arson by Year and Population

this agrarian society. And the evidence demonstrates not simply that local tensions were neglected as explanations but that misleading accounts were deliberately fabricated—perhaps in an effort to keep the peace, albeit at the expense of the Chinese, the Indians, and the odd Irishman.

In a broader sense, the practice of arson on the western frontier was a means, devised in civil society and derived from venerable tradition, for regulating conflictive situations where law was deficient. It was a form of *social control,* a concept sociologists use to describe the process by which people define and respond to deviant behavior: "Social control consists of the efforts of authorities, or of society as a whole, to bring deviants back into line" (Tilly 1978:99). The patterned, varied, modulated, acknowledged, and unspoken yet implicitly understood incidences of arson suggest that it was a means of collective self-help employed by western pioneers whose nascent public institutions had yet to develop the capacity for law enforcement. That situation would change in predictable ways. But as long as the law failed, alternative means prevailed. As Donald Black (1983:41) explains, "theory would lead us to expect more violence and other crimes of self-help in those contemporary settings where law—government social control—is least developed, and, indeed, this appears to fit the facts: Crimes of self-help are more likely where law is less available."

Quantitative data support the proposition, if we accept population increase as a valid proxy measure of the growing means of law enforcement. As the population of Inyo County grew from two thousand to seven thousand from 1870 to 1910, law expanded, sheriffs extended their authority, property lines were surveyed, titles were stabilized, an increasingly monetized economy relied on more formal rules of exchange, and civil courts provided the means to adjudicate disputes. With these developments, arson declined, from a high point of six or seven per year in the late 1870s to one or two per year by the turn of the century. New traditions superseded old ones. Yet old ones were not so much forgotten as they were shelved until new occasions for recourse to popular justice arrived—as they did with protests against the Los Angeles Aqueduct in the early 1900s. In the early years, arson provided an all-purpose means of social control on the lightly governed frontier.

THE CHINESE AND THE PLUTOCRATS

As homesteaders and prospectors began straggling into Owens Valley in the 1860s, Monterey was already celebrating its centennial with new optimism. Although the colonial capital had languished after U.S. acquisition of California in 1846 and the gold rush of 1849, settlers were now filling the coastal towns and interior valleys. Lying between the historic harbor and the fertile Salinas Valley, Monterey was well positioned for development. In the 1870s, local investors built a narrow-gauge railroad connecting agrarian producers with coastal steamers headed for San Francisco and Los Angeles. Equally endowed, Monterey Bay supported a growing and varied fishing industry: Portuguese whalers, Japanese abalone divers, and Chinese squid fishermen. Lumber was harvested from heavily wooded coastal ranges, sand and rock quarried on the shoreline. Local apiarists boasted the finest honey, made from sage blossoms, and Monterey Jack cheese immortalized its namesake, either local land baron David Jacks or the jack press used to make cheese—no one is quite sure which.

Monterey's greatest asset, however, was the place itself. Artists congregated to paint a landscape described as "the greatest meeting of land and water in the world." Writers from Robert Louis Stevenson to Robinson Jeffers and John Steinbeck drew inspiration from its dramatic scenery and rich folklore. Monterey's history was written, first as a Spanish pastoral story of gentle missionary priests and gay rancheros and later as a narrative of Yankee progress. The latter story was made by and for those who would develop the town and sell it to the world (Walton 2001).

Entrepreneurs soon realized the potential for holiday excursions and resort hotels. The decisive step came in 1880, when California's powerhouse

FIGURE 6.2

The luxurious Hotel Del Monte, built by the Southern Pacific Railroad in 1880, dominated the politics and reputation of Monterey. It also depended on a large local labor force.

Southern Pacific Railroad bought out the local line and established regular train service to San Francisco. Through its landholding subsidiary Pacific Improvement Company (PI Co.), the great SP acquired seven thousand acres in Monterey for a luxury hotel, parkland, and a real estate venture. Known pejoratively as the Espe or Octypus, the railroad soon dominated local life. By far the largest employer in town, the hotel built its own water and power systems, exempted itself from municipal taxes and ordinances, and called the tune in local politics. The hotel's address was given as Del Monte, California, suggesting that historic Monterey City was a mere appendage placed there for the entertainment of hotel guests. Billed as "the most elegant seaside establishment in the world," the Del Monte covered 150 acres of gardens and recreational facilities (a stable, polo field, Roman swimming pool, golf course, and tennis courts). Its centerpiece was the four-hundred-room Gothic-styled Swiss Chalet, which included elegantly appointed dining rooms and ballrooms surrounded by open-air porches. It soon became a redoubt of presidents, celebrities of stage and (later) film, visiting monarchs, and tycoons, including the three living members of SP's "big four": founders Leland Stanford, Charles Crocker, and Collis Huntington (Mark Hopkins having died the year the hotel opened).

The Hotel Del Monte perforce lived alongside the historic town of nearly two thousand people and drew its labor and provisions from the surrounding county of ten times that number. Monterey's population was traditionally diverse. Before statehood, Hispanic conquerors mixed with a large population of California Indians. In the early nineteenth century, European and American traders developed a thriving agricultural export economy in hides and tallow. Wage labor was always in demand. Initially, Indians were conscripted for construction and ranch work. But as their numbers decreased (owing to disease and assimilation into *paisano* culture), employers looked abroad for labor-force recruits. In successive waves, the working class grew with Mexican, Chinese, Japanese, and Filipino cohorts, as well as a good many white immigrants from other states and Europe. By the 1880s, Monterey had a thriving Chinatown at its center and several Asian fishing villages on the outskirts (Lydon 1985).

Tensions underpinned relations between the town, its employers, and the largely ethnic working class. The waterfront district housing minorities and low-income workers in the fishing industry came to be regarded as an eyesore by hotel visitors passing that way on carriage tours of the peninsula. Periodic "slum-clearance" campaigns focused on dockside shanties and "resorts" featuring prostitution and games of chance. Chinese washhouses that hung drying laundry in plain view were considered a nuisance and discouraged by local ordinances. Peddlers, including ambulatory Chinese produce vendors, were controlled by costly licensing. City fathers failed to appreciate the many functional activities performed by minority communities or the irony of labeling as undesirable such well-patronized services.

California and much of the Pacific coast suffered a virulent anti-Chinese movement in the late nineteenth century (Saxton 1971). Although the worst of the outrages took place in San Francisco and rural communities in northern California, Monterey experienced its own version of intolerance. Businesses employing Chinese laborers suffered boycotts and even arson. Chinese villages were relocated at a greater distance from expanding neighborhoods. Chinese fishing vessels on the bay were rammed, their nets cut, and their crews charged with violating fish and game laws. Yet these conflicts were also managed, negotiated. Chinese fishermen took their cases to court, defended their rights, and countersued bullies for damages to their boats. Stable ethnic communities developed and sought respect-ability through celebrations of cultural tradition. Indeed, Chinese and Japanese businesses prospered. Legend holds that some of Monterey's industrialists established their canneries with capital borrowed anonymously from Chinese merchant-bankers. Minorities achieved their place, albeit a place beneath respectable society and behind the scenes—but an essential place nevertheless. Their social contract rested on certain understandings of what was expected of them and what they might rightfully expect of their betters. They were not powerless in the relationship.

Late in the evening of April 1, 1887, the luxurious Hotel Del Monte broke out in flames. At the sound of the fire alarm around eleven at night, 275 guests were evacuated, some joining the hotel staff and the Monterey Fire Department in an all-night battle against the consuming flames. By morning, exhausted, sodden, and sooty volunteers beheld a scene of complete devastation. Only chimneys and beams rose from the smoldering foundation of the queen of American watering places.

As investigators assembled the evidence, it became apparent that the fire was the work of one or more arsonists. The blaze had originated on the basement floor, directly below the lobby and somewhere in the vicinity of the "circulating room" (providing access to water and gas pipes), an ice closet, and the "China (staff) dining room"—none of these places the likely source of an accidental fire. More incriminating, firefighting efforts were hampered because someone had closed a valve in the garden water system, not once but three times, causing a loss of pressure to the fire hoses.

In addition to these physical suggestions of arson, there were pointed suspicions. As it happened, April 1 was the date of a change in hotel management, involving the dismissal of E. T. M. Simmons, longtime clerk promoted to hotel manager during the previous year, and his replacement by the original manager, George Schoenwald, on PI Co. orders. Schoenwald accused Simmons of arson, telling police that his motive was revenge for dismissal. Schoenwald supported his suspicions with claims that Simmons needed money to support a style of high living (which further assumed that the fire was cover for robbery of the hotel safe), was seen moving about hotel corridors prior to the fire alarm, and had a bottle of turpentine that could have been used to start the fire in his quarters. Obvious ill will between the two managers prompted these suspicions.

On the strength of Schoenwald's denunciation and PI Co. pressure for decisive action, Simmons was arrested, charged with arson, and tried in June at the county courthouse in Salinas. Two weeks of testimony from 150 witnesses demonstrated to nearly everyone's satisfaction that there was no case against Simmons. Hotel employees accounted for his whereabouts up to the sound of the fire alarm, when he was seen salvaging the contents of the safe (which were intact) and assisting the fire brigade. The turpentine had been prescribed by a local physician for his daughter's asthma, and the limit of his high living involved purchase of a Pacific Grove lot that he could well afford on his comfortable salary of $200 a month (*People v. E. T. M. Simmons*, 1877). After the innocent verdict, Simmons countersued PI

Co. for $100,000 in damages. He won the case but was awarded only court costs of $741.

If Simmons was not the arsonist, who was? Local law enforcement never answered the question. Indeed, the malicious act and bad publicity were soon silenced as the hotel was rebuilt on an even grander scale and promoted anew in extravagant tones. Yet behind the facade of gracious living, trouble continued to plague the Del Monte. The events of April 1887 alone suggest tensions among the staff. Trial testimony indicated that Simmons was well liked; that others, including two chambermaids, were dismissed at the same time; and that Schoenwald was an abrasive man who, with the assistance of his fearsome wife, dealt abruptly with employees. Some, like stableman H. J. Palmer, reported previous "unpleasantries" with Schoenwald and F. S. Douty, who managed PI Co., which was headquartered at the hotel.

The Del Monte employed more than one hundred workers, from bookkeepers and front-office staff to waiters, chambermaids, and a number of Chinese described as "garden labor" (men) and "house cleaners" (women) by a census taker. The most nearly contemporaneous manuscript census of 1890 is lost to posterity, but data from 1900 indicate twenty-three Chinese servants living on hotel grounds, most of them (fifteen) adult males who worked in the landscaped gardens. Nea Lee was head gardener at the time, still unmarried at twenty-nine and the leader of a crew including many older men. Nea Lee had come to the United States in 1872 (at the age of fourteen), making him one of the longer-term residents within the immigrant population. The Chinese were resident aliens rather than naturalized citizens, yet most spoke English (in sharp contrast to other immigrants, such as Italians). They lived together in four communal households linked by kinship ties. They were, in sum, a close-knit group with the resources for collective action.

The fire was clearly an inside job and probably a collaborative effort, judging from coordinated action in the basement and garden water system. If some conspiracy of hotel workers was responsible, then who might they be? Of course, we do not know for sure. Yet one hypothesis incorporates the presumption of several arsonists (with some bond of mutual trust), who were likely to have had a grievance associated with the change of management, who had privileged access to the China dining room and hotel gardens, and who could move about unobtrusively shutting valves during the commotion. The arsonists were probably hotel workers, perhaps Chinese workers.

The hypothesis makes sense in light of historical precedents, labor relations, and intergroup sentiments. Protest arson was a common practice in nineteenth-century California. In Monterey, incendiaries had attacked boathouses and streetcar company stables. The Del Monte experienced unexplained fires prior to and after April 1887. During the previous year, specific conflicts had arisen when the PI Co. purchased and leased properties in Chinatown through a community agent.

The *Monterey Argus* wrote on November 13, 1886: "There is a great deal of jealousy and ill-feeling existing among Chinese just now, which had already led to several incendiary fires....The trouble grew out [of] the collection of rents there by the P.I. Co. through one Choy, who appears to be a sort of head man in the town, but who they think divides up the rent collections with the P.I. Co."

The Chinese working class in Monterey suffered varied forms of mistreatment, ranging from harassment of peddlers and laundries to evictions of whole communities. We do not know about labor conflicts involving Chinese at the Del Monte prior to the fire, but we might suspect their presence given the general local pattern. That inference is supported by a strike of Chinese workers two years later at the El Carmelo, a hotel built in Carmel and managed by the PI Co. The incident speaks to labor relations that were arguably similar to those prevailing at the troubled Del Monte. The *Monterey Cypress* of September 10, 1889, explained:

> When the guests at the El Carmelo sat down at breakfast Monday morning they found the course of events interrupted by the refusal of the waiters to serve Dr. Leonard because he had commented upon the character of the immigration pouring into the Golden Gate. The guests were convinced by this miserable manifestation of low spite that the Doctor was fully justified in his strictures....Mr. Seely [the manager] discharged the strikers at once but as the guests were hungry had to placate the strikers by a partial yielding to their contemptible demands.

In any event, someone—more likely some close-knit group of protesters—fired the Hotel Del Monte in April 1887. The point is to neither condemn the agents as lawbreakers nor romanticize them as avengers. Rather, it is to understand the historical circumstances in which protest arson flourished. Labor and ethnic relations were hostile. The combination of these conditions, precipitous dismissals, and the reintroduction of an onerous management may explain the otherwise mysterious fire. In any case, arson by hotel workers, perhaps Chinese workers, is a more plausible hypothesis than any offered at the time. It is a hypothesis, moreover, that opens up the world of working-class and ethnic groups to examination and understanding.

CONCLUSION

Arson cases in Owens Valley and Monterey present two phenomena, two instances of action with a common name but separate meanings. In the frontier community, arson took many forms, including acts of protest vengeance by miners and Indians but more commonly collective action conforming to a normatively regulated pattern. The greater number of incidents, their tactics, targets, and feigned ignorance of responsibility all suggest a practice of social control. Neighbors exchanged rough warnings when their legitimate interests were threatened. Justified or not, in every case the community sanctioned such pragmatic methods of rule enforcement. Exceptions prove the rule. Incendiaries from outside the community—those who existed beyond its borders of solidarity or sanity—were named, sometimes apprehended, and rarely punished. The system operated as long as required. As law developed and governmental means of formal social control superseded popular justice, incendiarism disappeared.

The Del Monte fire in Monterey seems a clear case of protest, although details of the grievance are lost. Like Indians and miners of the eastern Sierra, Monterey's ethnic working class labored under a system of economic and racial injustice. Solid evidence shows that bitterness developed over managerial actions, that the Chinese were capable of reciprocating aggression, and that the hotel fire was a case of sabotage from within. Some of the secrets are lost, but others are revealed and describe a pattern traced by recoverable facts. The Del Monte fire was either initiated by hotel workers or facilitated by their connivance. Chinese workers had the means, opportunity, motive, and organization. Yet even supposing their role was more passive, the pattern of protest arson associated with class conflict and racial oppression holds.

Discussion of these results and interpretations at the School for Advanced Research seminar provoked three general reactions. The first concerns my use of the term *social control* and the implication that it assumes some kind of strict regulation or domination. No such implication is intended in sociological uses of the concept that refer to *attempts* that society (or, more precisely, the social-control agents of society, such as police or moral authorities) makes to regulate behavior with more and less success, depending on a host of circumstances, including, as here, the relative advancement of law.

A second criticism is more serious and more interesting. My colleagues think I may be too cavalier in drawing inferences about the intentions, motives, and purposes or functions behind instances of arson for which the evidence is indirect and sketchy. To the charge, I plead guilty. Like Paul Eiss (this volume), who builds a story from a plaintive message inscribed long ago under exigent circumstances, I am constructing a narrative from fragments—a bit like the fragments of professors Beaudry, DeCorse, and Lightfoot. Is this interpretive practice justifiable outside the archaeological realms of necessity? That depends on the kind of risk a researcher wants to run. There are, after all, two kinds of risk we take in empirical research, two ways to go wrong, or what we know as type 1 and type 2 error. The first kind of error, the one we usually worry about, is to accept something as true when in fact it is false. To avoid this error, we set a high standard of evidence for our claims. But there is another way in which we may err. The second type involves rejecting something as false when in fact it is true—setting an evidentiary standard so high that only the most obvious truths are acceptable. Empirical work is always contingent. At some point, we make a choice about what we want to believe (or hypothesize), and we justify that choice as best we can. In the end, inference is our business.

In this study, I believe that we would miss something important by demanding a standard of proof about acts of arson that is customary for ordinary behavior. For in reality, there are what Thompson calls "crimes of anonymity" and, more generally, acts whose authorship is intentionally hidden in the very nature of the acts. To rule such action outside the realm of empirical investigation and inference would leave us poorer as the result.

A third reaction to the paper was summarized by Kathy Blee, who wisely noted that the term *arson* itself carries legalistic baggage and prejudges the act with this framing, and that my subject is perhaps a more generic form of "social burning." Although I accept the observation, I have chosen to retain the term *arson* because it is the language of the actors in these dramas and because it carries a certain rhetorical bite that admittedly helps me draw the contrast with popular justice.

Others (Paul Eiss and James Brooks) suggest that I have overdrawn the distinction between the forms of arson that I call protest and those I call social control. Once again, there is merit in the criticism. Certainly, one can argue that the Hotel Del Monte fire that I construe as protest arson is also an instance of "social control from below." Owens Valley miners and Indians burned in protest of wages, and later settlers mounted a protest movement against Los Angeles, employing arson in a larger repertoire of dissent. The distinction is imperfect, the types impure. What I hope to draw out with the contrasting terms, however, are two rather different phenomena: arson as a common, pervasive, and modulated practice for regulating disputes, as opposed to arson as a rare act of vengeance by an aggrieved class.

Finally, there are more questions about these case histories than the evidence is able to answer. As Richard Maddox notes, the case studies would benefit from more processual analysis of the circumstances leading up to the acts of arson. The Densmore–Walter feud is a rare case of a quarrel that developed from a property dispute, depredations of the land, and public warnings. Less directly, labor disputes at the Hotel Del Monte are at least suggested by a surrounding context of rent disputes, business harassment, and anti-Chinese sentiment. But direct evidence is thin. Little is recorded about vigilantism in the Owens Valley beyond the occasional sheriff's posse dispatched in saloon shootings, nothing comparable to the situation described in Linda Gordon's *Great Arizona Orphan Abduction* (1999). Chinese laborers left no account of their rebellion (if such it was) comparable to the memorial that peasants in Paul Eiss's study left to mark their insurrection. Microhistory typically contends with such gaps in the historical record just as it explores innovatively the ways in which documents, oral histories, archaeology, visual evidence, and official censuses may be combined to supplement one another. We pursue lost voices and elusive contexts with the means at our disposal. The challenge and the lure of microhistory lie precisely in the craft required for its realization. In the end, microhistory must also rely on heroic inferences, an alternative less to be avoided than elaborated upon and defended.

Returning to the theories of arson that introduced this paper, it is clear that the opposition of class action and individual initiative fails to exhaust the possibilities or capture the deeper meanings revealed by comparative microhistory. Some arson is individually conceived, some the result of group action, and a good deal more collectively prescribed and understood. This study suggests that arson may serve either as revenge against some injustice of the social order or as a means of maintaining order—as protest or as social control. A new interpretation emerges, an argument that social control and protest forms of arson exist in a reciprocal relationship orchestrated by the development of law and its legitimate enforcement. In the absence of effective government, popular justice develops to define and enforce rules in imperfect ways. As law develops, rule enforcement is regularized but also made to serve dominant or privileged interests. Inequality multiplies and ossifies. Communal regulation declines in favor of formal state mechanisms more effectively used by the powerful. Arson and similar means of illegal protest become furtive weapons of the weak.

This comparative microhistory of arson in nineteenth-century California accomplishes four explanatory ends. First, it reveals the social control form not previously noted or theorized in a large body of work on the subject. Second, it explores and contrasts the meanings of arson in the two cases. Third, it advances a new explanation for the occurrence of arson in the form of social control or protest based on the development of law. It suggests a generalization about broader processes, at least ones characteristic of the nineteenth-century American West. And, finally, the study reminds us that conventional terms such as *arson* or even *crime* are not self-evident, not reliable categories containing similar acts and meanings but often veils concealing the paradoxical nature of the empirical world. Microhistory is one way of lifting veils.

Note

For comments on an earlier draft of this chapter, I am grateful to Richard Maddox and the participants in the seminar "Place, Event, and Narrative Craft: Method and Meaning in Microhistory," School of American Research, Santa Fe, New Mexico, July 19–23, 2005.

7

The Floating Island

*Anachronism and Paradox
in the Lost Colony*

Michael Harkin

It's August 2001, about a month before the planes hit the Twin Towers. The temperature is in the high nineties, but, as everyone knows, it's not the heat, it's the humidity. And the mosquitoes. I am in a walled, Elizabethan-style garden, not at Hampton Court but at Roanoke Island, North Carolina, adjacent to the national park commemorating the first, failed attempt at English colonization. I am trying to enjoy the Queen Elizabeth hybrid tea roses, although I am soon forced into the air-conditioned and highly perfumed refuge of the gift shop.

The reference to 9/11 is not entirely gratuitous but suggests certain parallel lines of historical development: unexpected violence from afar, certainly, just as the coastal Algonquians of Albemarle Sound must have been similarly surprised when, on a sunny August day in 1585, Ralph Lane's brutal presence made itself felt. The reference also suggests permanently deferred or impossible projects: Islamic modernism, capitalist triumphalism. Finally, it suggests a process of symbolization that is never fully "consummated," in Greg Dening's (1996) words. Neither lower Manhattan's faded monument to grandiosity nor the attack itself were able to live up to the symbolic potential envisioned by their authors. It is as a failed symbol that we must approach the Lost Colony. But it is a particularly pregnant failure: one that invites or perhaps requires reinvention every generation or so.

Faulkner's adage that the past is not even past suggests an alternative reading to the one usually ascribed. Walking through the rose garden, planted in 1976 and situated within the larger garden complex, constructed in 1951 by the North Carolina Garden Club, it is impossible not to be aware of the pervasive anachronism of Roanoke. I am taken back to a warm summer evening in the early 1970s when my family and I attended a performance in situ of Paul Green's famous Depression-era play *The Lost Colony*. What struck me as much as the frequent loud reports of stage muskets and cannon, and the heavy Elizabethan costumes that seemed too hot for the circumstances (although actors have their secrets, and perhaps the clothes were not as hot as they appeared), was the collective aroma of OFF! insect repellant in its ubiquitous orange can. I remember (possibly incorrectly) that the repellant was available free to all patrons but that mosquitoes were little deterred by its florid scent. As the actors read their wooden lines of pseudo-Elizabethan dialogue, the smell of bug spray betrayed the fact that the central problem of the colony was not, as Green supposed, about freedom or class equality or protofeminism but about the question of survival in a pestilential swamp, in a location chosen specifically because of its isolation and marginality. If the Spaniards and the Indians did not get them, by God the mosquitoes would, and quite possibly did.

Across Doughs Creek from the town of Manteo lies the newer Festival Park. It has a variety of interactive diversions for tourists, including a wonderful folkways museum. There, at the duck-hunting display, visitors can sit in an authentic duck boat of local manufacture and shoot an infrared shotgun at duck-shaped targets. Another part of the park is an Elizabethan "settlement," in which costumed workers demonstrate Elizabethan-era crafts and lifeways. No attempt is made at reconstruction of the colony's physical plant, and the impression given is more that of a Renaissance fair than that of a living-history museum. However, a visit to the reconstructed "composite" bark *Elizabeth II* demonstrates the logic of the place. Like the vessel itself, the costumed crew members are intended not as simulacra of an actual past but as tokens of anachronism. This situation is captured in a clever way by the protocol interpreters follow when speaking to visitors. They use Elizabethan terms and, to the degree of their abilities, accents, but they do not pretend to be people living in the sixteenth century. Rather, they act like a particularly conservative sect of Renaissance people living in the twenty-first century.

Anachronism is a pervasive phenomenon in American perceptions of the past. Thus Renaissance fairs are a common component of middle-class urban and suburban recreation, and groups such as the Society for Creative Anachronism create communities around performances of medieval- and Renaissance-themed activities (see Handler and Saxton 1988). Another familiar example is the "hyper-reality" of constructs such as Williamsburg, Virginia, and Mystic Seaport, Connecticut, which are simulacra of an imagined and ideologically inflected past (Baudrillard 1988; Eco 1986; Handler and Gable 1997; Kirshenblatt-Gimblett 1998:189–200; Lowenthal 1985). A different problem is presented by wholly authentic sites and objects, whose curation requires an element of anachronism. Thus the major documents of the American republic are on display in a highly secure, high-tech facility at the National Archives building in Washington, DC. Even Revolutionary and Civil War battle sites are marked by an infrastructure of signage, access roads, toilet facilities, and the like.

What makes Roanoke different is the degree to which anachronism is foregrounded rather than hidden. While experiencing Roanoke, the visitor has access to at least three strikingly different interpretations of the Lost Colony, dating from the 1930s and the Depression (equality and freedom of the new society); the 1950s to 1976, leading up to the U.S. bicentennial (the connection between the white settlements in North Carolina and the mother country); and the 1980s to the 2000s, the quadricentennial of the Lost Colony (the commercialization of the mythmaking process). Moreover, each interpretive moment is allowed to persist on its own terms. The effect is not the palimpsest seen, for example, at other historical sites in North Carolina, such as the port of Wilmington, where previous meanings (such as those having to do with slavery) are erased or suppressed. Instead, the effect is a sort of collage or stratigraphy that allows all views to be perceived simultaneously.

A more controlled comparison may be made with Jamestown, the ultimately successful English settlement one hundred miles to the north. That site, which is institutionally completely under the control of a single entity, the Jamestown-Yorktown Foundation, suggests a more unified interpretation. While this interpretation has certainly changed over time—for instance, the role of Native Americans has been significantly revised, particularly in the context of extensive archaeological excavation—at any given moment, a relatively hegemonic discourse predominates. This situation is a function of the centrality of Jamestown in the national myth-history: its completeness and finality as a narrative of the English presence in the New World. In preparation for the quadricentennial year of 2007, a new museum opened. While explicitly emphasizing the "three currents" (African, European, and Native American) that contributed to Jamestown, it nevertheless does so with an air of inevitability, a teleological sense that the currents will indeed be joined into the larger river of Anglo-American civilization (of which the very museum, opulently decorated, is a prime example). By contrast, the heteroglossia of Roanoke is related to its status as an open-ended narrative of the sort that Mikhail Bakhtin called dialogic. Why this is so is a long and complicated story but can be limned along the following lines: The Lost Colony narrative has always required the interpretive efforts of its audience, in stark contrast to many national myths that do not readily permit alternatives.[1] It is inherently incomplete and ambiguous. It is a little like a postmodernist film with multiple endings, or perhaps even the prerelease cuts of Hollywood movies screened for focus groups, who then choose their preferred ending. The most obvious aspect of this situation is the lack of narrative closure: we do not know what happened to the colonists and to little Virginia Dare, but we can well imagine various scenarios. It was, after all, a colony that somehow was "lost," contrary to the first and fundamental rule of colonies. However, the narrative ambiguity has roots deeper than even this, going back to the conception of the project. It was ambiguously conceived as either a military or a civilian society or both. It was placed largely for strategic reasons out of the reach of both the Spanish and the powerful Chesapeake Indians, and it was, partly for this reason, located in the marginal space between land and sea, yet without deepwater access. This placement reflected, in turn, the ambivalence of Elizabethan elites toward America: was she to be a serviceable maid, providing codfish and shelter from the Spanish, or was she rather a tempting, if virginal, maiden, awaiting conquest (Fuller 2001)?

THE POLITICS OF REAL ESTATE PORN

John Donne, in "To My Mistress Going to Bed," provides the urtext for an erotics of America: "License my roving hands, and let them go / Behind, before, above, between, below. / O my America! my new-found-land, / My kingdom, safeliest when with one man mann'd, / My mine of precious stones, my empery, / How am I blest in thus discovering thee!" The parallelism is complete: the body of the lover, which exists for the pleasure of her explorer, is filled with precious hidden things (see Fuller 2001). It is also blessed with the promise of fertility, as Donne alludes to childbirth later in the poem: "Then since I may know / As liberally, as to a midwife, show / Thyself: cast all, yea, this white linen hence." These two themes, fertility and "precious stones," become the recurrent theme in the documents of early explorers to the area, which functioned much as an investment prospectus. Arthur Barlowe, who visited Roanoke in 1584, compares the country's fertility favorably to the landscape of the known world:

> The island has many large forests overrun with deer, rabbits, hares, and woodfowl, even in midsummer. The woods are not barren and fruitless like those in Bohemia, Moscovia, or Hercynia, but are thick with the highest and reddest cedars in the world, far better than the cedars of the Azores, of the Indies, or of Lebanon. (Barlowe [1584] 1965:126)

And while it could not feasibly be claimed that Roanoke was rich with gemstones, the presumed abundant pearls were a plausible substitute. In addition, precious metals were evident, although it was clearly copper that Barlowe observes on Granganimeo: "[He] wore a broad plate of gold about his head. As the metal was unpolished, we could not determine if it was really gold or copper, since he would not allow it to be taken from him. But when we felt it, it bent easily" (Barlowe [1584] 1965:128; Mancall 2007:198).

The people themselves provided further evidence of the attractions of the land: "[Granganimeo's] wife was very beautiful, small in stature, and shy. She wore a long cloak of leather, the fur side next to her body. Her forehead was adorned by a band of white coral, just as her husband's was. Her earrings of pearls as big as peas, hung down to her waist" (Barlowe [1584] 1965:128; Mancall 2007:198). Thus, on both literal and symbolic levels, this was a landscape of desire.

Thomas Hariot, a member of the first colony under Ralph Lane, provides an even more boosterish account of the land and its people, undeterred by the reality of a scrub pine landscape with a lack of freshwater or arable soil but with an abundance of mosquitoes and other pests. He catalogs the various resources available, divided into categories such as "fruites," "fishe," and "foule." A combination of wishful thinking and lack of knowledge of plants, animals, and especially minerals (like Barlowe, mistaking copper for gold and reporting the existence of silver as well) leads to an exaggerated assessment of the wealth of the land. Even the climate, hard to bear even with modern amenities, is proclaimed to be health giving. He explicitly encourages settlement of the area:

> Seing therefore the ayre there is so temperate and holsome, the soyle so fertile, and yielding such commodities as I haue before meontioned, the voyage also thither to and fro being sufficiently experimented, to bee perfourmed thrice a yeere with ease and at

> any season thereof: And the dealing of Sir Walter Raleigh so lib-
> erall in larger giuin and graunting lande three, as is already
> knowen, with many helpes and furtherances els. (Hariot [1590]
> 1991:385)

The critical problem of the 1587 colony is foreshadowed here. The resupply of the colony on a semiannual basis probably would have been required
in the early days for it to survive. Moreover, the lack of "English victual" was
a problem even for the Lane colony, whose members were forced "for
twentie daes" to "liue only by drinking water" not beer (Hariot [1590]
1991:383). Finally, Hariot does at one point more or less imply that
Roanoke itself is not the best location for a colony in this area but provides
access to the richer lands upcountry:

> Yet sometimes we made our iourneies farther into the maine and
> countrey; we found the soyle to bee fatter; the trees greater and
> to grow thinner; the grounde more firme and deeper mould;
> more and large champions [open fields]; finer grasse and as
> good as euer we saw any in England; in some places rockie and
> far more high and hillie ground; more plenty of their fruites;
> more abundance of their beastes; the more inhabited with peo-
> ple, and of greater pollicie & larger dominions, with greater
> townes and houses. (Hariot [1590] 1991:382)

David Beers Quinn argues that this is Hariot's honest and realistic
opinion, that in comparison with the richer upcountry lands, the coast was
relatively impoverished but nevertheless habitable (Quinn 1991:382). That
Roanoke was, in Hariot's view, to be a stepping-off point for access to the
lands and people inland is prescient and implies a grander and longer-
term perspective than that taken in other parts of the document. The city
of Raleigh, then, was being marginalized before it was even founded.
Colonization would, in this view, inevitably move inland. The lack of deepwater access at Roanoke would mean that it was also unsuitable for a port,
essentially conceding that future settlement would, when conditions (especially vis-à-vis the Spanish) were suitable, move northward, into the deeper
waters of the Chesapeake.

Nevertheless, the drumbeat of promotion is kept up throughout the
rest of Hariot's "Briefe and true report." Not only was the climate said to
be Mediterranean (comparable to "the South parts of Greece, Italy, and
Spaine"), but it was lacking the "violent" heat of the tropics. Indeed, the
"ayre" seemed to have curative powers in that only four members of the

Lane colony died, and they were said to be grievously ill from the voyage and lived longer than was to be expected (Hariot [1588] 1991:384). This information follows, as Quinn remarks, the Renaissance belief that similar latitudes produced similar environments (Quinn 1991:383n1). The Mediterranean was thought to have a more healthful climate than England. Thus, by association, so would Roanoke. In this connection, the famous drawings of the coastal Algonquians by John White, which are undisputedly valuable ethnographic documents, at the same time depict distinctly classical features (Egmond and Mason 1997:196). The implicit argument, processed through Richard Hakluyt's thoroughgoing optimism and Theodor De Bry's propaganda factory, was that Virginia provided a salutary, even ideal, environment for the development of civilization (Mancall 2007:204). Indeed, as Michael Zuckerman (1987) argues, the very insecurity of the British New World settlements (of food and from disease and attack) led to a sort of inferiority complex among settlers, leading them to exaggerate the resources and the ease with which they could be exploited. Thus began a line of argumentation closely linked to the development of Anglo-American identity, which, while changing, appears later in the eighteenth century in Jefferson's famous debate with the Comte de Buffon, in which he argues for the vitality of the American environment (see Egmond and Mason 1997:16; Wallace 1999:76–77). It resurfaces as late as the early twentieth century with Franz Boas's arguments about the plasticity of cranial form in immigrant populations due to the American environment (Gravlee, Bernard, and Leonard 2003; Sparks and Jantz 2003).

If the metonymic relation between environment and body was of primary importance in the articulation of a plan for English colonization, the metaphoric connections of the landscape to bodies were of even greater political significance in discourse about the New World. The term *Virginia*, given by Walter Raleigh to the lands referred to in his charter, was of course in honor of Queen Elizabeth and was given with her explicit permission (Quinn 1991:22). Such courtly gestures across the Atlantic imbued all discussion of the newly explored lands with a certain political gravity. The body of the sovereign becomes associated with a particular landscape—that of Virginia—which must perforce possess qualities appropriate to its exalted role. This idea is similar but not identical to the principle of the sovereign embodying the realm, which was developed slightly later by Hobbes and other monarchist political philosophers of the seventeenth century. Rather, the connection here is entirely metaphorical (whereas the sovereign in *Leviathan* is both metaphor and metonym). If anything, this metaphor makes the association more absolute and less subject to shades of meaning. Thus to speak ill of England in some sense (such as the weather) was not necessarily treasonous, whereas to speak ill of Virginia could be construed as such. Richard Hakluyt refutes reports of the barrenness of the land by connecting Virginia with Elizabeth and insisting that neither could be barren; to suggest otherwise would constitute lèse-majesté (Knapp 1993:284–85).

In this connection, the reticence of even a close observer such as Hariot to speak clearly of the limitations of Roanoke may be understood. Rather than point directly at deficiencies, which would become obvious to the colonists of 1587, it was necessary to suggest instead that proximity to superior territories was an absolute asset, much in the manner of real estate agents and developers today.

HOW TO LOSE A COLONY

The Lost Colony is the conventional name for the second Roanoke colony, financed by Sir Walter Raleigh and led by John White. It was the second colony at the site and, including the 1584 expedition, the third extended encounter with Roanoke and its inhabitants. The first colony, under the command of Ralph Lane, was a military outpost, abandoned because of supply problems and conflict with local Algonquians. The second colony was imagined differently: it was to be a civilian colony, reproducing an English village in the new world of Virginia (see Canny 1988). The "Lost Colony" would probably not have become so completely and paradoxically lost were it not for the failures of the Lane colony, and another famous historical factor: the Spanish Armada of 1588. Either one alone would possibly not have been fatal, but together they certainly were. Both circumstances can be viewed as part of a larger process of militarizing the eastern seaboard, just as the Caribbean had been similarly infected with violence in the ninety previous years. As Brian Ferguson and Neil Whitehead argue in *War in the Tribal Zone* (2000), the expansion of states into new territories produces a contact zone defined by escalating warfare and more pervasive violence. This, in turn, creates quickly evolving political situations in which indigenous societies "tribalize"—that is, they adopt higher-order political structures to better to prosecute war against other indigenous groups as well as colonizers. The colonists were quite clearly caught up in this dynamic. The murder of several Indians during the Lane settlement predisposed the local people to take a defensive stance against the new colony. At the same time, the local people would soon be feeling effects from the expanding Powhatan empire, as well as from Iroquoian groups from the mainland. Ironically, one plausible scenario has the colonists initially moving in with friendly locals, only to be absorbed, likely as slaves, into the Powhatan (Quinn 1984). This would explain reported sightings of fair-skinned Indians a generation later in the vicinity of Jamestown (Kupperman 1984:137–38). However, on this, as on all speculative matters concerning Roanoke, there is much debate (see Parramore 2001).

It is important to recognize that even the first Roanoke colony was by no means a "first contact," except perhaps in the sense of being an epitomizing event. The coastal Algonquians had certainly encountered the English before. Raleigh explored the coast in 1578. In 1584 he sent two ships, under the command of Philip Amadas and Arthur Barlowe, to site the colony. As a result of that voyage, two local Natives, Manteo and Wanchese (who become the hero and antihero of Paul Green's play), were taken to England. Although we know little of their voyage, we can assume that they were treated much as later indigenous dignitaries were. We do know that they lodged with Raleigh in his estate, Durham House, and that Hariot quizzed them on Algonquian language in order to create a means of communication (Oberg 1999:24–25; Quinn 1949). Thus Hariot's observations of 1585–86 benefited from some understanding of coastal Algonquian language and culture.

Working both for and against these attempts to ease relations with the local Natives was the unintentional factor of disease mortality. Earlier visits by English and Spanish had left the Native population weakened and reduced. Over time, the populations of eastern Algonquians would decline by 90 percent (Kupperman 1984:61–62). Although we do not have direct evidence for a causal connection, it is reasonable to assume that, as elsewhere in the Americas, disease mortality and suffering created their own dynamic of intergroup relations (Mallios 2006:64–66). Natives usually blamed Europeans for the disease, which was seen as a form of sorcery. At the same time, aboriginals were willing to borrow what they could from European culture, particularly medical practices and religious beliefs. The English of this era possessed little or nothing in the former category of greater value than that of the Natives, but they survived due to resistance to their own endemic pathogens. However, since aboriginal Americans universally viewed disease as having a spiritual etiology, the attractions of European spiritual beliefs were poignant. Moreover, as in other contact situations in other eras, this emphasis dovetailed completely with the Europeans' own emphasis on Christianity as the most important difference between themselves and the "savages." Indeed, in the version of colonialism preached, if not always practiced, by Renaissance Englishmen—in conscious contradistinction to the incipient "black legend" of Spanish conquest—lack of Christianity was the sole marker of savagery; hence the primacy of conversion over all other considerations (Oberg 1999:20–22; see Mancall 2007:202).

The coastal Algonquians' reception to the preaching of Thomas Hariot seems to fit with this model: people were receptive to Christianity, mimicking the motions of prayer and attaching great significance to objects, especially the Bible, as a means of preventing or curing disease (Kupperman 1984:61). This magical view was distressing to the Protestant Hariot, who very much held to a text- and belief-based version of Christianity and who regretted his poor command of Algonquian, with which he might persuade his listeners of the logical superiority of Christianity to other forms of belief (Hariot [1590] 1972:27–29).

Although the promise of superior spiritual power (much more so than technological power, which was not as clearly superior as it would later be) acted as an attractant for Natives, other aspects of this dynamic worked as a repellant. Thus if disease was a particularly potent form of English spiritual practice, then one logical response was to withdraw. This was effectively done in 1586, when the Lane colony was in need of food. Wingina, the *werowance* (local chief) of the Roanokes, whose brother Granganimeo had died over the winter, had subsequently changed his name to Pemispan.[2] The loss of Granganimeo was particularly unfortunate for the colonists, as he was one of the Natives most eager to engage in cultural exchange with the English. Although no evidence exists as to the cause of his death, it was quite likely due to illness; certainly, if he had met a violent end, it is unlikely that it would have escaped comment by Lane ([1589] 1991:285). It seems the name change may have signified a shift in stance toward one of war, or at least, as the name suggests, watchful vigilance (Kupperman 1984:76; Lane [1589] 1991:285; Oberg 1999:39; Quinn 1991: 893–94). In any case, the death of Granganimeo and the consequent peripeteia resulted in the complete withdrawal of aid from the colony at a critical time.[3]

The situation quickly became complicated by local politics, providing temporary respite for the colony. Menatonon, the werowance of the Choanokes, reported to Lane that Pemispan's intentions were bad. This report, curiously, resulted in Lane's kidnapping of Menatonon's son, Skiko, as insurance of the chief's truthfulness. However, Menatonon continued to support Lane, bringing in Okikso, werowance of the Weapemeocs, as a supporter. They even pledged their fealty to Queen Elizabeth and Walter Raleigh. At this point, the Roanokes were outnumbered; Pemispan backtracked a little, going so far as to build a fish weir for the colony. However, good relations did not persist. In June, satisfied that Pemispan was the source of their troubles, Lane had him killed. Although this action relieved the embargo on food supplies, it clearly had serious long-range consequences for the colony. When Francis Drake unexpectedly arrived at Roanoke in June and lost several small ships in a hurricane, the fate of the first colony was sealed. Lane left with most of the colony, leaving behind fifteen men. Their fate is uncertain, but we can assume they were victims of, as well as contributors to, the violence of the contact zone.[4] In addition, it is likely that Drake left several hundred freed slaves and Indians, whom he had picked up in the Caribbean, possibly to mix in with the local community (Kupperman 1984:92).

The Lane colony was set down in Roanoke as a toehold on the mid-Atlantic coast, as a means of undermining Spanish domination, and, certainly, as a base for piracy. A central consideration was that the base be hidden and relatively inaccessible. The shallow waters of Albemarle Sound prevented all but the smallest boats from putting in on Roanoke. Even pinnaces, the smallest category of oceangoing vessels, were sometimes stuck in the mud when attempting to land (Quinn 1991:166 n. 4). The plan was, as Hariot indicates, to move from Roanoke to a more permanent settlement inland. To that end, the first colony sent out an exploration party in the winter of 1585–86. We know little about that party—possibly owing to the suppression of the report for reasons of security or proprietary interest—but it likely made its way to Chesapeake Bay (Kupperman 1984:76; Quinn 1991:245–46). However, it is clear that such a colony could not be established with the resources possessed by the Roanoke colonies. A deepwater port in the heart of Powhatan country would have required a defensive capacity well beyond the means of the Lane colony.

Despite these serious drawbacks, and the fact that Spain claimed Chesapeake as Bahia de Madre de Dios de Jacán, the 1587 colony was indeed planned for Chesapeake Bay (see Mallios 2006:37–57). The plans were abandoned when pilot Simon Fernandez refused to take the colonists farther north. Despite Raleigh's explicit orders to the contrary, Fernandez insisted on depositing the colonists on Roanoke so that he could proceed with privateering in the Caribbean before the season became too advanced (Quinn 1991:503).

Roanoke can thus be seen as a default choice for a colony—not the place truly desired but the result of a series of compromises. Nevertheless, the second colony began with optimism, derived from the original vision of a Virginia colony as propounded by Thomas Hariot and John White. White was named the governor of the second colony, a fact that represents a significant departure from the model pursued in the first. Lane and other leaders of that venture were hard men, who had seen a great deal of violence in Ireland and elsewhere; they held to a view of cultural others as savages to be suppressed with brutality (see Mallios 2006). It is clear that the failure of Lane's colony had a great deal to do with his leadership. As Oberg (1999) argues cogently, this "frontier" perspective—counterpoised against the "metropolitan" view of people such as the Hakluyts, De Bry, White, and Hariot—often won the day, with frequently disastrous consequences for both indigene and colonizer. However, the alternative had its own problems.

JOHN WHITE'S VISION

As an artist, John White was a central figure in the scientific enterprise associated with the exploration and colonization of Virginia. White's drawings of coastal Algonquians provide the richest visual source on any culture of the sixteenth century (see Hulton 1984). The detailed depictions of everyday life are remarkable for their accuracy and informative content. They also, as engraved and published by De Bry, express a worldview that would culminate in the Enlightenment and comparative ethnography as a branch of natural history. Three thematic series are juxtaposed: the Algonquians and other coastal groups of North and South America (drawn after Le Moyne and Léry, respectively); other ethnic groups, including Picts and ancient Britons; and natural species, particularly birds and fish. The first two are part of White's interest in providing a "theatre of races" (Hulton 1984:194). In particular, he suggests a developmental, or proto-evolutionary, model; the Picts and Britons are shown to be equivalent to the Americans. Thus the essential ideology of colonialism—to be later developed into the apotheosis of the white man's burden—is present here (see Egmond and Mason 1997:158–60). One must agree with Oberg's assessment that such a view is optimistic and more benevolent than the alternative (Oberg 1999:23–24). At the same time, this perspective produces a technology of control, much as White's excellent maps of the area provided a template for navigation. The connection with the natural series is equally interesting. Operating here is not only a logic of universal classification—one that that implicitly links the natural and cultural as realms to be described and controlled—but also a concern for the interaction of culture and environment. Thus the plates titled "The manner of their fishing" (plate 43) and "The broyling of their fish ouer th' flame of fier" (plate 45) illustrate the ecological dimensions of Algonquian culture (Hulton 1984:73–75).

The most remarkable of White's drawings are the composite depictions of Algonquian villages, in particular the drawing of Secoton (plate 36) showing houses, fields, and several distinct activities of the inhabitants. This synoptic view of the village combines elements of White's maps—particularly the bird's-eye view—with his ethnographic pictures to create an imaginary landscape in which he, or the viewer, is in control of a place and its resources and inhabitants. (Such optimistic visual depictions of resource-rich landscapes are a leitmotif of the colonial experience, as Dale Tomich's paper in this volume so well reminds us.) The enhancements in De Bry's engraving give more detail, particularly of the gardens and the plant species grown, strengthening the visual argument of a way of life instantly comprehensible and controllable. Interestingly, in both White's and De Bry's versions, the view of Secoton is more developed than that of Pomeiooc, a palisaded, enclosed village. Hariot expresses his preference for the open village (Hulton 1984:190). On the most literal level, it is clear that the enclosed village would present greater barriers to beneficial exchange and could possibly reflect an equally closed view of the outside world. Visually, the closed village, with the houses and ceremonial areas separated from the fields, is less easily depicted synoptically. Rather than providing a landscape of apparent access and control, it is resistant to both the viewer and the colonizer.

Colonies are themselves largely "about" landscape. The view from the colony's center should ideally be neat and rational, with a visual catalog of the surrounding resources. Clear lines of sight and ease of comprehension make mastery of the environment possible (see Mitchell 1994). (We need not detain ourselves here with discussion of the many cases in the later history of British colonialism where the tropical landscape is not so easily mastered, a situation richly depicted by E. M. Forster and others.) The visual argument made by White and De Bry is that the landscape of Roanoke is straightforward and clear-cut. If the "savages," having attained a level of development comparable to the ancient Picts, could master it, then the Englishman certainly could. A second aspect of White's synoptic drawings is their familiarity. Although strange in detail to the European observer, the layout of the village, with its single-family houses and farms, was immediately graspable by viewers familiar with agrarian England. This image is the visual side of Hariot's argument that the land was rich and fertile and could be remade into something like the homeland. Recalling the observations of Tacitus in *Germania*, Hariot suggests that the existence of grapes, from which one could make wine, signaled a potential jump to civilization: "When they are planted and husbanded as they ought, a principall commoditie of wines may be raised by them" (Hariot [1590] 1991:330).

The land of Roanoke was not really so accommodating. With sandy, salty soil in many areas of the island, it was not an ideal place for agriculture—nor indeed did Hariot's and White's descriptions actually suggest that it was, since their examples came from the mainland. Exacerbating the basic problem of access to arable land was the severe drought of 1587–1589, which would have made an independent agricultural community impossible (Stahle et al. 1998). The survival of the colony thus depended entirely on the remaining two legs: good relations with local people and resupply from England.

Of the two familiar problems with the second colony, the lack of resupply is the easiest to understand. John White left the colony in August 1587 to argue forcefully for a relief expedition. He won the assent of Raleigh, but by October of that year, all shipping was stopped in view of the danger from Spain (Quinn 1991:554). In March 1588, after definite plans to send a fleet under Richard Grenville's command were set in motion, a counterorder was issued in view of the threatening Spanish Armada. Of course, it is not certain that the colony would have survived even on that schedule of resupply, since such aid would have arrived nearly a year after White left. In any case, by the time he returned, in 1590, the colony was no longer a priority for Raleigh, who had invested in the much easier colonization of Ireland. And famously, there was no trace of the colonists, only the name Croatoan inscribed on a post and the letters CRO carved into a tree trunk.

More complicated is the matter of relations with the local people. By all accounts, the early days began with a mutual wariness between the two groups. The Croatoans—the friendliest of the local groups, with whom the colonists may or may not have taken shelter—warned the colonists that they could not afford to feed them (Kupperman 1984:115; Mallios 2006:75–76). It can only be imagined that this problem became more acute during the drought year to come. Ironically, the Lane colony at full strength seems to have had more success with the local people; as powerful allies, the English were desirable, and the novelty of their tools and weapons was still great. By 1587, however, a different sort of colony, less immediately bellicose but in the long run more threatening, may have caused erstwhile allies such as Menatonon, no record of whom exists in the second colony, to abandon them. This conclusion in no way justifies the "frontier" attitude of men like Lane, who believed that the savage must be broken, but it does recognize the slow-motion violence inherent in colonization, even when espoused by "metropolitans" (compare Oberg 1999). It is likely that the Carolina Algonquians recognized this situation as well. Whatever became of the colonists—a debate I do not intend to enter into—it is not clear that either of the models presented a realistic possibility of success.

ANACHRONY, USA

Writing anything on the Lost Colony without espousing a theory of its fate has the advantage of putting one in the minority, rather like the subset of people who visit Paris without seeing the Eiffel Tower up close. Of all the speculations on the topic, the two main ones focus on absorption into the local population, or extermination at the hands of one or another group of Indians, either Algonquian or Iroquoian (see Parramore 2001; Quinn 1984). But this binary choice has not been sufficiently rich for the genius of American commentators, who over the years have proposed a range of scenarios, in which the colonists are picked up by Spaniards, who then sell the women into harem slavery or go on to found a new colony inland with greater or lesser degrees of intermarriage with aboriginals (see Arner 1982). Many of these scenarios connect with extant communities in North Carolina. Most famous of these were the Lumbee, who for a while called themselves Croatan (Blu 1980; Dial and Eliades 1975). Other visions, more consistent with Old South views on miscegenation, have the colonists moving to other parts of North Carolina (see, for example, Bailey 1991; see Stick 1983 for a survey of theories up to that time). Evidence such as a piece of quartz engraved with Elizabethan English—the famous hoax of the "Dare stone"—has been presented (Pearce 1938; White 1991). The very open-endedness of this situation has allowed people to fill in the gaps with their own interested projections.

One popular theme has been the "Elizabethan" quality attached to the Outer Banks, or eastern North Carolina, or the entire state, or indeed the white, English-speaking Southeast. Sometimes this ascription is merely a rhetorical gesture, as when one author writing in the *DAR* magazine ascribed the adventurous and independent spirit of the age (along with Pericles' Athens, "one of two periods of history [that] blaze with especial brilliance") embodied in the Virgin Queen to the character of the Old North State (Fletcher 1952). Other cases, such as the avocational writings of the prominent University of North Carolina geologist Collier Cobb (Cobb 1910), entail a somewhat more scholarly search for "survivals" of Elizabethan custom and language on the Outer Banks. Indeed, much is made of this connection even today, with popular guides to language and folklore of the area, along with trinkets reminiscent of Elizabethan and Jacobean England, widely available in tourist shops.

The apparent discontinuity between the Lost Colony and historic

North Carolina does not deter many from attempting to make these links with a useful past. The elision in fact makes possible a certain sort of historical claim. In particular, it allows a segment of the population—tidewater residents of English descent—to make claims of priority with respect to other groups in the state and region. It has also provided a template for other historical eras, especially the post–Civil War period of rapid social and economic change (see Harkin 2007). Anachronism in this context is thus less a naive misuse of history than its appropriation for a particular political agenda. The Queen Elizabeth hybrid tea roses are telling us that.

HISTORIOGRAPHY AND SHIFTING SCALES

As the case of the Lost Colony makes abundantly clear, the old Aristotelian unities—of time, place, and action—do not apply here. Rather, it is necessary to imagine the semiotic field of the Lost Colony as including various moments, spread out widely over time and space. This situation is certainly not unique to the Lost Colony but is shared broadly with other sorts of recursive historical fields, particularly those with a performative dimension, such as "living history," which invite anachronistic and transtemporal interpretations (see Handler and Saxton 1988). What is more, this phenomenon is one aspect of a more general problem in historiography, that of connecting events—always taking into account the double sense of *res gestae* (the facts themselves) and *historia rerum gestarum* (narratives)—which inevitably play out on a human scale, with other, similar events, and through this connection with macro-level phenomena, or morphology, to use the term of art (Egmond and Mason 1997).

Microhistory—the school of historiography focusing on the local and specific—and much ethnographically inspired historiography (including the majority of what is labeled ethnohistory) attempt to maintain the unities by circumscribing the frame of reference to a particular place and time. This effort can be quite successful in that it can richly evoke a particular lifeworld removed from both author and reader (for example, Ginzburg 1980a). At the same time, the very success of such approaches rests equally on their ability to point beyond themselves, to translate among contexts, including those of author and reader. Much like ethnography, which has conventionally come to be seen as a form of cross-cultural translation, historiography is always implicated in such a project of movement among contexts (Egmond and Mason 1997:79–81). This movement reaches beyond the triadic relationship of author, reader, and object; the very act of employing synthetic terms such as *shamanism* or *witchcraft* necessarily invokes other historical and cultural contexts (79–81).

In a second way, any attempt to preserve unity is undermined by a powerful principle of selection operating in historiography. I refer here to the notion of the "event," which rests at the center of most historical writing. The event can be defined as a disjuncture between successive states of a system, so that the world before and after the event is in some sense different (Pachter 1974; see Harkin 1988). The difference may be more or less fundamental, but it is never trivial if the event is truly an event. Thus one is forced to see the Lost Colony as separating a world *without* and a world *with* English colonization of Virginia, just as one must view the signing of the Declaration of Independence or the storming of the Bastille as similarly world changing. Of course, some of this is a function of the narrativization of the event; the storming of the Bastille was less significant as acted and more so as an epitomizing event of the French Revolution (see Fogelson 1985). However, the distinction between the two senses of "event" is never total; both action and narration entail pragmatic consequences.

Lévi-Straussian structuralism proposes an alternative reading of this problematic, in which events are not so much cause as effect, reflecting deeper structural oppositions and transformations. These structures, rooted in fundamental human cognitive-linguistic process, produce recurrent events, which in turn constitute crisis points in the reproduction of structure. In this sense, structuralism may be seen as a form of the common nineteenth-century notion of homology between phylogeny and ontogeny, which created similar notions of recurring events reflecting systemic crisis, as in Freud's Oedipal theory or Jung's theory of archetypes (Ginzburg 1989a:153–54). That is, connections between isomorphic but widely separated events are posited on a nonempirical basis, on the assumption of deep-structural similarities of the human mind. In a sense, humans are thus "programmed" to create structures based on fundamental oppositions and to react in predictable ways to crises in these structures (see Ginzburg 1991:20–22). Certain types of events, for instance regicide, are prone to recur in various times and places, driven by the posited structural dynamics of cultures.

Marshall Sahlins's work since the 1980s has extended this model in more empirical and dialogical dimensions. Thus the death of Captain Cook is an example of the "structure of the conjuncture," the meeting place between two cultural orders and pure accident (Sahlins 1981, 1985). Actors in both cultures act in a deterministic fashion shaped by cultural assumptions and the underlying dynamic of dualistic structures of outside–inside, heaven–earth, land–sea, civilized–savage. The resulting event creates an irrevocable break with the past as it produces discomfiture of the Hawaiian worldview while reinforcing certain aspects of the English one. However, as Obeyesekere's critique of Sahlins—although much less firmly grounded in the empirical details of Hawaiian ethnography—shows, this is only the beginning of nearly endless chains of association stretching into the present, to places far distant from Polynesia, and into the context of everyday life in the West and elsewhere, particularly in the form of primitivist and Orientalist discourses and their political ramifications. What is more, these chains of association are more than mere reinterpretations of a "settled" historical field; they have the capacity to constitute that field and to project it into the future (Obeyesekere 1992; Sahlins 1995).

Even if one is inclined to accept the view that events are produced by underlying structures of culture and, behind them, the human mind, it is impossible to delimit the historical field in an a priori manner or to fashion a convincing classification of events into formal categories based on structural similarity. The echo chamber of the modern world system, even before Google, has made that impossible. Beyond that, a contemporary model of mind based on principles of connectionism—rather than an outdated Chomskian structuralism—would tend to support a more open-ended notion of meaning creation, at odds with the structuralist insistence that recurrent forms of relations and actions can be stipulated.

If structuralism, in its way, addresses the disunities of time and action in a manner that attempts to show them to be secondary to the integrity of an underlying structure, a second anthropological approach has attempted to preserve the unity of space. The pioneering work of Keith Basso (1996), along with that of Simon Schama (1995) and others (see Feld and Basso 1996), has addressed the redolence of historical meaning in "place," which is seen as a meaning-infused inhabitation of landscape. Following Benveniste's revised notion of Saussurian "motivation," we could say that otherwise arbitrary features of landscape (or language) take on a deterministic quality to members of a cultural (or speech) community: what I have called topemes, or culturally defined landscape elements (Harkin 2004). Through a process of "inscription" on the landscape, communities over time invest place with layers of associative meaning, both collective and personal. In a manner of speaking, landscape elements become agents in historical time. While this perspective is quite valuable for certain contexts, particularly for the histories of aboriginal cultures, there are many cases in which the unity of place cannot reasonably be maintained. Even in the context of aboriginal cultures, once places, for instance sacred sites, become part of broader discourses, they inevitably become to some degree delocalized. Thus a site such as Devils Tower in Wyoming, iconized on a state license plate and in Hollywood films, is necessarily pulled out of its original meaningful context (see Harkin 2006).

Indeed, while the movement toward landscape studies in several disciplines has been beneficial and has relieved historical anthropology and historiography of some of the weight of their chronic (we might even say structural) crises, it can also be seen as a rearguard movement by a romantic form of localism that has been devastatingly criticized, especially within anthropology (Appadurai 1996; Gupta and Ferguson 1997). To achieve this unity of place, Basso, in his study of the Western Apache, is forced to minimize the translocality of the community (although he does not deny it) as well as the chains of association in which the Western Apache and the landscape of southwestern Arizona are already inevitably implicated. Rather than retreat to the conventional notion of a place-bounded culture, it seems more promising to adopt Appadurai's (1996) notion of "scapes" (ethnoscapes, mediascapes, and so on) as a means of constituting the field of study. "Scapes" suggest fields of meaning and action, which are necessarily translocal and transtemporal, unified rather by continuing interest and allegiance of groups of people.

The danger with Appadurai's approach is that it opens the door perhaps a little too wide. Is it necessary for Basso to consider, say, that the group of composers including Maurice Ravel was called les Apaches in prewar Paris? The chain of association leads there, but it is not necessarily relevant to a study of the Apache as opposed to French images of the other (see Harkin 2005). Here is where the craft of historiography comes in. As Ginzburg (1991:16) has argued, it is not necessary to show a simple causal relationship between two phenomena to consider them within a unitary interpretive framework; rather, some version of Wittgenstein's notion of "family resemblance" is sufficient (see Egmond and Mason 1997:5). At the same time, some limits must be placed on such connections, lest we find ourselves in a bewildering world in which all possible fields of meaning and action intersect, a bit like the occultist hero of Eco's *Foucault's Pendulum*. This hyperconnectivity may be an aspect of the reality of the mediated world in which we now live, or are soon moving toward, but it does not make for good writing or reading.

Ultimately, then, I favor our common term *narrative craft*. In shifting between frames, and constituting the object in one fashion or another, we are exercising authorial choice. The cases we decide to focus upon, the connections we make among them, are ultimately in the realm of art, not science. The phenomenon of anachronism, in the particular sense that I am using it, is thus more than a problem in the interpretation of one event or set of events, or indeed a historical field, but is also is an inherent feature of any historical interpretation. We cannot help but be reminded of other times and places. As Ginzburg's (1991) study of witches in Friuli reminded him of Baltic werewolves or Scandinavian berserkers, the Lost Colony points well beyond itself.

THE FLOATING ISLAND: DETERRITORIALIZATION AND RETERRITORIALIZATION

Like the floating island, the Lost Colony is fundamentally an oxymoron. The very notion of "colony" operating in the Elizabethan era and subsequently implied cadastral mapping, a pushing back of the frontiers of geographic knowledge and civil administration. In Ireland, colonization was thought of as bringing the benefits of civilization to new areas, much as today a city annexes rural land with the promise of roads and sewer lines (Canny 1988). To become "lost" in such a setting contradicts the very premise of the project and casts doubt on all such projects. This contradiction constitutes a running theme throughout the Lost Colony's history. The original colonists were put down in the "wrong" place initially and were absorbed into a landscape that was either unknown or was substituted for other, more familiar ones. John White's sketches of mainland Native towns are an act of propaganda to be sure but are also an example of Derridean *différence*, meaning "deferred," in this case at least until the English would establish a toehold on the mainland more than a generation later. One could argue that, as with Derrida's notion of language, such meanings were permanently deferred; the well-ordered Native town simply could not coexist with Europeans bent on colonial projects.

The current site of the national park may or may not be the location where Raleigh initially built his fort. It may in fact stand as a fairly arbitrary locational sign for a place that no longer exists; the shifting dunes and coastlines may well have carried this erstwhile place out to sea. If so, it merely dissolves a largely insupportable illusion of historical commemoration: that the essence of a historical event or personage can be immediately (that is, without mediation) apprehended by standing in the same place (Handler and Gable 1997; Kirshenblatt-Gimblett 1998:8).

Of course, many cultures possess elaborate mechanisms for constructing place, for inscribing a set of orthodox meanings into the landscape. The Apaches described by Keith Basso, although relative latecomers to the Southwest, set expressions of permanent cultural values into the land itself, in the form of places-cum-narratives. Through retelling across generations, meanings are maintained against the forces of geologic and cultural entropy. In the Lost Colony, a similar process has been undertaken, but with an additional dash of vehemence, expressed in the deictic formulations found frequently in speeches made in situ and speeches embedded within works of literature, such as Paul Green's *The Lost Colony* and Sallie Southall Cotton's *The White Doe*. Thus Governor Frank Porter Graham's speech on the occasion of the first performance of Paul Green's *The Lost Colony* affirms that "on *this* little island to which they came was built the first English home, the first English Chapel, was born and baptized the first English child in the new world" (Graham 1937; emphasis added). Even more forcefully, Judge Walter Clark, addressing a meeting of the North Carolina Literary and Historical Association at Manteo, stated: "Standing here we see the spot where first began on this continent the great race which in the New World in three hundred years has far surpassed in extent of dominion, in population and power, the greatest race known in the Old" (Clark 1902).

In one sense, however, the story of the Lost Colony is the inability of such performatives to adequately claim, define, and circumscribe the place. Just as Arner's (1982) survey of popular literature on the fate of the colonists points in every direction on the compass (a far from uncharacteristic version has the women sold into white slavery in North Africa), so the colony itself must be seen as inherently moving rather than stationary, a floating island of modern mythohistoriography.

This paradoxical formulation of place as movement—unlike the floating islands of classical myth, which were fantastic precisely because of their opposition to rooted, localized life—is rather a reasonably accurate formulation of life in the present moment. As Appadurai (1996:188) has stated the problem, it is one of producing and reproducing locality—reterritorializing—in the face of a world that is increasingly "deterritorialized," in Deleuze and Guattari's (1987) apt turn of phrase. The conflict between local and global itself destabilizes the very community that might be assumed to ground local discourse. That is, allegiances are not always what one would expect; the local person may have more subjective connection with distant places and discourses than with local ones. Another way of framing the matter is that the production of locality, if unsuccessful, leads to the dissolution of the sociological entity, the "neighborhood" as Appadurai calls it.

Local meanings in the neighborhood of tidewater North Carolina (and, in concentric circles, rural North Carolina and the rural South) are the product of a local praxis that both derives meaning from and adds it back into place-making discourse. In his masterly ethnography of the region, John Forrest (1988) depicts a way of living that in its aesthetic praxis reproduces key cultural values and reinforces notions of identity and place. Everyday practices such as quilt making, food preparation, religious piety, hunting, and related land uses shape identity and notions of place. However, even by the 1980s, this reproduction was threatened by the usual suspects of television, migration, and commercialization. Other notions of place compete with and ultimately defeat local ones. The interest of national governments in cadastral mapping is historically superseded by the demands of the neoliberal order for mobility of capital, commodities, and people (Hannerz 1996; J. Scott 1998:38–45). Such global flows directly threaten established local identities while opening the door for new possibilities of reterritorialization and identity formation. The current state of affairs is characterized by hyperinflation of waterfront real estate, the penetration of global media and commerce into local markets, and, perhaps most noticeably, the influx of Asian, eastern European, and especially Hispanic immigrants into the area and state. The Hispanic population of North Carolina increased more than sevenfold in the fifteen years following 1990 (U.S. Census Bureau 2006).

These pervasive changes destabilize local meanings based on place, occupation, religion, cuisine, and other practices of everyday life. The more these lifeways come under pressure, the greater the felt need to assert them through such mediated representations as folklife museums and locally published literature, including cookbooks, memoirs, folklore, dialect guides, and autoethnography. This material combines with a previous body of similar literature aimed at commemorating the Lost Colonists and later English settlers (above all, pirates). This activity all results in multiple discourses of place, which have specific counterparts in the memorialized landscape of the local area. The politics of memorialization are complex but tend to follow a logic of hybridity and anachronism rather than a hegemonic discourse of the past (compare Herzfeld 1991).

As a tourist site, Roanoke Island and its environs both resist and embody the centripetal and centrifugal forces at work in a globalizing world. Nearby monuments to the Wright brothers and to famous shipwrecks underscore the theme of long-distance travel, while Outer Banks beaches have increasingly been made over with references to Florida and the Caribbean. The floating island is open—for business above all—while retaining scraps of the past as both decoration and building material.

Notes

Research for this chapter was supported by a fellowship from the National Endowment for the Humanities.

1. An interesting comparison may be drawn with Fort Ross (see Lightfoot, this volume), which in similar ways challenges, or at least complicates, hegemonic national histories.

2. The werowance was a local peace chief who may or may not have effectively been a vassal to a regional chief, such as Powhatan. Prior to Powhatan, other, smaller confederacies existed (Gleach 1997:123–48; Rountree 1990:13; Rountree and Turner 2002).

3. Seth Mallios (2006) argues that the issue of exchange, of which violence is the negative image, determines the success of colonies. Thus he sites numerous examples of "exchange violations" in Roanoke, resulting from English hunger for food and Algonquian overeagerness for European goods, that undermine the exchange relationship.

4. The colonists of the second colony found one skeleton, which they took to be that of one of Lane's men (Kupperman 1984:114).

8

Biography as Microhistory,
Photography as Microhistory

Documentary Photographer Dorothea Lange as Subject and Agent of Microhistory

Linda Gordon

In a simple sense, biography is always microhistory, inasmuch as individuals are the "micro" in relation to the "macro" themes of social and political history. Biographies of the influential demonstrate in addition the force that the micro can exert on the macro. This force is not always immediately evident and certainly not predictable: no one who knew photographer Dorothea Lange in the first forty years of her life would have foretold that she would come to have fame and large-scale influence. Yet in her next five years, 1935 to 1940, she became the single most influential auteur of popular images of the Great Depression, images that in turn contributed to the political success of the New Deal and President Franklin Roosevelt. The microhistorical influence she exerted as an individual photographer was made possible by two equally micro phenomena: a tiny, almost accidental government agency, the Historical Project of the Information Division of the Farm Security Administration of the Department of Agriculture; and the (always inexplicable, always micro) personal chemistry between Lange and her unlikely second husband, Paul Taylor, an economics professor at the University of California at Berkeley.

Lange's microhistorical influence derives not only from her unusual government job but also from her photographic method. Popular documentary photography usually leans to the micro, because it communicates better about the specific than about the general. Of course, abstract photography exists, but the most gripping and remembered photography, with the possible exception of some of Ansel Adams's landscapes, brings us individuals, families, events, distinctive tragedies, singular joys. Dorothea Lange elevated the capacity of documentary photography to share individual stories with a broad public. She was above all a master of the specific, insistent on detailed contexts in every image. Her portraits of sharecroppers and migrant farmworkers provide information about their working conditions, living conditions, familial relations, possessions, health, and temperament. She tried to secure the specificity of her photographs by adding textual captions that related individual and family histories of employment, property, standard of living, migration, successes, and failures, often quoting her subjects verbatim. Sometimes these captions were paragraphs in length. She hated and resisted the universalizing and iconicizing of her images by those who distributed, published, and contemplated them.

Yet it was precisely these practices that she disliked and could not control—the transformation of her photographs into universals and icons —that made Lange famous. A similar contradiction lies at the heart of microhistory. Small, unique stories take on historical significance only when they connect with larger, more generic stories. Making such connections is the work that microhistory can do, should do. The unique details of a microhistory can not only interest the reader but also, paradoxically, draw the reader into understanding how macrohistorical processes work. In specifying those processes, historians do one of the tasks for which they are, or should be, trained: understanding process. And human processes of social and political change can develop only through individual action and interaction. As an example, consider the difference between historical sociologists and historians. The former can do large, multisociety comparisons of, for example, the emergence of welfare states; they can look at where they developed first and last, or at the correlation between more generous welfare states and other social indicators. To sociologists, historical narratives are often unsatisfying because by telling only one story, without comparison or control, they cannot produce theory or generalization. By contrast, historians often find these comparative sociological studies thin because they offer little insight into *how* change took place.

Some microstories can be great stories, however inconsequential, but they appeal to me only when they induce change in the macrostory. I hope that my last attempt, *The Great Arizona Orphan Abduction* (1999), did that, by revealing regional variation in racial formations, the function of both micro and macro—from individual families to international capital—in constructing race, the previously unnoticed role of women in stimulating vigilantism and their use of gender in doing that, and the fact that parent –child relations could be as racially provocative as sexual and reproductive relations. Now I would like Dorothea Lange's story to change, however slightly, the way we understand the Depression and the New Deal.

I came to microhistory from observing the media popularity of celebrity conflicts, fought out in public as reality soap operas. Contemplating the O. J. Simpson case, Anita Hill's testimony at the Clarence Thomas hearings, and the battle for the custody of Elián González, I observed that Americans often form and debate political opinions by arguing about particular, personalized controversies. Academic and other intellectual elites have often condemned this public interest in celebrity troubles and apparent disinterest in abstract principles of justice, but I no longer share that disdain. Sensational individual conflicts provide means of examining how the rule of law affects people in the concrete—and also means of criticizing the bias that impedes the rule of law. The "Brandeis brief" filed in the 1908 *Muller v. Oregon* case (actually written by social-justice feminists of the National Consumer's League) helped remake American jurisprudence by insisting that actual social conditions were as important as legal precedent in adjudicating competing claims. Many of us have criticized writing history as a parade of great men or as the motion of large-scale social forces. Our goal, however, should not be to ignore, underestimate, or deprecate those histories but to show how they connect to other, smaller historical happenings. Indeed, the very essence of citizenship, and with it hopes for democracy, resides in the capacity of individuals to see themselves at once as singular and as products of their environment, for only that recognition makes respectful political debate possible; and to see themselves at once as creatures of a social, political, economic culture and as capable of acting to change it, for only that recognition makes democracy possible.

So I want to tell a two-level story here: how one woman's documentary photography became a microhistorical influence, and how her own attraction to the microhistorical intensified that process. And to tease out the microhistorical workings, I will need to show them in relation to the macrohistorical.

To a startling degree, popular understanding of the Great Depression of the 1930s derives from visual images; among them, Dorothea Lange's were the most influential. Although many do not know her name, her photographs live in the subconscious of virtually everyone in the United States who has any concept of that economic disaster.[1] Her pictures gained purchase because she did the work for the U.S. Farm Security Administration

(FSA), which actively distributed the pictures through the mass media. If you watch the film of *Grapes of Wrath* with a collection of her photographs next to you, you will see the influence.

Lange's commitment to making her photography speak about injustice was hardly unique—thousands of artists, writers, musicians, dancers, and actors were trying to connect with the vibrant grassroots social movements and popular-front sensibility of the time. But she was an exemplary practitioner among the thousands, in both meanings of that term: her work exemplified a prevailing style and also provided the premier example of that style, thereby influencing it.

Dorothea Lange found her way to documentary photography on her own. Born in 1895 into a middle-class family in Hoboken, she migrated to San Francisco. There, from 1919 to 1935, she earned a living for herself and her family as a portrait photographer. Her romantic, flattering, individualizing, and slightly unconventional portraits drew in a prosperous, elite, and high-culture clientele. From her marriage to leading West Coast artist Maynard Dixon, she gained entrée into bohemian artistic circles and to the arts colony around Taos and Santa Fe, New Mexico. (To the end of her life, Dixon was a more celebrated artist than she was.) This crowd was what we would today call socially liberal but not particularly attuned to politics. That orientation began to change as the Depression deepened, social protest movements grew, and the art market, including the museum market, collapsed, leaving many artists penniless. At the same time, Lange was growing impatient with her rather demanding husband and confinement to her studio. This restlessness sent her out in the streets of San Francisco to photograph what was happening: homeless men sleeping on park benches, crowds lining up at relief stations, demonstrations, and pitched battles with police. Paul Taylor, an agricultural economist at UC Berkeley, saw her photographs and employed her for the California State Emergency Relief Administration in 1935, then saw to it that her photographs were noticed in Washington. When Roy Stryker, head of the FSA photography project, saw them, he recognized their power and immediately hired her. The most experienced of the FSA photographers and the only one who did not work out of the Washington, DC, office, she continued to live in California.

She divorced her artist husband and married Paul Taylor in 1935. In all her work from then on, her sensibility and strategy were indebted to his political intellectual approach. His political intellectual approach—quintessentially Progressive—thus becomes integral to this story.[2] In the tradition of Florence Kelley and Sophonisba Breckenridge, he combined rigorous research with public advocacy.[3] He devoted himself in the 1920s to studying Mexican labor and immigration, the first Anglo scholar to do so. As much an ethnographer as an economist, he talked with, listened to, and photographed his subjects, also collecting data about their immigration and work histories. He communicated to Lange his faith that uncovering facts, revealing reality, would produce good or at least better policy. Neither Taylor nor Lange systematically questioned the allegedly transparent authenticity of documentary photography, its power to reveal truth.

Nor did they question the compatibility of photographic propaganda and photographic truth. Taylor believed that the state ought to regulate the labor market and that policy should be made by well-educated, well-informed, objective experts. Since he also believed that his duties as a social scientist included advocacy as well as investigation, he thought it important, as had other Progressive-era reformers, that research be packaged and presented to reach a broad public. He understood just what Roy Stryker was trying to do.

As head of an agency, maneuvering to retain his budget and his control over the photographic project, Stryker was less committed to the idea of authenticity but equally committed to social justice. He turned his project into a historically unique and valuable one. His team of about a dozen photographers created a visual encyclopedia not only of the Depression's acute injuries but also of rural work and life in general, ultimately producing somewhere between 164,000 and 272,000 photographs before the project was abolished in 1942.[4]

It was a remarkable contingency that this project focused on agriculture. Had it been initiated, say, by Secretary of Labor Frances Perkins as opposed to Undersecretary of Agriculture Rexford Tugwell, it might have focused on urban life. Nothing about the photographers oriented them to the rural. Like Lange, the other FSA photographers were mainly of urban background; a remarkable proportion of them (five of eleven) were Jewish.[5] They have been accused of offering a superficial urban view of the rural, but their origins may have been a strength as well. Because they saw rural society anew, they took nothing for granted; because they needed to learn, they were better able to teach others. Lange's work fulfilled the FSA's project more thoroughly than any other individual photographer's, because she traveled to more regions than others, because she was married to and often traveled with her agriculture expert husband Paul Taylor, and above all because she had moved in 1918 from New Jersey to California, which represented in many ways the future of American agriculture.

Examining her work from this perspective challenges some scholarly appraisals of Lange's photography. Those scholars and writers who discuss her work categorize it mainly as art. Yet she did not consider her photography art or herself an artist until very late in her life. This reticence was overdetermined: by gender in the sense that artistry was an unwomanly aspiration; by gender in the sense that her first husband, Maynard Dixon, was the artist while she was the mere breadwinner; by the fact that photography had been her *business,* not her avocation; by her growing sense of social responsibility—she often described her photographs as "evidence" (Herz 1963:10). This "failure" of ambition freed her from the imperatives of the art market and of traditional art authorities and gave her space to develop a singular method and style, which became formative of the whole future of documentary photography.

Her systematic development of a communicative style has been masked, in part, by gendered clichés. Some critics have read the strong emotional content of her work as instinctive, in a way said to be characteristic of female sensibility. A "natural" feminine intuitiveness underlay her photography in this account of Lange: "Dorothea Lange lived instinctively…photographed spontaneously" (Cox 1981:5). At other times, she is described as a piece of white photosensitive paper, or "like an unexposed film," onto which light and shadow marked impressions.[6] Her oeuvre consists disproportionately of portraits, often described as particularly female, in line with the observation that women are typically more interested than men are in personality and private emotions. Critic George Elliot expressed the common imagining of female artists as passively receptive: "For an artist like Dorothea Lange the making of a great, perfect, anonymous image is a trick of grace, about which she can do little beyond making herself available for that gift of grace" (Elliot 1966:7).

Of course, there were gendered sources of Lange's photography—how could there not be? But femininity is no more instinctive or "natural" than masculinity. And male FSA photographers could at times produce work very similar to, if not indistinguishable from Lange's in its emotional charge, spatial composition, and insight into social relations. Lange, far from passively receptive, was an assertive visual intellectual, disciplined and self-conscious, working systematically to develop a photography that could be maximally communicative and revealing. Of course, the gender clichés derive from the photographs that were noticed and how they were read; today we have the opportunity to make another selection of photographs and read them differently.

Scholarly work on Lange has also been caught up in a dichotomizing "authenticity" debate about documentary photography. Documentary photography may be the only art or representational form that can sit directly on the divide between the empirical and the invented, between reportage and persuasion, between knowledge and artifice, in David Hollinger's (1987) terms. The chemical processes of making light register on paper have suggested, and still suggest to many, that photography reproduces the visible world. The phrase *social realism*, often applied to the popular-front style, is a misnomer that adds further to the notion of photography as transparent, merely "revealing" what is really there. (Yet I cannot avoid using the term because it remains a common descriptor of documentary photography.) Thus a distinction arose between "truthful" and "altered" photographs, or between documentary and "artistic" photography, a distinction not applied to paintings or novels. The FSA was particularly vulnerable to criticism regarding manipulating images because its mission was so instrumental: to mobilize support for its resettlement and rehabilitation programs. In other words, it was a propaganda outfit. But, as critics have had to emphasize, of course photography cannot replicate "reality"; it is constructed at every stage. As with history writing, "bias" starts with the frame—what is excluded, what included, what centered, what marginalized. Photographers manipulate shutter speed and aperture and filters and lenses and angle and choice of film and negative size to construct an image even before entering a darkroom, where there are almost endless further opportunities for manipulation of exposed film. Walker Evans composed his *Let Us Now Praise Famous Men* photographs by removing household clutter to simplify, "purify," his compositions. But for some critics, such as James Curtis (1986, 1989:ch. 3), Maren Stange (1986, 1989:ch. 3), William Stott (1973), and Mary Street Alinder (1996:228), the FSA was guilty of photographic dishonesty. The FSA was heavily attacked in 1936 when photographer Arthur Rothstein moved a steer's skull a few yards to make a more dramatic picture of drought. Stryker was furious when Lange arranged to have a stray thumb retouched out of her famous "Migrant Mother" photograph. Yet I think we must distinguish such editing from making photographs lie, as in erasing Trotsky from images of the Soviet leadership, or placing John Kerry next to Jane Fonda on a speaker's platform. FSA photographers always believed that they aimed at a foundational, deep reality; that they might need to alter details of individual environments to represent a large-scale reality.

The FSA's manipulation appeared even worse to critics influenced by new left and Foucauldian suspicion of "social engineering." Maren Stange charged that FSA photography "assisted the liberal corporate state to manage not only our politics but also our esthetics" (Stange 1986:xv). The fact that Stryker went to work for Esso's public relations office after the FSA was abolished in 1942 fueled further criticism of the underlying motives and function of New Deal documentary photography. Another critic argued that documentary photography in general produces "passive voyeurism, transforms misery into a luxury article, and flatters a feeling of impotent anguish among the members of relatively privileged societies who are able to see and buy it" (Tonkin 1986:162). This critique resembles that of social control in social policy, and it has the same weaknesses: it assumes unanimity among leaders, absence of initiative among other actors, and an entire lack of agency in self-presentation among subjects. The FSA archives thoroughly belie that assumption, filled as they are with evidence of political, ideological, bureaucratic, regional, and personal conflict and evidence of photographic subjects, particularly Lange's, characterizing their problems and beliefs in their own terms.

The macro also influences the micro, of course. Large-scale historical developments created the basis for Lange's choices. There was a historical logic (along with the illogic of love) in Lange's attraction to Taylor. In a poignant reversal of a more typical gendered story of liberation, Lange's move from a marriage in which she was the breadwinner to one of economic dependence on a husband brought her freedom—to step away from her rich clients and expand her photographic imagination. Even more significant, just as Lange was beginning to feel herself affected by historical change, she met a man who was confident that he could affect history and had a sense of responsibility to do so. It was Taylor's orientation to the world that seduced her.

Undersecretary of Agriculture Rexford Tugwell's ideas in launching the FSA also arose from long-term developments: the agricultural depression, which was already a decade long when the stock market collapsed. He wanted to treat agricultural *labor* as a fundamental part of America's working class and to demonstrate that agricultural labor relations were implicated in the economic depression. The Department of Agriculture had never had a labor division, and the department had long been dominated by large landowners. Tugwell wanted land reform and knew he needed to build political support for it; he thought photography could help.

Roy Stryker expanded the FSA photography project far beyond its formal charge. Not only did he distribute photographs aggressively, free of charge to publications, organizations, government agencies, and even individuals; not only did he insist that the agency, rather than individual photographers, be credited as the source of the pictures, he also encouraged his photographers to think of themselves as teaching Americans about

America in the most inclusive sense, guided by a populist attraction to agricultural workers rather than owners. This potentially controversial project was for a time protected by and understood through large-scale New Deal developments. The much larger Federal Art Project of the WPA was producing murals, public sculpture, theater, and arts classes. In other words, government programs radically increased public exposure to art through a degree of decommodification—removing it from the market and making it, like the national parks, part of the appropriate responsibility of the federal government and, therefore, the birthright of all Americans.[7] Under the Federal Art Project alone (within WPA), approximately thirty-six hundred artists produced sixteen thousand works shown in one thousand cities and towns (M. Brown 1981:7). The federal arts programs also trained many artists and raised the level of professional competence among many more, thereby introducing into the art world the perspectives of those who would have been excluded previously. That FSA work could be accepted as appropriate federal activity, and that it could be categorized as art, resulted from this larger context.

Combined with many artists' own sense of responsibility to address social injustice in their work, this decommodification has to be understood not only as allowing greater access but also as altering common expectations of, and thus the meaning of, art itself. Professional easel painters knew, however unconsciously, that their paintings were at best destined for the homes of the wealthy or for museums. Neither fate encouraged artists to defy academic and market conventions. Creators of painting and sculpture for public spaces were less constrained. Influenced now by Mexico City in addition to Paris, their art could desert its Europeanist models and explore styles consonant with the American vernacular.[8]

The restrictions that came with public funding—no abstract art, for one—also shaped the photographic work. And some artists, particularly the muralists, ran up against bureaucratic and political censorship. "To paint Section" meant to paint something pleasant and agreeable, reported Lewis Rubenstein, who worked for the Treasury's Section of Fine Arts. Paul Cadmus got in trouble for painting drunken, raucous sailors. These conflicts were uncommon, in many cases because artists didn't need to be told to avoid provocative subjects. They thought the compromise was worthwhile. Jackson Pollock, for example, was eight years on the government payroll (Barnett 1988; Rosenzweig and Melosh 1990). The conflicts that did happen became well known quickly, often through personal grapevines, and created further self-censorship.

As art became more ordinary, it also became less mysterious—and that meant less subjective, more referential. Whether inspirational, instructive, or descriptive, it was *about* matters of the "external" world. Moreover, the fact that some government projects created public works that were at the same time useful and decorative—the many lovely WPA bridges come to mind—strengthened the presumption that things nice to look at could appropriately be created by government. Correspondingly, photographs that were useful and informative could also be nice to look at. Of course, the public also understood this artistic production as a temporary measure of emergency relief for artists, but nevertheless the availability of art in the public sphere increased geometrically.

As decommodification influenced art in a nationalist direction, an inverse trend worked to the same end. Photographs contested the monopoly of the luxury market in art, paradoxically through the rise of new commodity forms: first, the new photographic magazines such as *Life* and *Look*, both born in the 1930s; second, the increasing use of halftone screens to reproduce photographs in newspapers. These outlets encouraged photographers to desert the self-consciously arty style of the early twentieth century in favor of vernacular subjects. These commoditized photographs were no longer luxury goods. In fact, they traveled so widely that they created new kinds of property and authority. Thanks to Margaret Bourke-White's clout and personal relationship with Henry Luce, *Life* began to publish photographers' names with their pictures (Goldberg 1987:194). Eventually, in a new auteurism, photographers formed guilds such as Magnum, agencies to construct ownership rights and maximize earnings from their pictures. By contrast, when FSA prints were first distributed, few took note of the individual photographers. Photographs then seemed authoritative, because very few people noticed that photography could lie or that its framings and perspectives produced its facts. The very anonymity of photographic creators strengthened this authority by drawing the mind away from questions of individual bias. Thus the FSA photographs appeared at a historical moment at which they exerted maximum influence.

Lange was invigorated by the opportunity to create a photography that could be influential as well as relevant and critical. But this was easier said than done. She faced substantive hurdles—intellectual and political as well as artistic and emotional ones. First, it was the FSA, not individual photographers, that decided what pictures to promote. Thus there is a substantial difference between Lange's oeuvre and her contemporaneous published or exhibited photographs. In popular memory, Lange's photographs are most associated with the dust bowl. This identification derived not from the drought's relative importance in Lange's photography but from the politics of what the FSA distributed. It is true that Lange and Taylor were the first to call Department of Agriculture attention to the mass migration of "Okies" traveling west to seek employment. Even as some hundreds of thousands of Mexicans and Mexican Americans, high proportions of them farmworkers, were expatriated, the big growers were advertising in the dust bowl area in their search for the cheapest labor. The great migration was so unmonitored that Taylor decided to pay a gas station attendant to count migrants entering California and their origins. And it was Taylor who explained insistently that the catastrophic drought and dust storms were not strictly "natural" calamities but resulted from pressure from agribusiness to plow up the plains for cash crops, denuding the soil of the flora that held it in place.

Lange had to conform her work to the "shooting scripts" Stryker sent. At first they were open-ended and inquiring, in part the result of an early meeting Stryker held with Robert Lynd to seek advice. From Lynd came ideas such as: "Where can people meet?" "Do women have as many meeting places as men?" "[R]elationship between time and the job." "How many people do you know?" Later outlines became more restrictive, for example,

I. Production of foods...

a. Packaging and processing of above

b. Picking, hauling, sorting, preparing, drying, canning, packaging, loading for shipping

c. Field operations—planting; cultivation; spraying

d. Dramatic pictures of fields, show "pattern" of the country; get feeling of the productive earth, boundless acres.

e. Warehouses filled with food, raw and processed, cans, boxes, bags, etc.

Later, political pressure forced Stryker to ask his photographers to de-emphasize poor people and the Depression and instead to get "pictures of men, women and children who appear as if they really believed in the U.S....Too many in our file now paint the U.S. as an old person's home ...everyone is too old to work and too malnourished to care....We particularly need...More contented-looking couples—woman sewing, man reading; sitting on porch; working in garden" (Stryker 1973:188).

Other problems grew out of the medium itself. The "straight" photography style of the New Deal documentarians shows, by definition, surfaces, appearances.[9] Their cameras had no X-ray vision. A photograph of people, family, or fields of labor could actually disguise the social relations that produced them. This stillness and superficiality of photographs, then, made it difficult to show that the economic crisis had social-structural origins and was not created only by acts of God or nature or individual improvidence.[10]

Furthermore, documentary photography is also by definition representational and concrete, and it cannot communicate concepts precisely. The problem was "constructing [visually] an event—the 'Great Depression' —that was beyond the control of those without jobs but that was sufficiently tangible that it could be seen as the cause of their unemployment" (Landis 1999:285).

Another issue: Aggregating data, and then naming aggregate patterns with abstract terms such as mass migration or racism, is necessary for analysis. But photography that shows only large aggregates of people or things tends to be dry and/or abstract, nonrepresentational and thus not "straight" photography. Yet if photographs of individuals are to illuminate social and economic structure, these individuals must become "types": the migrant, the sharecropper, the Mexican, the impoverished child. Lawrence Levine (1988) pointed out that some degree of iconization seemed the only way to discuss a problem at a level greater than the individual.

The documentary form implies that the individuals or episodes portrayed are representative, or at least are not wildly exceptional, and the latter charge has been a common defense to documentary photography's exposure of injustice. But even without the critics, FSA photographers met quandaries in trying to make accurate representation: John Collier Jr., for example, complained that "only rarely did the workmen in an industrial plant look like the symbolic workman is supposed to look like."[11] Collier's honest expression of confusion suggests not only the received stereotypes in his mind but also his sense of a responsibility to be sociologically accurate.

Another dilemma of the documentary: how to show the poor as needy (this is the easy part) without making them ugly or beyond repair (the hard part). Poverty is rarely beautiful. But if the people looked too good, didn't look like victims, then how to justify the New Deal's massive government spending?

The necessity for the right kind of victimhood made it difficult to show victims' resistance, diversity, and imperfections without delegitimating them as appropriate beneficiaries of help. Part of the power of nonviolence as a protest strategy derives from its resolution of that tension. But in practice, treating the poor and the oppressed as real requires acknowledging and accepting their human imperfections—violence, anger, dishonesty, jealousy, manipulativeness.

The FSA photographers also had to worry about the label "propaganda," applied so often by anti–New Deal media and politicians. Many of them understood the term as ideological. Ben Shahn: "I cannot separate art from life. Propaganda is to me a noble word. It means you believe something very strongly and you want other people to believe it…art has always been used to propagate ideas and to persuade."[12] Lange: "Everything is propaganda for what you believe in, actually, isn't it?…I don't see that it could be otherwise. The harder and the more deeply you believe in anything, the more in a sense you're a propagandist.…I never have been able to come to the conclusion that that's a bad word" (Riess 1968:181). But they could not so easily brush off attacks that threatened the very existence of the photographic project, because they were in it not only for the income but also out of a commitment to the principles and programs for which they agitated.

Lange managed these constraints unevenly—sometimes transcending them, often not. She could not control what Stryker's office distributed. For example, she would have preferred groups of photographs telling a story, but Stryker privileged single images so as to get them into mass-circulation publications.[13] Lange tried to distribute some photographs personally and through the San Francisco regional FSA office, and she antagonized Stryker in doing so. Her efforts failed, for Stryker remained unalterably committed (and many would say rightly so) to centralizing the distribution of all FSA work from headquarters.

Lange was remarkably compliant with Stryker's shooting scripts, always willing to do even the most boring photography, but she frequently tried to sell him other scripts, usually without success. Her reputation as pushy, and her loss of the job in 1939, derived in part from this flow of suggestions and demands. For example, in letters to Roy Stryker in 1938, she proposed a photography series on the poll tax and the resultant disfranchisement of many southerners, white and black (Stryker 1936–42). Stryker would have none of this idea; he thought, probably correctly, that it would make powerful southern Democratic politicians determined to crush the FSA. The Department of Agriculture's work was administered through local representatives dependent on local politicians and landowners.

The limitations of photography itself were actually more tractable to Lange's efforts. She succeeded in replicating New Deal principles by integrating neediness and deservingness in her subjects. For example, under Harry Hopkins, emergency relief programs rejected the old Progressive and scientific-charity view that poverty arose from inferior character as well as lack of money. Progressive-era welfare programs often combined minimal

FIGURE 8.1

Tulare County, California. Cheap auto camp housing for citrus workers, February 1940.
(Lange's caption.) National Archives ARC 521799.

material support with surveillance, supervision, and moralizing. New Deal relief provided only money and jobs. Because the Depression had abruptly plunged into poverty so many respectable working-class and middle-class people, living in normative families, assumptions had to change; poverty implied no character flaw. It was through a visual embodiment of this premise that Lange solved the problem of showing people as broke and even broken, but simultaneously attractive and interesting. Her photographs insisted that there was no contradiction between destitution and virtue, between damage and potential, between misery and beauty. They did so through the tension they maintained between the poverty and deprivation they exposed and the integrity and stability of their composition.

This kind of portraiture was entirely uncommon at the time. Poor and working-class people often got their portraits made, but always in their Sunday best.[14] Upscale photography viewers were accustomed to pictorialist versions of landscapes and portraits, romanticized through mistiness,

FIGURE 8.2

*Mexican migrant fieldworker, Imperial Valley, 1937. (Lange's caption.) Library of Congress
LC-USF34-016425-C.*

blurred edges, draped fabric. Ansel Adams's detailed, sharp-edged views of
the American West were virtually unknown. Lewis Hine's documentary
photographs were known only to those in reform networks, like that
around *Survey Graphic*, and his pictures rarely attained the emotional power
or beauty of Lange's.

Lange's photographs began to draw journalistic attention to the terrible conditions of farmworkers, and the words of journalists—"loathsome,"
"unimaginable filth," "festering sores"—echoed her pictures.[15] But editors
wanted eye-catching close-ups. Many viewers react, as I do, with greater dis-
tress to her image of a toddler covered with flies than to a picture of a filthy
encampment. It is as if the visual desecration of an individual child's satiny
skin, shot close up, works as a symbol more forcefully than photographs of
groups or pictures with more empirical information about wretchedness.
So Lange returned to portraiture, turning toward the poor the same eye,
the same patience, the same flattering angles and easy-to-read composition
that she had previously directed toward the rich. In the portraits, she was

FIGURE 8.3

Nursing mother. (Lange's caption.)

able to maintain another productive tension, between the clarity, even simplicity, of her composition and her subjects' complexity of character, a complexity that resisted sentimentality (figs. 8.2, 8.3). Her subjects typically could not be described by thin or homogeneous labels. Her victims were often sexy; the destitute women walking the highway were well dressed; the workers smile, even laugh, and they are almost always thoughtful, intelligent; they are using intellectual as well as emotional faculties to figure out how to survive.[16]

Lange evolved a way to portray both individuals and social conditions. Consider how much information lies in the photographs here. We learn how migrant farmworkers built shelters out of scraps; how they insisted on dressing up for photographs; how sharecroppers' homes were constructed; how orderly even the poorest homes could be kept. If she could not integrate the individual and the social in a single photograph, she made images in series, the most famous of which yielded her "Migrant Mother." In six exposures (only five of which she sent to the FSA), she began with a view taking in the family's whole lean-to—a half tent of canvas supported by branches that sheltered a family of six. In this image, we see a suitcase and a wooden produce box, a beautiful bent-elm rocker holding a sullen teenager, and a depressed and possibly resentful mother with her face

FIGURE 8.4

Migrant agricultural worker's family. Seven hungry children. Mother aged thirty-two. Father is native Californian. Nipomo, California. (Lange's caption.) Library of Congress 009098.

FIGURE 8.5

Migrant agricultural worker's family. Seven hungry children. Mother aged thirty-two. Father is native Californian. Nipomo, California. (Lange's caption.) Library of Congress 009097.

161

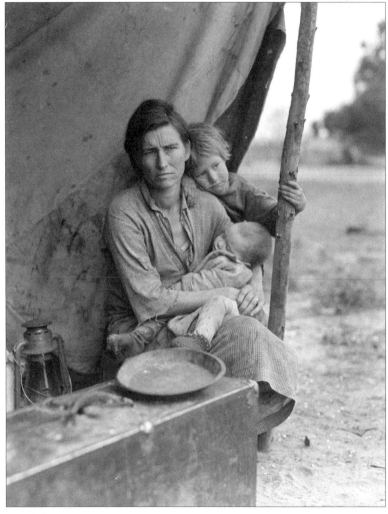

Figure 8.6

Migrant agricultural worker's family. Seven hungry children. Mother aged thirty-two. Father is native Californian. Nipomo, California. (Lange's caption.) Library of Congress 009095.

averted. In the next image, Lange had gotten the teen-ager to move outside and the mother to turn her head toward the camera, while still looking down. In the third, the mother allows Lange to get closer, and we see
the baby nursing at an exposed breast—no other photographer at the FSA
dared show a breast. Now we see a kerosene lamp and tousled linen, the
torn and dirty clothing of the mother and the baby she is now nursing,
and her worry. Next Lange backed up again to bring one of the younger

FIGURE 8.7

Migrant agricultural worker's family. Seven hungry children. Mother aged thirty-two. Father is native Californian. Nipomo, California. (Lange's caption.) Library of Congress 009093.

FIGURE 8.8

Destitute pea pickers in California. Mother of seven children. Aged thirty-two. Nipomo, California. (Lange's caption.) Library of Congress 009058.

163

children into the picture and, in the analysis of one scholar, found a way to keep the girl from moving by asking her to lean her chin on her mother's left shoulder. As the exposures continue, we see the subject, Florence Thompson, visibly relax, but without losing the anxiety that lines her beautiful face (Curtis 1986).

Integrating the social and the individual is neither easy nor always possible. Lange's first great strength, critics agree, was her eye. Among her favorite sayings was, "A camera is a tool for teaching how to see without a camera." Lange was disabled as a result of childhood polio and almost always worked with an assistant. She would instruct the assistant to drive very, very slowly, so they could stop suddenly when she saw a photo op. Her second strength was an ability to get subjects to cooperate and relax. Ironically, this skill derived precisely from her long experience as a portrait photographer and her success in making portraits that appealed to the elite and high-cultured. She had two approaches: either she conversed with her subjects until they fell into what she called their "natural body language," or she fiddled with setting up her equipment for so long that they forgot about her and returned to what they had been doing. She never rearranged background objects—unlike Walker Evans and Margaret Bourke-White—but she was quite willing to ask her subjects to move into a position that allowed her to photograph individual and background together.

One reason Lange's systematic approach is often missed is that her photographs were in many ways so conventional. Her composition was never avant-garde. She used no montage or surprising angles. Instead, her pictures were comfortably inside vernacular and even commercial Christian visual culture, and this made her work speak to the uneducated as well as the elite, the religious as well as the urban sophisticate.

Yet in several dimensions, Lange's worked pushed beyond popular-front conventions. Consider, for example, her gender sensibility. While almost every New Deal policy rested on family wage assumptions and aimed to strengthen the male-breadwinner family, and while the usual popular-front artistic icons stereotyped women as helpmates and earth mothers (Melosh 1991), Lange often scrambled the gendered structure of her photographs. She visualized women as independent, to the degree that her work could be considered protofeminist. Here again, her rural subject matter was partly responsible, because the sexual division of labor was more blurred among farmworking people. She did love maternal images, but she photographed men with equal tenderness. A mistiness that had characterized some of her studio portraiture disappeared entirely. The Depression women were sharply etched—often thin, often delicate, always tough. Photography critic Sally

FIGURE 8.9

Street scene. Macon, Georgia. (Lange's caption.) Library of Congress 009467.

Stein has pointed out how often Lange's work decentered nuclear families
—not only in showing countless mothers and sisters caring for children without the presence of husbands and fathers but also in her strikingly numerous photographs of fathers and children (S. Stein 1994). Lange rose to the
challenge of presenting idle, unemployed men as worried and despondent
yet manly nonetheless. She not only faced the gendered tensions created by
the economy, in contrast to the New Deal's denial, but represented them
with sympathy and in some cases approval.

Her antiracism, by contrast, was more than "proto." It was conscious
and considered, shaped by her West Coast experience. Lange was the first
American photographer to include people of Mexican, Filipino, Japanese,
and Chinese origin in her portrait of America. Altogether, she made hundreds of photographs of farmworkers of color. In the South, she made
dozens of compelling, close-up portraits of African Americans. Overall in
her FSA work, she made more pictures of people of color—31 percent of
her total output—than any other FSA photographer until Gordon Parks
joined the staff (Natanson 1992:9, 61–62, 72).

Figure 8.10

Member of the Delta cooperative farm at Hillhouse, Mississippi. (Lange's caption.) Library of Congress 017299.

Her photographs drew people of color into citizenship. I argue this primarily on the basis of the visual evidence. Her subjects are thoughtful, deliberative, even cerebral. She gives them gravitas. But she also used verbal evidence when she could. She copied into her notebook the words of a female laborer: "I want to go back to Mexico but my children say, 'No we all born here we belong in this country. We don't go'" (Dorothea Lange Collection n.d.).[17] She captioned one lovely portrait of father and baby, "Future voter & his Mexican father."

Lange's attempt to create not only inclusive but specifically antiracist photography was less successful. She wanted to illustrate racism, as a relationship and as a structure. She tried to use visual relationships to show social ones. She made a few pictures of "bad guys": the plantation owner, the brutal southern overseer, the sheriff's thug. But these were mostly agents, not authors, of racism—or class relations, for that matter—as a structure. The several photographs in which she was able to make spatial relations metaphoric of power relations are rare, and not legible as such without captions.[18]

FIGURE 8.11

Plantation owner. Mississippi Delta, near Clarksdale, Mississippi. (Lange's caption.) Library of Congress 009599.

Lange herself was conscious of this ambiguity in still photography. She wrote lengthy captions, often providing brief life histories of her subjects or economic data about landownership, earnings, standard of living. She insisted that photographs needed words—without them, pictures could too easily be decontextualized. Like Stryker, she thought of the photograph as "the little brother of the word" (Stryker 1973:8). She cared about specificity as a microhistorian does, always looking for the relation between the individual and the social, always interested in the intersection between the personal experience of change and the vast historical process. In some ways she could be said to be creating photographic microhistories. Before she joined the FSA, her visual style was already conducive to representing change. To illustrate with a comparison: Walker Evans would line up his subjects and hold them still, as in an old-fashioned portrait studio; his subjects appear timeless, fixed, often intense but rarely active. His many close-ups of vernacular architecture intensified the stability of his photographs.

Lange wanted her subjects in motion. This had to be slow motion, of course, given the relatively slow speed of the film she used. It revealed the personality of the body in conversation, gesture, and the heavy, repetitious motion of field labor, but her subjects often seemed unsettled, uncertain, disrupted, deracinated, and this was exactly what she wanted to communicate about the agricultural political economy.

But Lange's captions did not travel with the photographs, and sometimes the FSA staff defanged them. In this caption, for example, the FSA struck out one phrase: "Old Negro—the kind the planters like. He hoes, picks cotton, and is full of good humor."[19] Lange hated the way her photograph known as "Migrant Mother" was removed from its context and turned into a universal image of motherhood. The plantation-owner picture can serve as a vivid example of this ambiguity and deracination; the photograph shows the relations of power and deference on a southern plantation. But Archibald MacLeish (1938) took it, cropped out all the blacks, and used it in his *Land of the Free*, turning the white man into a symbol of salt-of-the-earth, hard-working Americanism. (The photo as used by MacLeish can be in seen in Gordon 2006.) Lange was helpless to prevent this action, as her estate was helpless to prevent the thousands of appropriations of her work—to symbolize deserving poverty and self-sacrificing motherhood, and to sell products—after her death.

Yet Lange's own photographic temperament helped make these appropriations possible. Her political aesthetic leaned toward heroism rather than open conflict. For example, she made several attempts to photograph organized protest—the San Francisco longshoreman and general strike of 1934, the 1938 lettuce workers' strike, even secret meetings of the Southern Tenant Farmers Union. Some of these efforts yielded fine photographs, but none that communicated collective resistance. During the 1930s, Lange's home state experienced some of the most intense class conflict in US history, a virtual war in the fields. California's big growers used every available means of law, violence, and intimidation to prevent farmworker unionization. Her portraits of individual leaders and militants in these struggles, such as Tom Mooney, are vibrantly sympathetic. But on the whole, these photographs are among her weakest. No doubt it was difficult to get close to the action. Moreover, sympathetic photographers such as Lange may have shied away from exposing strikers' violence or even the chanting and shouting that often renders faces as distorted. Historian Nicholas Natanson wrote (of another photographer), "an angry camera becomes a demeaning camera" (1992:26).

Lange also was personally uncomfortable with open conflict, and Paul Taylor influenced this. His Progressive-era progressivism relied on expertise, surveys, facts that would convince and create the political will for reform. His reform goals required soft-pedaling conflicts of interest, trying to help farmworkers by persuading those who directly benefited from exploiting farmworkers.

Some who knew Lange suggest that she was more drawn to the left and to militancy than Taylor was.[20] But if this is so, she restrained herself from arguing and deferred to Taylor on these matters. This deference derived both from the gender culture of her time and from her complex adaptation to it, another example of the intersections that microhistory and biography can reveal. Lange felt a great deal of anxiety about her drive and ambition, which were marked as unwomanly in her time. She was guilt-ridden about being away from her children so much. She soothed herself (and quite possibly her husbands) by bracketing her areas of independence and hewing to conventionally feminine activity: intensive, slightly obsessive housewifery (cooking, decorating, entertaining). With her boss, Roy Stryker, her means of combat involved performance of femininity, even deference. (On September 30, 1936, she signed a letter to him "your little stepchild" [Stryker 1936–42].) And she typically worked at controlling her world through her verbal eloquence and charm. We see this approach throughout her documentary photography. Her photographs do not exhort activism. They are so calm, her subjects so contained, that they seem to advocate patience and even forbearance.

I can't tell yet if my biography of Dorothea Lange will be (or could be) a microhistory tout court, but it will surely contain tendencies in that direction. It is assuredly a "life and times" biography, in which Lange becomes in part a vehicle for examining often-neglected cultural aspects of the period. My task is to use Lange in that way without sacrificing any of the drama of her personal story. As a microhistorical subject, her failures are perhaps more important than her successes—the failures occur at the moments when her own aspirations meet the concrete wall of the macrohistorical balance of forces. Yet at other moments her individual work was a historical force in itself. These intersections vary: at times the micro and the macro become fellow travelers; at other times they clash; most of the time they rub against each other, producing both irritation and stimulation.

Notes

1. Her most famous picture, often known as "Migrant Mother," had by the late 1960s been used in approximately ten thousand published items, resulting in millions of copies in the estimation of *Popular Photography* magazine (Levin and Northrup 1980:42).

2. See my biographical sketch of Taylor for *American National Biography* at www.anb.org/articles/14/1114-01138-print.html.

3. A most unconventional economist, Taylor had studied labor economics under John Commons at the University of Wisconsin and connected with Paul Kellogg and other Progressive-era social reformers at Hull House. Like other Progressive reformers, Taylor did not believe that objectivity required neutrality with respect to policy on the part of social scientific investigators—the stance of most of today's poverty scholars. On the contrary, precisely because policy should follow directly from reliable data, he thought it important for scholars to follow the logic of their findings to the recommendations that they should yield, and to advocate actively for these recommendations (Gordon 1994).

4. The Library of Congress offers the lower estimate, while Stryker gave the higher. Lange's papers also include approximately forty thousand negatives in the Oakland Museum, and negatives from her work for other government agencies are in the National Archives.

5. Arthur Rothstein, Carl Mydans, Ben Shahn, Jack Delano, and Edwin Rosskam are the five major Jewish photographers. Also Jewish were Esther Bubley, Louise Rosskam, Charles Fenno Jacobs, Arthur Siegel, and Howard Liberman. By contrast, many key FSA administrators—Will Alexander and C. B. Baldwin, for example—were southern. All the major photographers were formed through urban experience: Lange in New York and San Francisco; Collier and Lee in San Francisco; Evans, Rothstein, Shahn, and Post Wolcott in New York and Paris; Mydans in Boston and New York; Delano in Philadelphia.

6. Weston Naef, interviewed by Therese Heyman in Keller 2002:101.

7. This decommodification was cheered on by most artists involved, but the photographers struggled against it in one dimension: control and ownership of negatives. Lange was among several FSA photographers (Walker Evans being another) in fighting to be able to develop and retain her own negatives, make her own prints. This conflict was unique to photography because photography is unique in that it is produced in several stages: shooting, developing, printing. Lange and Evans had no quarrel with letting the government distribute their prints freely but wished to retain control of the negatives.

8. When painter George Biddle first proposed a federal art project to his friend

and former classmate President Roosevelt, he specifically used the Mexican murals as a model (O'Connor 1986:170). Many scholars agree on the powerful influence of Mexican art on New Deal artists (Contreras 1983; Hills 1983; Hurlburt 1989; Ware 1991).

9. Photographers in the early twentieth century coined the term *straight* to differentiate their work from an earlier style, pictorialism, which featured soft focus, fuzzy borders, and romanticized portraiture. "Straight" photography, by contract, used sharp focus and contrast and in theory required no "manipulation" of film or negatives. In fact, "straight" photographers such as Ansel Adams used filters on their lenses and engaged in extensive manipulation in the darkroom. But the documentary photographers did not use montage, deliberate distortion, multiple exposures, and so on.

10. Although, as Michele Landis (1999) shows, a great deal of argumentation for New Deal relief rested on metaphorical identification of the crisis with a natural disaster.

11. Quoted in Peeler 1987:83.

12. Forrest Selvig, AAA interview with Ben Shahn, September 27, 1968, page 14 (Hurley 1972:50).

13. Paul Vanderbuilt, quoted in Stange 1991:212.

14. Therese Heyman interview with Pare Lorentz; Dorothea Lange Collection n.d.:10.

15. Quoted in W. Stein 1973:48.

16. It is largely this attraction to complexity that protected her work from sentimentality. As curator Judith Keller wrote, "She never provides any superficial suggestion that we understand that person immediately. Typically these faces resist easy understanding" (Keller 2002:100).

17. Accompanying image RA825B.

18. She wrote many captions about racism. For example, she quoted a Mississippi delta planter: "Hours are nothing to us. You can't industrialize farming. We in Mississippi know how to treat our niggers." But these captions were rarely published along with the photographs.

19. I have the original caption in Lange's own hand and compared it to that in the FSA-OWI Collection, Library of Congress, image 017079.

20. Henry Mayer, interview with Alice Hamburg and Tanya Goldsmith, April 22, 1999.

9

"Above Vulgar Economy"

The Intersection of Historical Archaeology and Microhistory in Writing Archaeological Biographies of Two New England Merchants

Mary C. Beaudry

"You say, in finishing the life of Daniel Gookins, that his family is extinct: This is a mistake, he was my mother's great-grandfather" (Tracy 1793). In composing this admonitory letter to the Massachusetts Historical Society, Nathaniel Tracy revealed a preoccupation with genealogical research that he had had little time for in earlier years. The son of a wealthy Newburyport merchant, Tracy became a successful, rich man in his own right, an able and active merchant, public figure, owner of many mansions, fabled host among the most brilliant of Massachusetts's glittering Revolutionary-era elite. But the revolution that won Tracy great fortune in the end brought about his economic downfall. By 1793 he and his family had spent several years living in retirement in an "ancient" house in Newbury.

After Tracy's death, his widow, Mary Lee Tracy, sold the farm to Offin Boardman, another Newburyport merchant, an ambitious self-made man. Boardman commanded privateers that had been outfitted by Nathaniel Tracy. The profits he made from his share of prizes of captured ships enabled him to set up his own mercantile enterprise and to purchase ships, a wharf and warehouse, and eventually the country estate of his former employer. Boardman moved to the farm with his wife in 1799, after spending lavishly on its improvement. His family lived there in grand style, entertaining frequently and maintaining the latest fashions. Yet at his death in

FIGURE 9.1

Nathaniel Tracy (1751–1796), painted in 1784 by John Trumbull. Privately owned by a direct descendant of Nathaniel Tracy; reproduced with permission.

1811, Boardman was deeply in debt; the Jeffersonian Embargo was an economic disaster for American shipping, and a fire that swept through Newburyport's waterfront destroyed Boardman's wharf and warehouse and, in the end, his business.

Neither of these men are famous Americans; their lives have not been chronicled in books about American history. I encountered them because I am an archaeologist and was hired to excavate at a place where they had lived. I became interested in their lives because I found myself sifting through their rubbish and wondering what to make of it. There were contradictions in what I'd been told about these men by the representatives of the historical agency that was restoring the Spencer-Peirce-Little House as a museum.[1] Nathaniel Tracy, I was repeatedly told, had been one of the richest men in early America. Not only had I never heard of him, I found little in the archaeological record that revealed much about the time he and his family spent at the site. On the other hand, everywhere I excavated,

FIGURE 9.2

Captain Offin Boardman (1748–1811), painted in 1787. Attributed to Christian Gullager.
Courtesy Worcester Art Museum, Massachusetts, museum purchase.

it seemed, there were traces of Offin Boardman. But Boardman, too, while
a figure of some renown in local history, had not made it into history
books. I was confronted with a dilemma that historical archaeologists face
almost daily: my excavations were leading me into the realm of "archaeological biography"—the reconstitution of forgotten or little-known lives
that would never be of interest if an archaeologist did not happen to be
invited to explore a particular site, not because certain people had lived
there but because proposed construction, restoration, or renovation might
have an impact on unspecified archaeological deposits.[2] Once the archaeologist puts shovel to soil, she is hooked, both by obligation and by interest, to pursue the stories that come to light as the residues of past lives
begin to emerge from the earth. The task is to collect and collate the

archive, composed as it is of artifacts and documents, houses, landscapes, and memories; the real feat is to synthesize and make sense of all the various lines of evidence and to construct interpretations that move between the particular and the more general, between the microscopic or microhistorical and the morphological.[3]

As I researched the lives of Nathaniel Tracy and Offin Boardman, I began to realize that both men had tried in their own ways to become part of the emerging elite in America's early republic. The archaeological record for Boardman's years at the farm produced extensive evidence of landscaping, conspicuous consumption, and social display. Without recourse to documents, I would have probably inferred that he succeeded in his pursuit of elite status and dynastic longevity. Tracy's tenure at the Spencer-Peirce-Little Farm left only the faintest of traces in the archaeological record. But what little there was seemed to indicate wealth and high social standing. But as Tracy's self-conscious preoccupation with family genealogy in his waning years suggests, his concern with historical identity and legitimacy was motivated by loss of social standing arising from a financial setback of thundering finality. In a way, he was attempting both as actor and as narrator to participate in the construction of his own history (Trouillot 1995:2). As an interpretive historical archaeologist, I found myself confronted with disparate bodies of evidence about two very strong personalities who despite having once laid claim to elite status were invisible in grand narratives of American history and powerless in efforts to inscribe their lives into those narratives. I needed to hold the archaeological evidence up to scrutiny against documents and social histories to interpret the artifacts in the wider context of the sociohistorical process (Trouillot 1995:6).

Interpretive approaches in historical archaeology employ multiple lines of evidence and multiple readings of what we choose to consider as evidence to get beyond superficial, ostensibly unfiltered, neutral readings of "obvious facts" about the past. Practitioners of interpretive archaeology, like microhistorians and historical anthropologists, are interested not solely in "knowing" the past but in how it is "known" and how it is "refracted over time through successive modes of communication" (Darnton 2004). It is a pursuit aimed at attempting to comprehend how people in the past construed their experiences rather than how those people fit into preconceived analytical structures (compare Egmond and Mason 1997), and it is based on concern for the immediacy of experience and for the meanings attributed to it by real people in the contexts of their daily lives.

Rosemary Joyce, in her book *The Languages of Archaeology*, notes, "[T]hat archaeological *writing* is storytelling is a commonplace observance by now, although it continues to be resisted.... [E]ven archaeologists most sympathetic to this point have for the most part overlooked the storytelling that is purely internal to our discipline and that precedes the formalization of stories in lectures, books, museum exhibitions, videos, or electronic media" (Joyce 2002:4–5, emphasis in original). Archaeological productions are not and can never be merely transcriptions of what is in the ground; all forms of archaeological transcription involve negotiation of meaning, a "re-presentation of some things in the present as traces of other things in the past" (Joyce 2002:5). In other words, all archaeology is storytelling, all archaeological narratives are constructed. The same is true for modes of representation and narration in disciplines such as history, historical sociology, and historical anthropology, but archaeologists face special challenges in writing accounts of the past because their work compels them to weave together simultaneous interpretations not just of texts but also of inscriptions in material and corporeal form. This process calls for experimentation, a sense of playfulness, and more than a dash of imagination (Joyce 2006). It also means that historical archaeologists cannot "do" microhistory the same way historians do; rather, we need to adapt the methods of microhistory to suit the demands of our own discipline.

Because it begins with a focus on the small scale and the everyday, microhistory is often highly biographical in its approach. Microhistorians face the criticism, as Jill Lepore (2001) puts it, that they "love too much"—they become enamored with the actors in their historical dramas, identify with them, and at times even transform themselves from author into character. Robert Darnton (2004) notes that most microhistories start with an event and employ something of a detective's cleverness and insight to expose the underlying meanings of supposedly single events. The researcher treats the "incident" as part of a chain of events situated in a particular historical context and examines the ways in which individuals with different backgrounds, motivations, and standpoints experienced, reacted to, and recounted an event.

The forensic metaphor of "incident analysis" in many ways fits archaeology better than it does history; archaeologists can be crime scene investigators, more or less, because our work often begins with the "scene of the crime," as it were, and we have a battery of methods that allow us to understand how our sites were formed and perhaps how things got to be in the ground in just the way we find them. The problem is to take the obvious and the not so obvious and situate both in the contexts of the lives of the people we are studying and then try to understand what a particular congeries of artifacts and other evidence is telling us about what it all meant to those people. This situation forces us to construct narratives that do more than just tack back and forth between sources but that weave together the various strands of evidence into strong cables of inference (Wylie 1999). This sort of exercise cleaves closely to the evidence and constitutes a first step in the process of constructing alternative narratives.

Here I offer an intersecting pair of archaeological biographies that I think of as constituting an alternative narrative to the usual histories of the rise of American elites, American capitalism, and American identity. My stories are about losers, not about winners. I cannot call them subaltern narratives because my characters were surely not subalterns. But to my mind, the stories of those who did not "make it" are as revealing and instructive as the stories of those who did. Through the orientation or practice of microhistory, I aim to place my microscopic observations of two lives lived in part at one physical locale into a wider narrative by looking for meaning both within the microcosm and within the larger sociohistorical processes that post-Revolutionary Americans set into motion in their struggles with issues of class, power, identity, and historicity (see Walton, Brooks, and DeCorse, this volume).

Nathaniel Tracy and Offin Boardman were *sedentary merchants*; they operated from a fixed headquarters, transacting affairs at distant points through agents such as captains, supercargoes, and commission merchants. Sedentary merchants performed a number of economic, administrative, and managerial functions and relied upon the record-keeping skills of head clerks and apprentice clerks. Such merchants contrasted sharply with the small shopkeeper or general country storekeeper, for whom they may have been sources of goods for sale (Porter 1937:4–5).

In the seventeenth, eighteenth, and early nineteenth centuries, it was taken for granted that successful merchants enjoyed a grand and opulent lifestyle. The Marquis de Chastellux, visiting Newburyport in 1781, evinced no surprise at the sumptuousness of the surroundings in which merchants like the Tracys lived. He recounted an evening's hospitality hosted by John Tracy:

> [H]e came with two handsome carriages, well equipped, and
> conducted me and my aid-de-camp to his country-house. This
> house stands a mile from the town, in a very beautiful situation;
> but of this I could myself form no judgment, as it was already
> night. I went however, by moonlight, to see the garden, which is
> composed of different terraces. There is likewise a hot-house
> and a number of young trees. The house is very handsome and
> well-furnished, and every thing breathes that air of magnificence

accompanied with simplicity, which is only to be found among merchants. (De Chastellux [1780–82]1963)

Before the Revolution, there were two routes for men in training for the mercantile life in the Massachusetts Colony. One was "by way of the countinghouse," in which a young man of good family graduated from a prestigious academy and Harvard College. After his schooling, he served a brief apprenticeship under a prominent merchant before drawing upon family capital to set himself up, either independently or with partners, as a sedentary merchant. A young man of lesser means and connections could become a sedentary merchant "by way of the quarterdeck," working his way up "through various grades of seamen, becom[ing] a captain, accumulat[ing] capital through privilege," becoming a shipowner, and, eventually, becoming a merchant (Porter 1937:7). Similarly, acceptable courses of action for a merchant whose success proved fugitive were limited: he could begin again at the bottom of the commercial ladder and try to work his way up; he could undertake an entirely new career unconnected with business; or he could go into dignified retirement (Porter 1937:120). The two late-eighteenth-century owners of the Spencer-Peirce-Little Farm, Nathaniel Tracy and Offin Boardman, exemplify these differing career trajectories in various ways, and the archaeological record reflects the business failure of one and the relative success of the other.

Newburyport was never a serious rival to the larger ports of the Atlantic seaboard, but in its eighteenth-century heyday, it was a bustling entrepôt and home to some of Massachusetts's wealthiest and most powerful merchant families. Newbury, Massachusetts, has a history tied intimately to that of adjacent urban Newburyport, for Newbury's port broke off from its parent town in 1764 after bitter rivalry between competing interests of merchants who controlled the port, or "waterside," and farmers tilling "land side," or rural backcountry (Benes 1986; Labaree 1975:2–3).

At the mouth of the Merrimack River on Boston's North Shore, the port of Newbury was an ideal locale for both agricultural and mercantile enterprise; here, the point of land known as Plum Island curves in a protecting arm across the mouth of the river, forming a safe harbor. Settlers arriving in 1635 took up lands cleared by Native American horticulturalists (Russell 1982:13–15). The river and ocean teemed with fish that could be dried or salted for export to the West Indies; inland and upriver, timber was abundant. Newbury's waterside bustled with commercial activity exploiting these plentiful resources. Shipping and shipbuilding predominated, and the riverfront became heavily built up with wharves, shipyards, ropewalks, chandlers' yards, warehouses, and shops. The land stretching away from

FIGURE 9.3

The Spencer-Peirce-Little House, Newbury, Massachusetts, built in the late seventeenth century. Photographed in the 1880s by Wilfred A. French. Courtesy Historic New England.

the waterfront served as an agricultural hinterland for the concentrated population of the waterside. Fertile alluvial soils along the Parker River, to the south of the Merrimack, provided generous crop yields as well as ample pasturage for livestock. Acreage in salt marsh produced rich fodder, in the form of salt hay, for expanding herds (Labaree 1975:1–3).

The land conveyed to Daniel Peirce Sr. in the 1660s, now the Spencer-Peirce-Little Farm, was granted originally to John Spencer, one of the founders of Newbury, in 1635. Documents reveal that Peirce and his family lived at the farm, but only ephemeral traces of any pre-1680 structures have been found to date. It is likely that his oldest son, Daniel Peirce Jr., built the surviving house in the decade following his father's death in 1677 (see Beaudry 1993b). For its time, it was a grand and imposing home.[4]

In the seventeenth century, the Peirces established a pattern of discontinuous residence at the farm; through several generations, the family had at least one residence at the waterside, using the farmhouse as a summer home. By the late eighteenth century, the house had acquired a patina of sufficient age to be considered an appropriate country seat for urban merchants who had amassed great fortunes through shipping and privateering, among other pursuits, and who heretofore had lived in grand houses in town.

One such individual was Nathaniel Tracy. While Nathaniel's father, Patrick Tracy, had begun his career by going to sea as a cabin boy ("coming in by the hawsehole"), his sons benefited from his success (Patrick became one of Newburyport's most prosperous and prominent merchants) and found a far smoother path to advancement (Porter 1937:7, 10). Nathaniel "prepared" at Boston Latin, then attended Harvard College (class of 1769) and Yale College (in 1772). He received an honorary AM from the College of New Jersey (Princeton; 1773), making many friendships and forging alliances that served him well throughout his business career (Lee 1916; Shipton 1975). Nathaniel's partner Jonathan Jackson married Nathaniel's sister Hannah, while Nathaniel married Mary Lee, daughter of a leading merchant family of Marblehead (Lee 1906:63; Shipton 1975:248). Mary Lee Tracy's sisters all married into other merchant families, forming a tight network of kin-based alliances within the mercantile elite (Lee 1917; Porter 1937). In 1778 Nathaniel Tracy purchased the Peirce Farm from two Peirce heirs who had acquired it after their petition to dock the entail placed on it by Daniel Peirce Sr. was successful.

Tracy entered international trade as a sedentary merchant after a short apprenticeship in his father's countinghouse. He formed a partnership with his younger brother John and college friend Jonathan Jackson. The firm, which specialized in duck, hemp, glass, cod lines, and nails, shifted to coasting trade as tension between Britain and the colonies heightened prior to the Revolution. The partners' closest connections were with Philadelphia. They exchanged rum, molasses, and flaxseed from New England for flour, iron, corn, rusk, crackers, loaf sugar, Russia duck, turpentine, hemp, coffee, and cocoa and sold these goods on commission in Newburyport (Porter 1937:7, 16).

Tracy, Jackson, and Tracy received a commission from the government to act as privateers in 1776 (Allen 1927:48). Privateering in the Revolutionary period was a high-risk venture—a form of entrepreneurial patriotism—that could produce vast fortunes or financial disaster. Expenses and half the returns would be divided among and allotted to the owners in proportion to the number of shares each had taken out; investors tended to protect themselves by taking out relatively small shares (Porter 1937:20).[5]

Tracy fitted out the first privateer to sail in the Revolution, eventually owning or having interest in 110 merchant vessels and twenty-four cruising ships (Allen 1927; see also Eastman 1928). In the end, Tracy had a hand in the capture of 120 vessels that were sold for $3,950,000. Tracy made a large loan ($167,000) to the new government of the United States; it was never repaid. And despite having had millions during the Revolutionary years, he suffered financial setbacks that reduced his fortune substantially. After 1785 he was forced to mortgage or sell much of his property, which included more than half a dozen houses and, briefly, the title to the farm. He and his household "retired" to the Peirce Farm in Newbury and, after a series of complex transactions (see Grady 1992), regained title to the property.[6]

Nathaniel's decision to resolve the dilemma of his business failure through dignified retirement was, as noted earlier, one of the acceptable courses of action a merchant in his position might take. That he elected to do so at the Peirce Farm is not without import. The property, the house, and its associations served as an instrument in the long-term social and economic strategies of the Tracys. The prestige of the "house" (in the sense of family continuity) and the power relations signified in the interplay between kinship, property, and movable wealth could be preserved in this context.

In the late 1780s and early 1790s, travelers and diarists, including Thomas Jefferson and John Quincy Adams, recorded their visits to Tracy and his wife, then living in relative seclusion at the farm (Grady 1992:30–35). Adams spoke of him with high regard:

> This gentleman was in the course of the war peculiarly fortunate and accumulated an immense fortune; but he has since been equally unlucky and is now very much reduced. The generosity of his heart is equal to any estate whatever; and although he has not been so prudent as might be wish'd, yet everyone who is acquainted with him must lament his misfortunes, and heartily wish he may retrieve his affairs. (Adams [1788]1902:397)

Although visitors reported that Nathaniel and Mary Lee Tracy lived in reduced circumstances, Nathaniel's probate inventory, made at his death in 1796, reveals that the house was furnished with the trappings of genteel life, including mahogany furniture, decorative mirrors, silver, branch candlesticks, curtains, floor covers, easy chairs, worked chairs, a sofa, a great chair, and large case pieces (Dempsey 1993b:5). The Tracys thus lived in a setting familiar to them, but their lifestyle was no longer "numinous" or brilliant.[7]

Tracy's dignified retirement did not preclude his participation in public affairs: he was repeatedly elected to local office and continued his activities as a charter member of the American Academy of Arts and Sciences and as trustee and treasurer of Dummer Academy in Byfield. He was a Mason, serving as master of St. John's Lodge of Newbury.

In 1793 Tracy wrote a letter, published in the *Collections of the Massachusetts Historical Society*, that reveals his concern with lineage and with preserving the family line, and his own connection with illustrious and pious ancestors:

> You say, in finishing the life of Daniel Gookins, that his family is extinct: This is a mistake, he was my mother's great-grandfather. This Daniel Gookins had a son Daniel, who was ordained minister at Cambridge. He died at twenty-two years of age, but left a son Nathaniel, who was afterwards minister in Hampton, and was my mother's father. He left a son Nathaniel, who was a minister in North-Hill parish (Hampton,) and many other children, two of whom are now living in Portland. A cousin of mine, Capt. Daniel Gookins, served in our army the last war, with a good reputation. And a Captain's commission was given to him, when we were about rasing a new army in 1786 or 1787.

Tracy's emphasis on genealogical continuity and good reputation and his efforts at public clarification of his family's good name are far from surprising given that, in his retirement, he would have had ample time to reflect on such matters.

At the height of his mercantile success, Tracy and his family lived in a grand and luxurious manner and underscored their position and wealth through overt display as well as subtle imagery.[8] The reverse in Tracy's fortunes meant that, after 1786, he no longer was able to indulge in the elaborate entertainments and public display for which he had once been celebrated.

Soon after he acquired the farm, Tracy undertook a limited remodeling of the house: a modified "Georgianization," giving symmetry to the fenestration and reworking the fireplaces and center chimney stack. Excavations beneath the floor of the kitchen ell in advance of restoration work in this room explored the crawl space. A sealed feature of considerable depth, a filled-in stairwell, was found along the northern edge of the central chimney stack (Beaudry 1992).

Artifacts from the fill of the abandoned stairwell provide a *terminus post quem* circa 1780 (Scarlett 1992), suggesting that it was deposited early in the Tracy ownership, while Tracy was one of the richest men in the new republic, still flush with the success of his privateering ventures.

Tracy's rebuilding of the central chimney stack included relocating the internal entry to the cellar via an opening in the kitchen floor. This was effected by stoning up the doorway in the cellar wall; extracting the wooden steps from the clay ramp, leaving only the filled-in mold of a support post; and then pitching into the hole some of the broken brickbats, stones, and fireplace fittings generated by the dismantling of the original chimney stack and its hearths. While the stairwell cavity was open, it was used to dispose of kitchen waste, including numerous animal bones that seemed almost fresh and perfect as they came from the soil, having suffered not at all from exposure or weathering (Landon 1991a, 1991b, 1992). It appears that cooking activities went on even in the midst of the disruption and inconvenience caused by the renovations. Artifactual material within the stairwell fill included ceramics, half a small grindstone, cutlery, and wine-bottle glass (Scarlett 1992); charred seeds were abundant (Pendleton 1990).

The ethnobotanical, pollen, and faunal evidence all suggest that the feature was filled in over the course of a few days or up to a week in spring (Kelso 1992; Landon 1992; Pendleton 1992). Despite having been created as a result of remodeling, the stairwell deposit provides evidence of the Tracy lifestyle in its heyday. In the faunal assemblage, butchered squirrel and woodchuck were complemented by poor-quality cuts represented by cattle bones and by a large number of pig foot bones with butchery marks that testify to the consumption of pigs' feet. In contrast to this seemingly humble fare, the assemblage also contained the remains of three suckling pigs with cut marks on the jawbone, likely made by cutting open the mouth to stuff it—perhaps with an apple. This would have been part of a formal presentation of roast suckling pig for a banquet or other very special meal. The archaeological evidence suggests that Tracy celebrated his newest acquisition of property with a splendid banquet—even though this event would have forced his servants to struggle with the hindrances and disarray of a renovation in progress.[9]

Mary Lee Tracy sold the Spencer-Peirce Farm to Offin Boardman in 1797. Boardman became one of Newburyport's leading merchants after serving as a ship captain. Unlike Tracy, whose route to the mercantile life had been via the countinghouse, Boardman established his career by way of the quarterdeck. Boardman captained Tracy privateers during the Revolution.[10] In 1776, at age twenty-nine, posing as a pilot, Boardman tricked a British ship into Newburyport Harbor. Captured at sea later the same year, he was taken to Mill Prison in Plymouth, England, from which he escaped twice, eventually making his way to France. There, he recorded in his diary how impressed he was by the grandeur of country estates of the nobility. He met outside Paris with American commissioners Franklin and Adams and became involved with John Paul Jones's plans to outfit a fleet of privateers; he sailed home on one of the ships in the resulting convoy (Boardman 1779–80). Back in Newburyport, he built up a good-sized estate, for the most part through straightforward business dealings—his ships sailed to ports in the Baltic as well as to Surinam and the Caribbean—and through inheritances from his own and his first wife's family. Boardman apparently attempted to defraud his siblings out of their inheritances, however, by tricking his father on his deathbed into signing a will that gave the entire Boardman estate to Offin only. The other heirs successfully brought suit against Offin, but the rift was so deep that the rest of the Boardman family refused to have anything further to do with him. Hence, during his years at what he called the Tracy Farm, where he took up full-time residence with his second wife, Sarah Tappan Boardman, in 1799, his social connections were maintained largely through his wife's family rather than his own (Dempsey 1993a).

Boardman made extensive changes to the external appearance of the estate. These included construction of a wooden addition to the west wing of the stone house, with an up-to-date Federal-period parlor and a sleeping chamber for his wife, who was often ill and bedridden. The additions to the stone house left it intact, although the extensions modified its external appearance and increased interior living and sleeping spaces. Boardman also built a new house (later known as the Tappan House) on the western edge of the property, near the High Road, for his in-laws.

The rift with his consanguineous family did not dampen his energies or his ambitions. The diary he kept of his time at the farm

> reflects a variety of interests and activities....He describes farm
> activities as well as town interests, barreling apples and caulking
> a sloop, huskings and Marine Society meetings. He gives equal
> time to the description of his work and his leisure, making par-
> ticular note of comings and goings of members of his family and
> his household, and of parties and visits he hosts and attends.
> Winter months were especially social ones, with sledding easing
> the transport to and from town, and long family visits extended
> by snowstorms. (Dempsey 1993c:9)

Most frequent among visitors were his own children and their families, as well as his immediate affinal relations, chiefly Sarah Tappan Boardman's siblings and their families. The diary entries reveal "how kinship reinforced friendships and business relationships...[through a] web extending and thickening through the years" (Dempsey 1993c:10).

After Boardman's death in 1811, Sarah Boardman sold the property to Edward Pettingell, another Newburyport merchant, reserving her dower rights. She moved in with her relations down the lane at the Tappan House. Boardman's estate proved to be considerably in arrears; his assets were insufficient to settle outstanding bills.[11]

Boardman's will gives no indication that he was aware of potential difficulties, but it was written in 1808, three years before his death (Boardman 1811). He suffered losses during the Jeffersonian Embargo, which paralyzed Newburyport shipping (Labaree 1975:151–52), and could scarcely have recovered after it was lifted before his wharf, shop, and other property were destroyed in the Great Fire that swept through the waterfront in May of 1811 (compare Faulkner et al. 1977:128; Gilman and Gilman 1811). Boardman's estate, both real and personal, was sold at auction in 1813. In the end, the profits from the sales did not cover his debts. The proceeds were divided proportionally among his heirs and creditors.[12]

A plat map of the property generated by the estate settlement shows the farm and its many outbuildings, fences, and fields. The plan represents Offin Boardman's vision for the farm. Boardman made many improvements and changes to the landscape and farmyard that apparently went well beyond what Tracy had been capable of during his retirement. Nathaniel Tracy's family had employed a professional gardener to design and build gardens at their homes in town as well as at their country seats (M. Moore 1988; recall Marquis de Chastellux's moonlight visit to John Tracy's terraced garden), so it seemed logical that Nathaniel and Mary should have been able to comfort themselves with strolls through a formal pleasure garden. However, excavations conducted in 1994 confirmed that the flower garden depicted on the 1812 plan of the property was created by Boardman, not Tracy (Beaudry 1995a).[13]

The plan depicts a small structure just to the east of the house; it is the only unlabeled area or structure on the map. In 1990 a crew of volunteers completed excavation of this unlabeled structure (Beaudry 1987). It was a very large privy vault, lined with stone and about ten feet (about 3.03 meters) square in plan. At the bottom of the vault was a layer containing hundreds of fragments of ceramics and glass, as well as other items such as a coin, buttons, fragments of a writing slate, and a few pieces of animal bone —including several vertebrae from a mature, oceangoing shark. Several lines of evidence indicate that the privy was constructed several years after

FIGURE 9.4

A selection of liquor and condiment bottles from the Boardman privy. Photograph by Michael Hamilton, Department of Archaeology, Boston University.

the Boardmans moved to the farm in 1799 but before Boardman's death in 1811.[14]

Most of the ceramic and glass vessels from the privy were manufactured between 1800 and 1810 (compare G. Miller 2000), although numerous items predate this period; the plates especially bear evidence of heavy use in the form of scratches and cut marks. Local redwares, English refined earthenwares, and English wine and case bottles predominate, but local stonewares, Chinese porcelain, Silesian wine glasses, and blue French condiment bottles are also present in the assemblage, giving it an unmistakably international character.

It is impossible to say how the items in the privy were assembled for disposal; it is possible that all the ceramics and glass were discards from the Boardman household. For example, Boardman mentions in his diary that he supervised repairs to his dairy between June 30 and July 6, 1808 (Dempsey 1993a); the renovations may have been extensive and may have involved replacement of dairying utensils. This could, perhaps, account for the many dairying vessels found at the base of the privy and for the thousands of fragments of redware vessels forming part of the midden around the privy foundation. The many plain creamware vessels, having seen much use, had become unfashionable and may have been overdue for replacement at the time of their disposal. But it cannot be stated with certainty that Boardman did not mine rubbish heaps formed before he and his wife moved to the farm; it is possible, therefore, that some items may have been discards from the Tracy occupation—or even earlier.

The plant remains were varied, with a minimum of twenty-two species, almost all of which could have been used for food or medicine. There were cultivated species such as table grapes, which may have been brought to the site, and white clover, which was probably grown there (Boardman mentions the "New Clover Field" in his diary entry for July 26, 1809). Blueberries, elderberries, blackberries, and raspberries may have been cultivated, although they grow wild in brushy areas at the farm today. Bulrushes and sedges are likewise found in the nearby marshes. Most of the macrofossils fall into the category of herbs (although many would today be thought of as weeds) and could have been gathered from the wild or cultivated. In recounting his own ailments in his diary, Boardman alludes to herbal preparations several times. Once he mentions drinking herbal tea for medicinal purposes: "Wednesday, December 22, 1802. For the night full of pain. At 7 am had the bed fixed for a sweat with penial [pennyroyal?] tea. Lay till 4 p.m. when all the pain off. Got up & took soup. Found myself well."[15] He frequently took a dose of salts to relieve the pain of his aching joints; on one occasion he administered an emetic to himself, perhaps a home remedy (Dempsey 1993a).

The ceramic vessels deposited in the lowest, Boardman-era stratum of the privy were intact or nearly so.[16] They included utilitarian items related to hygiene—chamber pots of debased scratch blue stoneware and plain cream ware. Vessels for dairying, although extremely bulky, comprised a small percentage of the ceramic assemblage; food preparation and food storage vessels for kitchen use, made of local redware and stoneware, constituted only a tiny fraction of the total. The preponderance of the assemblage was for entertaining, or at least feeding and refreshing, large numbers of people; Boardman's diary reveals that he and his wife entertained lavishly, at least once serving eighty guests at dinner. Vessels for food consumption dominated the assemblage, followed by those for beverage consumption. The forms included serving and punch bowls, tureens, platters, sauce boats, pitchers and jugs, and multiple sets of dinner plates and muffin plates.

Tea wares comprised a large proportion of the beverage consumption vessels, but punch bowls dominated that category, indicating a household in which formal entertainments included tea parties as well as evenings "passed rapidly with the aid of agreeable conversation and a few glasses of punch" (De Chastellux [1780–82]1963:245). This fact notwithstanding, it is clear that tea could be served fashionably and from sets of differing quality, ranging from hand-painted and transfer-printed pearlwares to Chinese porcelain. The ceramic vessels are not fully representative of the Boardmans' stylishness in this regard; a silver teapot is among the objects that were handed down in the Boardman family. It was acquired by Offin and his first wife, Sarah Greenleaf Boardman, in the 1780s or early 1790s. Made by London silversmith Hester Bateman, the teapot represents the height of "advanced English taste" at the time. It has a boxwood handle, "applied beaded edges, a domed lid, oval straight-sided body, and bright-cut engraving," including the cipher OB (Benes 1986:132). The silver teapot and other pieces that survive in collections are "object lessons" indeed, reminding the archaeologist that it is all too easy to lose sight of the fact that she is picking over a household's discards, devoting inordinate attention to things people hoped never to see again.

The glass vessels complement and round out the beverage distribution and consumption categories in the form of wine glasses and tumblers as well as decanters.[17] Glass bottles of both English and French origin are present; the food containers of blue-green French glass testify to the use of commercially distributed yet nonetheless exotic foodstuffs such as olives and capers (Harris 1978; O. Jones 1993:33; Jones and Smith 1985).

The range of spirits represented by the bottles in the privy assemblage is just as impressive, for it includes not just wine and beer but aquavit and gin bottles as well. These, the nearly thirty punch bowls in the privy, and Boardman's diary entries revealing that he brewed his own beer and regularly put up hundreds of gallons of cider (Dempsey 1993a) lead to the conclusion that he was well prepared to extend hearty and bibulous hospitality to his guests.

The diary entries reveal a seasonal pattern to entertaining and visiting, with the majority of social visits and house parties occurring during the coldest winter months, when "snow was well packed on the roads," making travel easier (Nylander 1993:237–38; compare Carson 1990:75). The Boardmans hosted husking parties in the fall, offering a feast to guests who assisted in shucking the newly harvested corn. Boardman recorded, for example, that on October 22, 1799, a "company of 30" stayed on after husking was done; he noted that they were fed on "5 mutton roasted & pudding" (Dempsey 1993a).

Here, it is useful to explore ways of thinking about the privy contents in a multifaceted progression of ever-widening contexts that begins with the most minute and particular and works outward toward the more general. This feature provides insight into the Boardmans and their life at the farm. But by the very process of placing artifactual contents in their social context, it is possible to show how they signify a much broader world of social connections and cultural practices.

A recontextualization of the objects involves "reconstructing the emic" (compare Beaudry 1993a:94) or, to put it another way, establishing the ethnographic context that links material culture to the people who used it.[18] A framework for interpreting the assemblage from the Boardman privy attends to both the context of the site—a rural setting closely tied to an urban entrepôt—and the lifestyle that its late-eighteenth-/early-nineteenth-century inhabitants enjoyed as part of the North Shore's wealthy elite.

Historical anthropologists Comaroff and Comaroff (1992:27) note that "the place to begin is with the idea of culture itself." Emphasis on careful construction of context arises out of employing a definition of culture as something other than a means of adaptation or a set of mental rules or constructs producing broad regularities that are wholly independent of circumstance, situation, and actors. The Comaroffs define culture as

> the semantic space, the field of signs and practices, in which human beings construct and represent themselves and others, and hence their societies and histories. It is not merely an abstract order of signs, or relations among signs. Nor is it just the sum of habitual practices. Neither pure langue nor pure parole, it never constitutes a closed, entirely coherent system. Quite the contrary: Culture always contains within it polyvalent, potentially contestable messages, images, and actions. It is, in short, a historically situated, historically unfolding ensemble of signifiers-in-action, signifiers at once material and symbolic, social and aesthetic. (Comaroff and Comaroff 1992:27)

Sometimes the signifiers that convey culture will be integrated into a relatively explicit worldview; in other circumstances, worldviews may be overdetermined, "heavily contested, the stuff of counterideologies and 'subcultures'" (Comaroff and Comaroff 1992:27). Yet others may be non-fixed and interdeterminate.

The excavated material culture provides an entry point for interpreting rituals for establishing and maintaining elite status. It is important to "read" the Boardmans' assemblage from the privy in terms of the social frame in which the objects functioned, which in part, at least, was one of negotiation of elite status. Artifacts can be interpreted in terms of the roles they play in the discourse of prestige negotiation—rituals of exchanging visits, dining, taking tea, and attending church services, as well as meetings of voluntary associations such as the Marine Society. To participate in these rituals, the Boardmans and others of their milieu constructed for themselves a material life "above vulgar economy," as Jane Austen put it: "In the meantime for Elegance & Ease & Luxury...I shall eat Ice & drink French wine, & be above vulgar economy" (quoted in Ellis 1982:2).

An explicit code of behavior dictated that elite families should live in luxury and ostentation; inability to display wealth would be humiliating in the extreme. Historical anthropologists Villamarin and Villamarin (1982:135) note of elites that "their display of wealth served to mark them off from the rest of society. A considerable amount of money and energy was spent in competition among families of high position, and was expressed in terms of large expenditures on houses, clothes, dowries and festivities." Boardman's deliberate pursuit of "bourgeois personhood" (compare Barker 1984; Bourdieu 1987; Comaroff and Comaroff 1992) and indeed the very fact that, like most members of his class, he recorded his actions in a diary reflect a self-conscious construction of his own subjectivity, incorporating the outward projection of an image of gentility and control over personal destiny.

Construction, negotiation, and maintenance of elite status required display and a certain visible measure of extravagance. But, as many scholars have pointed out, it was not enough merely to possess the trappings of elite status: the observances and artifacts had to be the right ones and had to be deployed in the right ways if they were to serve as appropriate indicators of gentility and refinement (compare Bushman 1993; Carson 1990; Martin 1996).[19] The demonstration of gentility was an outward form of social competition via consumption (McKendrick 1982:11) involving actions *as well as* artifacts. Bushman (1993:xix) notes that

> Gentility bestowed concrete social power on its practitioners. It was a resource for impressing and influencing powerful people, frequently a prerequisite for inspiring trust. All who sought worldly advancement were tempted to use refinement as a bargaining chip in social negotiations. Moreover, it afforded a convenient identity and a definition of position in the confusing fluidity of democratic society.

What made an old and unfashionable house such as Spencer-Peirce-Little suitable as a country seat for a succession of Newburyport's merchants when it was common for most urban elites who took up country life to build for themselves grand homes in the latest style and to undertake sweeping landscape improvements (compare Thornton 1989)? It seems evident that the house itself played a role in prestige negotiations and rituals among Newburyport's post-Revolutionary elite: its "antique" status was remarked upon by visitors in the late eighteenth century. One of the Tracys' visitors, Alice Tucker, wrote in her diary on October 20, 1789, that "this antique building is situated in the very bosom of retirement, and is surrounded by well cultivated fields and gardens.... I found Mrs. Tracy, dress'd genteelly, sitting at her tea table with her children about her. She is a very handsome accomplished woman, and knows very well how to keep up her dignity." On another visit, on December 13, 1790, she again found Mrs. Tracy at her tea table in "the dining chamber, which is spacious and has a genteel and an airy appearance considering its antiquity. Mrs. Tracy received with that politeness which is so natural to a well bred woman. Our repast was slender; two cups of tea, and one small piece of biscuit."

Tucker's diary entries employ tropes stressing the maintenance of family dignity and reputation in circumstances such as the Tracys' retirement and highlight the critical role Mary Lee Tracy played in this process. Indeed, visitors invariably mentioned her and stressed her stoical demeanor and comportment. J. P. Brissot de Warville ([1791]1964:363–64) visited in 1788:

> We arrived at Newbury at noon and had dinner at the home of
> Mr. Tracy, who owns a small country house two miles out of town.
> This American once had a fortune of over two millions, but he
> was ruined in a number of various enterprises....Mr. Tracy...now
> lives retired in the country, where he stoically bears his misfor-
> tunes, comforted and sustained by his good wife, who maintains
> great dignity in the midst of their adversity.

Thinking of Wolf's notion of funds,[20] it appears that, finding their economic fund diminished beyond recourse, the Tracys husbanded their social fund carefully through the scrupulous maintenance of a dignity and respectability that underscored their gentility. Mary Lee Tracy, from her tea or dinner table, was the ultimate broker of this fund as she steered the course of conversation and oversaw social interaction in her role as hostess.

Thornton, in *Cultivating Gentlemen*, explores the meaning of country life among Boston's post-Revolutionary elite, noting that "the connotations of urban commerce and manufacturing were in the main negative, whereas those of rural life and agriculture were largely positive" (Thornton 1989:2). Historians have concluded that the subsistence-level family farm is largely a myth, yet neither were farmers unbridled capitalists (Kulikoff 1992:13–18). No one in the eighteenth or nineteenth century would have expected farmers to operate outside of the market or to eschew opportunities to make a profit, but the ideology of the values intrinsic to agrarian life was firmly entrenched long before English people set foot on the shores of North America. Trade and manufacture generated wealth, but "these fields of enterprise lacked the historic prestige and political privileges attached to land"; back in England, "gentry still defined themselves primarily by the tenure of manors and the accompanying political and military obligations" (Vickers 1994:17). Elite status in England and New England alike was linked firmly by tradition to land tenure, while for yeoman farmers, owning and working the land vouchsafed a measure of independence not granted to other freemen. All the same, farmers aimed not so much to make a profit but to attain a *competency*, a comfortable independence that was a household affair and permitted family continuity; "competency had an undeniably collective family dimension" (Vickers 1994:19; see also Kulikoff 1992:16; Vickers 1990).

For the late-eighteenth-century owners of the Spencer-Peirce-Little Farm, the age of the house and its association with an agrarian life and its virtues vitiated the negative connotations of the urban commerce upon which their fortunes had been based and overrode the farm's lack of stylishness and failure to meet the standards of taste for the time. McCracken refers to this phenomenon as the "patina" system of consumption: "Patina, as both a physical and a symbolic property of consumer goods, was one of the most important ways that high-standing individuals distinguished themselves from low-standing ones, and social mobility was policed and maintained" (McCracken 1990:31). Although largely supplanted by the "fashion" system of consumption by the late eighteenth century (exemplified by the once-fashionable goods thrown into the privy), patina remained a status strategy among the very rich. Among the items in the Boardman privy assemblage dated to circa 1800 were two mid-eighteenth-century vessels of Chinese export porcelain: a Batavia tea bowl and an Imari dinner plate. They were at least half a century old before they were discarded. The symbolism of the age of objects, houses, and perhaps even landscapes served not just to represent high standing, wealth, and taste but also to legitimate status claims through implications of longevity and generational continuity (McCracken 1990:32). More than anything else, the house's association with the town's founding families provided its near-mythical patina; the aura of antiquity was associational and largely overrode the reality of renovations and remodelings that successive owners undertook to assure their comfort or to provide themselves with a fashionable parlor. The house's quality as a "genealogical mnemonic" carried with it not just the implications of antiquity and rootedness, however; it was a medium that carried the status of former owners—four generations of descendants of a town founder—and conveyed it in some measure upon new ones. It was also a medium that helped maintain the prestige of owners such as the Tracys, whose reversal of fortune rendered them unable to participate fully in the rituals of prestige negotiation, or Boardman, who lived grandly until his death but burdened his widow with egregious debt. In the socially fluid and economically challenging decades after the Revolution, both the Tracys and the Boardmans participated in dual systems of consumption, engaging in fashionable consumerism while at the same time employing patina to bolster their attempts to consolidate their identity and power as part of the elite.

For elites negotiating their social position in the early republic, to economize was vulgar. Extravagance in service of social display and competition could lead to debt and social decline—as it did in the cases of Tracy and Boardman—but those who pulled it off assured themselves membership in the "consolidated elite" that emerged in the early nineteenth century. Families like the Derbys of Salem ascended to the upper echelon as members of the North Shore's consolidated elite (Thornton 1989); descendants of Nathaniel Tracy and Offin Boardman did not. Tracy's dignified retirement preserved the family's social fund, assuring that the family name continued to be respected. The archaeological record at the site reveals, through lack of evidence for the Tracy occupation beyond the confines of the house, just how complete his retirement was in other regards. Boardman had both economic and social funds when he moved to the farm, although he jeopardized his social fund through his sleight of hand with his father's will. He nevertheless kept strong ties with his affinal relations and his own children and grandchildren, was active in local affairs, and took great interest and pride in erecting new buildings and renovating others at the farm while maintaining his shipping business. The Embargo Act of 1807 and the Great Fire in Newburyport in 1811 depleted Boardman's fortune, leaving no economic fund to pass down to his family. But Boardman's time at the farm was anything but a retirement; his household's impact on the archaeological record is a pronounced one that reflects outlay on the trappings of elite country life.

The take-home lesson for the archaeologist is that interpreting "the trappings of genteel country life" is not a straightforward exercise. Absent the context provided by a microhistorical approach that tacks among and brings together various lines of evidence, I initially interpreted materials recovered from sealed Tracy- and Boardman-era deposits (the filled-in stairwell and privy, respectively) as clear evidence of successful merchants enjoying elegant, luxurious lifestyles and high status. This is how historical archaeologists normally interpret these very sorts of remains. But by using the "exploratory stance" of microhistory (Maddox, this volume), my search for meaning in tea wares, punch bowls, food remains, and other archaeologically recovered forms of historical debris, I was able to comprehend how Tracy's and Boardman's lives and practices fit within the broader world of power relations and identity construction in the early republic. As a result, I now see the archaeological remains not as irrefutable indicators of achieved status but rather as evidence of ambition, as expression of desires for elite acceptance and social prestige.

Notes

1. Historic New England, formerly the Society for the Preservation of New England Antiquities.

2. The concept of archaeological biography was initially developed by Mary and Adrian Praetzellis (1989) as a means of using historical archaeology to illuminate the lives of nineteenth-century women.

3. There is an extensive literature on sources for historical archaeology and methods for analyzing and interpreting them. See, for example, Beaudry 1988, 1995b; D'Agostino et al. 1995; Little 1992; Wilkie 2006.

4. The house is built of stone in a cruciform plan. The porch entry is built entirely of brick, and there was brick trim around the original arched casement window openings. The asymmetry of the early fenestration and the use of molded brick for decorative detailing have led some architectural historians to use the term *Mannerist* to characterize the architectural style of the house (Grady 1992).

5. Half the value of a prize went to the officers and crew of the privateer making the capture, half to the owners. The former half would be divided according to rank. For instance, prize shares for capture of the *Yankee Hero* by a Tracy ship were as follows: five for the captain; five for the prize masters; descending proportions for the lieutenants, sailing master, surgeon, petty officers, and gunners; and one share each for the seamen (Porter 1937:20).

6. Tracy initially sold the farm to Thomas Russell (Essex Deeds 1786), who leased it to Patrick Tracy (Essex Deeds 1787). It seems Patrick Tracy's lease permitted Nathaniel to remain in residence at the farm. Finally, in September 1791, Thomas Russell exchanged the Peirce Farm with Nathaniel for a brick house in Boston (Essex Deeds 1791).

7. Oliver Putnam's blacksmith accounts reveal that the wheeled vehicles the Tracys owned were old and in frequent need of repair and that the Tracys hired a chaise from him on several occasions when they made visits to their in-laws at Marblehead. It is telling that on the rare occasions when Tracy "settled" his accounts with his blacksmith, he paid not with cash but with scrap iron salvaged from outbuildings and farm implements beyond repair, or by providing pasturage for Putnam's cow or a few bushels of corn grown in his fields (Putnam 1794–1800). Putnam's account book offers no indication that Tracy ever settled the account fully before his death.

8. On the bookplate designed for Tracy by Boston engraver Nathaniel Hurd, a scallop shell figures prominently alongside armorial devices. The scallop shell is often a symbol of Christian pilgrimage (Lewis and Darley 1986), but its likely import in this instance derives from its association with Venus, who, being born of the sea, represents good fortune derived from the sea (J. Hall 1974). Tracy's partner Jonathan Jackson's bookplate, also engraved by Hurd, features scallop shells as well (Benes 1986:157).

9. For a fuller interpretation of the evidence for feasting and entertaining by both Tracy and Boardman, see Beaudry in press.

10. In 1775 Boardman was listed as commander of a Tracy schooner, the *Washington*, an armed vessel of forty tons. Offin Boardman, "mariner, and Abner Greenleaf, merchant," gave bond for the ship (Allen 1927:321). On May 11, 1782, Offin Boardman Jr. of Newburyport was listed as commander of the *Lark*, a Tracy-owned brigantine with four guns and a crew of fifteen men (Allen 1927:202).

11. Possibly because the estate was mishandled by its administrators (Claire W. Dempsey, personal communication, 1994).

12. The Salem Registry of Probate (1813:29) decreed that "whereas said deceaseds estate is insolvent, the debts due therefrom amounting to forty six thousand four hundred seventy dollars forty one and half cents; and the whole of said estate, after charges of Administration, widows dower &c, being but twenty nine thousand one hundred ninety four dollars six cents: Giveing the creditors to said Estate sixty two cents eight mills one fourth (Nearly) on A Dollar." There were more than one hundred creditors: individuals, relatives, business firms, insurance agencies, and others. The list of goods sold at auction includes land, wharves, turnpike shares, houses, livestock, crops, church pews, agricultural utensils, and household furnishings such as linens, looking glasses, candlesticks, a warming pan, bedsteads, desks, tables, chairs,

and carpets. Items such as wooden ware, teaspoons, soup spoons, salts, pepper boxes, and so on also were sold (Salem Registry of Probate 1813:27–28). Goods purchased by the widow included dairy utensils, agricultural implements, and building materials (Salem Registry of Probate 1813:27).

13. The chief evidence is that the garden deposits do not occur beneath the wood-frame addition that Boardman constructed against the west wing of the house, and the presence in the garden strata of late-eighteenth-century ceramic fragments and machine-cut nails with applied heads. Such nails were used in the west wing to attach lath to studs (Grady 1992:37); some of them must have been lost or discarded during construction and subsequently incorporated into the garden deposits. Boardman was an investor in a woolen mill in nearby Byfield, where an ancillary industry involving the manufacture of machine-cut nails was begun by Jacob Perkins in 1795 (Bathe and Bathe 1943:14). This date provides a *terminus post quem* for the garden deposits.

14. The depiction of the privy on the 1812 map drawn from the 1811 survey provides a *terminus ante quem* of 1811 for the basal deposit. Several nearly intact vessels, among them a hand-painted Chinoiserie pearlware teapot missing only its handle and lid, lay *underneath* the stones making up the north wall of the privy. This placement suggests that the crocking material was deposited after the hole was dug but before the walls were built up. How this was done without crushing all the ceramics and glass is a mystery. But the wood mentioned above consisted of planks set on end around the perimeter of the hole at its base and planks *overlying* the northern portion of the crocking deposit; there was no wood on the "floor" of the privy. The stone walling sat upon the horizontal planks that lay atop a portion of the crocking. Hence the laborers working on the privy may have constructed a sort of boxlike platform over the crocking deposit for their convenience and as a base for the stones *before* they stoned up the walls of the vault. It is highly unlikely that artifacts, especially nearly intact vessels, could have gotten below the stones of the privy vault *after* it was constructed. Around the top of the privy pit, the "builder's trench" was backfilled with soil containing fragments of pottery, some of which cross-mend to vessels from the bottom of the privy. The unfortunate collapse of the south wall of the privy after excavation but before it could be backfilled provided the serendipitous opportunity to collect additional items from the installation trench. These, too, mended with or matched vessels from the crocking layer at the base of the privy. It seems clear that Offin Boardman was responsible for the privy construction and used an accumulation of household debris for a drainage layer in the bottom, although the excavators discovered to their discomfort that water wells up and recedes in the privy vault with local tide levels, in a sort of self flushing action that might well have rendered crocking unnecessary. This situation

may also account for the fact that there is no evidence that the privy was ever cleaned out. This is not wholly unexpected, for on farms it was often the practice to relocate the privy when the old one became unusable; cleaning privies out produced only minimal amounts of manure compared to the tons of dung contributed by livestock. The majority of artifacts at the base of the privy were deposited intentionally to provide drainage (compare Roberts and Barrett 1984), but a good many items (for example, chamber pots, coins, and buttons) found their way into the privy while it was in use.

15. Pennyroyal is a "species of mint (*Mentha Pulegium*) with small leaves and of prostrate habit; formerly much cultivated and esteemed for its supposed medicinal virtues" (Oxford English Dictionary 1971:2122).

16. The minimum number of vessels is 272.

17. These were 102 in number.

18. For discussions of the concept of "active voice" analysis of material culture, see Beaudry 1996 and Beaudry, Cook, and Mrozowski 1991.

19. See Shackel 1993 for an archaeologically oriented example, albeit one with different emphases and different conclusions than those presented here.

20. Wolf's (1966:7–10) concept of funds is interpreted by historical anthropologists Villamarin and Villamarin (1982:144) as constituting "the purposeful setting aside or apart of personnel and quantities of material or other resources for their accumulation, from which present and future generations might draw rewards to maintain or increase their wealth and highly valued, culturally sanctioned style of life." Wolf distinguished four types of funds: one for wealth accumulation; a social fund; a religious fund; and a political fund.

10

What Influences Official Information?

Exploring Aggregate Microhistories
of the Catasto of 1427

Rebecca Jean Emigh

The "micro" part of microhistory can be a liability. Scholarship in this tradition may be too narrow to attend to macro-level social processes. Or it can focus on a population or geographical area that is too small to be of more general interest. One possible solution to this problem is to develop "aggregate microhistories" that combine individual microhistories to increase their scope and to create links to larger processes and issues. In this chapter, I take this approach. I combine three microhistories about patterns of information gathering in the Catasto of 1427, a set of fiscal documents collected in Tuscany for the purposes of collecting government revenue, with Herlihy and Klapisch-Zuber's findings (1985) from their more general but less detailed examination of this Catasto. These individual microhistories either focused on small areas in Tuscany or used some particular feature of the documents (Emigh 1996, 1999b, 2002). While these features made it possible to make strong conclusions about a specific aspect of information gathering, combining these insights will make it possible to draw broader conclusions about it.

CAPTURING THE EVERYDAY LIVES OF ORDINARY INDIVIDUALS

One of the hallmarks of microhistory is its focus on ordinary individuals and the meaningful interpretation of their lives (Ginzburg and Poni

1991:3–4). When enough information can be gathered, the in-depth examination of single individuals or families, often using a biographical method, can be very revealing. For example, subjects who are still alive can be observed or interviewed (see Maddox, Gordon, Blee, this volume). For some historical subjects, there is a substantial amount of documentary or archival material (for example, Davis 1983). Microhistory based on archival documents has an august Italian tradition, which includes the tales of the exorcist from Piedmont, Giovan Battista Chiesa (Levi 1988), and the heretical Friulian miller Menocchio (Ginzburg 1980b). Several works entail Tuscans, including the history of a family of sharecroppers, the Del Massarizia (Balestracci 1984); the love story of Giovanni and Lusanna (Brucker 1986); and the life of the lesbian nun Benedetta Carlini (J. Brown 1986). Indeed, the richness of the Italian archives allows microhistory to flourish there because it is possible to locate enough documentation to tell the story of individuals' lives (Ginzburg and Poni 1991:2; Muir 1991:ix).[1]

Yet microhistories often focus on individuals who are not particularly ordinary (Lepore 2001:131–32; Muir 1991:xv), including "normal exceptions" (Grendi 1977:512). Although such cases may be especially revealing precisely because they are exceptional (Ginzburg and Poni 1991:7–8), they may not directly illuminate everyday life. One of the primary obstacles to studying ordinary people, especially those who lived in the distant past, is the relatively little documentary material available for any given individual or family.[2] Thus, instead of a biographical focus on individuals or families, another method is needed to explore ordinary historic lives. In this volume, for example, DeCorse, Beaudry, and Lightfoot turn to historical archaeology. While an archaeological method may not provide the richness about any particular individual that a biographical method does, it can provide evidence about ordinary individuals lost from the written record, as well as microhistories of locations.

In fifteenth-century Tuscany, there is a considerable written record for individuals in the form of fiscal records and legal (notarial) documents. However, for most ordinary rural inhabitants, the available documentary evidence is fragmentary; relatively little of it exists for any given individual or family (for an exception, see Balestracci [1984]). It is therefore quite difficult to use this evidence, especially biographically. On the one hand, there are vast amounts of it to sift though. On the other hand, it often consists of discrete pieces that do not easily combine into a coherent whole (Emigh 2005).

Despite these limitations, it is possible to create microhistories of rural inhabitants and their families (although they are much less detailed and

shorter than the ones in the classic Italian tradition). I have done so to illustrate how property devolution among rural smallholders is linked to markets (Emigh 2003) and to show how sharecroppers had long-term
associations with their landlords (Emigh 1999a). These microhistories were
created by matching different documents that related to the same individual or family, either across different types of sources (legal and fiscal documents [Emigh 2003]) or across time (fiscal documents [Emigh 1999a]). I
have also created microhistories of geographical locations by combining
documentary and visual evidence to illustrate how the growth of urban
markets paradoxically eroded rural market institutions (Emigh 2005).

The microhistories I present here, however, take a different approach.
My intention is to discover how ordinary rural Tuscans used numerical
information. Yet I have never encountered a single document in which
such an individual provided direct evidence—such as a reflection or discussion about numeracy—that would allow me to examine this topic
through a biographical or narrative method. Thus the microhistories presented here, and the aggregate microhistory that they lead to, are not in-
depth narratives or stories of particular individuals, families, or locations,
because these sorts of microhistories would require different methods (see
Emigh 1999a, 2003, 2005). Instead, in each of the three individual microhistories, I focus on how an event—a death, the payment of rent, or the
provision of a loan or livestock to a sharecropped farm—was recorded in
the Catasto. Each event can be viewed from two different perspectives: I
compare deaths recorded in the Catasto to mortality patterns that might
be expected in a preindustrial population; I compare how landlords and
tenants recorded rents, loans, and livestock. The comparisons of the two different perspectives can then be aggregated to illuminate patterns in information reporting. In turn, these patterns can be interpreted to suggest how
individuals used numerical information in meaningful ways. These comparisons do not necessarily reveal who actually died, how large of a loan or
how much livestock was actually provided, or how much rent was actually
paid. However, as I show below, they will provide a considerable amount of
otherwise inaccessible information about how and why numeracy was
important in everyday life in rural Tuscany.

In this sense, my microhistories are of events, not persons. Event analysis also has a microhistorical tradition but often focuses on the unraveling
of a single event (Eiss, this volume; Ladurie 1979; compare incident analysis, which Darnton [2004] contrasts to microhistory). Like Eiss (in this volume), I take advantage of the recording of events as text. Eiss draws
meaning and interpretation from an inscription that occurred during a

single event and is able to narrate a history of a rebellion through this event. I also rely on this movement from event to text; but in my case, I look at records that reflect multiple, often mundane events to discover what the patterning of the records of such events suggests about individuals' intentions in creating the records. Like Eiss's study, the context for my study is one in which knowledge of the practice of writing and the power that it held was widespread, even among the formally illiterate (Emigh 2002). Rural Tuscans used numerical information for a wide variety of purposes, including property devolution and participation in local markets, which helped coordinate household provisioning and agricultural production (Emigh 2002). Thus both Eiss and I show how ordinary individuals harness writing for their own purposes in a historical context in which the written word had a long history.

My microhistories rely on quantitative analysis—sometimes simple, sometimes more complex. This approach may be somewhat surprising, because microhistory as the study of individual lives, along with the cultural turn and the return to narrative, were historiographical movements that reacted against the use of quantitative methods (Brucker 1986:viii; Ginzburg and Poni 1991:2–3; Stone 1979:4–6). Such methods have been sharply critiqued for their lack of transparency, their obfuscation of reality, their overly technical nature, and their reliance on a hierarchical team of researchers because of the vast scale of research (Comaroff and Comaroff 1992:20–22; Ginzburg and Poni 1991:2–3; Stone 1979:4–6). At the extremes, quantitative history and microhistory can certainly look quite different —when the former presents final analyses several levels of abstraction away from individuals' actions (compare Abbott 1992:56), and the latter concerns the intimate details of an individual's life that tell a story through narrative. In my work, however, through an imaginative and somewhat unconventional use of quantitative methods, they find a rapprochement.

In this chapter, I do not use quantitative methods to make a claim for the power of "scientific history."[3] Instead, I use them in an interpretive way, to illuminate patterns that suggest how individuals meaningfully and intentionally engage in social interaction through numeracy. Thus I do not use quantitative methods in a positivist sense, to test directly a theory with evidence (indeed, as I note above, I am not even particularly concerned with whether the events I compare actually occurred or not), but in the historical ethnographic and microhistorical sense that a thorough and detailed understanding of particulars (here, events) creates the possibility of understanding the subjective orientation of historical actors.[4] By understanding these subjective orientations, it is possible to explain the causes and consequences of social action (M. Weber 1978:4). I find this quantitative approach necessary to understand some aspects of social reality—here, the examination of numeracy, to which I next turn. Sometimes all that exists of ordinary people and their everyday lives are the traces they leave in documents; these must be collated, the aggregate patterns presented using quantitative methods, and these patterns must be interpreted, or there will be no story to be told.

STATES, SOCIETIES, AND INFORMATION GATHERING

Which social actors influence patterns of enumeration? States' demands for information can shape the categories of thought that individuals use to process and deploy information (Emigh 2002:654). At the same time, the level of knowledge available in societies at large influences how governmental bureaucracies can collect information (Emigh 2002:659). After all, highly detailed and accurate written information cannot be obtained through coercion in a population that is not literate and numerate (to give an extreme example). Thus the process of enumeration is influenced by states and societies, but different aspects of information may be influenced by different actors. Furthermore, how do states and societies exert influence? The methods used to collect information may influence their results (Starr 1987:8). Furthermore, states' demands for revenue may produce certain types of reporting or patterns of information as individuals respond to financial incentives. However, individuals' own economic incentives may be more important than tax incentives in shaping information. Finally, both states and individuals may draw on broad cultural patterns that shape information in diffuse but important ways. Here, I look specifically at these influences by considering the relative influence of states and societies on patterns of information and by considering the type of influence (economic incentives, cultural patterns, and methodological practices).

Examining the influences on information gathering in the regions that are now Italy is important, because society's influence on information gathering was strong there vis-à-vis the state's influence (for example, in Tuscany; Emigh 2002:689). A comparison to England makes this point clearer. In England the growth of the national state was tied tightly to the growth of official information gathering because much information gathering was conducted explicitly for the purposes of this state (Starr 1987: 15–16). In contrast, in the Italian city-states, merchant activities stimulated widespread numeracy and accounting practices upon which states could then capitalize. In rural regions, smallholders' agricultural production was intertwined with partible inheritance and local markets, both of which necessitated extensive record keeping (Emigh 2002). These practices produced widespread and diverse local—not national—practices of official record keeping. A national census was introduced very late in Italy and did not replace local records for many practical purposes. Since England is often taken as the prototypical case of the development of record keeping, it is important to examine other cases with different relative influences of the state and society. Tuscany provides an important Italian case. Not only is it the site of the Catasto of 1427, one of the first systematic and comprehensive European cadastral surveys, it is also worth remembering that fifteenth-century Tuscany was the birthplace of the Renaissance, one of the key historical periods for subsequent developments. Here, I focus mostly on the rural population, which was the vast majority of the population during this period, even in relatively urbanized Tuscany.

THE SEX RATIO AND AGE ROUNDING IN THE CATASTO OF 1427

In 1427 the Florentine government overhauled the system of direct taxation and forced loans. The previous system had been based on distributing a tax burden in rough proportion to ability to pay (Herlihy and Klapisch-Zuber 1985:3–4, 6–7). In contrast, the Catasto of 1427 was based on lists of households' actual members, assets, and debts. Households were required to submit their *portate*, or original declarations, to tax officials, who then recopied this information into official versions called *campioni*. Taxation was based on capitalized income from assets and the number of household members. Households were allowed to deduct certain expenses and debts from their total assets. As a consequence, the Catasto contains a relatively complete list of Tuscans' assets (including real estate, cash, other movable property, credits in various public funds and debts, and investments in commercial ventures) and debts (including commercial loans) and an enumeration of the Tuscan population.

Not surprisingly, the resultant information contained in the Catasto was shaped by many factors, including the level of knowledge of assets, debts, and demographic information among the general populace, the methods used by tax officials to collect the information, and widespread Tuscan cultural categories. Herlihy and Klapisch-Zuber investigated several influences on the demographic information in the Catasto, including age and sex. The government's practice of collecting information about age in the tax records influenced the population's record keeping with respect to this information. Over time, as additional tax surveys were collected, more and more Tuscans recorded their biological ages. For example, in a survey of 1371, about 44 percent of the population of the villages around Prato and about 12.5 percent of the population in the town of Prato declared no age at all. In contrast, in 1427 only about 1.6 percent of the Tuscan population declared no age. Similarly, over the course of the fifteenth century, with the subsequent collection of *catasti*, the degree of age rounding (the preference for reporting ages ending in a 0 and to a lesser extent in a 5) declined, resulting in a lower proportion of ages ending in a 0 as the century progressed (Herlihy and Klapisch-Zuber 1985:164). Furthermore, in 1427 the regions in which the Florentines had previously collected taxes that required individuals to report age information showed less age rounding than regions in which such information had not been collected (Herlihy and Klapisch-Zuber 1985:181). Thus, where Tuscans were required to report such information, they became used to doing so. In addition, tax officials' practices helped Tuscans do so. Tax officials compared, where possible, current declarations to previous ones. The information given in the Catasto of 1427 could be compared to the previous tax survey, the Estimo of 1422 (where it had been assessed); households had to report the tax from this Estimo on their 1427 declarations (Herlihy and Klapisch-Zuber 1985:7; see Emigh 2000:39–40). Catasto officials attempted to check fraudulent ages and correct errors (Herlihy and Klapisch-Zuber 1985:165).

In the Catasto, the sex ratio, the ratio of reported males to females, was influenced by cultural expectations about the appropriate marriage age for women. Females tended to cluster around age eighteen, the typical age of marriage for Tuscan women (Herlihy and Klapisch-Zuber 1985:141). In fact, heads of Florentine households lowered the ages of their unmarried daughters to improve their marriage chances (Molho 1988:194). In comparison to ages calculated on the basis of the Dowry Fund (Monte delle doti), the ages of unmarried females in the Catasto are lower (Molho 1988: 201). This pattern of age reporting was influenced by notions of honor and by widespread cultural expectations, especially among wealthy families, that women should be married soon after sexual maturity (Molho 1988: 194). Delay threatened the reputation of the entire household (Molho 1988:209). To make time for the lengthy negotiations that marriages and dowries generally entailed, fathers lowered their daughters' ages (Molho 1988:211–12).

The sex ratio and ages in the Catasto were also shaped by tax incentives. Florentine and Pisan males between the ages of eighteen and sixty and male residents of the *contado* (the rural regions closest to Florence and tied most tightly to its jurisdiction) between the ages of fifteen and seventy were subject to a head tax. The depressed sex ratio just after the ages of the imposition of the head tax illustrates that household heads tried to avoid paying this tax by reporting males to be females or by lowering the ages of their male children nearing the age of eligibility for the head tax (Herlihy and Klapisch-Zuber 1985:138–42). Similarly, men had incentives to reach the age of exemption from the head tax. Thus the male population increased relative to females at older ages (Herlihy and Klapisch-Zuber 1985:143).

Herlihy and Klapisch-Zuber's analysis of the Catasto of 1427 thus points to the ways in which methodologies of enumeration, cultural practices, and economic incentives influenced official statistics. While invaluable, their summaries do not necessarily provide information about the relative influence of the state and society on these factors or the differential impact of these factors on different types of information (assets as opposed to demographic information). Most of their evidence, however, suggests that the state had a larger influence on information than society did, by spreading numeracy through repeated requests for information or through tax incentives that gave individuals financial rewards for keeping records. The overall thrust of their argument also suggests that one reason the state had such a strong role was that rural inhabitants, who were the majority of the Tuscan population and were generally poor, had little exposure to numeracy except where they were subject to Florentine taxation through the Catasto (Herlihy and Klapisch-Zuber 1985:164, 182). They show that urban residents, men, and the wealthy reported their ages more accurately than rural residents, women, and the poor (Herlihy and Klapisch-Zuber 1985:179–82). The former, of course, were the Florentine elite—male merchants and officials who would have learned numeracy through their occupations or formal schooling (Emigh 2002:664–65) and were steeped in the humanist culture of literacy (Graff 1987:76–90).

Do Herlihy and Klapisch-Zuber's findings suggest that rural inhabitants had no use for numerical information, were not culturally sophisticated enough to use it, and learned it only when forced to do so by the urban elite, and, as a consequence, that numerical information played little role in their everyday lives? Cohn's (1996:156) finding that some rural residents living farther from Florence reported their ages more accurately than those living closer to the city suggests a different pattern and points to the need for more investigation. Thus, to consider the possible uses of numeracy in everyday life, as well as to provide more detailed and specific information about the influences on numeracy (for example, the relative weight of states and societies, the relative role of economic incentives, cultural patterns, and methodological practices), I needed much more micro-historical information about specific individuals' patterns of reporting information. I found such information embedded within three of my studies of Tuscany that focused on different locations, using somewhat different information and sometimes oriented toward somewhat different debates (Emigh 1996, 1999b, 2002). Each study considers a different pattern of reporting. By here considering these three studies together, the influences on official information can be understood more thoroughly.

DEATH AND TAXES

The Catasto of 1427 was collected between 1427 and 1430. After the redaction of the initial declarations, there was a period of time, about three years in the contado, during which households were allowed to make corrections and additions to their declarations, including reporting the deaths of household members. Reporting the deaths of males eligible for the head tax in the contado unambiguously lowered households' tax liabilities (unlike in Florence, where deaths had mixed effects because each household member received a sizable tax deduction, and in the district [the rural regions beyond the contado], where the head tax was not always imposed) (Conti 1966:76; Emigh 1999b:184; Herlihy and Klapisch-Zuber 1985:18–19, 257–58). The number of reported deaths, however, is quite small. Based on this number, the death rate would have been about 4.4 per 1,000 persons (about half the death rate in modern, developed countries) (Herlihy and Klapisch-Zuber 1985:258).

Thus, although there were financial incentives to report deaths, only some households did so. Their reasons are not transparent. Households may have been unclear about the regulations; tax officials may have implemented them unevenly; or reporting a death may not have been worth the trouble of returning to the tax officials. Although the tax incentives did not induce a complete reporting of deaths, they did influence the information that was reported. The deaths of males eligible for the head tax were much more likely to be reported than other deaths.

Herlihy and Klapisch-Zuber (1985:257–60) noted the influence of tax incentives on this overall pattern, but they did not analyze other possible influences. They did not account for underlying differences in age at death; nor did they explore the possible influence of tax officials' use of heads of households as a methodological device for collecting and organizing information. This methodological device was based on a widespread cultural pattern of patriarchy, the authority of the eldest male head of the household, and the relatively high frequency of large, extended households that included the parental couple, adult married offspring, and their married siblings. Formal and informal authority was generally transferred to the eldest coresident male when the head of the household died (Emigh 2003:391).

Thus the category "head of household" was a widespread cultural concept that tax officials used to organize the registers. The household, or coresidential group, was the unit upon which the Catasto was based and around which the physical registers were organized, at the level of each household's campione and portata and at the level of the summary registers. The tax officials required that all heads of households in the Estimo of 1422 submit Catasto declarations. The physical records of the Catasto of 1427 began with the name of the head (or heads) of household (along with the assessed tax in 1422) (Emigh 1999b:186).

Because the tax officials compared the newly submitted Catasto declarations to the previously recorded Estimo declarations, and the subsequently submitted catasti declarations throughout the fifteenth century to the ones from 1427, they may have been more likely to notice and record the deaths of heads of households than those of other household members (Emigh 1999b:186; see Emigh 1999a:367, 369 for examples of comparisons among later catasti). This conjecture would help explain why Herlihy and Klapisch-Zuber (1985:258) found that the deaths of seventy-year-old males were reported more thoroughly: older males were more likely to have been heads of households and thus perhaps more likely to have been noticed by tax officials. Thus, if heads of households were canceled more often than other household members, this pattern may stem from the effects of the methodology used to redact the Catasto of 1427—namely, its organization on the basis of household head, which in turn reflected the widespread use of this cultural pattern to organize social life.

To investigate this possibility, I used Herlihy and Klapisch-Zuber's machine-readable data set (1981) to locate the cancellations of males in the contado, the group of individuals for whom the tax incentives would have been strongest and most unambiguous. Then I coded some information from the campioni that was not in Herlihy and Klapisch-Zuber's data, including the amount of the head tax. In addition, I used Herlihy and Klapisch-Zuber's data to select a matched sample of males who had not been canceled to compare them to those who had been canceled. I used a statistical technique called logistic regression, which makes it possible to consider the impact of different factors—here, headship status, eligibility for the head tax, whether the individual was actually charged for the head tax, and the age-specific probability of dying, on the likelihood that an individual was canceled from the declaration because of death (for additional methodological details, see Emigh 1999b:186–94).

The results show that net of the underlying probability of dying, heads of households were more likely than other household members to have been canceled. Thus the methodology of the Catasto of 1427 had an influence on the resulting information. Those eligible for the head tax were more likely to have been canceled than those who were not eligible for the head tax. However, this effect was not simply a matter of avoiding payment assessed by tax officials. Net of the effects of the probability of dying, headship status, and eligibility, those who had been charged the head tax were less likely to have been canceled than males who had not been charged the head tax. This finding is contrary to the tax incentives, which suggest that those households that had been charged the tax would be the most likely to take advantage of the tax relief offered by the death of the male charged for the tax. Thus the results suggest that Tuscans' knowledge of whether their household members fell into the category of being eligible for the head tax was more important than whether this person had been charged the tax. The tax incentive was important, but at the level of eligibility, not actual payment. A sizable proportion of households (about 30 percent of the cancellations) seemed to have anticipated that the death would affect their tax calculations and reported the death prior to the tax collectors' assessments. Thus these Tuscans were not merely responding to tax officials' requests for information and improving their reporting on that basis but were anticipating demands for information that they already had available. However, among those who had actually been charged the head tax, the size of the payment did affect cancellation status: cancellations were more frequent among males who had been charged a higher payment than among those with smaller payments (Emigh 1999b:192–94).

These results extend Herlihy and Klapisch-Zuber's findings by examining a set of declarations in more detail than they did. These results show that financial incentives and the methods used to collect information simultaneously affected Tuscans' reporting patterns. Deaths of heads of households were more likely to be reported than those of other members, in part because the Catasto itself was organized around the names of heads of households. This methodological device was in turn based on widespread cultural practices associated with Tuscan household formation and the household head's formal and informal authority. The death of the household head would have held considerable importance for the household itself.

Tax incentives also affected the reports of deaths, although in complicated ways. First of all, such incentives were not sufficient to induce most Tuscans to report deaths. In fact, the reported deaths often emerged from households with a relatively thorough knowledge of the tax implications and whose members reported deaths even before tax officials calculated their taxes. They may have been the best informed households and most sensitive to tax regulations. Financial incentives were important in a more specific way. Among those households that were charged the head tax, those with the largest assessments were more likely to report deaths.

COMPARING RENTS DECLARED BY LANDLORDS AND TENANTS

The previous sections focused on influences on demographic information, including deaths, sex ratios, and age distributions. The Catasto, however, contains much more information about assets, and in particular agricultural properties, than about demographic factors, since assets were the primary basis for taxation. This and the following section, then, consider some of the influences on reports of agricultural income and assets. This section considers the influence of different types of economic incentives on patterns of reports of rural rents, namely whether tax incentives or individuals' other economic incentives had more influence.

Here, I use the declarations from Montecatini, a small town in the Valdinievole, northwest of Florence. The Valdinievole was one of the more urbanized and prosperous regions of rural Tuscany (Herlihy and Klapisch-Zuber 1985:350–51). Montecatini was part of the Florentine district and had been under Florentine control since 1339, after a series of wars with Lucca (J. Brown 1982:14–21; Repetti [1839] 1969:354–56). The Catasto declarations indicate that most individuals were smallholders who worked their own plots of land. Rural inhabitants often leased small plots of land from their neighbors (Emigh 2002:672).

Tuscans were required to report the rental income from any real estate holding they owned. Thus landlords of rented houses were required to give the amount of the rent, usually a fixed rent in cash. Similarly, landlords of sharecropped tenancies were required to list the rent, usually their portion (generally half) of the harvest from the property. Fixed-term landlords were required to report the amount of the rent, either in cash or kind. Thus Catasto declarations throughout Tuscany provide information about rents for houses and agricultural properties. In addition, households living in rented houses were allowed to deduct the rent, capitalized at 7 percent, from their total taxable wealth. Thus the Catasto also contains information about households that rented their dwellings (Emigh 2002:678–79).

However, the Catasto declarations from Montecatini (and throughout the Valdinievole) exhibit an unusual feature. Tenants often listed the amount they paid in rent in the section in which the debts (*incharichi*) were listed, although this was not required by the tax regulations (and was not common elsewhere). There was obviously some systematic confusion about tax procedures in this region. Perhaps tenants hoped that tax officials would lower their assessments on the basis of these amounts. However, since the landlords were required to list their rents, the tenants' practice of listing the rents makes it possible to compare the amounts declared by the landlords to the amounts declared by the tenants. This comparison can be used to consider different influences on the information in the Catasto (Emigh 2002:678–79).

Comparing the rents required that I find the pieces of rental property in both the landlords' and tenants' declarations with reasonable certainty. I used all the declarations from Montecatini (Emigh 2002:672). I matched pieces of land for which both the tenant and the landlord gave the name of the other party and that seemed identical. I also matched pieces of land for which one of the parties gave the name of the other party and that I could identify on the other party's declaration with a reasonable degree of certainty. In matching the pieces of land, I relied primarily on the campioni. Although I might have obtained more matches with the portate, the information might have been inconsistent. There were two sets of portate for the Valdinievole (Herlihy and Klapisch-Zuber 1985:22–23), making it difficult to determine, for any pair of landlord and tenant, which, if either, set of declarations matched. Thus the campioni yielded more consistent information. However, when the campione was ambiguous, I did refer to the portata, making sure to use the one that matched the campione (Emigh 2002:679).

This process yielded sixty-two matches for which the same piece of land could be found in the landlord's and the tenant's declarations and for which there was enough information to compare the landlord's and tenant's declarations of the rent. Of these sixty-two cases, six were rentals of houses and fifty-six were rentals of agricultural holdings. The six cases representing the rental of houses corresponded to the tax regulations for both landlords and tenants, since such information was pertinent to the tax officials' calculations. However, in the other fifty-six cases, although the landlords' information was pertinent to the tax calculation, the tenants' information was not. Thus these tenants were not just responding to information requested by the tax collectors but had the information already available for some other purpose (Emigh 2002:679).

The rents from these properties could be declared in fixed or share terms, in money or kind. To compare the rents from these pieces of land,

I converted all the rents in kind into monetary values by assigning to the rent in kind, generally reported as amounts of crops, the standard prices used by Catasto officials (Emigh 2002:680).

There were three possible patterns of reporting rents. In the first pattern, the one corresponding to tax incentives, landlords might have declared a lower rental income in hopes of lowering their tax assessment based on income, while tenants might have declared a higher rent, hoping that tax collectors would interpret the rent as commercial debt and give them a tax deduction for it, even though this type of rent was not an allowable deduction. In the second pattern, one corresponding to the short-run income incentives of the landlord and tenant, the landlord might have declared a higher rent, hoping to extract more income from the tenant, while the tenant might declare a lower rent, hoping to lower the eventual amount of payment. Finally, in the third pattern, one corresponding to long-run incentives of landlord and tenant, the amounts declared by them would have matched. In the long run, it may have been important to establish a reputation as an honest, reliable landlord or tenant, who declared obligations fully and met them responsibly, in a way that agreed with the other party's assessment of the obligation. This reputation may have been especially important in regions such as the Valdinievole, in which landlords and tenants did not form distinct agrarian classes. Instead, they engaged in reciprocal leasing with their neighbors, depending on their income needs and stages of their life cycles. As a consequence, they could anticipate being both landlords and tenants (sometimes simultaneously on different properties).

The majority of the matches followed the third pattern. In thirty-seven of the sixty-two cases (almost 60 percent), the amount declared by the landlord matched the amount declared by the tenant. For example, Nanni di Mazzeo Barruci was a smallholder in Montecatini and owned about ten pieces of land, some of which he worked himself and some of which he leased to others. He also leased several pieces of land, one of which was owned by another inhabitant of Montecatini, Antonio di Guasppare. Both declarations gave an annual fixed rent of two *staia* of grain. Thus the monetary value of the rent would have been twenty-eight *soldi*, using the standard price of fourteen soldi per staia that Catasto officials used for grain in the region (Emigh 2002:680).

In a minority of cases, eighteen of the sixty-two (about 29 percent), however, the rent declared by the landlord and tenant did not match. Of these, eleven of the sixty-two cases (about 18 percent) followed the second pattern corresponding to the short-term income incentives of landlords and tenants. In these cases, the amount of rent declared by the landlord was larger than the amount declared by the tenant. For example, Giovanni di Antonio declared that he rented a piece of land from the works of San Michele for an annual rent of .5 staia of grain. Giovanni was listed as a tenant in the declaration of the religious institution, but the rent was given as 1.5 staia of grain each year (Emigh 2002:684–85). Finally, in the smallest category of cases, the pattern of reporting corresponded to the tax incentives. In seven of the sixty-two cases (about 11 percent), the landlord declared less rent than the tenant did. For example, Meo di Agostino declared that he rented a piece of land from Papo di Benintendi for an annual rent of seven staia of grain. Papo declared Meo di Agostino to be one of his tenants, who paid an annual rent of one staia of grain (Emigh 2002:682).

Thus these patterns suggest that overall, individuals' own economic incentives were more important than those of the tax officials. Although there were clearly cases in which the rents did not match (although some of these mismatches may have been affected by different redaction dates of the Catasto; see Emigh 2002:683–84), even in these cases, more of them corresponded to the rental contract incentives than to the tax incentives.

Of course, individuals did respond to tax incentives. As Herlihy and Klapisch-Zuber showed, Tuscans did falsify their Catasto returns to lighten their tax burdens. However, more detailed analyses show that tax incentives were not necessarily paramount in declaring income. The tax incentives may have been relatively unimportant with respect to the landlord's interest in receiving the entire rent from the tenant; after all, the amount saved by lowering the amount of tax would not, in most cases, have made up for the loss of income, because households were taxed at a relatively small percentage of the total amount of their taxable wealth. Thus, if there were any chance the other party in the contract would discover the discrepancy, there was relatively little reason for a tenant to overreport or a landlord to underreport the amount of rent. If tenants declared a larger rent to try to lower their tax burdens, and landlords discovered these reports, landlords might demand the higher rents. Furthermore, the loss of reputation as a reliable contractual partner might be more damaging than paying taxes on the entire income (Emigh 2002:684).

COMPARING LOANS AND LIVESTOCK DECLARED BY LANDLORDS AND TENANTS

In this section, I examine another dimension of agricultural production, the provisioning of share tenancies. Sharecropping was a common form of rental contract in rural Tuscany; landlords leased properties to tenants for a share of the harvest (commonly one-half). In some locations in rural Tuscany (in contrast to the Valdinievole), landlords and tenants of sharecropped properties formed different classes. Landlords tended to be Florentine urban merchants who owned consolidated farms leased to rural inhabitants, who owned little land of their own. Where these arrangements prevailed, landlords commonly provided loans to their tenants for capital for working the land and provided livestock, oxen, and sometimes other animals for the properties (see review in Emigh 1996:707–8). Written leases preserved as notarial documents suggest that landlords provided inputs on nearly 86 percent of sharecropped tenancies (Emigh 1998:362).

What affected how landlords' inputs were recorded on the Catasto declarations? As Herlihy and Klapisch-Zuber (1985:119) noted, sharecroppers' own declarations mention oxen in a minority of cases. In nearly 65 percent of the cases, sharecroppers' declarations did not mention oxen. In about 14.5 percent of the cases, their declarations indicate that sharecroppers leased oxen; in nearly 21 percent of the cases, sharecroppers owned oxen. From the perspective of the tax regulations, this pattern is not surprising. The Catasto regulations stated that livestock and loans on all farms were supposed to be declared (although certain categories of them were exempt) (Herlihy and Klapisch-Zuber 1985:13–14, 118–19; Karmin 1906: 21–22). However, it is not clear whether both the landlords and the tenants were supposed to declare the values (see Karmin 1906:21–22). Landlords were taxed on the livestock on their farms but were allowed to subtract a one-florin tax credit for each team of oxen (Herlihy and Klapisch-Zuber 1985: 14). Livestock held by rural inhabitants was taxable, but oxen used for cultivation were tax exempt. However, the tax officials were not consistent about recording this deduction (Herlihy and Klapisch-Zuber 1985:119). Loans contracted between landlords and tenants were not considered to be commercial debts, and tenants were not given a tax deduction for them (Herlihy and Klapisch-Zuber 1985:17, 119). In addition, these loans were not always considered commercial assets, so landlords were not always taxed for them. Given that these loans and livestock, then, were relatively unimportant from the point of view of tax regulations and incentives (that is, they were mostly tax exempt) and in any event that these regulations were enforced irregularly, do the declarations exhibit any consistent pattern? If they do, it may suggest that landlords' and tenants' own incentives were motivating such a pattern, since tax regulations and incentives were not paramount.

To investigate this question, I used the same strategy as above. I focused on a relatively small region, in which it would be possible to match landlords' and tenants' records. I focused on two small rural parishes, San Piero a Sieve and Santa Maria a Spugnole, in the Mugello, north of Florence. These parishes provide examples of sharecropping communities in which wealthy Florentines leased land to local residents. The region was prosperous and the soil fertile (Herlihy and Klapisch-Zuber 1985:51). Landlords in these parishes were involved in their tenancies, and sharecropping was a productive form of agricultural production, at the leading edges of a capitalist agricultural transformation (Emigh 2000:43). Thus it is quite likely that tenants in these parishes had access to landlords' inputs in the form of loans and livestock.

Here, I used both the campioni and portate, which were similar but not identical. The portate contained some information about loans and livestock that the tax officials did not bother to recopy to the campioni, probably because it was irrelevant to tax calculations. To match landlords to tenants, I first looked through all the Catasto declarations in these parishes for possible landlords named on tenants' declarations as debtors, landlords, or owners of properties listed in the boundaries of tenants' own properties. I then used Herlihy and Klapisch-Zuber's data (1981) to search for the landlords' declarations, which were generally among the Florentine registers. When I identified a landlord, I searched through his or her portata and campione for the property worked by the rural resident. In some cases, this search was relatively straightforward, because the landlord's declaration provided the name of the tenant or a household member of the tenant. In other cases, the worker's name was not given, but the property was in the appropriate parish and the match seemed unambiguous. Once a landlord was located, I also looked through his or her entire declaration for other pieces of land in these parishes and for possible landlords' names among the boundaries of property. Certainly, some farms remained unmatched to their tenants, but this strategy provided a reasonably exhaustive way to match tenants to farms. I matched forty-six landlords' holdings to tenants in these two parishes. Then, on the basis of this match, I coded any information about loans and livestock from both the tenants' and the landlords' declarations (Emigh 1996:710–11).

There was considerable agreement between landlords and tenants with respect to loans. For these forty-six holdings, the mean value of loans declared by landlords was 19.27 florins, while the mean value declared by tenants was 12.73 florins. In half the cases (twenty-three of forty-six), the landlords and tenants declared an identical amount. In twelve cases, both landlord and tenant declared the identical nonzero amount. In another eleven cases, neither landlord nor tenant declared any loan. In another ten of the forty-six cases, the discrepancy between the landlord's and tenant's declaration was relatively small, less than five florins (Emigh 1996:711). In thirty-three of the forty-six cases, then, the landlords' and tenants' declarations were identical or similar.

In contrast, in eleven of the forty-six cases, there was a large discrepancy between the landlord's and tenant's declarations. In seven of these discrepant cases, one of the two parties declared no debt at all (in six cases, the tenants declared no debt; in one case, the owner declared no debt). In these cases, it is not clear whether landlords and tenants disagreed about the amount of the debt or whether one party, generally the tenant, simply did not bother to list the loan. In the other four discrepant cases, landlords' and tenants' declarations greatly diverged (by more than five florins). However, one of these large discrepancies, and several of the others, may stem from the different redaction dates of landlords' and tenants' declarations. (In the remaining two cases, the amount of the loan could not be determined.) If so, then the number of discrepant cases may be even smaller (Emigh 1996:711–12).

In sharp contrast, landlords' and tenants' listings of livestock diverged widely. The mean value of livestock declared by landlords was 18.34 florins; that of tenants, only 2.49 florins. In contrast to the loans, where the declarations were similar in thirty-three cases, the listings of livestock were similar in only seventeen of the forty-six cases. The value of the livestock declared by landlords and tenants matched exactly in only one case. In another thirteen cases, the declarations matched because neither landlord nor tenant declared any livestock. In another three cases, the landlords and tenants declared amounts that differed by only five florins. In the majority of the cases, however, twenty-five of forty-six (about 54 percent), the landlords, but not the tenants, declared a value for livestock. In another four cases, the landlords declared livestock, but the value cannot be determined (the livestock was not listed on the tenants' declarations). Although it cannot be determined for sure whether landlords and tenants disagreed about the value of the livestock or whether or not it was provided, it seems more likely that tenants simply did not bother to list the livestock (Emigh 1996:714).

These data suggest that the usual practice in these parishes was for landlords to provide either loans or livestock, or both, for their sharecropped tenancies. In thirty-eight of the forty-six tenancies, about 83 percent, either the tenant's or the landlord's declaration indicated that a loan or livestock had been provided. This is approximately the same percentage given by an analysis of notarial documents, suggesting that 86 percent of landlords provided inputs for their share tenancies (Emigh 1998:362). These data make it possible to draw different conclusions than those based on Herlihy and Klapisch-Zuber's figures based on only tenants' declarations, which suggested that sharecroppers did not have access to livestock. However, a careful analysis shows that the analyses are providing complementary information. The data from these parishes show that in twenty-nine of the forty-six cases, about 63 percent, tenants did not list livestock on their declarations. This is just about the same as the percentage (about 65) of sharecroppers throughout all of rural Tuscany who did not mention livestock, according to Herlihy and Klapisch-Zuber (1985:119). These comparisons also suggest that landlords' practices in these parishes were similar to those in Tuscany more generally.

What explains this pattern of reporting? The tax regulations explain relatively little. Theoretically, landlords and tenants were supposed to declare all loans and livestock, but there were few reasons to do so. These loans were not considered commercial assets. Tenants were not given a tax deduction for them, and landlords often were not charged for them. Further, some livestock was either exempt or was subject to a deduction, and was generally irrelevant to tax calculations. Even further, these regulations were not applied consistently, suggesting that there was general confusion about them (Emigh 1996:717).

In these particular parishes, the reporting patterns do not seem to follow tax regulations, although the calculations were often ambiguous. It is often difficult to determine how the taxes were calculated on the loans and livestock, because these assets were sometimes recopied from the location on the document where the farm was given to the location where the credits were listed. Where the workers' names were not given, the loans and livestock from any particular farm cannot be matched easily to the names in the lists of credits. In other cases, it is difficult to determine exactly what had been taxed because lists of credits were summarized in the campione, and the workers' names had not been recopied from the portata. However, it appears that most landlords in these parishes were not assessed taxes on the value of the loan or the oxen but were assessed taxes on any other livestock. In other cases, landlords were assessed taxes on some but not all the loans and all the livestock except the oxen. Some landlords, however, were assessed taxes on the loans and the oxen. The tenants, however, were not subject to taxes on either the loans or the livestock, and such taxes were not generally assessed (Emigh 1996:717–18). Thus neither the tax regulations in the abstract nor their concrete application in these parishes explain why landlords and tenants generally reported loans but only landlords generally reported livestock.

The tax incentives do not explain this pattern either. The specific incentives for loans and livestock are quite unclear. If the landlord's loan was to be considered an asset, and taxed as such, then landlords would have had incentives to omit them. However, loans to tenants were not always considered assets. Furthermore, even if oxen were considered assets and taxed as such, landlords were supposed to receive a deduction for them. But given the value of oxen, it is unlikely that this deduction was an incentive to list them, because the remainder of their value was taxable. Tenants had no incentives to list livestock or loans, since they received no deductions for them. Thus the tax incentives also provided little motivation for landlords and tenants both listing loans but only landlords listing livestock.

Given the general level of confusion about how these assets would be taxed, it is possible that Tuscans followed more general tax incentives: underplay assets; accentuate liabilities (allowable or not). However, these general incentives also explain little. The mean value of loans and livestock reported by landlords (assets) was considerably higher than the mean value of loans and livestock reported by tenants (debts or liabilities). Thus landlords and tenants in these Mugellan parishes, like the landlords and tenants in Montecatini, do not seem to be following a general pattern of hiding assets and declaring debts.

Instead, like the landlords and tenants in Montecatini, they seem to be recording financial assets and debts to keep records of their obligations and interests. The amounts of the loans between landlords and tenants frequently matched; obviously, both landlords and tenants felt that the debts were genuine ones, for which tenants were obligated. However, since tenants did not generally record livestock, it is quite possible that they did not consider themselves to be obligated or responsible for the monetary value of these animals in the same way as they were for loans. Thus, although it is impossible to determine for certain, the most consistent interpretation of these documents is that landlords were declaring these animals as their own assets while tenants felt relatively little financial obligation for them. Perhaps landlords and tenants considered livestock to be similar to other fixed capital assets on the farm (the house, the outbuildings) that were listed on the landlord's declarations for the tenant's use. While the tenants had to care for these assets, they may not have been financially responsible for them as they were for loans. This explanation is consistent with the interpretation of the pattern of reporting rents in Montecatini. The Catasto was a public document in which individuals were careful to record their major assets and debts to preserve their interests or to limit their liabilities, regardless of tax incentives (Emigh 1996:718). Failure to declare an asset might call into question its ownership (Herlihy and Klapisch-Zuber [1985:18] give the example of land, although this was likely to be true of all assets). Thus landlords and tenants were careful to record loans, for which they both felt responsible, but only landlords recorded livestock, as it was generally the landlord's asset, not the tenant's asset or liability.

ASSESSING THE RELATIVE INFLUENCES ON THE CATASTO OF 1427

I assessed three sets of influences on the Catasto of 1427: economic incentives, cultural patterns, and methodological practices. To do so, I combined information from three microhistorical studies. These microhistories examined in detail a relatively small number of documents that were restricted either topically (for example, only death records of males) or regionally (for example, only for a few small towns). These microhistories make it possible to examine specific patterns of influences on the Catasto that were not apparent in Herlihy and Klapisch-Zuber's more summary research on the Catasto as a whole (although the microhistories would not have been possible without their pathbreaking work).

The microhistories show that economic incentives were important but that individuals' own financial incentives were generally more important than tax incentives, when the two conflicted. Herlihy and Klapisch-Zuber (1985:138–42) showed that Tuscans responded to tax incentives, which affected the age and sex distribution in the Catasto. However, the microhistories show that when some other financial interest was at stake, it generally trumped the tax incentives. I illustrated this by comparing rents declared by landlords and tenants in Montecatini and loans and livestock declared by landlords and tenants in San Piero a Sieve and Santa Maria a Spugnole. The patterns based on these comparisons did not generally conform to what would be expected on the basis of tax incentives, which should have induced Tuscans to underreport their assets and overreport their debts. Instead, the most common pattern—matching records of landlords and tenants—suggested that the more powerful influence on the information in the Catasto was individuals' interests in maintaining records of their assets and debts to preserve their interests or limit their liabilities. Thus, while tax incentives were important, they were not paramount, especially with respect to assets and debts. It is possible that the tax incentives had more influence on age reporting than on asset and debt reporting, precisely because this information had relatively few other financial implications that might have produced conflicting incentives with respect to reporting in the Catasto.

The examination of death records also showed that while Tuscans paid attention to tax incentives, they were not necessarily paramount. Although reporting deaths of adult males eligible for the head tax would have reduced Tuscans' taxes, most deaths went unreported (Herlihy and Klapisch-Zuber 1985:258). Furthermore, the analyses show that whether the tax had been paid or not was not the most important influence affecting reports of deaths. Householders' knowledge of eligibility for the tax and tax officials' methodological practices of using the names of heads of households as an organizing principle were more important than whether the deceased male had been charged the tax. Thus it appears that Tuscans who reported deaths were anticipating payment, not responding to whether the payment had been made or not. Although the tax incentive certainly shaped individuals' actions through eligibility for the tax, the results suggest that individuals were not responding to immediate taxation so much as anticipating possible payments.

Cultural influences were also apparent. The widespread cultural category of household head was deployed by tax officials as a methodological device, which in turn affected the results. Similarly, unmarried females were systematically reported to be younger in the Catasto to improve their marriage chances (Herlihy and Klapisch-Zuber 1985:141; Molho 1988:201). Such practices were based on cultural expectations about women's appropriate marriage age. Finally, the redaction of the Catasto was possible only because of widespread cultural practices of literacy and numeracy. The collection of information, given the level of detail, would have been impossible if Tuscans did not have specific knowledge of their assets, debts, and demographic information (Emigh 2002:666).

NUMERACY IN EVERYDAY LIFE

The level and detail of this information also illustrates that in the Tuscan case, the Florentine government had to be capitalizing to a large extent on information that Tuscans already knew (Emigh 2002:688–89). The microhistories comparing landlords' and tenants' declarations show that Tuscans generally had more information at their disposal than tax officials wanted them to report. In this respect, the microhistories again suggest that information about ages may have had different influences than information about assets. Herlihy and Klapisch-Zuber's analysis (1985:164, 181) suggests that Tuscans learned to report their ages more accurately over time, in response to the need to provide this information to tax officials. While the state may have influenced age reporting, for assets and debts it seems that society, not the state, had the larger influence on the information in the Catasto. In fact, Tuscans' knowledge of their assets and debts overwhelmed the tax officials. It took much longer than officials expected to redact the Catasto of 1427. Some procedures were simplified as its collection progressed because they were simply too labor intensive, and the Florentines never again attempted to collect such a detailed survey (Herlihy and Klapisch-Zuber 1985: 11, 26; Petralia 2000:68–69). While the Catasto of 1427 was certainly linked to state-building processes, the Florentine government was largely dependent upon information that its populace had already developed on the basis of engaging in financial transactions for its own purposes.

Herlihy and Klapisch-Zuber's seminal work, although it pointed out the influence of methodologies of enumeration, cultural categories, and tax incentives, could not illustrate the relative importance of these influences. Furthermore, because they suggested that rural inhabitants, in particular, had little reason to be numerate except when information was requested by the government, their work can be interpreted as suggesting that the government's role in assessing and collecting taxes was the most important influence on numerical information. Indeed, given the deficiencies of the Catasto (for example, the scant recording of deaths and the multiple contradictions between the postings and the tax regulations), it is easy to assume that the inhabitants' numerical knowledge was deficient and that perhaps numerical knowledge was a part of elite culture that only slowly penetrated rural regions through repeated tax assessment and collection. Such a view might be consistent with Herlihy and Klapisch-Zuber's findings (1985:164, 182) that numeracy spread from urban to rural areas, and Graff's argument (Graff 1987:76–90) that literacy flowered among Florentines, who had opportunities for education and exposure to a humanist culture. This view is also consistent with the more general argument that states are the prime reasons individuals learn to be numerate and that, as a result, tax incentives are the primary incentives for individuals' patterns of reporting and use of numerical information (see Emigh 2002:654).

In contrast, I argue here against this possible interpretation. By combining three detailed microhistories, I argue that rural individuals had their own reasons for using numerical information and when their own incentives conflicted with those of the tax system, their own incentives prevailed. Numeracy was part of everyday life in rural regions (Emigh 2002). The results presented here—based on the patterning of events reported in the Catasto—suggest that rural inhabitants had strong incentives to report transactions to preserve their interests and limit their liabilities, or to show more generally that they were honest and reliable parties in transactions. The results also show that rural inhabitants frequently had more numeric information at their disposal than the tax officials requested. More generally, rural inhabitants knew the value of their credits and assets (land, rents, livestock, loans) because of broader social practices of partible property devolution (including partible inheritance for men at a father's death and dowry payments for women at the time of marriage) and local markets for land, labor, and commodities. These social practices assured that rural inhabitants frequently exchanged assets and debts with each other through sale, gift, or deed and recorded their values to preserve their or their off-spring's interests in them. These practices necessitated extensive knowledge of numerical information as well as careful recording of it (Emigh 2002, 2003, 2005).

I argued that a microhistorical comparison of records of events could illuminate how rural individuals used numerical information. The three microhistories, each based separately on sets of comparisons, although interesting, are much more powerful when combined. Alone, each one provides less information than the combination, because the findings of each one largely confirm the findings that tax incentives, while not disregarded, are not paramount. Thus the combination shows that each separate microhistorical analysis of some particular feature of a document (for example, how landlords and tenants recorded loans, livestock, and rents; or how rural inhabitants recorded deaths) or some particular small community (the two Mugellan parishes or Montecatini di Valdinievole) is not idiosyncratic. The particular details of each study illustrate more generally how rural inhabitants used numerical information for their own purposes.

Microhistorical studies of this genre will continue to be important in the historiography of late medieval and early modern Europe. Given the nature of the archival evidence (plentiful, but fragmentary), it is unlikely that the level of detail needed to draw conclusions about everyday rural life can be amassed for larger, comprehensive geographical units, such as all of Tuscany, or that biographical narratives can be constructed for many topics of substantive interest. The microhistorical methods presented here suggest some alternatives that can be used to explore the lives of everyday, ordinary individuals.

Notes

1. Therefore, several microhistorical sources were discovered while authors were looking for something else (J. Brown 1986:3; Brucker 1986:vii).

2. From Trouillot's (1995:26–27) perspective, the lack of source material creates historical silences that need to be deconstructed through a variety of methods.

3. Opponents of quantitative history argue that quantitative historians use quantification to argue for the scientific rigor and validity of their research (for example, Stone 1979:5–6); whether or not this is true is another issue.

4. Compare Eiss's discussion of microhistory, positivism, and interpretation in this volume and Magnússon's (2003:712–14) discussion of microhistory and social science methodology.

11

Anomalies, Clues, and Neglected Transcripts

Microhistory and Representations of the Cuban Sugar Frontier, 1820–1860

Dale Tomich

The practice of microhistorians is significant not only for its rich and innovative interpretations of singular historical phenomena but also for its distinctive approach to the use of documentary evidence. What has come to be known as *microhistoria* in Italy developed as a response to serial history practiced by the French Annales school, most prominently Fernand Braudel, with which it has maintained a complex relation even while following an independent and, in a certain sense, opposite path of development (Ginzburg 1993; Ginzburg and Poni 1991). For Braudel and the *annalistes*, serial history offers a scientific and strongly quantitative approach to historical analysis that seeks to identify spatial-temporal structures and establish causal relations between them. Its evidentiary paradigm is concerned with repetition, regularity, and quantity. Serial history is not interested in the individual document, but in series of documents and the relations between them. It selects and constructs documents as a function of their repetitive character (Furet and Le Goff 1973:231, cited in Ginzburg 1993:18; Ginzburg 1993:21). Through what Carlo Ginzburg refers to as a process of "equalization of individuals," it disregards particulars and cognitively recognizes only what is homogenous and comparable. Thus serial history has no place for the documentarily unique. The individual document is significant only through its relation to the other documents in the series.

In contrast, microhistory embraces the singular, the peculiar, the out of series, the anomalous. Microhistorical methods are particularly appropriate for close analysis of highly circumscribed phenomena, such as a village community, a group of families, or an individual person, event, or object. In contrast to the scientific criteria claimed by serial history, the evidential and conjectural approaches with which microhistory is concerned are highly qualitative. They employ interpretive techniques to examine objects, situations, and documents that are understood as singular objects of study rather than repetitive and quantifiable phenomena. The purpose of their inquiry is not to establish general laws but to derive scientific knowledge from such individual instances. They pursue this end not by incorporating the object of inquiry into a series but by interpreting its relation to its contexts.

This approach accepts the evidentiary and theoretical limits imposed by the reduction in scale of its subject matter. At the same time, it remains alert to new, often fragmentary sources and seeks new ways of interpreting them (Ginzburg 1993:28). For microhistorians, the exceptional or improbable document offers the richest interpretive potential (Ginzburg 1993:33). Carlo Ginzburg emphasizes the importance of clues or traces in the practice of microhistory. He recalls the hunter, the diviner, the detective, the art critic, and the psychoanalyst whose skill in "reading" apparently insignificant, infinitesimal, and highly individual evidence leads to comprehension of a complex and otherwise inaccessible reality. By the nineteenth century, the human sciences, strongly influenced by the epistemological and social prestige of medicine, increasingly accepted what Ginzburg refers to as "the conjectural paradigm of semiotics." Because of the individualizing perspective that characterizes such disciplines, they produce results that possess what Ginzburg describes as an "unsuppressible speculative margin" (Ginzburg 1989a:96–125, esp. 105–7).

In such contexts, Ginzburg argues, analysis of particular clues or traces may serve as "indications of more general phenomena: the worldview of a social class, a single writer, or an entire society" (Ginzburg 1989:123–24; for examples of this approach, see Ginzburg 1976, 2000). Yet such indications of more comprehensive phenomena are not achieved by a logic of analogy or by insertion into a series. The relation between microhistorical and macrohistorical levels is necessarily discontinuous and heterogeneous. The results of fragmentary and singular microhistorical analysis cannot automatically be transferred to the more general sphere and vice versa. Consequently, microhistory establishes broader meanings by narrating the relation of its research to its specific contexts. The irreducible margin of speculation of microhistorical accounts and the discontinuity between them and their macrohistorical contexts necessarily introduce lacunae, uncertainties, and misrepresentations into such accounts. Rather than attempting to eliminate such ambiguity, doubt, and speculation, microhistorians insist that these elements form part of the narrative. Thus microhistorical analysis is unavoidably incomplete, conjectural, and uncertain (Ginzburg 1989:23–24, 33).

LOS INGENIOS AND MICROHISTORICAL STRATEGIES

This chapter examines what can only be described as an exceptional document of nineteenth-century Cuban economic and social history. *Los Ingenios: Colección de vistas de los principales ingenios de azúcar de la isla de Cuba*, by Eduardo Laplante and Justo Cantero, provides an incomparable record of the technological transformation of the Cuban sugar industry through precise visual and textual descriptions of representative sugar plantations (*ingenios*). Laplante's striking lithographs of sugar mills and their machinery are accompanied by Cantero's detailed inventories of the productive organization of each plantation. Taken together, image and text allow us to comprehend the dramatic technical and spatial reorganization of sugar production realized by Cuban planters at the moment they first dominated world production.

Not inappropriately, economic and social historians have integrated the information contained in *Los Ingenios* into documentary series constructing the history of the Cuban sugar plantation and slavery (Moreno Fraginals 1978, 1: esp. 198, 223, 231; 2: 31, 69, 71, 73). On the other hand, art historians have viewed the images as part of the history of representations of nineteenth-century Cuban life and the development of lithography in Cuba (Juan 1985:28–29, 32–39; Rigol 1982:152–55). However, close examination of *Los Ingenios* discloses anomalous elements that resist incorporation into these serial accounts. As economic and art historians pursue their own ends without particular regard for one another, such disregarded elements appear precisely in the relation between modes of representation and the objects presented. These materials lend themselves to the analytical and interpretive strategies of microhistory. They provide clues to historical discourse that fall outside the constituted serial histories and have been neglected by scholars with other interests. Microhistorical analysis of these anomalies suggests neglected transcripts that deepen our understanding of both the work and the historical transformation of the Cuban sugar frontier. Juxtaposition of microhistorical and macrohistorical narratives discloses the multifaceted and complex construction of *Los Ingenios* and suggests ways in which the neglected transcripts subtly shape reception of the book's technological and economic information. *Los Ingenios* thus provides a privileged site for examining how different evidentiary and narrative paradigms may operate together in a single work to produce distinct but interrelated levels of meaning. In this way, microhistorical perspectives contribute to new terrains of historical knowledge by reinterpreting the results of other approaches.

THE MAKING OF *LOS INGENIOS*

Regarded by many as the most beautiful book ever published in Cuba, *Los Ingenios* was published in 1857 by the Havana press of Luis Marquier. It was the product of the collaboration of French lithographer and engineer Eduardo Laplante and Cuban sugar planter Justo Germán Cantero Anderson. Cantero, patron of the project, was one of the most prominent planters in his native city of Trinidad. Born in 1815 in the midst of the sugar boom in Trinidad, he went to Boston to complete his education. In 1837 he obtained a medical degree from Harvard University (Venegas 1966:90). Upon his return to Cuba, the young surgeon played an important social role in the society of Trinidad. Nonetheless, he lacked the resources to start his own plantation. However, in 1842 Cantero married María de Monserrate Fernández de Lara, widow and heir of his friend Pedro Iznaga, owner of several sugar mills. Cantero began to invest rapidly in sugar production. He joined together three of the five sugar mills under his wife's control and purchased the newest technology available, including a vacuum pan manufactured by the French firm of Derosne and Cail. Cantero was one of the first three planters in Cuba to acquire one of these machines (at a cost of one hundred thousand pesos). He installed it at his Güinía de Soto plantation under the personal supervision of Charles Derosne.

Los Ingenios was intended both to provide a testimonial to the scientific and technical progress of the Cuban sugar planters and to propagate technological innovations in the Cuban sugar industry. Initially sold by subscription in *separadas*, it clearly had sugar planters as its primary intended audience. The book is distinguished by twenty-six superb color plates, created by Laplante, showing the most important sugar mills in Cuba. These images are accompanied by detailed descriptions of each mill, written by Cantero. *Los Ingenios* took full advantage of the possibilities for the mass production and circulation of images offered by the new art of lithography. No expense was spared in the production of the book. Its oversized format, high-quality paper, strikingly colored plates, and carefully documented text created a deluxe volume. *Los Ingenios* was the first book of its type to be published by a Cuban press. Until its appearance, there had been no body of specialized work about sugar, only isolated articles and memorials. However, Cantero cautioned that the book was not a detailed chronological or natural history of cane, or a systematic treatise on sugar manufacture. Rather, he stated, "we will only limit ourselves to the notes we took for each estate in order to provide some interesting information, to make a brief analysis of each, and to practically demonstrate the mode of operation, the terrains in which the cane thrives best, and the refining equipment that is now in use in the island."

The format of the book was novel. It was presented in the form of a travel book, a genre made popular by lithography. Superficially, it appeared as a tour of the great sugar plantations, replicating the social calendar of the planter elite. But instead of having the customary content of a travel book, it conveyed information about the advantageous effects of technological innovation in sugar manufacturing (Venegas 1966:88). Laplante's images were made in the region around Havana, Matanzas, the heart of the new sugar frontier, and in Cantero's native province of Trinidad. According to Cantero, the mills that were selected are "those that are most notable for the large scale of their production, those that have established some improvements or reforms of recognized utility, and those that because of their particular circumstances shed some light on the sphere of production and elaboration or give some useful idea for its history." In a certain sense, *Los Ingenios* might be seen as an early attempt at industrial advertising or economic propaganda. Technically precise information is here presented in a way that appeals as much to the senses as to the intellect. At the same time, the presentation of the material in the book has affinities with the trade fair or industrial exposition. (It is perhaps worth remembering that 1851 was the year of the Great Exhibition in London.)

Eduardo Laplante was particularly well qualified to execute the images in *Los Ingenios*. Born in France around 1818, he moved to Cuba about 1848. Lithography was well established in Cuba, in part because of the tobacco industry's need for decorative images to be used on cigar bands and boxes; Laplante was one of many French lithographers responsible for its precocious development. As well as a distinguished painter and lithographer, he was the representative for a construction firm that erected machinery for sugar mills. Laplante resided in Havana and traveled throughout the interior, visiting the principal cities of Cuba. His work for the construction firm brought him into contact with some of the most important planters of the period, including Cantero, and made him familiar with sugar production and Cuban sugar mills. In 1849 he established himself as a lithographer and dedicated himself principally to lithography.

Laplante's images in *Los Ingenios* celebrate an industrialized and economically rationalized countryside as an emblem of progress. He develops a distinctive documentary style that in some ways anticipates photography in detail and precision of image and is particularly appropriate for the technological character of his subject matter. The twenty-eight images drawn from nature that he created for *Los Ingenios* are intended to accurately depict the sugar mills and their productive apparatus. These unsentimental images combine illustrative elements with a topological and documentary approach that emphasizes accurate observation and measurement. Laplante offers what is clearly among the nineteenth century's most complete graphic accounts of a process of manufacture and distribution.

Laplante's knowledge of the sugar industry and his approach to lithographic representation allow him to document the technological transformation of the Cuban countryside and to accurately depict new techniques of sugar production. More particularly, Laplante's lithographs visually represent the spatial articulation of material processes of production, the new milling and refining machinery, and the architecture of the slave plantation on the Cuban sugar frontier. Laplante's images are accompanied by Cantero's notes on each plantation. These include brief descriptions of each property and its buildings, but they concentrate on providing precise data about the amount of land cultivated, the types of cane, the technical features of the machinery, the capacity of the mill and refinery, the size and composition of the labor force, how the production process is organized, and the output of each ingenio. Cantero's text complements Laplante's images by providing technical information that cannot be readily conveyed visually, and it allows a comparative analysis of the technical characteristics and political economy of each mill. According to Manuel Moreno Fraginals, the preeminent historian of the Cuban sugar industry, *Los Ingenios* offers extremely valuable information on the largest sugar mills in Cuba in the 1850s, and the plates are beyond reproach from a technical point of view because of the meticulous attention to detail with which the machinery is reproduced (Moreno Fraginals 1978, 3:189–90). (From the point of view of technical representation, the book may be compared with Charles

Derosne's treatise on sugar manufacturing, with its precise engineering drawings of some of the same apparatuses depicted by Laplante. Derosne's manual was translated into Spanish and published in Cuba in 1844, one year after its original appearance in France.)

THE CUBAN SUGAR FRONTIER, 1820–1860

Los Ingenios appeared at the end of the first phase of Cuba's rise to domination of world sugar production. Beginning in 1792, around the time of the Haitian Revolution, the emergent Cuban planter class, centered in Havana, engineered perhaps one of the most dramatic transformations in the history of Latin American agriculture. On the basis of free trade in sugar and slaves, the extension and intensification of slave labor, and the systematic application of science and industry to agriculture, the planters created the most dynamic zone of sugar production in the world during the first half of the nineteenth century. Cuban planters had to place their product in expanding and increasingly competitive world markets that were driven by industrialization, urbanization, and the erosion of economic protectionism. Through the creation of an open commodity frontier (J. Moore 2000), they successfully mobilized land and slave labor on a massive scale and harnessed them to the most modern sugar refining technology available. Cuban planters realized unprecedented economies of scale and levels of productivity and efficiency, which enabled them to dominate world sugar production and set world prices. Cuba's output doubled each decade from the 1820s until the 1860s. By 1830 Cuba had emerged as the world's leading sugar producer, with an output of more than one hundred thousand metric tons. By 1848 Cuba accounted for one-fourth of the world's sugar supply.

New milling and refining technologies were first developed in the European beet sugar industry and were later adapted to tropical sugarcane. The technological transformation of cane sugar production entailed systematic application of physics and chemistry to manufacturing, the deployment of steam power and large-scale machinery, and the adoption of new varieties of cane. Produced in factories in Lille, Glasgow, and West Point, New York, the new industrial technologies included not only extremely large and powerful steam mills but most importantly the vacuum pan and centrifuge. These devices revolutionized sugar production and transformed it from an artisanal craft into a scientific process subject to precise measurement and control. They extracted more juice from the cane and obtained more and higher quality sugar from the syrup. However, these new technologies required an exponential increase in capital investment and scale of production. The successful utilization of these machines was possible only by proportionally increasing the area under cultivation and the size of the labor force.

The availability of extensive lands in the interior of the island with ideal conditions for sugarcane cultivation enabled Cuban planters to successfully adopt the new refining technologies and allowed the sugar boom to occur. However, these territories could be opened to sugar cultivation only with new means of transportation. The formation of the Cuban sugar frontier directly required and was made possible by the railroad. In 1837, thirteen years after the first railroad in England, a rail link was completed between Havana and Güines. It was the first railroad in Latin America. Built for and financed by the emergent sugar elite, rail transport opened new territories in the interior of Cuba to sugar cultivation (Zanetti and García 1998:18–124). The railroad gave Cuba a "frontier advantage." The only obstacles to the expansion of sugar production were dispersed cattle-raising *hatos*, which were quickly converted into more lucrative sugar plantations. The forest was destroyed, and non-sugar-producing populations were displaced (Funes Monzote 2004:213–74). With each increase in productive capacity of technology, Cuban planters could bring new lands under cultivation, increase the scale of plantations, and bring more labor to bear on production. The unprecedented combination of land, technology, and slave labor created enormous new sugar estates and shaped the remarkable plantation landscapes depicted in *Los Ingenios*.

LOS INGENIOS: DOCUMENTING THE INDUSTRIALIZATION OF CUBAN AGRICULTURE

Los Ingenios offers what is in some ways an unsurpassed record of sugar production and the transformation of the Cuban countryside. Not only the technical accuracy of the images but also the book's representational strategies establish its documentary character. The way in which the images are presented, what is included, what is excluded, the order, emphasis, and modes of representation are necessarily part of the text. Careful attention to such representational devices discloses an analysis of the technological, spatial, and social transformations of the Cuban ingenio and enables us to understand the relations and processes ordering the social landscape of sugar.

Although at first glance the album appears to represent a wandering journey through the Cuban countryside, the images and text are arranged in a way that provides an analytical and symbolic cross section of the sugar plantation. (This combination of illustration and scientific observation and analysis recalls Alexander von Humboldt. The use of the cross section also suggests the botanical drawings typical of the traveler-artists of nineteenth-century Latin America [Catlin 1989b:41–62].) The presentation begins with an image of new warehouses in Regla, from which sugar was shipped abroad. These modern structures were designed to facilitate the transshipment of an unprecedented quantity of sugar. After emphasizing the countryside's link to world markets in the first image, the authors present two sugar estates. These serve as typological markers for the subsequent treatment of individual plantations. The next image is a wide panorama of the Valley of Magdalena outside Matanzas, one of the first areas to be incorporated into the new sugar zone. It gives an overview of the transformation of the landscape by the sugar boom and depicts the dense distribution of ingenios across the valley. Portraits of individual sugar estates follow this image. These alternate between exterior views of the plantation complex, which significantly emphasize the productive organization of the estate rather than the planter's house, and interior views of the mill and refinery that focus on the technologies and processes of sugar manufacture. Careful attention to the interior views reveals that each is presented from a different perspective. Taken together, they offer a systematic exposition of the machinery and work processes entailed in each step of the manufacturing process, much in the style of a cyclorama.

The detailed pictorial and textual descriptions of individual plantations combine to form a typological account that documents the technical evolution of the ingenio as a productive enterprise and the productive spaces and geography of the Cuban sugar economy. From this perspective, the sugar mills appear as repetitive and quantifiable economic units. Together, text and images provide an inventory of agro-industrial techniques operative in mid-nineteenth-century Cuban sugar mills. The objective, detailed, technically accurate representations allow measurement, the formation of typologies, and systematic qualitative and quantitative comparison of inputs and outputs, mills, and machinery at each stage of sugar production.

The overall effect of the work is to present an image of the achievements and advantages of technological innovation and of the planters as agents of science, progress, and modernity (at the expense of adequately representing the other condition of the new plantation zone—slave and indentured Chinese labor). Indeed, the machines are the centerpiece, if not the purpose, of the entire exposition. The images depict the harvest season, when the impact of the machines is most evident. The representations of milling and refining technologies give order and meaning to the other images. On the one hand, the other images are arranged to increase the dramatic presentation of the machines, which are the culmination of each sequence. On the other hand, the organization and sequencing of the images demonstrate how the machines order the spaces of the plantation; the scale and location of the fields, form and disposition of the buildings, arrangement of interior space, and organization of the transportation system are all determined by the productive capacity of the new milling and refining techniques and the speed and continuity required for their operation. Machines appear as the animating force of the plantation. They articulate the particular spatial and social organization of production on each individual estate and unify the overall composition of the landscape. The plantation is presented as virtually a self-activating agro-industrial mechanism.

THE PICTURESQUE: AN ANOMALOUS TRACE

Los Ingenios offers its readers a sophisticated and highly effective visual and textual document of the technological and productive characteristics of the Cuban sugar mill at mid-century. Yet in the midst of the text, brief passages are at variance with the technical descriptions that Cantero offers. For example, he notes the picturesque qualities of the Valley of Magdalena:

> Indeed, when seen from the nearby heights, that magnificent prairie, bounded in the distance by picturesque hills, presents such an enchanting view that the imagination cannot easily conceive of a more beautiful one. It is especially so at sunrise or at sunset or in the morning when it shows itself covered with a light mist that gives it the appearance of an immense circular lake above which rise both the crowns of palms swaying softly in the breeze and the roofs of sugar-mills which, here and there, display their high towers crowned by steam and smoke, while at their feet the waving cane, principal foundation of the wealth of our island, spreads its brilliant green.

This brief passage runs against the grain of the text and is easy to overlook. Indeed, Cantero's description of the Valley of Magdalena appears in the midst of an account of the geological formation of the valley, an enumeration of the ingenios located there, and a report on the quantity of sugar shipped annually from the port of Matanzas. Yet a closer reading of *Los Ingenios* reveals that Cantero persistently describes the sugar mills and the industrialized countryside that they created as "picturesque." Throughout the text, he uses this term to evoke an image of the vast sweep of green cane fields, dotted by the orderly clusters of plantation buildings and clumps of palms, all enveloped in the distant hills under the tropical sun.

Initially, Cantero's repeated use of the term *picturesque* seems curious but insignificant. Indeed, his use of the concept appears to be merely ornamental and has no documentary function. Yet, on further reflection, its discordance with both the textual and visual narratives is evident. The term not only signals a break from Cantero's emphasis on the technological and economic characteristics of the ingenio but also seems to be at variance with Laplante's images of machinery and the industrialized landscape. Cantero's repeated reference to the "picturesque" landscape appears as an anomaly in the text and cannot be assimilated into the documentary series constructing the technological and economic history of the Cuban sugar mill. At the same time, it has drawn little, if any, attention from art historians, whose interest is in the images and the history of lithography. Hence the term has not been the subject of scholarly discussion. Yet it is precisely the anomalous character of Cantero's use of *picturesque* that reveals it as a verbal trace, a clue to the presence of another level of meaning contained within *Los Ingenios*. This term calls attention to the relation between industry and nature, an implicit but neglected dimension of the book's industrial narrative. It thus offers a key to another interpretation of the images and text of *Los Ingenios*, permitting us to understand the symbolic construction of the work and to reexamine conventional understandings of both the book and the historical processes that it documents.

SPECIFYING THE PICTURESQUE IN CUBA

It is difficult, however, to interpret Cantero's anomalous and fragmentary references to the picturesque. No documentary evidence is available to let us examine Cantero's motives and purposes with regard to his use of this concept. The paucity of documentary evidence remains a limit for any attempt to recuperate Cantero's use of the term *picturesque* and calls attention to the necessarily uncertain and speculative nature of any such endeavor. Further, the term *picturesque* is itself highly plastic. Nonetheless, it is difficult to associate the subject matter of *Los Ingenios* with the picturesque of eighteenth-century English landscape painting (Bermingham 1986). Conceptions of the picturesque, with regard to what it entails and the objects to which the name is applied, underwent profound transformation in the Americas during the first part of the nineteenth century. Central to this reconceptualization of landscape was Alexander von Humboldt, but it is equally difficult to assimilate *Los Ingenios* into the tropical picturesque of nineteenth-century artist-travelers in Latin America such as Humboldt, Debret, and Rugendas (Catlin 1989a, 1989b). In addition, various travel albums published in Cuba at the same time as *Los Ingenios* used the term *picturesque* in their titles (Lapique 1974), but none depict the starkly industrial landscapes of the sugar frontier or employ such consciously technical and documentary modes of representation. Thus Cantero's use of *picturesque* appears anomalous with regard to more broadly accepted uses of the term.

However, from the perspective of microhistory, the problem is not to recover Cantero's conception by integrating into it the serial history of planter *mentalité* or the picturesque idea. His use of the term is singular and circumscribed. There is no evidence of similar texts or that any other planter deployed the term in an analogous manner. It remains a specific mode of expression of a single individual that cannot be automatically transferred to a larger sphere. It cannot be taken as a typical representative of a broader or more general collective phenomenon or integrated into a series of evidence constructing planter consciousness or the Cuban picturesque. (Here we may say that Cantero could have been only a Cuban sugar planter but that not all Cuban sugar planters were Cantero.) Thus, given the singular and anomalous nature of the evidence, microhistorical practices allow us to attempt to recuperate the role and meaning of Cantero's usage by interpreting it within the specific textual and historical contexts provided by *Los Ingenios* and by the conjuncture of the Cuban sugar boom.

In the absence of other evidence, we might approach the specificity of Cantero's use of *picturesque* by contrasting it with the conception of English landscape painting discussed by Ann Bermingham (1986). The purpose of this comparison is not to recover an authentic meaning for the picturesque, to insert Cantero's usage into the history of the picturesque idea, or to criticize him for degrading or banalizing the term. Rather, the purpose of the comparison is to ascertain, as far as possible, how Cantero implicitly or explicitly construes the concept of picturesque, as well as the justifications and functions of his usage. By thus examining the role of the picturesque in *Los Ingenios*, we may to some degree illuminate the relations between culture, industry, and nature that structure the work and shape its meaning. Such a reflection is especially interesting and germane because Bermingham posits that the English picturesque of the late eighteenth and early nineteenth century was itself a response to agrarian enclosures, economic improvement, and capitalist agriculture.

During the 1790s, picturesque theory developed in England both as a category of painting and as a category of landscape based on an aesthetic valorization of nature and the natural. It posited an exceptionally close, precise, and formal relation between artistic representation and nature. According to Bermingham, "[A]pplied to landscape, the term picturesque referred to its fitness to make a picture; applied to pictures, the term referred to the fidelity with which they copied the picturesque landscape" (Bermingham 1986:57). The Reverend William Gilpin, an important figure in articulating the picturesque aesthetic, distinguished between the beautiful and the picturesque. In his view, "the picturesque referred to those objects which please the eye in their *natural state*, in contrast to those, which please from some quality, capable of being illustrated by *painting*" (cited in Bermingham 1986:63). Gilpin insisted that "rough, irregular, and various" objects were more appropriate for picturesque painting than beautiful ones, whose smooth, neat qualities lacked pictorial definition (Bermingham 1986:64).

Bermingham argues that Gilpin's conception of the picturesque changed the focus from painting nature to observing the picturesque in nature. This valorization of nature operated a double displacement away from art and the painterly reproduction of nature. On the one hand, picturesque sensibility became a mark of cultivated taste, the capacity to observe and record the "real" landscape in the countryside itself. On the other hand, the picturesque landscape in nature was necessarily superior to its representations. In Gilpin's conception, art derives its validity from nature, and nature becomes the standard for judging art. This dependence on the authority of nature closely linked the picturesque to place. The picturesque ideal referred to the native English landscape, which was regarded as its embodiment, just as the Alps were the embodiment of the sublime. The harmonious vision of the countryside represented by the picturesque landscape itself became a fundamental symbol of English identity and English virtues.

The tension between art and nature engendered by Gilpin's notion of the picturesque reached its climax in Uvedale Price's concept of the landscape garden. Price criticized the inadequacy of human artifice and regarded the picturesque as the product of nature. He set the picturesque aesthetic against the improved, economically productive landscape, industry, and commerce. The picturesque landscape was created by time and accident, not human industry and investment. Although he was a gentleman farmer, his ideal countryside appeared old, timeless, and worn out, its overgrown and irregular features dotted with tumbledown cottages and peopled with vagabonds and beggars. Bermingham contends that Price's preference for the picturesque did not represent a protest against the effects of enclosure on rural society or the longing for a past golden age. Rather, Price sought to create an aesthetic ideal that provided a privileged refuge from the operation of agrarian capitalism on the landscape. The aestheticization of the countryside was intended to mute the injustices that caused popular unrest and democratic leveling in neighboring France (Bermingham 1986:66–68).

In contrast to the English landscape theorists, Cantero does not construe the picturesque as a natural property of landscape and hence as an anti-industrial motif. For him, culture in the Cuban sugar zone does not find its justification in nature. Rather, it finds justification in production, in the "rational exploitation" of nature—improvement and progress. (As Bermingham argues, this production is exactly what English landscape painting seeks to conceal.) The nature presented in *Los Ingenios* is a "second nature" dominated by a nonnative plant—sugarcane—that is industrially produced for the world market. By implication, tropical nature (*el monte*) may perhaps be seen as profligate, primeval, degraded, and unproductive. The story of the Cuban sugar frontier is the story of taming, or more precisely destroying, this primal nature.

Cantero's picturesque contributes to the creation of an agrarian industrial aesthetic based on the direct economic rationalization of agriculture and the countryside. The aesthetically pleasing landscape is the productive one. In contrast to the English picturesque, the distinction between art and nature collapses here, not because nature assumes authority over art but because human artifice is represented as nature. In interpreting the thoroughness of industrial transformation and the remaking of both physical and social-economic space, Cantero unifies and orders the documentary elements in the work through their relation to his conception of picturesque nature. He posits a harmony between transformed nature and the machine. Picturesque nature is made through industrial rationality that is then naturalized in a way that presents the landscape as the self-evident and inevitable combination of nature and reason. On the one hand, it aestheticizes transformed or second nature. On the other hand, it sanctions industry and the industrial landscape by incorporating them into nature and treating them as if they were natural phenomena. Industry transforms nature: nature provides the material for industry, becomes its geophysical foundation, and finally absorbs industry into it as one of its constituent elements. Each mediates the other. From the perspective of Cantero's picturesque, technology appears to organize nature as though it were itself a natural process of creating order. By thus regarding the economic ratio-

FIGURE 11.1

Ingenio San Rafael. Reproduced from J. G. Cantero and E. Laplante, Los Ingenios de Cuba. *Barcelona: Levi Marrero, 1984.*

nalization of space as natural and depicting the countryside as the harmonious union of sugar and nature, Cantero's picturesque validates the subordination of nature to private property, industry, and the distinctive geometry of sugar cultivation and manufacture (fig. 11.1).

The aesthetic interpretation of the industrial landscape made by Cantero's picturesque deemphasizes the role of labor in the productive processes of the sugar estate. As the laborers involved are slaves and indentured workers, this absence is clearly highly charged and gives an ideological caste to the whole presentation. But there may be diverse aesthetic, ideological, and political motives for the underrepresentation of labor: the conventions of landscape painting play down the presence of human figures (see Barrell 1980); the presence of slaves may be seen as incompatible with the work's discourse of industrial progress and modernity; and, finally, the proslavery authors may simply have wished to avoid calling attention to slavery, and therefore the potential fragility of the sugar regime, at a time when servile labor was heavily contested by abolitionism and slave resistance. In contrast to the prominent position of the machines, field workers are extremely difficult to find. Indeed, there are far fewer field workers depicted than would be required by the scale of the mills. Laborers in the mills and refineries appear to epitomize "machine tenders." They appear in leisurely postures and activities, almost as if they were ornaments decorating the works. Cartage and transport are more prominent in the images, but they are present as the anonymous flow of cane from field to mill, not as the physical activity of humans and animals. Although virtually every task entailed in the sugar harvest is depicted, the underemphasis on slave workers in itself idealizes plantation labor.

In both the English and Cuban landscape, nature is the sign of property and property is the sign of nature. But in Cuba, nature is subsumed by industry. Nature signifies class in Cantero, but nature is the justification of class only insofar as it is the bearer of progress, civilizing reason, and accumulation—that is, it is a transformed, rational, and productive nature. Class signifies a dominated and particular nature and an attendant set of cultural values, not a universal nature that itself justifies class. In the Cuban landscape, the representation of rationalized nature refers directly to the wealth and power of the owners and celebrates their agency (even as it obscures the exploitation of the slave and contract labor upon which the whole enterprise depends). The señor transforms nature; land valorizes power and wealth. Landed proprietors appear not as directors or managers but as the productive agents of capital whose productive wealth sets in motion and sustains the transformative power of machine technology. This process allows the formation of an ideology of universal progress. The Cuban planters' claim to universality is made not through nature or the dominion over slave labor but through science and technology. They are simply agents of a universal march of scientific and technological progress.

ORDERING IMAGE AND TEXT: THE NATURALIZATION OF INDUSTRY

Cantero's use of the term *picturesque* calls attention to a neglected dimension of *Los Ingenios*. Whether intentionally or unintentionally, this term constructs a specific conception of the relation between nature and industry. This conception not only subtly shapes the meaning of the textual materials in the book, it also calls attention to the representational elements that integrate the industrial and natural motifs in Laplante's landscapes and codifies a logic of representation that is also operative in his images. Laplante's lithographs aestheticize and naturalize the tedious geometry of this rationalized agro-industrial countryside (even as they of course provide valuable documentary material). The focal point of his landscapes is the cluster of manufacturing buildings presented in minute detail. Beyond them are endless plantings of sugar divided into regular quadrangles to facilitate calculation of daily production quotas during harvest and transportation of raw material to the mill. In a great many of Laplante's images, long lines of oxcarts carrying cane to the mill unite field and factory and demonstrate the material coherence of the countryside. These images are visually framed, ordered, and unified by means of a variety of representational techniques whose origins go back to Dutch landscape painting of the seventeenth century. Laplante's choice of perspective, horizon, and construction of foreground, middle ground, and background, together with his use of trees, smokestacks, and other devices as *repoussoir* elements, creates a distinct sense of space. The number, type, and placement of human figures, together with the stylistic conventions for depicting them, contribute to an almost theatrical setting, while color, season, and time of day shape the viewer's response to the image. The interplay of representational techniques and documentary information visually unifies machine technology and nature and presents a harmonious image of the sugar factory that reconciles industrial and natural orders in a manner congruent with Cantero's use of the picturesque.

The way text and image work together through Cantero's conception of the picturesque to interpret the relation between nature and sugar production may be seen in the treatment of the Valley of Magdalena. Cantero notes that the valley is remarkable for its fertility and its picturesque landscapes. Seen from the top of Paraíso Hill, it offers the viewer "a magnificent panorama." Cantero describes the valley as

> a softly undulating terrain of green hills five leagues across. Charming groves of trees crowned by slender palms and the picturesque buildings of a great number of sugar-mills stand out like oases in a desert of verdure. In the background, the city of Matanzas, the bay with its woods, and finally the sea with its unfathomable immensity frame everything. This magnificent picture gives a perfect idea of the rich vegetation of the tropics.

Laplante's lithograph of the valley is a broad panorama of a specific location, seen from a prominence at the valley's edge, perhaps the heights of Paraíso Hill. Its organization first draws attention to the foreground. There, a gentlemanly figure on horseback passes along a rough roadway in front of a clump of trees. The trees, evidently part of a grove that clings to a rocky and uncultivable hillside, dominate the picture. They divide the image and create the picture's perspective. In contrast to theatrical settings, which frame the sides and center a distant horizon, here the eye moves from the foreground out to a broad vista that is almost imperceptibly framed by distant hills and the sea. This perspective visually unifies the landscape in a way that delineates the valley's natural features as a great bowl opening to the sea. (This effect is accentuated by the diagonal plane of light illuminating

FIGURE 11.2

Valley of Magdalena. Reproduced from J. G. Cantero and E. Laplante, Los Ingenios de Cuba.
Barcelona: Levi Marrero, 1984.

the hills and leading the eye to the far right horizon and by the extension
of the curve of the road, which leads the eye toward the city of Matanzas on
the far left horizon.) The topography frames the picture (fig. 11.2).

This organization of perspective heightens the dramatic impact of the
image's content—the industrialized and rationalized landscape of the valley itself. The valley appears literally as a sea of sugarcane punctuated by
the chimneys of sugar mills scattered across its surface. (There are eighteen mills, each of which Cantero identifies in the text.) Aside from those
in the foreground, the only trees that appear in the picture demarcate
property lines or are planted along roadways. They thus emphasize the
geometry of property and cane planting that organizes the valley floor. Off
in the distance, on the left side of the image, is the port city of Matanzas,
and beyond it is the sea. Here the picture portrays, and indeed emphasizes,
the economic geography and unity of the valley (as opposed to its physical
unity)—sugar mills, the port city, and the sea that carries its produce to
world markets. Seen from this perspective, the landscape indicates industry (and, by means of the smokestacks, modernity), commerce, and prosperity. On the other hand, the tranquility of the countryside suggests the
unity and harmony of industrial order with nature.

There are two visual tensions here. The vestigial trees that organize this
perspective can recall only the original forest that was destroyed by the

arrival of the cane fields (Funes Monzote 2004). (The forest was cleared both for planting cane and to supply fuel to mills.) This scene, of course, confirms the massive reworking of nature by human intervention. The industrial background provided by the image also belies the aristocratic associations of the caballero in the foreground. Indeed, closer examination reveals that the rider shares the highway with a *tropero* (driver), who is driving what appear to be oxen, or more likely a pack train of mules.

This image of the Valley of Magdalena creates the visual frame of reference for the exterior views of the individual plantations in the rest of the book. These images focus on the buildings (*batey*) of particular estates. Although these properties are distant from the Valley of Magdalena, they are portrayed in a similar topography and landscape of uninterrupted cane fields that extends to (often identifiable) neighboring estates. The continuity of cane fields is broken only by occasional hills or lines of palms that demarcate property boundaries. It is as though we are zooming in from the broad view of the sugar belt for a closer and more detailed view of particular mills. This organization of the images calls attention to the uniformity of landscape, the economically rational organization of space created by the geography of sugar, and the seriality of the sugar mill.

The concept of the picturesque and the treatment of nature in Cantero's text and Laplante's lithographs project the congruity and harmony of the natural landscape and the sugar landscape. Together, they structure the representation of vegetation—cane fields, residual forests, and pasture—and the geometric patterns of cultivation as they are broken by natural features—waterways, sky, and light—and punctuated by architectural features in ways that depict the preeminent suitability and adaptability of nature to the needs of the sugar industry. Sugar and nature are made to conform to one another. The natural landscape seems to be made for sugar, and sugar appears as the natural destiny of the land. The picturesque gives authority to this association and stamps the fateful union as the mark of inevitable progress. Thus, far from being simply a curious anomaly that can be neglected without consequence, Cantero's picturesque creates and interprets the meaning of the documentary information presented in *Los Ingenios*. Through it, Cantero's text and Laplante's images participate in the aesthetic appropriation of the geographical space of Cuba and symbolically construct it as the space of the "sugar island" par excellence.

CONCLUSION

Cantero's use of the picturesque offers a clue that, through the perspective of microhistory, reveals the complex evidentiary and hermeneutic structure of *Los Ingenios*. This anomalous fragment intrudes, almost unconsciously, on the consciously documentary account of the industrial transformation of the Cuban countryside presented in *Los Ingenios*, and it is easily overlooked. Yet this neglected and inassimilable element can be ignored only at great risk, for it subtly interprets the textual and visual materials presented in the work and shapes their meaning.

Cantero's conception of the picturesque—whether deliberately or not—creates a specific interpretation of the relation of the sugar industry to the natural environment and slave labor. By means of the aesthetic appropriation of the landscape, Cantero's conception of the picturesque assimilates the physical environment into the industrial order in ways that construe Cuba as the natural space of sugar. It naturalizes and legitimizes the sugar industry and physical appropriation of the countryside by the planter class and presents the planters as agents of industry, progress, and modernity. The harmonious relation created by this interpretation suppresses tensions and antagonisms that are inextricably part of the formation of the sugar frontier through the production of silence. Cantero's use of the picturesque does not merely remove from consideration the destruction of the forest (Funes Monzote 2004:213–74) and the intensified exploitation of slave labor (Moreno Fraginals 1978, 2:7–75) that were conditions for the creation of the Cuban sugar frontier. Perhaps more decisively, the emphases created in its presentation mask the complex and specific historical interdependence of physical geography, slave labor, and technology and the ways in which each factor of production shapes the development of the others in the process of industrial transformation of sugar production in Cuba. The plantation appears in *Los Ingenios* as virtually a self-activating agro-industrial mechanism set in motion by the planters.

From this perspective, Cantero's picturesque is an ideological construct. It subtly gives specific content to the narrative of science, industry, and progress and creates a transcript of symbolic meanings that support the claims of the planter class for continued transformation of the countryside and hegemony within the Cuban socioeconomic formation. Here, a microhistorical approach discloses how this ideology operates within the evidentiary paradigms of *Los Ingenios* and shows how a single individual in an extremely circumscribed setting may produce, from diverse and in many ways contingent materials, a statement that expresses the collective worldview of a group. If we remain unaware of how, through Cantero's interpretation of the picturesque, *Los Ingenios* produces the significance of its own documentary evidence and places it within an order of symbolic meaning, we may simply remain within the ideological construction of the problem and take these materials at face value.

Note

Research on this project is supported by a collaborative research grant from the Getty Foundation. Discussions with Charles Burroughs of Case Western Reserve University contributed greatly to the elaboration of the ideas in this chapter. I would also like to thank the participants in the seminar "Place, Event, and Narrative Craft: Method and Meaning in Microhistory," held at the School of American Research in Santa Fe, July 20–22, 2005, for their comments and criticisms.

12

Seductions and Betrayals

La frontera gauchesque, Argentine Nationalism, and the Predicaments of Hybridity

James F. Brooks

In 1949 the lion of Argentine literature, Jorge Luis Borges, published an essay of historical and philosophical reflection entitled the "Story of the Warrior and the Captive Maiden." Using one of his trademark devices, he juxtaposed two vignettes vastly separated by time and culture; for Borges, the conflation of these seemingly disconnected stories might reveal their poetic unity. We first meet Droctulft, a barbarian warrior, who in the sixth century AD is sweeping down the plains of Italy with his Germanic tribesmen to lay waste to the Holy Roman Empire. Yet as Droctulft stands before the gates of Ravenna "suddenly blinded and renewed by the City," he comes to understand, in Borges's words, "that this city [was] worth more than his gods and the faith he [had] sworn to and all the marshlands of Germany." Deserting the barbarian host, Droctulft dies in the defense of Ravenna. He could not have read the grateful Latin epitaph the people of Ravenna chiseled upon his tomb: CONTEMPSIT CAROS DUM NOS AMAT ILLE PARENTES, HANC PATRIAM REPUTANS ESSE, RAVENNA, SUAM (He was contemptuous of his beloved ancestors while he loved us like parents, believing Ravenna to be his motherland). Yet some deeper intelligence allowed the barbarian to grasp the enlightened architecture of civilization. In doing so, Borges argued, Droctulft became an *illuminatus*, a convert, anticipating in a single instant the later transformation of these "Longobardi" invaders into the Lombards of northern Italy (Borges 1998:209).[1]

Thirteen hundred years later, we see Borges's own English grandmother strolling the rustic streets of Junín, a frontier outpost west of Buenos Aires, where her husband, Francisco Borges, held a military command in the 1870s. One day she saw "an Indian girl slowly crossing the town square," barefoot, wearing two red ponchos. The roots of her hair, however, were blond. Her coppery face, "painted with fierce colors," held eyes of the "half-hearted blue that the English call gray." Enunciating carefully, Borges's grandmother spoke to the girl, who replied haltingly, searching for words and then repeating them, "as if astonished at the old taste." From that conversation we learn that the girl had been born in Yorkshire and had emigrated with her parents to Buenos Aires, where on the Pampas they had died and she been carried away in an Indian raid. She was now the wife of a minor Araucanian chieftain, whom she had given two sons. Behind her tale, says Borges, "one caught glimpses of a savage and uncouth life: tents of horsehide, fires fueled by dung, celebrations in which the people feasted on meat singed over the fire or on raw viscera, stealthy marches at dawn; the raid on corrals, the alarm sounded, the plunder, the battle, the thundering roundup of stock by naked horsemen, polygamy, stench, and magic." When offered rescue and redemption, the girl refused and "returned that night to the desert." Borges's grandmother thought she saw the girl some years later. In passing a squalid hut in the swampland she beheld a man slitting a sheep's throat. An Indian woman, riding by on horseback, "leapt to the ground and drank up the hot blood." We are left to wonder whether the girl did so "because she was no longer capable of acting in any other way" or "as a challenge, a sign" to her erstwhile English sister. The question of whether this is a tale of seduction or betrayal Borges leaves unresolved (Borges 1998:210).

He concludes his story by uniting the two figures: "the figure of the barbarian who embraced the cause of Ravenna, and the figure of the European woman who chose the wilderness—they might seem conflicting, contradictory. But both were transported by some secret impulse, an impulse deeper than reason, and both embraced that impulse that they would not have been able to explain." Had he stopped here, Borges would have simply displayed his commitment to the poetic philosophy of the Unitaristas—a school of Spanish poets who devoted their work to showing the essential unity of the human condition—a cause he had long embraced. But he goes on (I would argue) to hint that these juxtaposed tales created a powerful metaphor that not only encapsulated the very essence of Argentine history and national identity but also stood ready to resolve the bloody tensions of his country's past: "It may be that the stories I have told are one and the same story. The obverse and reverse of this coin are, in the eyes of God, identical" (Borges 1998:211).

Thus a full century after the publication of Domingo Sarmiento's *Facundo: Or Civilization and Barbarism* (1845), Argentina's greatest writer still saw his country engaged in an almost metaphysical dialectic between seduction and betrayal, between the "civilizing" influences of the western European tradition and the "savage" allure of indigenous life. His poetic solution was to conflate the enticements of civilization and the yearning for barbarism in a "single impulse deeper than reason," the comprehension of which might bring understanding and forgiveness to a people long torn between the two positions. For as Nicholas Shumway has argued, nineteenth-century intellectuals such as Sarmiento who first framed the *idea* of Argentina did so by creating a "peculiarly divisive mind-set" that resulted in a "'society of opposers' as dedicated to humiliating each other as in developing a viable nation through consensus and compromise." On the one hand stood the *porteños* of Buenos Aires, forever attempting to cast Argentina as a nation of cosmopolitans whose "civilized" heritage derived from Europe. Arrayed against them were the peoples of the provinces and their caudillo leadership, forever determined to maintain regional autonomy and control over the pastoral economy of the vast Pampas grasslands. Their staunchly independent mind-set derived, at least in theory, from long and complex associations with the indigenous peoples of the frontier, *los indios barbaros* (Shumway 1991:x–xi).[2]

Of course, the center place in this dialectical tension was presumably occupied by those people we know as the gauchos—rough-hewn, free-living, and culturally intermediate frontier pastoralists whose way of life and political affinities vacillated somewhere between the poles of barbarism and civilization. From Bartolomé Hidalgo's early efforts to create the literary form known as *el genero gauchesco*, through Sarmiento's scathing indictment of the gaucho as cultural impediment to Argentine modernity, to José Hernandez's resuscitation of the gaucho Martín Fierro as Argentina's cultural wellspring, this icon has worked in various ways to link barbarism and civilization (Goodrich 1998; Hernández 1974; Slatta 1983). Whether this literary vision is borne out by on-the-ground history is one question I hope to rethink in this essay, thereby testing two horizons of historical comprehension and expression that hold promise for multiscalar interpretation.[3] Like Maddox, Eiss, Gordon, and Beaudry in this volume, I place biography and structural analysis in conversation with one another.

In a nutshell, I argue that literary fascination with the figure of the gaucho silences and erases a more interesting history—an indigenous Argentine history vastly more complex and meaningful to the pressing concerns of today's world than the classic framing.[4] I'll also suggest that creoles themselves could embrace a more finely grained cultural politics than the civilization–barbarism dualism has implied. Thus I attempt to divert the center of analysis away from the intermediate qualities of the gaucho and refocus in two directions at once: the project of indigenous Argentine nation-building on the one hand and creole Argentine nation-building on the other, in the early nineteenth century. Both focal points—microhistorical in their essence—will illuminate what I term herein the predicaments of hybridity.[5]

Let us look at another story that suggests a more complicated Argentine past. This story comes from the field journal of Luis de la Cruz, a Spanish officer who set out in 1806 to survey a route over the Andean cordillera between Santiago, Chile, and Buenos Aires. A few weeks out of Santiago, a woman was brought before him. He first believed her to be a Pehuenche (People of the Pines) Indian. But her Spanish proved fluent, and in questioning her he discovered that her name was Petronila Pérez, once a resident of Pergamino, west of Buenos Aires. Like Borges's captive maiden, as a child she had lost her parents in an Indian raid, when she, her sister, and two stepbrothers were carried into captivity. When de la Cruz expressed his amazement at her fine Spanish, she explained that she had enjoyed the companionship of many "other women captives who taught me to speak as they did." Now a grown woman, she had married twice among the Pehuenche, once to the brother of the cacique and after his death to the Indian Mariñan. And again, like Borges's maiden, when asked why she did not "return to the Christians," she responded that she "didn't want to leave because I love my children."

Yet there are significant departures in Petronila's tale as well. That she not only retained her childhood Spanish but *increased* her fluency through conversation with other captive Spanish women suggests that either assimilation to a Pehuenche Indian identity did not require the abandonment of her natal tongue, or there existed a relatively durable Spanish-speaking community of women within those Indian peoples. Indeed, later censuses of Spanish captives redeemed from their Indian captors showed a remarkable consistency in this element: while women had generally been held twice as long as their male counterparts, their language shift was only half that of males. We'll see that female Spanish captives were so numerous among Indian groups that a virtual subsociety of such women existed on the Pampas across the nineteenth century. But additional factors played into this enduring cultural liminality. When asked if she did not miss her Spanish kinsfolk, she confessed that her stepbrothers, who had long been freed from captivity, actually visited her annually in her Pehuenche *toldería*, or encampment, at the Salinas Grandes (the great salt pans that provided the principal source for salt in the region). It seems that in one case at least, the boundaries between barbarism and civilization were porous and that dynamic relations of kinship proved the key to membership in the indigenous community, as well as passage between Spanish *and* Indian society.[6]

These two stories—Borges's attempt to find poetic unity in barbarism and civilization, and Petronila's account of her own life—provide a point of entry into larger questions at work in this volume. These involve uncovering the relationships among the intimate experiences of women like Petronila, the middle-range set of negotiations and conflicts between Indian and European peoples along *la frontera pampero*, and the larger acts of imagination and state-building that ultimately cycle back to constrain the way we remember the smaller-scale histories. All these horizons of analysis express themselves—albeit fleetingly, and often multiply—in the form of identities: A Spanish captive woman simultaneously the wife and mother of Pehuenche Indians, a Pehuenche "tribe" composed in no small part of creole captives, or Argentine "nations" at once constituted in the *ayuntamientos* of Buenos Aires or the tolderías at Salinas Grandes. Each presents a predicament of hybridity—a growing realization that the hybrid seldom synthesizes into stable forms but rather maintains a volatile shape-shifting quality that confounds the easy generalization or literary resolution we see attempted in the *gauchesque*. As the editors of another advanced seminar volume argue, "dialogically constituted identities are always re-forming somewhere between positions institutionalized on social terrain and their habitation as it is made meaningful in intimate terms. Identities live through practices of identification" (Holland and Lave 2001:29). And these identifications (I would add) are at once intimate, local, global, and vexingly energetic.

Luis de la Cruz's field journal hints at such larger linkages and destabilizations. Lest we read the foregoing incident as indicative of generally benign relations between these Indians and their creole neighbors (however much that condition was predicated upon violent exchanges of women), we should note another of his observations: from the same Salinas Grandes toldería where Petronila Pérez made her home, he saw three Indian men driving "1,500 or more head of cattle and sheep [westward] to the cordillera." These livestock bore creole brands and clearly had been recently liberated from estancias in Buenos Aires Province. While Petronila's creole

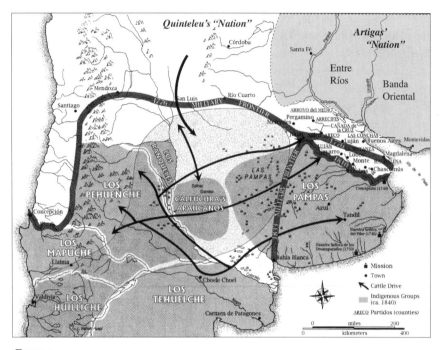

FIGURE 12.1

Locations of the Quinteleu and Artigas "Nations." Map adapted from "The Buenos Aires Region" from Contested Ground, *edited by Donna Guy and Thomas Sheridan © 1998 The Arizona Board Regents. Reprinted by permission of the University of Arizona Press.*

kinsmen might visit her during annual salt expeditions, other creoles would see her encampment as a den of thieves. Indeed, ten years later, Colonel Pedro García (from whom we'll hear more) reported that

> It is no exaggeration to say that in all the frontier lines (from Mendoza to Buenos Aires) cattle theft amounts to more than 40,000 head annually, and perhaps the same amount or more of horses, mares, and mules...making [for] an active seasonal trade selling and exchanging the animals to the Araucanians of the Andes.[7]

Captives and cattle. This is a familiar alliteration to those who study intercultural borderlands across the eighteenth and nineteenth centuries. My own curiosity has led me to engage similar dynamics in the American southwestern borderlands, the Russian Caucasus, and Transorangia in southern Africa. In each case, the pairing is ubiquitous and suggests heretofore hidden histories. But the sheer volume of these victims and commodities becomes overwhelming when we turn to the Argentine Pampas.[8]

Indeed, the colonization of the vast grasslands south of the rivers Paraná and La Plata was first accomplished not by Spanish conquistadores but by the few livestock left behind when Querandí Indians destroyed Pedro Mendoza's first settlement at Buenos Aires in 1537. By the time we take up our story in the late eighteenth century, Spanish observers estimated that the Pampas held some forty-two million head of wild horses and cattle and an indigenous population of perhaps one hundred thousand. By way of comparison, the North American Great Plains at this time saw some twenty million head of bison and horses providing a way of life for approximately eighty thousand equestrian Indian peoples. And just as the Cheyenne, Comanche, Kiowa, and Apache elaborated their distinctive cultural profiles amid pastoral abundance, so too did Pehuenche, Mapuche, Tehuelche, Araucanian, and Pampas peoples experience specific cultural florescence consequent to the pastoral transformation of *their* lands.[9]

Yet they did not do so "naturally"—the social evolution of Argentina's indigenous peoples from horticulturists or transhumant hunters and gatherers to equestrian pastoralists demanded real and often painful social transformation. One distant measure of what must have been momentous social adjustment may again be read from estimates of livestock on the Pampas—by 1800, it seems, only six million head still roamed free. In a period of less than twenty years, fully 85 percent of those once-wild horses and cattle found themselves under the control of creole ranchers south of Buenos Aires or maintained in massive herds by recently "pastoralized" Indian groups. Creoles and Indians leapt into the pastoral economy with a vengeance, for the broader economic vitality associated with the era of the Bourbon reforms provided ready markets for both sides. Creole *estanceros* exported an average of six hundred thousand hides per year through the port of Buenos Aires in the two decades leading up to 1800, while their Indian counterparts delivered their products on the hoof across the cordillera to the west, where buyers in Mendoza and Valdivia, both licit and illicit, purchased them for their meat and hides (Bechis Rosso 1983:70–72; Cooper 1946; Mayo 1995:31; Villalobos 1986:51–60).

Pastoral engagement with market economies—whether through the formal mercantile circuits of Buenos Aires or informal transfers through Mapuche and Huilliche middlemen for resale in Chile or Peru—meant the creation of new labor regimes. Creole ranchers met this need in part through the importation of African slaves (more than 60 percent of late-colonial livestock estancias included such slaves among their workforces) or the bound labor of poor mestizos. Indian groups also recruited unfree labor, first from among their weaker neighbors or from the *gente perdida*—fugitive Africans and militia deserters who fled confinement in the Spanish colony—and finally from the women and children who dwelt on the isolated farms and ranchos that extended beyond the line of protective *fortines* in Buenos Aires Province (Barros 1975; García Enciso 1979). Real numbers of unfree laborers in the Indian pastoral economy are of course impossible to determine, but in those few cases where we can compare redemptions of Spanish captives with the estimated populations of their captors, those victims alone number some 10 percent of the population. When we factor in Indian slaves from other groups, and whole bands subordinated in the Araucanian expansions of the nineteenth century, it seems clear that, as with their creole counterparts, entrance into market-driven pastoral economies introduced major new dimensions of inequality among the Indian peoples of the Pampas.[10]

Yet for all the resonance between creole and Indian systems of bound labor, certain cultural distinctions pertained as well. While African slaves and indentured workers in creole households and ranchos performed labor essential to market success, they did so in an ideological domain that disparaged their racial and class status. A rather more variegated world of work and prestige obtained among Indian-held slaves. Female and child captives performed labor across the whole range of the Indian economy—herding cattle, sheep, and horses; cultivating wheat, barley, and beans; preparing rawhides and fleeces for sale; weaving textiles; creating finished leather goods; gunsmithing and silversmithing. In the 1820s, the English traveler Maria Graham Calcott noted that "their flocks and herds are entirely managed by the women and slaves (Christian women), who watch alternately during the night, mounted on horseback, going the rounds among the cattle. The occupation of the women during the day is to catch and saddle the horses of the Indians, and cook their food." Lest we interpret this diffuse delegation of labor as indicative of secure social standing among women and slaves, she cautioned, "if a sheep or any animal should be missing, the unfortunate woman is stripped and flogged in the most barbarous manner" (quoted in K. Jones 1998: 99–100; see also Socolow 1992:89).

Yet the kinship and quasi-kin systems of many Pampas Indians cast a wider web of affinal connections and social mobility than could be sanctioned among the Catholic creoles. Widespread customs of marital exogamy and bride-price and intergroup diplomacy meant that captive women entered into a "marriage economy" in which they constituted valuable social currency. Since polygamy served as one method by which headmen among the Pampas, Pehuenches, and Tehuelches could make public their wealth, and marriage to a Spanish woman constituted a slap at the honor of Spanish men, captive consorts seem to have been highly prized. Petronila Pérez's marriage to the brother of the Pehuenche cacique suggests just such social value, as does her quick remarriage after his death. Even where formal extensions of kinship were denied to captive women, they could find themselves culturally elevated. Araucanians assigned particular prestige to the possession of Spanish slave-concubines, whose purported sexual skills brought social wealth, power, and prestige to their captors.

The ambivalent position of captive women in Indian society also extended into the world of Indian political culture. Those women and the mixed-descent children they bore to their husbands or masters were only the most immediate and intimate example of the complex hybridities at work among the indigenous peoples of the Pampas in the first decades of the nineteenth century. The political upheavals attendant to the eruption of republican independence movements throughout Spanish America after 1810 found creoles and Indians alike engaged in dramatic rethinking of relationships among elites, commoners, and slaves, between colony and metropole, and between Indians and creoles themselves.

Colonel Pedro García provides our best window into these changes in Indian country. The revolutionary junta formed in Buenos Aires in May 1810 sent García on several expeditions to the Salinas Grandes over the next several years to take the temper of the Pampas vis-à-vis the ongoing struggle between republicans and royalists across the southern cone. García's reports were rich in ethnographic and political observation, as well as ambiguity. Although in 1806 Luis de la Cruz had found Petronila Pérez's Pehuenche kinsfolk settled at the Salinas Grandes, by 1810 they seem to have been absorbed into a territory shared by two contending groups, the Ranqueles (or People of the Reeds), under their headman Carripilúm (Green Ears), and a Huilliche people known as the Salineros (People of the Salt Lakes), under a man named Quinteleu. This man exercised extraordinary powers among his people, who were assumed in the colonial era to have organized themselves in bands under chieftains who led more by persuasion and charisma than by force or hereditary rank. Yet García reported that Quinteleu was revered as an "ulmen," or "cacique gobernador," of whom there were "only two in the whole area [between] the ocean and the cordillera from the northern frontier to the Rio Negro." When these "'ulmenes' come to attend meetings with subordinate Indians and caciques," García wrote, "a group of musicians go in front of them playing flutes and bows of strings that play with other strings very similar to the ones used by the Blacks and he is followed by all of his slaves. Everybody welcomes the ulmen and I have seen some of them undress themselves to present their gobernador with their own garments." The second ulmen may have been Quinteleu's brother, Epumer, a Huilliche from the Chilean side of the Andes who had "been raised near Valdivia." Quinteleu was also related by marriage to the Ranquel subchief Quidulef—just one segment of a "confederation of twelve Indian chiefs related through kinships," according to García. Thus through fraternal ties and marriage diplomacy the network of this Indian leader stretched for some three hundred miles from the heart of the Pampas to the Pacific Ocean. If we consider that Spanish women like Petronila, whether wives or concubines to their Indian masters, continued to maintain informal ties with some of their Spanish kinsmen, the web of intercultural relations probably extended even to the outskirts of Buenos Aires.[11]

García enjoyed the protection and hospitality of Quinteleu during his visits and later brought the ulmen to Buenos Aires to meet with the ayuntamiento itself. These occasions afforded him time to discuss the Salineros' vision of *his* people's future as an indigenous "nation." Not unlike the tumults then racking centers of creole power, old Quinteleu found his own people in social flux. "These days," he said, "everybody wants to be a chief." Ill discipline and challenges to authority were rampant, especially, he said, because of "the bad influence that the many Christians among the Indians had on some chiefs," forever "counseling them to oppose any expedition to harvest salt and to raid the white ranchers for cattle." This is one of the rare acknowledgments in official sources that Indian tolderías held not only Spanish slaves but also deserters, fugitives, and transcultural entrepreneurs who were attempting to craft their own multiethnic enterprises. Quinteleu resisted these efforts, however. Although he might welcome the presence of Huincas, as the white "Christians" were called, his imagined community hewed to a different path.

First he declared that the salt lakes were the property of all—Spaniard and Indian alike. In fact, Quinteleu believed it would be best for everybody if the Spaniards would establish fixed settlements nearby, even to the point of garrisoning a *fortín* at the lakes. Thus territoriality, sovereignty, and identity were not synonymous in his mind. From these mercantile and military outposts, his people would find not only efficient markets for their pastoral production but assistance in developing an appreciation for "the joyousness of tilling the land," which in 1812 he said was well under way. He implicitly acknowledged common notions of law and property when he offered to return fugitives from justice and stolen cattle to creole authorities, if they in turn would guarantee safe passage of Indian livestock drovers to and from purchase points. But he made no mention of the captive women and children, and García remained significantly silent on the issue. When in 1815 a Spanish fleet threatened to invade Buenos Aires itself, Quinteleu sent Epumer to the city to offer "arms, people, and horses to the government to be used whenever they were needed." The authorities failed to respond. However, García continued to appeal to the republican government that it must endorse and underwrite Quinteleu's vision, or face war on two fronts—from royalists bent on arresting creole independence, and from Indians disgusted with a fledgling state unwilling to treat them as equal sovereign nations.[12]

The moment, we now know, was lost. Crises internal and external beset the creoles. In 1815 García, even as he journeyed again to meet with Quinteleu and his caciques to "define the spots for the fortines and to agree with the Argentine government" on political relations between the two nations, found himself arrested and imprisoned. Likewise, in the 1830s, Quinteleu's Salineros would be defeated and absorbed by a new wave of Araucanians under Calfucurá, who would himself establish a lineage that survived until the final pacification of the Pampas in the years after 1870. But the pregnant contingencies of those few years should not be overlooked. We see from hindsight that the Argentina taking shape thereafter would be dominated by political conflicts between the "cattle oligarchy" of creole ranchers such as the caudillo Juan Manuel Rosas and porteño modernizers such as Domingo Sarmiento, both of whom would need to "barbarize" Indians in order to define themselves as "civilizers." So too would Indians consolidate power in stronger, yet narrower chiefdoms like that of Calfucurá and the Ranquel cacique Llanquetruz. But these reductions were not yet in play in 1815. We will return to Quinteleu's "nation" and place it in the context of what Paul Eiss (this volume) might call a "microhistory of the possible"—the theoretical extension of specific cases from the past into the potential cultural politics of our present, especially in terms of intriguing analysis on the nature of premodern empires. But first, let us visit a similarly contingent and creative movement among the creoles themselves, unfolding in the very years that Quinteleu and García were exploring the indigenous vision of the future. The comparison of these two exercises in borderland cultural politics will, I hope, allow us greater extensions and insights than would either one alone.

Like Quinteleu, José Gervasio Artigas was a man of the country, in his case the western borderlands of the Banda Oriental, which would become the nation of Uruguay in 1830. For twenty years he had led a division of *blandengues* (rural militia) charged with defending his rich cattle region from Indian and cross-border Portuguese raiders. With the 1810 rebellion in Buenos Aires, he journeyed to that city and offered his services to the revolutionary junta. His success in recruiting a diverse multiethnic army, coupled with that army's success in the field, won him both a substantial popular following and the hatred of the porteño elite who had gained control of the government. By 1814 he found himself with a price of six thousand pesos on his head. When royalists offered him the rank of general if he would adopt their cause, he responded, "I am not for sale, nor do I want any greater reward for my work than to see my country free of Spanish control" (Shumway 1991:58). By 1815 Artigas claimed the title El Protector de los Pueblos Libres. He set out to create a federation of autonomous provinces from Santa Fe to the Banda Oriental.[13]

Artigas may have been nearly illiterate, but that did not prevent him from dictating a sociopolitical program apparently so radical that he remains today the darling of leftist historians and the demon of the right. But again, just as Quinteleu does not fit into the simple dualism of "barbarism" and "civilization," neither can Artigas settle easily into a left–right dichotomy. Certainly, his call for land expropriation "from Europeans and bad Americans" and redistribution to "free Negroes, zambos [people of mixed Indian-African blood], Indians, and poor Creoles" that they might "work toward their happiness and that of their province" was revolutionary. So too was his remarkably sympathetic Indian policy, born perhaps of the relationship with his adoptive Guaraní Indian son, Andrés Artigas. In 1815 Artigas declared:

My desire is that the Indians in their communities govern themselves, so that they can tend to their interests as we tend to ours. Thus they will experience a practical happiness and escape from that state of annihilation to which misfortune has subjected them. Let us remember that they have the principal right and that it would be a shameful degradation for us to keep them in the shameful exclusion that until now they have suffered because they were Indians.

Yet replication of the colonial *republicas de indios* was not enough. Artigas actively sought to recruit nomadic Indians to his fledgling state with promises of land, tools, and starter herds. He put Andrés in charge of the Indian-dominated province of Misiones to help implement the policy. Little wonder that his opponents raised an alarm about the "barbarian democracy" building north of Buenos Aires (Shumway 1991:60–61).

But this situation was neither barbaric, as is now clear, nor democratic, at least not in the sense that we heirs of liberal democracy understand the term. Artigas's charismatic popular vision, while inclusive of the most marginal members of society, retained some elements of customary power relations that Quinteleu might have recognized, and not only the lateral extension of leadership through his fictive kinsman Andrés. While he abolished the African slave trade and provided for the emancipation of children born to African slaves, he remained curiously quiet on other forms of bound servitude, especially that of Indians such as those he maintained as family servants. This shading between liberal norms of individual autonomy and customary notions of patrimonial deference extended to other realms. Those "most unfortunate" who received redistributed land, for instance, could neither "transfer ownership nor sell these kinds of estancias, nor contract against [these properties] any kind of debt." Artigas himself seems to have been the ultimate trustee for such lands. Like Quinteleu, he supported free-market access for his people, but he undertook a protectionist trade policy by imposing detailed tariffs on European imports that might undercut their production. Democratically elected *cabildos*, or town councils, might address local concerns but remained subject to binding instructions from *el protector* on "national" matters (Rock 1985:90–93).

And as with his Indian counterpart, we will never know what might have become of Artigas's "nation." His experiment also proved short-lived, since by 1820 Portuguese troops had seized Montevideo. Opponents in Buenos Aires drove Artigas into exile in Paraguay, where he would quietly live out the remaining thirty years of his life. But if we step back a bit and place these two cases in the wider context of events then occurring in other nineteenth-century borderlands, we may be able to draw some general lessons from the Quinteleu and Artigas failures and play with some extensions to our own twenty-first-century world.

During precisely these same years, on the Orange River of southern Africa, a diverse and contentious mixed community of Khoikhoi, Dutch, Bastaard, San, and Xhosa peoples established themselves as a "tribe" and a "nation" under the identity of Griqua. They even drafted a constitution that produced a "democratic oligarchy," under which they thrived for two generations and expanded to settle nearly four hundred miles of intercultural borderland. In central Canada at this time, a mixed British-Cree people known to us as the Home Guard Cree fashioned a community that fused Indian notions of polyandry (whereby Cree women engaged in second marriages with Hudson's Bay Company factors to gain preferred trading access) with a corporate-military political organization borrowed from the Hudson's Bay Company. Along the Terek River and into the foothills of the Caucasus Mountains, both Terek Cossacks and the various Muslim communities of Chechnya and Daghestan formed enduring communities inclusive by ethnicity or religion, sometimes both, under powerfully charismatic leaders and amid endemic military conflict. And in North America's southwestern borderlands, we see the formation of creative and volatile "communities of interest," through which New Mexican *comancheros*, *ciboleros*, and *nacajalleses* worked in concert with marginal members of Comanche, Kiowa, and Navajo societies to plunder the wealth of each other's elites (see Brooks 2002a, 2002b).

None of these cases could come close to qualifying as culturally pluralistic utopias, for all came to be under conditions of intercultural conflict or warfare. Although egalitarian in some respects, all were premised upon systematic violence against women. Whether such cruelty was born of the intersection of long-standing customs among indigenous and colonizing men or produced as uniquely original borderland "technologies of violence" requires deeper analysis across time and space (Barr 2007; Bennett and Manderson 2003; Block 2006). Yet somehow the cases seem potent with promise, too. Ethnically and religiously diverse peoples did coexist in these families, tribes, and nations, not under some vapid multiculturalism but as discrete cofunctioning members of a larger polity. Kinship seemed often to intercede and mediate between violence and social assimilation. Children born of sexual trauma became "citizens" and leaders in these mixed communities. These local cases bear surprising conceptual resemblance to recent reassessments of premodern empires like those of the Aztecs, Mongols, and Ottomans, wherein ethnic bargaining, marriage diplomacy, and state-sponsored religious tolerance all produced, in Karen Barkey's words, "political systems where ethnicity, language, and religion did not have much national content" (Barkey and Von Hagen 1997:103; see also Stoler and McGranahan 2007). In a sense, all might qualify as examples of what the philosopher Charles Taylor has called "deep diversity"—conditions under which "a plurality of ways of being and belonging," of difference and discord, become social fabric in some inscrutable fashion (quoted in Geertz 2000:224).

However much the political promise of these uneasy hybridities, they gave way quickly to the simpler narratives of nineteenth-century nation-states. The emergence of the "guiding fictions" of American nationalism (North and South) was part and parcel of the ideological cementing of modern nationhood, where the production of ethno-racial difference involved troweling over the variegated surfaces of the past in favor of less

FIGURE 12.2

Angel Della Valle, La Vuelta del Malón, *1892. Image courtesy of Museo de Bellas Artes, Buenos Aires, Argentina.*

abrasive stories of the barbarous and the civilized (Duara 1995; White and Limerick 1994). Narratives of women's captivity and "white slavery" among the barbarians emerged across the American hemisphere as an early and anxious form of today's bodice busters (Namias 1993; Operé 2001; Tinnemeyer 2006). The reciprocal exploitation of women lost ground to stories of white women's victimhood at the hands of savages—even in painterly narratives such as Angel Della Valle's *La Vuelta del Malón* (The Return of the Raid) of 1892. Riding at the break of dawn across the swampy ground of the *pampas humidas,* perhaps even to the Salinas Grandes, these *malones* have taken possession of the twin symbols of Argentine nationalism: Catholic liturgical paraphernalia and a sole white woman. Breasts bare and pinioned behind her captor's lance, perhaps only Borges's Yorkshire girl could have been quite so alabaster in tone. Violation personal and national awaits.

But not so quickly. Also obvious in Valle's painting is the "swoon." Has the captive fainted in terror, or in anticipation? Is the seduction complete while in the captor's horsehide *toldo* betrayal portends? Surely, beneath the velvety discourse of the nation, there rested in family and community memory stories, like those of Petronila Pérez, that held the promise of unorthodox interpretation. Even while portraying—in words or brushstrokes—

the essentials of simplified national narratives, an eroticism barely able to catch its breath hints at remnants of "some secret impulse, an impulse deeper than reason" that once held the promise, however ambiguous, of alternative social worlds. However much modern nation-building required that indigenous peoples be reduced to barbarism and white women become the ghostly icons of a ghastly transgression, the depth of field provided by multiscalar methods and meaning-making leaves open the possibility of revitalizing the past toward ends of twenty-first-century social consequence. To recall Borges: "Tradition is the work of memory and forgetting." In these stories from the Argentine Pampas, we have recourse to alternative "traditional" narratives —microhistories of the possible, to borrow from Eiss in this volume—that allow us access to the recovery of memory, and resistance to forgetting.[14]

Notes

1. For Borges's singular literary heritage and intellectual style, see Parks 2001.

2. For the "barbarian Indian" in the Spanish imagination, see D. Weber 2005; for the place of the Indian in the Argentine imagination, see Alminaque 1981 and Mandrini 1983; for a synthesis of the conquest and pacification of the Pampas and Patagonia, see Walther 1973.

3. For a similar exploration of literary and historical narratives for the US-Mexican borderlands, see Brooks 2000.

4. An effort informed by Michel-Rolph Trouillot's call that to gain a "richer view of historical production...we cannot exclude in advance any of the actors who participate in the production of history or any of the sites where production may occur." See Trouillot 1995:25.

5. For the notion's application to cases in the Caucasus, Canada, and South Africa, see Brooks 2002b.

6. For de la Cruz and Pérez, see Socolow 1992:88; for similar evidence of transcultural attributes of captives, see Lopez 1977.

7. For Cruz and García, see Bechis Rosso 1983:73–74.

8. For the North American southwestern borderlands, see Brooks 2002a. For other regions, see Brooks 2002b.

9. When Juan de Garay reestablished that settlement in 1580, he reported that within thirty leagues around the site there roamed some eighty to one hundred thousand stallions and mares. Twenty years later, Governor Diego Rodríguez de Valdes y de la Vanda estimated more than one million horses, more than all the horses in Spain,

France, and Italy combined. For livestock estimates, see K. Jones 1984:12. For the southern plains, see Flores 1991. For a definitive transhemispheric narrative across the eighteenth century, see D. Weber 2005; for comparative perspective between Argentina and Canada in the nineteenth century, see Adelman 1994.

10. For slaves on estancias, see Mayo 1995:39. For Indian recruitment of *vagos* and enslavement of other Indians, see Rock 1985:25, 37–38, 47–48. For 707 Spanish captives among eight thousand Araucanians in 1833, see Socolow 1992:99 and K. Jones 1998:112. In the period 1810–1820, especially to 1815, Pedro García's ethnographic reporting on Quinteleu and his Huilliche brothers (centered at Salinas Grandes and south) suggests strongly that Indians were reworking all their internal and external arrangements—economy, society, politics—in "national" ways that in many respects mirror the frantic experimentation and positioning at work among the porteños. As European immigration was one solution to porteños' problems, the same population recruitment in the form of captive assimilation proved the case among the Indians. One key indigenous element, however, was the persistence and increase in marriage diplomacy. While on the other hand, we will see that the Artigas/Hidalgo movement shows strong elements of attention to indigenism.

11. García [1836]1974. For Araucanian political organization, see Bechis Rosso 1983:77–78. On ulmenes, see Bechis Rosso 1983:230–31. For Epumer, see Bechis Rosso 1983:63. For Quinteleu's affinal relation to Quidulef, see Bechis Rosso 1983:231; for a classic contemporary ethnographic report on the Ranqueles, see Mansilla [1870]1997.

12. García [1836]1974:74–75. On the January 1812 visit to Buenos Aires, see Bechis Rosso 1983:200–201.

13. For Artigas, see Shumway 1991:52–67.

14. On imperial negotiations of sex and intimacy, see Stoler 2006 and Borges 1998:208.

13

Oral Traditions and Material Things

Constructing Histories of Native People
in Colonial Settings

Kent G. Lightfoot

The Russians established Colony Ross, perched on an uplifted marine terrace next to a small cove in northern California, in 1812. For the next three decades, it served as the administrative center of a lively mercantile enterprise. Here the Russian-American Company attempted to turn a profit by the intensive harvesting of sea otters, whose pelts were traded to China for a plethora of Asian goods. The merchants also established farms and ranches in the nearby region, traded goods to the Spanish (and later Mexican) missions and presidios in nearby Alta California, and even manufactured a limited range of merchandise for sale to their neighbors to the south. The company recruited an amalgamation of craftsmen, artisans, and laborers from across eastern Europe, the North Pacific, and northern California to work at Colony Ross. Until the waning years of the Russian venture in the mid- to late 1830s (the colony closed in 1841), Native Alaskans, who served as sea mammal hunters and skilled artisans, comprised the largest segment of the colony's population. Sizable work crews of Native Californians, primarily Kashaya Pomo, Coast Miwok, and Southern Pomo men and women, toiled in the outlying agricultural fields and grinding mills, manufactured bricks, and hauled timber to the small shipyard.

Since 1906 the old Russian settlement—mostly reconstructed by the California Department of Parks and Recreation since the 1950s—has been the centerpiece of Fort Ross State Historic Park. With its stout redwood walls enclosing a distinctive Russian Orthodox chapel and gable-roofed log houses with fine paned-glass windows, the stockade complex makes a strong Russian imprint on the contemporary landscape. In the late 1980s, archaeologists began to expand the historical investigation in the state park to include the broader mercantile settlement of Ross, which once surrounded the stockade walls and where the majority of the workforce lived and labored. As a participant in these excavations, I often reflected on the irony of how Russia still maintained an imposing beachhead only one hundred kilometers north of San Francisco in the twilight of the cold war.

I was fortunate to direct an archaeological study of the old Native Alaskan village, situated directly south of the eight-sided southern blockhouse in an open, grassy field above the surf of the Pacific Ocean. Here resided between one hundred and two hundred people in households composed of single Native Alaskan men (when they were not out hunting sea otters), Native Alaskan families, and interethnic families comprised of Native Alaskan men and Native Californian women, and their children. The investigations proved successful in detecting intact archaeological materials, from two separate areas of the site, that appear to be the remains of interethnic households. Employing this archaeological information and pertinent historical sources, our research team produced a detailed monograph of the Native Alaskan village (Lightfoot, Schiff, and Wake 1997). But I always felt that more could be done with this extraordinary site.

My participation in the SAR seminar offered me a golden opportunity to revisit the Native Alaskan village. I wanted to see if a microhistorical analysis of this place could generate new perspectives about people on the front line of colonialism. As outlined in the introductory chapter by Walton, Brooks, and DeCorse, renewed interest in event, biography, and local vantage—the stuff of microhistory—is bringing into focus the lives of ordinary people not previously appreciated in traditional histories. More importantly for me, detailed analyses of the small worlds of individuals and families can provide fresh insights about broader historical events and processes. What impressed me most about the SAR seminar was how the participants worked at diversifying the writing of history to include the stories of people who were failures, who were disenfranchised, and even one who was a celebrity (but little understood in her own lifetime) and made them meaningful to the broader social, political, and economic contexts in which these people lived. As demonstrated in this book, the writing of a more inclusive history must involve innovative ways of defining, finding, and working with new sources of data—whether one is writing about insurgent uprisings in the Yucatán in the early 1900s; about the Roanoke Colony, which failed to survive two separate colonization efforts; or about the initial activities of a social movement that never really took off in contemporary Pittsburgh.

My purpose is to write a microhistory of Colony Ross that focuses on indigenous women and their daily experiences and that touches upon two different but related goals. One goal is to examine critically how these women were treated in this colonial endeavor; the other is to generate a better understanding of the broader power dynamics of the Russian colony. We typically rely on meta-narratives constructed from studies of colonial policies, demographic trends, and statistics on rebellions, incarcerations, and litigation cases to evaluate how specific colonial regimes treated indigenous populations. This kind of meta-narrative has painted the Russian treatment of its Native workers within the mercantile enterprise of Ross as relatively benign, especially compared to the contemporaneous Franciscan missions located to the south in Alta California (see Lightfoot 2005b:9).

My intent is to evaluate this common perception by focusing on the treatment of Native women who were recruited into the Russian mercantile community as laborers, spouses, and Russian Orthodox converts. A relatively large number of local Indian women entered into interethnic households with colonial men. In undertaking a microhistorical analysis of these women during the course of their daily lives, we should obtain an excellent vantage about the overall social and political climate of Colony Ross. I hope to examine critically how women were treated in the course of their day-to-day activities, how they interacted with their spouses, how they negotiated with other colonial laborers and administrators, and how much freedom to continue their Indian cultural practices they enjoyed within the colonial settlement.

METHODOLOGICAL ISSUES IN MICROHISTORY AT COLONY ROSS

In participating in the SAR seminar, I was inspired to write an archaeological biography about one or more of the women who lived in the excavated house areas in the Native Alaskan village. In chapter 9, Mary Beaudry demonstrates how the combination of archaeology and specific kinds of historical documents—personal letters, journals, wills, and so on—can be skillfully employed to reconstitute the lives of forgotten or little-known people. However, in sharp contrast to her case study, where a diverse range

FIGURE 13.1

The Ross settlement as drawn by Auguste Duhaut-Cilly during his visit to California in 1827. The Russian village is illustrated to the right of the stockade; company houses and gardens in front of the stockade and chapel. The three long, low structures, along with several flat-roofed structures to the left of the southern blockhouse, are probably related to the Native Alaskan village, although they may be industrial or agricultural outbuildings. Courtesy of the Bancroft Library, University of California, Berkeley.

of historical records pertain to Nathaniel Tracy and Offin Boardman (who penned some of the documents themselves), there is precious little written about the Indian women living with colonial men at the Ross settlement.

I scoured available archival documents for information about the Native Alaskan village, but my extensive investigation revealed few descriptions—primarily snatches taken here and there from longer passages that elaborate upon other physical characteristics of the colony (see Lightfoot, Schiff, and Wake 1997:6–8). Several censuses from the 1820s and 1830s list the names and ethnicities of workers and spouses, including members of the interethnic households at Colony Ross. Period drawings of the Ross settlement sketched by the French visitor Auguste Duaut-Cilly (1827) and the Russian naturalist I. G. Voznesenskii (1841) emphasize the stockade complex, but also the Russian village, where many of the lower-class Russian and creole workers lived, along with other outlying houses, fences, and garden plots that made up the broader Ross settlement. But it is interesting that little is shown of the Native Alaskan village; the vantage point of both pictures tends to minimize a clear view of this place. It is also interesting that neither picture depicts the Native Californian villages that were apparently located a short distance to the north of the stockade complex.

There are excellent eyewitness accounts written about the local Kashaya

Pomo and Coast Miwok people at Colony Ross. But these representations follow a natural-history genre commonly employed by European travelers in the late 1700s and early 1800s. By presenting these groups as relatively pristine ethnographic examples described within the context of the flora and fauna of colonial regions, the writers deliberately filtered out the destructive consequences of colonial entanglements (see Vansina 1990:21). The French and Russian authors portrayed the Indians in their natural habitats and villages, largely segregated from the colonial interlopers (see, for example, Kostromitinov 1974; Laplace 2006:34–38; Wrangell 1974). These writings provide exceptional information on hunting methods, clothing, physical appearances, and use of plant and animal resources, as well as houses and domestic activities. There is also an incredible set of paintings of the Coast Miwok community adjacent to Port Rumiantsev (today's Bodega Harbor) drawn by Mikhail Tikhanov in 1818 (see Farris 1998 for a detailed ethnographic analysis of the paintings). What is largely missing in these writings and paintings are discussions or depictions of Native interactions with the colonizers—whether as visitors to the colonial settlements, as laborers in colonial mercantile or agrarian enterprises, or as spouses in interethnic households.

NATIVE ORAL TRADITIONS

Although there is a paucity of firsthand written accounts about Indian women's interactions with colonial men, investigations of Colony Ross are blessed with a rich array of Native oral traditions. The Kashaya maintain oral narratives that encompass stories about their creation, myths, the supernatural, and their history. Some of the latter stories pertain to their first sightings of Europeans, their encounters with Russian colonists, and their later interactions with Anglo-American ranchers and timber companies. In the 1950s, Robert Oswalt, a linguistic anthropologist from UC Berkeley, initiated interviews with tribal elders in the Kashaya Pomo language. These interviews provided information on various stories, which Oswalt later published in both the Kashaya and English languages in his pioneering monograph *Kashaya Texts* (Oswalt 1964). Recently, archaeological researchers have been building upon this corpus of stories by initiating interviews with Kashaya elders and tribal scholars. Otis Parrish, a member of the Kashaya Pomo tribe and a practicing anthropologist in the Phoebe Hearst Museum of Anthropology at UC Berkeley, is spearheading the oral tradition project.

In chapter 5, Christopher DeCorse outlines the various methodological and theoretical issues involving the use of historical documents and archaeological materials in microhistorical studies of colonialism in Africa. My intention is not to repeat his excellent analysis, which highlights the "different tongues" spoken by historians and archaeologists in their respective research programs for studying the past. Rather, I will focus my attention on the uneasy relationship that practitioners of archaeology have with oral traditions.

Scholars certainly recognize the great promise of working with both archaeological materials and Native oral narratives to generate a more balanced and multivoiced perspective of the past. As both Mary Beaudry and Christopher DeCorse emphasize in their chapters, the study of archaeological remains provides a window into the past concerning ordinary people and ordinary things that are often not described in historical documents. A similar claim has been made with respect to the use of oral narratives—that these sources allow us to get beyond official, elite histories by giving voice to underrepresented, disenfranchised people and in doing so making the past more democratic (Finnegan 1996:890; Howarth 1998:6; Purser 1992:26–27; P. Thompson 2000:9). Furthermore, oral narratives can provide a wealth of information about subjects that are largely unrecorded in early written accounts. This information includes detailed observations of daily life and mundane domestic activities, family organization and relations, community structures and political organizations, gender relations, and even underground or resistance movements (see Erdoes and Ortiz 1984:xv; Purser 1992:27; P. Thompson 2000:8, 109, 154). And as Paul Thompson (2000:8) further elaborates, even when family relations or colonial workers are described in written sources, there is a tendency to use aggregate statistics. This is certainly true for Russian accounts of family units or colonial workers at Colony Ross; the most frequent references are census records. In contrast, oral narratives often articulate detailed accounts of the involvement of individual actors in family affairs, social relations within the community, and routine activities (see Purser 1992:27; P. Thompson 2000: 8–9), which makes them ideal sources for use in microhistorical analyses.

The use of oral traditions by archaeologists has a long and checkered history. Here I define oral traditions as stories that have been transmitted from one generation to another, often over extensive periods of time, while oral histories are people's reminiscences or accounts of events that happened in their lifetimes (see Vansina 1985:11–13, 27). Oral traditions may be memorized messages or speeches that are recounted on ceremonial occasions to honor past events and ancestors (as exemplified in some African kingdoms; see Reid and Lane 2004). Other oral traditions are myths, legends, folktales, and historical remembrances that have been passed down over generations (see Simmons 1992). Oral traditions, commonly used by American archaeologists in the late 1800s to examine migration routes and the culture history of Indian tribes (for example, the fieldwork of Fewkes, Cushing, and Bandelier in the American Southwest), became largely taboo in the following decades when the veracity of the accounts was questioned by such distinguished anthropologists as Robert Lowie and Alfred Kroeber (Anyon et al. 2000:61).

By the 1970s and 1980s, with the advent of processual archaeology and a more scientific bent to the field, Native oral traditions were rarely incorporated into mainstream archaeological research. But since the 1990s, there has been a growing interest among some archaeologists in incorporating oral narratives into their research. This interest has been stimulated, in part, by the Native American Graves Protection and Repatriation Act (NAGPRA), which recognizes oral traditions as one of the legitimate sources of evidence for determining the cultural affiliation of skeletal remains and associated funerary objects, an important step in the repatriation of museum collections back to Indian tribes. There is also a growing recognition among historical archaeologists that oral testimonies can provide a powerful source of information for evaluating many kinds of research questions (Purser 1992).

Yet despite the growing interest in using oral narratives in archaeological research, the number of scholars implementing this kind of work remains limited. Historical archaeologists are the most common users of oral narratives, although they tend to collect and work primarily with oral histories. Even among scholars working in Africa, who are the recognized leaders in incorporating oral sources into archaeological and historical projects (Purser 1992:26; P. Thompson 2000:166), there remains considerable tension about the use of oral traditions (DeCorse 2001:3, 2004:2; Helm 2004:61; LaViolette 2004:145–53; Reid and Lane 2004:18; Vansina 1990:31). While scholars recognize the tremendous promise of using these sources, most practicing archaeologists are uneasy about using them to evaluate historical and anthropological research issues, as exemplified by Christopher DeCorse in chapter 5.

SKEPTICISM ABOUT ORAL TRADITIONS

There is an extensive literature about the challenges of employing oral traditions to reconstruct historical events and to investigate historical processes. My purpose here is not to summarize this large body of work in detail but to highlight five major issues about the efficacy of using oral traditions in historical research.

Remembrances of the Past in the Present

Oral traditions are remembrances of the past as told by people in the present. As such, they are not static historical documents but are dynamic testimonies. They are subject to revision and modification depending upon perceptions of the past, which may change under new social and political conditions (Cruikshank 1992:14; Helm 2004:78; Purser 1992: 33–34; Vansina 1985:xii). Some scholars view the use of oral traditions in archaeological research as problematical because they are more an artifact of contemporary culture than an accurate record of past events (Mason 2000:242). Traditions are always in the process of being re-created and invented (Finnegan 1996:891). Over time, some stories may be forgotten or intentionally discarded; other stories are combined into one narrative; while still other stories are restructured and even stereotyped to fit current views of the past (Erdoes and Ortiz 1984:xiv; P. Thompson 2000:167; Vansina 1985:8, 170–71). DeCorse (2001:3) also emphasizes the problem of "feedback," in which contemporary communities read about their history and incorporate this knowledge into indigenous renditions of the past (see also Purser 1992:32). Oral traditions can never be taken at face value, but like any historical source, they must be critically examined and evaluated for veracity, internal consistency, and concordance with known historical events (see, for example, Echo-Hawk 2000a:270–72; Finnegan 1996:889).

Memory

An important concern about the historical integrity of oral traditions (as well as oral histories) is the ability of storytellers to recollect events, people, and places from many years ago (Purser 1992:27; P. Thompson 2000:129; Vansina 1985:176–78). There is a general consensus about the crucial role time plays in the memory of individuals and communities, but there is no agreement about the length of time that has to transpire before stories are forgotten or transformed into something entirely new. Echo-Hawk (1997, 2000a, 2000b) champions a long chronology for some kinds of historical events and remembrances, arguing that some Native American oral traditions may date back to the late Pleistocene. Mason (2000), in contrast, believes in a shallow time line, suggesting that most oral traditions are accurate in their remembrances of past events only within a generation or two (see also Vansina 1990:31). Of course, how long historical remembrances remain alive within a community or group will depend on various factors, such as the kind of story being transmitted, how information is exchanged from one generation to another (the existence of storytelling specialists; the practice of reciting memorized messages, speeches, or poems), and how much information is lost and manipulated from one generation to the next.

Chronology

A widely recognized limitation of oral traditions is the "weakness in chronology." That is, it is difficult to accurately date people, places, things, and events recounted in most oral narratives (P. Thompson 2000:167; Vansina 1985:56). Vansina (1985:173, 185–86) argues that there is typically no direct way to date oral traditions. He notes that we must employ other sources of information (written sources, archaeology, geology) to date specific events recited in stories.

Performance

Oral histories and oral traditions are public narratives that typically involve performances for various kinds of audiences (Purser 1992:28–29). Folklorists and oral historians caution that any critical analysis of oral narratives must take into account the context of storytelling (Finnegan 1996: 890–91). The emphasis and content of a story may change from one venue to another, depending on the kind of performance, the place or social function at which stories are told (the home, the workplace, the pub), and the composition of the audience (Cruikshank 1992; Purser 1992:27; P. Thompson 2000:124–26, 140). Vansina (1985:34) notes that the performance of oral stories is never simply a recitation but that the storyteller and audience develop a symbiotic relationship in the creation of the story every time it is told.

Culturally Sensitive Texts

Oral traditions are often culturally sensitive texts that have sacred or spiritual meaning to descendant communities. As such, oral narratives may be encoded with cultural meanings that outsiders may not understand or may interpret incorrectly. Folklorists, cultural anthropologists, and oral historians define multiple genres of oral traditions (myths, legends, folktales, proverbs, songs, prayers, and so on), only some of which may contain historical remembrances of actual events (Dundes 1980; Finnegan 1996; Winthrop 1991). Among North American tribes, there is also considerable debate and concern about the use of oral traditions, especially sacred texts, by non-Indian scholars and laypeople (Anyon et al. 2000; Ferguson et al. 2000).

KENT G. LIGHTFOOT

TENSIONS BETWEEN ARCHAEOLOGISTS AND INDIAN SCHOLARS

The skepticism about using oral traditions in archaeological research is compounded by current tensions between archaeologists and Indian scholars, the primary practitioners who employ archaeological materials and Native oral traditions, respectively, in North America. Despite important strides in ameliorating friction between Indians and archaeologists with the recent emphasis on "indigenous" or "collaborative" archaeology, the incorporation of archaeological remains and Native narratives to reconstruct historical narratives remains deeply politicized and polarized. Some Native scholars continue to be skeptical about the use of archaeological data because of ethical concerns about whether its collection involved the desecration of cemeteries and other sacred sites. They resent past practices that excluded Indian people from participating in archaeological research or kept indigenous people from speaking as rightful stewards of the past (Lightfoot 2005a:38–39). With Native narratives now recognized as a legitimate source of information in repatriation claims, some archaeologists remain suspicious about information that may ultimately be used to remove human skeletal remains and archaeological objects from museums and archaeological collections.

In reality, oral traditions and archaeology represent "two separate but overlapping ways of knowing the past" based on different kinds of data and scholarly research methods (see Anyon et al. 2000:78–79). And these two ways of knowing the past can lead to significant discrepancies about our understanding of the past. We only have to turn to tribal creation stories and compare them to archaeologically derived interpretations for the initial colonization of the Americas to see significant differences in how and when people first arrived on this continent. For example, one creation story in *Kashaya Texts* ("The Creation of the Ocean") recounts how in "ancient times" Coyote, who "presided just like a heavenly being with his people," created the ocean; turned logs into whales, small seals, and porpoises; "cast down edible foods to grow on the rocks...[l]impets, small chitons, large chitons, sea anemones—he didn't miss making anything for people to eat"; and then created people (Oswalt 1964:37–41). This oral tradition differs significantly from the standard archaeological interpretation for the movement of the Hokan-speaking proto-Pomoan people into northern California (Moratto 1984:530–74). Furthermore, our earliest dates for Native occupation of land that would become Fort Ross State Historic Park are from only about six thousand to eight thousand years ago (Lightfoot, Wake, and Schiff 1991:110–11). I have been involved in other interpretive discrepancies in Fort Ross State Historic Park: archaeological investigations at an important Kashaya Pomo village indicate that the site was occupied during recent historic times, whereas oral traditions suggest this important ancestral site has roots that extend back into ancient history.

A MICROHISTORICAL APPROACH FOR COLONY ROSS

In working with both archaeological materials and oral traditions, I am struck by several commonalities. Both sources can provide information on family life, social relations, and underground resistance movements not highlighted in written documents. Both sources are capable of registering significant historical events, such as natural calamities (earthquakes, tsunamis) or cultural catastrophes (massacres, wars). Every archaeologist dreams of uncovering another Pompeii, where an event, in that case a volcanic eruption, has been perfectly preserved within the archaeological record. Important events are certainly recorded in oral traditions. For example, Glenn Farris (1988, 1992) has demonstrated how Kashaya Pomo oral traditions carefully recorded Indians' encounters with a Hudson's Bay Company brigade that passed near Colony Ross in April 1833. But neither case is typical.

The nature of most archaeological deposits and ancient oral traditions is that individual events may not be captured as discrete historical happenings that can be dated precisely. Although I have spent my entire life looking for a Pompeii-like site, my time has been spent mostly on archaeological sites that have been built up over time and where the stratigraphy does not reveal specific episodes or events. In both oral histories and oral traditions, it is not uncommon for separate events to be collapsed and recombined to fit within a specific story (P. Thompson 2000:159). As Anyon et al. (2000: 79) stress, oral traditions and archaeology are both palimpsests of history; events are often smeared and blended together, which makes the reconstruction and study of events very difficult (see also Fleisher 2004:94–95).

Rather than arguing about the merits of using archaeology and oral traditions to accurately reconstruct specific historical events that can be pinpointed precisely in time, I believe it may be more constructive to employ a more "practice-oriented" approach that emphasizes the study of redundant cultural practices that took place day after day. Paul Thompson (2000:158–59) argues that people generally tend to be much better at recounting processes that took place on a daily basis, such as the methods farmers used to plow fields, than at remembering or recalling isolated events that did not reoccur over time. I think the strength of archaeology and oral traditions lies in the study of daily routines and cultural patterns that are encoded within the archaeological records and narratives. Elsewhere I have noted that patterned accumulations of material culture resulting from routinized daily activities are among the most interpretable kinds of deposits that archaeologists commonly work with (Lightfoot, Martinez, and Schiff 1998:201). Oral traditions that I have been privileged to hear are rich with memories of daily life: mundane domestic activities such as cooking or cleaning houses; social interactions between people; family life; and the teaching of children (see also Simmons 1992). Oral traditions also relate well to cultural practices that unfolded at specific places; landscapes, localities, and even archaeological sites often serve as mnemonic devices for many stories (Basso 1996; Helm 2004:61, 78; Vansina 1985:45).

In highlighting the investigation of daily practices, I employ a micro-historical approach that examines the routinized activities and social relations of Native women residing with colonial men at Colony Ross. In working with Native stories, archaeological findings, and pertinent census data, I believe it is best to examine each source separately, rather than forcing Native narratives, archaeological findings, and historical texts into a single "master" spatio-temporal framework (contra to Kowalewski 1997). Interpretations can be constructed independently for each data source, taking into account potential biases and analytical constraints for each source. Using this approach, we can then systematically compare and contrast interpretations generated from different data sources in a diachronic framework (see Lightfoot 2006). Vansina (1990:28–29) describes a method of "cross-checking" sources to spot discrepancies in accounts as a way to develop a rough index of reliability. This is pretty standard practice in historiography.

But as I have outlined elsewhere (Lightfoot 2006), the common practice of checking sources with one another, especially checking archaeological findings and oral accounts with already-accepted written documents, may be too limiting. Should we assume from the outset that our diverse sources will neatly converge into a single scenario? I argue that interpretations drawn from oral, archaeological, and documentary sources will probably not merge into a single historical interpretation for colonial contexts such as Colony Ross. We should not be surprised to see deep discrepancies in these diverse sources, given the different viewpoints of history that were recorded and the varied reasons why these sources survive in our contemporary world. Rather than marginalizing oral or archaeological sources that do not neatly correlate with written records, we should pay particular attention to them. These discrepancies may prove insightful for writing alternative histories of colonial communities from the vantage of history's disenfranchised or forgotten people.

Currently, there are significant discrepancies in how we account for the formation of interethnic households at Colony Ross. On the one hand, Russian accounts emphasize how local Indian chiefs freely offered their daughters as mates to Ross employees (Golovnin 1979:163; Kotzebue 1830:124). Scholars (including myself) have tended to view these interethnic households as part of a broader process of alliance formation through kinship networks that linked together Indian groups and employees of the Russian-American Company (Lightfoot, Wake, and Schiff 1991:24). On the other hand, as a consequence of my involvement with elders of the Kashaya Pomo tribe in the oral history project, I have recently heard a very different story about the Russians and the formation of interethnic households. During several interviews with Kashaya women, it became clear that they view the Russian merchants and their colonial program with great bitterness, especially regarding the treatment of Native women. One consultant remarked that the "old Russians took our girls," while another noted that the Native women were forced to work for the Russians and to live with the foreign men. A tribal scholar in her early seventies recounted that her grandmother told her that the introduction of liquor to tribal members was a significant factor in male relatives allowing young women to be taken by foreigners. Some women were reportedly raped and abused in domestic relationships with colonial men.

Can a detailed microhistorical analysis focusing on Native women at Colony Ross make some sense of these significant discrepancies in interpretation? Below I consider pertinent Native oral traditions, archaeological findings, and census data to address this question.

KASHAYA POMO ORAL TRADITIONS

In the late 1950s, Robert Oswalt recorded Kashaya Pomo narratives about myths, the supernatural, and folk history from two key consultants: Herman James and Essie Pinola Parrish. Herman James recounted stories about Colony Ross that he had learned primarily from his maternal grandmother, Lukaria, who helped raise him. Lukaria was reportedly about eight years old when the Russians founded their California colony. Essie Parrish acquired much of her knowledge about Kashaya history from her maternal grandmother as well. Her grandmother was born about ten years after the Russians left California (circa 1851). The stories told by Herman James and Essie Parrish relate three basic themes: how Kashaya Pomo women responded to foreign cultural practices; how they were employed as laborers for the colonists; and how they interacted with foreign and Indian men within the power structure of the Russian colony.

The first theme concerns deep suspicion about foreign cultural practices. In text 55, "The First White Food," Essie Parrish described Indian reactions to "white food":

> Never having seen white men's food before, they thought that they were being given poison. Having given [the Indians] their food, they left and returned home but [the Indians] threw it in the ditch. Some they buried when they poured it out. They were afraid to eat that, not knowing anything about it—all they knew was their own food, wild food. They had never seen white people's food before then. (Oswalt 1964:251)

In another story, text 56, "The First Encounters with Coffee Beans," Essie Parrish related how the Kashaya had been given coffee to drink by a white man, who also left them a grinder and beans. A Kashaya woman then experimented with the coffee beans:

> She boiled it too. Just the way they used to cook their acorns, that's how she boiled [the coffee beans], thinking they would become soft—she boiled them whole. She let it boil and boil—let it boil all day long. She tested them with her fingers but they never did get soft—they weren't cooked. Then, saying that they must have been bad, that they were just like rocks, she poured them out. (Oswalt 1964:251)

Herman James recounted in text 63, "Two Underseas Youths Freeze to Death," how two colonial ("underseas") children died by exposure while hunting coots at a place called Shohka. His story stressed how Kashaya material culture was superior to that of the foreign colonists:

> They sat there like that at first. Many coots were lying there in the sacks they had been packing around. Then one said, "I wonder how it would be if we stuffed the feathers against our bodies." "Perhaps if we did that, it would warm us up," said the older one. "Let's try it," he said. Taking the coots up out of the sack, they plucked them and stuffed them inside their clothes. They stuffed that way.
>
> The rain pelted down steadily. There wasn't a dry spot on their bodies—they were all soaking wet. They sat there like that. They

stuffed like that. The feathers having got wet, they never warmed up. They really began to freeze stiff when the middle of the night came. At the stroke of twelve it got so that they couldn't talk.

Then, probably at one o'clock, one suddenly just died, fell over and lay there, having frozen stiff from the great cold. The other one must have died soon afterwards....

Because of that, the Indians said that cold was a terrible thing. Even if he wore a lot of clothes, a person would die if he got drenched in the rain. "When the body's blood grows cold, one becomes numb," said the Indians. They [Indians] wore a bear skin underneath so that the cold could not get in. Even the rain couldn't penetrate that bear skin or panther skin—or the buckskin that they wore in summer time. That's why the Indians never sickened from the great cold, even when the rain beat against them. [The Russians] asked why it didn't happen to them [the Indians]. Then they told the undersea people. (Oswalt 1964: 274–75)

A second theme of the Native narratives is how hard the Kashaya Pomo labored for the Russian-American Company and that some of this work was dangerous, resulting in fatalities. A couple of excerpts from text 60, "Grain Food," told by Herman James, illustrate this point:

My grandmother told me this too about what the undersea people did. What I am going to tell about now is how they ground their flour when they raised and gathered wheat.

Where the land lies stretched out, where all the land is at Métini, they raised wheat which blanketed the land. When it was ripe everywhere, then the people, by hand, cut it down, tied it up, and laid it there. Then, in a sea lion skin, they dragged it to their houses....

In order to make it turn into flour, they had something that spun around for them in the wind—they called it a "flour grinder." When they got ready to grind with that, they poured [the wheat] down in there to be ground, while tossing the sacks up—that they did all day long. Then they filled the sacks with flour, and hauling it away as before, they piled it up in a building. There was a lot for them to eat in the winter.

Once, while a woman was walking around there, she

happened to get too close while the wind was turning [the grind-stone]. At that time, women's hair was long. [The woman's hair] got caught and turned with it. The woman, too, was spun around, all of her hair was chewed off, and she was thrown off dead.

They picked her up, carried her home, and cremated her—at that time they still cremated. That is the way it happened; the flour grinder snared the woman and she died. (Oswalt 1964:267)

A third theme stresses the problem of spousal conflicts among interethnic and Indian couples and the swift measures taken by Russian administrators to punish abusive men. In text 62, "The Suicide of a Wife," Herman James told Robert Oswalt about the mistreatment of an Indian woman by her colonial husband:

This, too, my grandmother told me of what she saw herself. That was at a time when the undersea people had come up [from the ocean].

One time, a woman arose early in the morning. That Indian woman was married to an undersea man. They had been quarreling with each other. The man walked out saying, "If I find you here at home, I will kill you." Then he left to go to work.

When she had finished eating, she gave food to her children, went into the bedroom, and put on her good, new clothes.

"Where are you going, Mother?" said her oldest girl. She replied, "I am going to walk over to coastal cliff for a little while." "Let me go along, Mother," said [the girl].

"No," she said at first. But still, when she left, when she had gone some distance, [the child] followed. When [the mother] reached her destination, [the child] came closer to her mother. She stopped at the top of the coastal cliff.

"What are you going to do?" she asked her mother. "I am going to die today," she replied to her daughter. "No," said the daughter. "Who would take care of us?" "Your father growled at me so much that I can't go home any more," [the mother] said.

Then the child grabbed her dress. When she did so, [the mother] didn't listen. After a while, she suddenly threw herself way down onto the gravel beach. When that happened, when she threw herself down, the child let go.

Then she ran home and told. The others came, carried her up, and laid her down over at her house. The next day they buried her—at that time they already buried people [no longer cremated them].

Then her husband arrived home and she wasn't there. Subsequently, they locked him up as a prisoner—the undersea people did. One week later, they took him out, led him off a little way from the houses, and arrived at the place where they used to whip people. Then they whipped him; they whipped him for almost a whole day.

When they did so, he fainted and fell to the ground. He didn't regain consciousness; he died. Then they buried him.

This is also a true event that was told to me. [My grandmother] really saw it herself. This is all. (Oswalt 1964:271)

Herman James's grandmother Lukaria not only stressed the vulnerability of Native women in this colonial context but also recounted, in another story, "The Wife-Beater" (text 61 in *Kashaya Texts*), how the company disciplined a husband for abusing his Kashaya spouse:

This that I am about to tell about was also at Métini. This my grandmother also told me—it, too, is true. People lived there, in the manner I have described.

One time there was a man and an Indian woman living there together. Once, early in the morning, he arose cranky. He growled at his wife. He got meaner and meaner, and suddenly grabbing an axe, he cut her head with it.

At that time, the undersea people already lived there. They already had a sheriff then, and when they told him, he led him [the husband] away. He was shut up at a place where a little house was standing. They locked him up for about one week.

Then, in the woods, they cut off small hazel switches to whip him with. They brought them to the settlement. They laid them there.

Then, leading the man out, they made him stand at a certain place. So that he couldn't run away, they had tied his hands, tied his feet, and stood him up. Next they started in to whip him. When one [switch] wore out, they took another, and thus whipped him for half a day. He fell down unconscious. Then they carried him home.

Unexpectedly he became conscious. After a while he recovered. When he had recovered, he told what had happened to him. He said that that was the only thing that could tame him. After they whipped him, he said that he started to think of good, righteous things. Intending to tell about that, he caused the people to assemble and spoke. "Don't ever want to try that," he said. "I am telling you that I could only stand going through that because I am strong," he said.

That woman left the man. They separated. Then they lived there like that. For a long time the man was alone. The woman, too, was alone. She didn't want to stay with him any more.

This is what was told to me. It, too, is true. This is all. (Oswalt 1964:269–71)

ARCHAEOLOGICAL FINDINGS

A four-year study of the Native Alaskan village focused on the areal excavation of two house areas where we think Native Californian women and Native Alaskan men resided (Lightfoot, Schiff, and Wake 1997). An analysis of the artifacts, faunal remains, and architectural features provides an intimate glimpse of the daily practices undertaken in interethnic households, especially the preparation and cooking of meals, the cleaning of domestic spaces, and the furnishing of houses. Significantly, our interpretation of the spatial structure of the archaeological materials suggests that Kashaya conventions and organizational principles underpinned many of the day-to-day cultural practices carried out in the houses and outlying extramural spaces. It appears that Native Californian women continued to use traditional culinary methods, particularly underground pit ovens, to prepare and cook meat and vegetable dishes. They butchered and prepared sea mammals hunted by their Native Alaskan spouses in largely the same fashion that they traditionally cooked deer and other large terrestrial game.

Native women employed Kashaya Pomo conventions of cleanliness and order in sweeping house floors and disposing of refuse in discrete house dumps. Little evidence of traditional Native Alaskan household equipment or furniture was recovered during the excavation, in contrast to the remarkable material culture unearthed from the manufacture and maintenance of the sophisticated marine hunting equipment of Native Alaskan men. With respect to the household domestic equipment, we found primarily Native Californian material culture, including milling stones, cooking rocks, and chipped stone tools. Finally, although European materials such as glass and ceramics were recovered in the excavations, they appear to be associated with the transformation of broken foreign objects into Native artifact forms, such as pendants and projectile points.

Our investigation indicates that Native Californian women were asserting their own distinct social identities within interethnic households. Although Native women left their own homeland villages to move into the Native Alaskan village, they maintained their separate lives in their performance of daily activities centering around houses and nearby extramural space. They reconstituted their Indian conventions during the daily acts of processing and cooking meals, producing Native objects from European materials, cleaning and caring for residential space, and furnishing their homes with familiar items.

CENSUS DATA

The Kuskov censuses of 1820 and 1821 and the Veniaminov censuses of 1836 and 1838, recently published by Alexei Istomin (1992) and Sannie Osborn (1997), respectively, provide longitudinal data for examining the nature of interethnic unions in the Ross Colony. Here, I summarize three major trends resulting from my analysis of the census data.

First, significant numbers of households in the Ross settlement were composed of local Indian women and colonial men, but these decreased over time. In the Kuskov censuses of 1820–1821, the majority of the households at Ross with two or more people consisted of Native Californian women, colonial men, and their children. Of the ninety-five households with two or more members, fifty-six (59 percent) had Native Californian women residing with Russian, creole, or Native Alaskan men. In the Veniaminov censuses of 1836 and 1838, interethnic households with Native Californian women no longer comprised the dominant type of family residence. Of the seventy-three households containing two or more members, only twenty (27 percent) were the abodes of Native Californian women and colonial men. Furthermore, the composition of the interethnic households changed over time. Of the fifty-six Native Californian women listed in the 1820–1821 censuses, fifty (89 percent) resided with Native Alaskan men, five (9 percent) with Russian men, and one (2 percent) with a creole man. By the time Veniaminov made his observations in 1836, the majority of Native Californian women were residing with Russian men. Of the twenty Native Californian women identified in ethnically mixed marriages in the late 1830s, eleven (55 percent) resided with Russian men, four (20 percent) with Native Alaskan men, three (15 percent) with creole men, one (5 percent) with a Yakuts man, and one (5 percent) with a man whose ethnicity was not identified. The sharp drop in the number of Native women cohabiting with Native Alaskan men is due, at least in part, to the decline in sea otter hunting in the 1830s and the transfer of many Native Alaskan workers back to Russian colonies in the North Pacific.

Second, interethnic unions involving Native Californian women were relatively brittle affairs, with couples often separating after only a short time together. In 1824 Khlebnikov (1990, 35:194) observed:

> All the Aleuts have Indian women, but these relationships are unstable, and the Aleuts and the Indians do not trust each other. An Indian woman may live for a number of years with an Aleut and have children, but then, acting on a whim, will drop everything and run off to the mountains.

None of the fifty-six Native Californian women involved with colonial men in the early 1820s were still living with their partners in the 1836 or 1838 censuses (Osborn 1997:213, 297). The longest documented relationship for a Native Californian woman at Ross was between Paraskeva (an "Indian wife") and Isai Adamson, a Finnish cooper who was sent to Colony Ross in 1823. Their relationship apparently lasted thirteen years (1823 to 1836). But most relationships were much more fluid and short term. My tabulation of whether couples were married for one or both years during census years indicates that most women stayed with their colonial husbands for only one year in either the two-year census cycle of 1820–1821 or the three-year cycle beginning in 1836 and ending in 1838. The pattern did not appear to vary by the ethnic identification of the male partner. For the fifty Native Californian women residing with Native Alaskan men in the early 1820s, twenty couples remained together for only 1820, eight for only 1821, and twenty-two for the entire two-year cycle. A similar pattern is shown for the four Native Californian and Alaskan couples documented in the late 1830s; one couple was recorded for 1836 and another two for 1838. Only one couple remained together for the entire three-year cycle.

Of course, many of the interethnic unions recorded for a single year may have lasted longer, as the couples may have been together for varying lengths of time either before or after the censuses were taken. But the above information does highlight the capricious nature of the ethnically mixed households, since more than half did not last the full two years of the 1820–1821 censuses (thirty-two of the fifty-six couples) or the full three-year cycle of the 1836 and 1838 censuses (eleven of the eighteen couples). Furthermore, there is some indication that sequential, serial monogamy was being practiced by at least some of the colonial men and Indian women at the Ross settlement. I counted eleven Native Californian women who were married to a particular colonial man for one year of the census cycle and then either entered into a second relationship with a colonial man at Ross or moved back to their home villages when their former partner became involved with another woman in the second year of the census cycle (1820 and 1821 or 1836 and 1838).

Third, there is a significant difference between the 1820–1821 and 1836 and 1838 censuses in the presence of a cohort of baptized Indian women and children who apparently were not attached to the households of colonial men during the waning years of the colony. In the 1820–1821 censuses, all but one of the fifty-seven Indian women listed were residing with colonial men, and most were probably not members of the Russian Orthodox Church. In the 1836 and 1838 censuses, twenty Indian women, some of whom had converted to the Orthodox faith, were members of interethnic households, while another fifteen to twenty were baptized females not currently residing with colonial men. The latter included widows, heads of single-parent households, and single women with no record of previous marriages or children.

DISCUSSION

A microhistorical analysis of available oral traditions, archaeological materials, and census data provides a much more nuanced and complicated perspective about the treatment of Kashaya Pomo women at Colony Ross than one would glean from Russian sources alone or from the perception of contemporary Kashaya Pomo elders. Some women may have entered into undesirable relationships with colonial men at the request of family patriarchs or because of inequitable power dynamics exerted by foreign suitors. There appear to have been underlying tensions in joint households composed of Indian women and colonial men: spousal abuse existed among some couples, most relationships did not last for more than a relatively few months, and, based on limited archaeological excavations, Indian women could and did maintain very separate lives and identities from their husbands. While social interactions with foreign men may have been inevitably stressful, it is clear that Kashaya Pomo women exerted considerable agency in negotiating their lives at Colony Ross. If relationships did not work out, Native Californian women could return to their homeland villages, take up with other colonial men, or gather at the Ross settlement with other Indian women and children. In maintaining their own cultural practices, furnishings, and cleanliness in interethnic households, it is clear that some of these women maintained a sense of home within a foreign social setting. However, it is not yet clear how much the lives of Indian women who converted to the Russian Orthodox faith changed, especially in the last years of the colony, when a few of these converted women married Russian men or lived by themselves at the Ross settlement.

Even though my attempt at a biographical study of Native women at Colony Ross lacks the specificity and detail of Mary Beaudry's chapter on sedentary merchants in New England, we can still hear individual voices of people who never penned a letter or journal about themselves. Lukaria, the maternal grandmother of Herman James and eyewitness of Colony Ross, is probably recorded as "Luker'ia" in the list of baptized Indians prepared by Father Veniaminov in 1836 (see Lightfoot 2005b:159–60). She would have been about thirty-two years old and part of the cohort of Indian women who had converted to the Russian Orthodox faith. Significantly, several of the stories told by Herman James make observations about Christian practices at Colony Ross. In text 63, about two colonial youths who freeze to death, Herman James concludes his story with their burial:

> This that my grandmother told me is also true; she saw it herself. She also saw when they buried them in the ground. Before they buried them, they had borne them into the church. Having prepared them, they set the two youths down into the ground. This is what she told me she herself saw—saw with her own eyes—this is also true. That's the way she told me the story. I know a lot of the true stories that she told me. This is the end. (Oswalt 1964:275)

In text 58, "The Last Vendetta," Herman James presents a poignant story about an Indian group from Métini avenging the death of one of their men murdered by enemies from the "Forest Depths." But you can definitely sense Lukaria's presence in his recounting of this oral tradition. After raiding a house in the Forest Depths and shooting an Indian man, the people from Métini decide to live peacefully, an action that is attributed to their participation in the Russian Orthodox faith:

> Then the Indians, having slung their bows and put their arrows in their quivers, returned home. They set off to go back to Métini. They lived there. "Let this now be the end," said the old people in council. "We aren't going to kill any more; we aren't going to be enemies with Indians any more. Now we'll just live peacefully. Battling enemies comes out to be a bad deal—people keep dying."
>
> Into what we call a "cross-house" [church] some people

drifted in. Some people drifted into the church belonging to the undersea people. Thereafter there was no more killing of people—what was called enemy-killing.

My grandmother told this, saying that she herself saw and heard it. (Oswalt 1964:259)

By focusing on the small worlds of the Kashaya Pomo women, we also obtain important insights for understanding the broader political setting of Colony Ross. There is no question that the managers of the Russian-American Company were tough taskmasters. Native laborers worked long, hard hours during the harvest season, at potentially dangerous tasks. Company administrators maintained tight discipline within the Ross Colony. But it is also evident that the company punished both colonial and Indian men for the abuse or ill treatment of Native women. The perception that the company would whip men to death for infractions against Native women may have been a significant reason why some Kashaya entered into interethnic households and/or converted to the Russian Orthodox faith.

CONCLUSION

In the future, students writing microhistories about colonial people and places, no matter what discipline they are trained in, will need to learn to work with multiple sources of oral, visual, material, and documentary data and to grapple with the challenges of integrating these varied sources into their research projects. In this paper, I highlight some of the issues that have made archaeologists skeptical about using Native oral traditions in historical research. Oral traditions can be influenced by contemporary social and political matters, memory loss, chronological issues, the performance of narratives and the places where stories are told, and the encoding of cultural meanings that outsiders may not understand. But I believe that archaeologists have focused too much on the problematical side of oral traditions, often failing to see the many strengths that these sources may bring to archaeological and historical research. True, we must be extremely critical about the use of Native narratives, scrutinizing them for potential biases, shortcomings, and interpretive pitfalls when we address specific kinds of research questions in specific historical contexts. But this is true of all sources of information we use in our investigations, be they historical documents, archaeological findings, pictures, or paintings, as the chapters in this book nicely demonstrate.

Kashaya Pomo oral traditions provide crucial Native perceptions of the Russian colony—not available from any known written source—about how life unfolded for ordinary laborers and spouses undertaking daily tasks, domestic practices, social interactions, and family relationships. Rather than trying to use these rich texts to reconstruct specific historical events or to date historical happenings in the Ross settlement, I believe they are best employed to obtain a sense of what life was like for Native Californians as they encountered foreign people, alien foods, and new kinds of cultural practices and religious beliefs. Although oral traditions, archaeological findings, and census documents represent different ways of knowing about the past at Colony Ross, I found that they can relate to each other in a complementary fashion. While the oral traditions and archaeological findings elicit fresh insights about the daily practices of Indian people at Ross, the census data provide the means of securing these happenings into a broader chronological framework. The rich trappings of daily life exposed by these diverse sources are the meat and potatoes of microhistory. In using these multiple sources of information, we obtain new insights about the complicated social interactions that took place within interethnic households, as well as the elaborate power structure that underpinned Colony Ross.

Note

I thank James Brooks, Christopher DeCorse, John Walton, Alan Taylor, Roberta Jewett, and an anonymous reviewer for their constructive comments on an earlier version of this paper. I also appreciate greatly the advice and helpful comments provided by other participants in the SAR seminar. I commend the entire staff of the School for Advanced Research for the fine food, drink, company, and accommodations that made our stay in Santa Fe a memorable time.

References

Abbiateci, Andre

1978   Arsonists in Eighteenth-Century France: An Essay in the Typology of Crime. *In* Deviants and the Abandoned in French Society, Selections for the Annales, vol. 4. Robert Foster and Arest Ranum, eds. Pp. 157–79. Baltimore: Johns Hopkins University Press.

Abbott, Andrew

1992   What Do Cases Do? Some Notes on Activity in Sociological Analysis. *In* What Is a Case? Exploring the Foundations of Social Inquiry. Charles C. Ragin and Howard S. Becker, eds. Pp. 53–82. Cambridge: Cambridge University Press.

Adams, John Quincy

[1788]   The Diary of John Quincy Adams. Collections of the Massachusetts Historical
 1902   Society, 2nd series, vol. 16.

Adelman, Jeremy

1994   Frontier Development: Land, Labour, and Capital on the Wheatlands of Argentina and Canada, 1890–1914. New York: Oxford University Press.

Agorsah, Emmanuel Kofi

1983   Social Behavior and Spatial Context. African Study Monographs 4:119–28.

Aguilar, Paloma

2001   Justice, Politics, and Memory in the Spanish Transition. *In* The Politics of Memory: Transitional Justice in Democratizing Societies. A. Barahona de Brito, C. González Enríquez, and P. Aguilar, eds. Pp. 92–118. Oxford: Oxford University Press.

2002   Memory and Amnesia: The Role of the Spanish Civil War in the Transition to Democracy. Oxford: Berghahn Books.

Alinder, Mary Street

1996   Ansel Adams: A Biography. New York: Henry Holt.

Allen, Gardner Weld

1927   Massachusetts Privateers of the Revolution. Published for the Massachusetts Historical Society. Cambridge, MA: Harvard University Press.

References

Alminaque, Conrado
1981   El indio pampero in la literatura gauchesca. Miami: Ediciones Universal.

Anyon, Roger, T. J. Ferguson, Loretta Jackson, and Lillie Lane
2000   Native American Oral Traditions and Archaeology. *In* Working Together: Native Americans and Archaeologists. K. E. Dongoske, M. Aldenderfer, and K. Doehner, eds. Pp. 61–87. Washington, DC: Society for American Archaeology.

Appadurai, Arjun
1996   Modernity at Large: Cultural Dimensions of Globalization. Minneapolis: University of Minnesota Press.

Armando, Adriana Beatriz
1994   Un acercamiento al chaco austral a mediados del Siglo XVIII: El relato de Dobrizhoffer y los conflictos fronterizos. Anuario Del Instituto de Estudios Histórico-Sociales 9:215–26.

Arner, Robert D.
1982   The Lost Colony in Literature. Raleigh: North Carolina Department of Cultural Resources.

Atherton, John H.
1983   Ethnoarchaeology in Africa. African Archaeological Review 1:75–104.

Auyero, Javier
2004   When Everyday Life, Routine Politics, and Protest Meet. Theory and Society 33:417–41.

Bailey, Josiah
1991   Was the Lost Colony Really Lost? Some Carteret Countians Tell a Different Version of John White's Historic Expedition. The State 58(9):12–14.

Balestracci, Duccio
1984   La zappa e la retorica: Memorie familiari di un contadino toscano del Quattrocento. Florence: Salimbeni.

Ballong-Wen-Mewuda, J. Bato'ora
1984   Sao Jorge da Mina (Elmina) et son contexte socio-historique pendant l'occupation portugaise (1482–1637). Doctoral thesis, Center for African Research, University of Paris.
1993   La vie d'un comptoir portugais en Afrique Occidentale. Lisbon and Paris: École des Hautes Études en Sciences Sociales, Centre d'Études Portugaises: Fondation Calouste Gulbenkian/Commission Nationale por les Commémorations des Décourvertes Portgaises.

Barker, Francis
1984   The Tremulous Private Body: Essays on Subjection. London: Methuen.

Barkey, Karen, and Mark Von Hagen
1997   After Empire: Multiethnic Societies and Nation-Building. Boulder, CO: Westview Press.

Barlowe, Arthur

[1584]   Narrative. *In* The New World: The First Pictures of America, vol. 1. Stefan
1965   Lorant, ed. Pp. 125–34. New York: Duell, Sloan and Pearce.

Barnett, Catherine

1988   The Writing on the Wall. Art and Antiques 11:90–99, 124–28.

Barr, Juliana

2007   Peace Came in the Form of a Woman: Indians and Spaniards in the Texas
          Borderlands. Chapel Hill: University of North Carolina Press.

Barrell, John

1980   The Dark Side of the Landscape: The Rural Poor in English Painting,
          1730–1840. Cambridge: Cambridge University Press.

Barros, Álvaro

[1872]   Fronteras y territorios federales de las Pampas del sur. Buenos Aires:
1975   Hachette.

1975   Indios, fronteras, y seguridad interior. Buenos Aires: Solar/Hachette.

Basso, Keith H.

1996   Wisdom Sits in Places: Landscape and Language among the Western Apache.
          Albuquerque: University of New Mexico Press.

Bathe, Greville, and Dorothy Bathe

1943   Jacob Perkins: His Inventions, His Times and His Contemporaries.
          Philadelphia: Historical Society of Pennsylvania.

Baudrillard, Jean

1988   America. Chris Turner, trans. New York: Verso.

Beaudry, Mary C.

1987   Limited Archaeological Reconnaissance of the Spencer-Peirce-Little Property,
          Newbury, Massachusetts. Boston: Center for Archaeological Studies, Boston
          University.

1993a   Public Aesthetics versus Personal Experience: Worker Health and Well-Being in
          19th-Century Lowell, Massachusetts. Historical Archaeology 27(2):90–105.

1993b   Puzzling Over the Pieces: The 1992 Field Season at Spencer-Peirce-Little Farm.
          Context (newsletter of the Center for Archaeological Studies at Boston
          University) 11(1–2):5–7, 24.

1995a   The Boardmans' Flower Garden: Archaeological Testing in the Proposed Dry
          Well Area, Spencer-Peirce-Little Farm, Newbury, Massachusetts. Boston:
          Department of Archaeology, Boston University.

1995b   Introduction: Ethnography in Retrospect. *In* The Written and the Wrought:
          Complementary Sources in Historical Archaeology. Mary Ellin D'Agostino,
          Margo Winer, Elizabeth Prine, and Eleanor Casella, eds. Pp. 1–15. Kroeber
          Anthropological Society Papers 79. Berkeley: Department of Anthropology,
          University of California.

REFERENCES

1996   Reinventing Historical Archaeology. *In* Historical Archaeology and the Study of American Culture. Lu Ann De Cunzo and Bernard L. Herman, eds. Pp. 473–97. Winterthur, DE: Winterthur Museum.

In press Privy to the Feast: Eighty to Supper Tonight. *In* Table Settings: The Material Culture and Social Context of Dining in the Old and New Worlds, AD 1700–1900. James Symonds, ed. Oxford: Oxbow Books.

Beaudry, Mary C., ed.

1988   Documentary Archaeology in the New World. Cambridge: Cambridge University Press.

1992   Beneath the Kitchen Floor: Archaeology of the Spencer-Peirce-Little Farm. Interim Report 3. Boston: Department of Archaeology, Boston University.

Beaudry, Mary C., Lauren J. Cook, and Stephen A. Mrozowski

1991   Artifacts and Active Voices: Material Culture as Social Discourse. *In* The Archaeology of Inequality. Randall H. McGuire and Robert Paynter, eds. Pp. 150–91. Oxford: Blackwell.

Bech, Niels, and Hyland, A. D. C.

1978   Elmina: A Conservation Study. Occasional Report 17. Kumasi, Ghana: Faculty of Architecture, University of Science and Technology.

Bechis Rosso, Martha

1983   Interethnic Relations during the Period of Nation-State Formation in Chile and Argentina: From Sovereign to Ethnic. PhD dissertation, New School, New York.

Becker, Howard

1995   The Power of Inertia. Qualitative Sociology 18:301–9.

Benes, Peter

1986   Old-Town and the Waterside: Two Hundred Years of Tradition and Change in Newbury, Newburyport, and West Newbury, 1635–1835. Newburyport, MA: Historical Society of Old Newbury.

Benjamin, Walter

1969   Illuminations. New York: Schocken Books.

1978   Reflections. Peter Demetz, ed. New York: Schocken Books.

Bennett, Linda Rae, and Lenore Manderson, eds.

2003   Violence against Women in Asian Societies: Gender Inequality and Technologies of Violence. New York and London: Routledge.

Bermeo, N.

1997   Myths of Moderation: Confrontation and Conflict during Democratic Transitions. Comparative Politics 29(3):305–22.

Bermingham, Ann

1986   Landscape and Ideology: The English Rustic Tradition, 1740–1860. Berkeley: University of California Press.

Billings, Dwight B., and Kathleen M. Blee

2000   The Road to Poverty: The Making of Wealth and Hardship in Appalachia. New York: Cambridge University Press.

Black, Donald

1983   Crime as Social Control. American Sociological Review 48 (February):34–45.

Blake, John William

1942   Europeans in West Africa, 1450–1560. London: Hakluyt Society.

1971   West Africa: Quest for God and Gold, 1454–1578. London: Curzon Press.

Blee, Kathleen M.

1991   Women of the Klan: Racism and Gender in the 1920s. Berkeley: University of California Press.

2002   Inside Organized Racism: Women in the Hate Movement. Berkeley: University of California Press.

Blee, Kathleen M., and Ashley Currier

2005   Character-Building: The Dynamics of Emerging Social Movement Groups. Mobilization: An International Journal 10(1):129–44.

Block, Sharon

2007   Rape and Sexual Power in Early America. Chapel Hill: University of North Carolina Press.

Blu, Karen

1980   The Lumbee Problem: The Making of an American Indian People. New York: Cambridge University Press.

Boardman, Offin

1779–80 Diary of Offin Boardman, January 4, 1779 to March 18, 1780. Transcript prepared by Mrs. John Bradbury. Historical Society of Old Newbury, Newburyport, Massachusetts.

1811   Will of Offin Boardman, March 1, 1808; proved September 5, 1811, Essex County Registry of Probate. Massachusetts State Archives, Boston.

Boas, Nancy

1988   The Society of Six: California Colorists. San Francisco: Bedford Arts.

Borges, Jorge Luis

1998   The Warrior and the Captive Maiden. *In* Collected Fictions. Andrew Hurley, trans. Pp. 208–11. New York: Penguin.

Bourdieu, Pierre

1987   The Biographical Illusion. Working Papers and Proceedings of the Center for Psychosocial Studies 14. Chicago: Center for Psychosocial Studies.

Bourque, Nicole Marie

1997   An Analysis of Faunal Remains from Elmina, Ghana. BA honors thesis, Department of Anthropology, Syracuse University.

REFERENCES

British Parliamentary Papers
1970   Correspondence Concerning the Gold Coast and the Ashantee Invasion, 1873–1874. Irish University Press Series of British Parliamentary Papers, Colonies Africa Volume 58:44–47.

Brooks, James F.
2000   Served Well by Plunder: *La Gran Ladronería* and Producers of History Astride the Río Grande. American Quarterly 52(1):23–58.
2002a   Captives and Cousins: Slavery, Kinship and Community in the Southwest Borderlands. Chapel Hill: University of North Carolina Press.
2002b   Life Proceeds from the Name: Indigenous Peoples and the Predicament of Hybridity. *In* Clearing a Path: Theorizing the Past in Native American Studies. Nancy Shoemaker, ed. Pp. 181–205. New York: Routledge.

Brown, Judith C.
1982   In the Shadow of Florence: Provincial Society in Renaissance Pescia. New York: Oxford University Press.
1986   Immodest Acts: The Life of a Lesbian Nun in Renaissance Italy. New York: Oxford University Press.

Brown, Milton
1981   Introduction. *In* Social Art in America, 1930–1945. New York: ACA Galleries.

Brucker, Gene
1986   Giovanni and Lusanna: Love and Marriage in Renaissance Florence. Berkeley: University of California Press.

Burke, Peter
2001   New Perspectives on Historical Writing. 2nd ed. Cambridge: Polity Press.

Burton, Richard
1863   Wanderings in West Africa from Liverpool to Fernando Po. London: Tinsley Brothers.

Bushman, Richard L.
1993   The Refinement of America: Persons, Houses, Cities. New York: Vintage Books.

Bustos, Jorge
1993   Indios y blancos, sal y ganado mas alla de la frontera: Patagones 1820–1830. Anuario del Instituto de Estudios Histórico-Sociales 8:27–45.

Canny, Nicholas
1988   Ireland as Terra Florida. *In* Kingdom and Colony: Ireland in the Atlantic World: 1560–1800. Pp. 1–29. Baltimore: Johns Hopkins University Press.

Carson, Barbara G.
1990   Ambitious Appetites: Dining, Behavior, and Patterns of Consumption in Federal Washington. Washington, DC: American Institute of Architects Press.

Catlin, Stanton L.
1989a   Nature, Science and the Picturesque. *In* Art in Latin America. Dawn Ades, ed. Pp. 63–99. New Haven, CT: Yale University Press.

1989b   Traveler-Reporter Artists and the Empirical Tradition in Post-Independence Latin America. *In* Art in Latin America. Dawn Ades, ed. Pp. 41–62. New Haven, CT: Yale University Press.

Cetina Aguilar, Anacleto
1996   Breves datos históricos y culturales del municipio de Hunucmá. Mérida, Mexico: Tallers Gráficos del Sudeste.

Chartier, Roger
1982   Intellectual History or Sociocultural History? The French Trajectories. *In* Modern European Intellectual History: Reappraisals and New Perspectives. Dominick LaCapra and Steven L. Kaplan, eds. P. 32. Ithaca, NY: Cornell University Press.

Clark, Walter
1902   On Roanoke Island. Address of Judge Walter Clark at meeting inaugurated by the state literary and historical association, Manteo, July 24, 1902. North Carolina Collection, UNC–Chapel Hill.

Clifford, James
1990   Notes on (Field)notes. *In* Fieldnotes: The Makings of Anthropology. Roger Sanjek, ed. Pp. 3–33. Ithaca, NY: Cornell University Press.

Cobb, Collier
1910   Early English Survivals on Hatteras Island. North Carolina Booklet 14:91–99.

Cohn, Samuel K., Jr.
1996   Women in the Streets: Essays on Sex and Power in Renaissance Italy. Baltimore: Johns Hopkins University Press.

Colomer, Josep
1998   La transición a la democracia: El modelo español. Madrid: Editorial Anagrama.

Comaroff, John, and Jean Comaroff
1992   Ethnography and the Historical Imagination. Boulder, CO: Westview Press.

Conti, Elio
1966   I catasti agrari della repubblica fiorentina e il catasto particellare toscano (secoli XIV–XIX). Rome: Istituto storico italiano per il Medio Evo.

Contreras, Belisario R.
1983   Tradition and Innovation in New Deal Art. Lewisburg, PA: Bucknell University Press.

Cooper, John M.
1946a   The Araucanians. *In* The Handbook of South American Indians, vol. 2. Julian Steward, ed. Pp. 687–767. Bulletin 143. Washington, DC: Bureau of American Ethnology.
1946b   The Patagonian and Pampean Hunters. *In* The Handbook of South American Indians, vol. 1. Julian Steward, ed. Pp. 127–69. Bulletin 143. Washington, DC: Bureau of American Ethnology.

REFERENCES

Cox, Christopher
1981   Introduction. *In* Dorothea Lange. New York: Aperture.

Crone, G. R.
1937   Cadamsoto and Other Documents on Western Africa in the Second Half of
         the Fifteenth Century, series 2, vol. 80. London: Hakluyt Society.

Cruikshank, Julie
1992   Life Lived Like a Story: Life Stories of Three Yukon Native Elders. Vancouver:
         University of British Columbia Press.

Crumley, Carole L., and William H. Marquardt, eds.
1987   Regional Dynamics: Burgundian Landscapes in Historical Perspective. San
         Diego: Academic Press.

Curtis, James C.
1986   Dorothea Lange, Migrant Mother, and the Culture of the Great Depression.
         Winterthur Portfolio 21(1):1–20.
1989   Mind's Eye, Mind's Truth: FSA Photography Reconsidered. Philadelphia:
         Temple University Press.

Daaku, Kwame Yeboa
1970   Trade and Politics on the Gold Coast, 1600–1720. London: Oxford University
         Press.

Daaku, Kwame Yeboa, and Albert Van Dantzig
1966   Map of the Regions of the Gold Coast in Guinea. Ghana Notes and Queries
         9:14–15.

D'Agostino, Mary Ellin, Margo Winer, Elizabeth Prine, and Eleanor Casella, eds.
1995   The Written and the Wrought: Complementary Sources in Historical
         Archaeology. Kroeber Anthropological Society Papers 79. Berkeley:
         Department of Anthropology, University of California.

Darnton, Robert
2004   It Happened One Night. New York Review of Books, June 24, 60–64.

Davis, Natalie Zemon
1983   The Return of Martin Guerre. Cambridge, MA: Harvard University Press.
2006   Trickster Travels: A Sixteenth-Century Muslim between Worlds. New York: Hill
         and Wang.

De Chastellux, François Jean, Marquis
[1780–82] Travels in North America. 2 vols. Chapel Hill: University of North Carolina
1963   Press.

DeCorse, Christopher R.
1987a   Excavations at Elmina, Ghana. Nyame Akuma 28:15–18.
1987b   Historical Archaeological Research in Ghana, 1986–1987. Nyame Akuma
         29:27–32.
1989a   An Archaeological Study of Elmina, Ghana: Trade and Culture Change on the

Gold Coast between the Fifteenth and Nineteenth Centuries. PhD dissertation, University of California, Los Angeles.

1989b   Material Aspects of Limba, Yalunka and Kuranko Ethnicity: Archaeological Research in Northeastern Sierra Leone. *In* Archaeological Approaches to Cultural Identity. Stephen Shennan, ed. Pp. 125–40. London: Unwin Hyman.

1992a   Archaeological Research at Elmina. Archaeology in Ghana 3:23–27.

1992b   Culture Contact, Continuity, and Change on the Gold Coast, AD 1400–1900. African Archaeological Review 10:163–96.

2001   An Archaeology of Elmina: Africans and Europeans on the Gold Coast, 1400–1900. Washington, DC: Smithsonian Institution Press.

2004   The Mouse that Roared: Historical Archaeology as Microhistory. Paper presented at the Symposium Villes anciennes en Afrique Histoire et archeologie: La complementarité imparfaite, University of Paris.

2005   Coastal Ghana in the First and Second Millennia AD: Change in Settlement Patterns, Subsistence and Technology. Journal des Africanistes 75(2):43–52.

DeCorse, Christopher R., and Gerard L. Chouin
2003   Trouble with Siblings: Archaeological and Historical Interpretation of the West African Past. *In* Sources and Methods in African History: Spoken, Written, Unearthed. Toyin Falola and Christian Jennings, eds. Pp. 7–15. Rochester, NY: University of Rochester Press.

Deleuze, Gilles, and Félix Guattari
1987   A Thousand Plateaus: Capitalism and Schizophrenia. Brian Massumi, trans. Minneapolis: University of Minnesota Press.

De Marees, Pieter
1987   Description and Historical Account of the Gold Kingdom of Guinea (1602). Albert van Dantzig and Adam Jones, trans. and ann. Oxford: Oxford University Press.

Dempsey, Claire W.
1993a   Extracts from Offin Boardman's Farm Diary, Transcribed and Annotated. Boston: Society for the Preservation of New England Antiquities.

1993b   Nathaniel Tracy and Mary Lee Tracy. Boston: Society for the Preservation of New England Antiquities.

1993c   Offin Boardman and Sarah Tappan Boardman. Boston: Society for the Preservation of New England Antiquities.

Dening, Greg
1996   Performances. Chicago: University of Chicago Press.

Derosne, Charles
1844   De la elaboración del azúcar en las colonias y de los nuevos aparatos destinados a mejorarla. Havana: Imprenta del Gobierno.

de Warville, Jacques Pierre Brissot
[1791]   New Travels in the United States of America, 1788. Cambridge, MA: Belknap
1964   Press of Harvard University Press.

Dial, Adolf L., and David K. Eliades

1975   The Only Land I Know: A History of the Lumbee Indians. San Francisco: Indian Historian Press.

Dorothea Lange Collection

n.d.   Oakland Museum, Oakland, California.

Doumanis, Nicholas, and Nicholas G. Pappas

1997   Grand History in Small Places: Social Protest on Castellorizo (1934). Journal of Modern Greek Studies 15:103–23.

Duara, Prasenjit

1995   Rescuing History from the Nation: Questioning Narratives of Modern China. Chicago: University of Chicago Press.

Dundes, Alan

1980   Interpreting Folklore. Bloomington: Indiana University Press.

Eastman, Ralph M.

1928   Some Famous Privateers of New England. Boston: State Street Trust Company.

Echo-Hawk, Roger C.

1997   Forging a New Ancient History for Native America. In Native Americans and Archaeologists: Stepping Stones to Common Ground. N. Swidler, K. E. Dongoske, R. Anyon, and A. Downer, eds. Pp. 88–102. Walnut Creek, CA: AltaMira Press.

2000a   Ancient Histories in the New World: Integrating Oral Traditions and the Archaeological Record. American Antiquity 65(2):267–90.

2000b   Exploring Ancient Worlds. In Working Together: Native Americans and Archaeologists. K. E. Dongoske, M. Aldenderfer, and K. Doehner, eds. Pp. 3–7. Washington, DC: Society for American Archaeology.

Eckert, Andreas, and Adam Jones

2002   Historical Writing about Everyday Life. Journal of African Cultural Studies 15(1):5–16.

Eco, Umberto

1986   Travels in Hyper Reality: Essays. San Diego: Harcourt, Brace, Jovanovich.

Edles, Laura Desfor

1998   Symbol and Ritual in the New Spain: The Transition to Democracy after Franco. Cambridge: Cambridge University Press.

Egmond, Florike, and Peter Mason

1997   The Mammoth and the Mouse: Microhistory and Morphology. Baltimore: Johns Hopkins University Press.

Elliot, George P.

1966   Introduction. In Dorothea Lange. New York: MOMA.

Ellis, Monica

1982   Ice and Icehouses through the Ages, with a Gazetteer for Hampshire. Southampton, UK: Southampton University Industrial Archaeology Group.

Elordi, C.

2002   Los años difíciles: El testimonio de los protagonistas anónimos de la guerra civil y la posguerra. Madrid: Aguilar.

Emigh, Rebecca Jean

1996   Loans and Livestock: Comparing Landlords' and Tenants' Declarations from the Catasto of 1427. Journal of European Economic History 25(3):705–23.

1998   The Mystery of the Missing Middle-Tenants: The "Negative" Case of Fixed-Term Leasing and Agricultural Investment in Fifteenth-Century Tuscany. Theory and Society 27:351–75.

1999a   The Length of Leases: Short-Term Contracts and Long-Term Relationships. Viator 30:345–82.

1999b   Traces of Certainty: Recording Death and Taxes in Fifteenth-Century Tuscany. Journal of Interdisciplinary History 30(2):181–98.

2000   Forms of Property Rights or Class Capacities: The Example of Tuscan Sharecropping. European Journal of Sociology 41(1):22–52.

2002   Numeracy or Enumeration? The Uses of Numbers by States and Societies. Social Science History 26(4):653–98.

2003   Property Devolution in Tuscany. Journal of Interdisciplinary History 33(3):385–420.

2005   The Unmaking of Markets: A Composite Visual History. Vectors: Journal of Culture and Technology in a Dynamic Vernacular 1. Electronic document, http://vectors.usc.edu/index.php?page=7&projectId=5, accessed October 3, 2007.

Erdoes, Richard, and Alfonso Ortiz, eds.

1984   American Indian Myths and Legends. New York: Pantheon Books.

Essex Deeds

1786   146:215, November 17. Essex County Registry of Probate, Salem, Massachusetts.

1787   146:215, January 1. Essex County Registry of Probate, Salem, Massachusetts.

1791   153:210, Tracy to Russell and Russell to Tracy, etc., September 7. Essex County Registry of Probate, Salem, Massachusetts.

Fabian, Johannes

2002   Time and the Other: How Anthropology Makes Its Object. New York: Columbia University Press.

Farris, Glenn J.

1988   Recognizing Indian Folk History as Real History: A Fort Ross Example. American Indian Quarterly 13(4):471–80.

1992   The Day of the Tall Strangers. The Californians 9(6):13–19.

1998   The Bodega Miwok as seen by Mikhail Tikhonovich Tikhanov in 1818. Journal of California and Great Basin Anthropology 20(1):2–12.

Faulkner, Alaric, Kim Mark Peters, David P. Sell, and Edwin S. Dethlefsen

1977   Port and Market: Archaeology of the Central Waterfront, Newburyport, Massachusetts. Prepared for the National Park Service, Interagency Archeological Services, Atlanta, Georgia. Newburyport, MA: Newburyport Press.

REFERENCES

Feinberg, Harvey Michael

1989   Africans and Europeans in West Africa: Elmina and Dutchmen on the Gold
        Coast during the Eighteenth Century. Transactions of the American
        Philosophical Society 79, part 7.

Feld, Steven, and Keith H. Basso, eds.

1996   Senses of Place. Santa Fe, NM: School of American Research Press.

Ferguson, Brian, and Neil Whitehead, eds.

2000   War in the Tribal Zone: Expanding States and Indigenous Warfare, rev. ed.
        Santa Fe, NM: School of American Research Press.

Ferguson, T. J., Kurt E. Dongoske, Mike Yeatts, and Leigh J. Kuwanwisiwma

2000   Hopi Oral History and Archaeology. In Working Together: Native Americans
        and Archaeologists. K. E. Dongoske, M. Aldenderfer, and K. Doehner, eds.
        Pp. 45–60. Washington, DC: Society for American Archaeology.

Finnegan, Ruth

1996   Oral Tradition. In Encyclopedia of Cultural Anthropology, vol. 3. D. Levinson
        and M. Ember, eds. Pp. 887–91. New York: Henry Holt and Company.

Fleisher, Jeff

2004   Behind the Sultan of Kilwa's "Rebellious Conduct": An Archaeological
        Perspective. In African Historical Archaeologies. A. M. Reid and P. J. Lane,
        eds. Pp. 91–124. New York: Kluwer Academic/Plenum Publishers.

Fletcher, Inglis

1952   The Elizabethan Background of North Carolina. Daughters of the American
        Revolution Magazine 86(3):274–75.

Flores, Dan

1991   Bison Ecology and Bison Diplomacy: The Southern Plains from 1800 to 1850.
        Journal of American History 78(2):465–85.

Fogelson, Raymond

1985   Night Thoughts on Native American Social History. Occasional Papers in
        Curriculum 3:67–89. Chicago: D'Arcy McNickle Center for the History of the
        American Indian, Newberry Library.

Forrest, John

1988   Lord I'm Coming Home: Everyday Aesthetics in Tidewater North Carolina.
        Ithaca, NY: Cornell University Press.

Fuller, Mary C.

2001   Images of English Origins in Newfoundland and Roanoke. In Decentring the
        Renaissance: Canada and Europe in Multidisciplinary Perspective, 1500–1700.
        Germain Warkentin and Carolyn Podruchny, eds. Pp. 141–58. Toronto:
        University of Toronto Press.

Funes Monzote, Reinaldo

2004   De bosque a sabana. Azúcar, deforestación y medio ambiente en Cuba:
        1492–1926. Mexico City: Siglo XXI.

Furet, François, and Jacques Le Goff

1973   Histoire et ethnologie. *In* Mélanges en l'honneur de Fernand Braudel. Vol. 2: Méthodologie de l'histoire et des sciences humaines. Toulouse, France.

García, Colonel Pedro A.

[1836]   Diario de un viaje a Salinas Grandes, en los campos del sud de Buenos Aires.

1974   Buenos Aires: EUDEBA.

García Enciso, Isaias J.

1979   Tolderías, fuertes, y fortines. Buenos Aires: Emecé Editores.

Garrard, Timothy F.

1980   Akan Weights and the Gold Trade. New York: Longman.

Geertz, Clifford

1983   Local Knowledge. New York: Basic Books.

1988   Being There: Anthropology and the Scene of Writing. *In* Works and Lives: The Anthropologist as Author. Stanford, CA: Stanford University Press.

1996   Afterword. *In* Senses of Place. Keith Basso and Steve Feld, eds. Pp. 259–62. Santa Fe, NM: School of American Research Press.

2000   The World in Pieces: Culture and Politics at the End of the Century. *In* Available Light: Anthropological Reflections on Philosophical Topics. Princeton, NJ: Princeton University Press.

2006   Among the Infidels. New York Review of Books, March 23, 22–25.

Genovese, Eugene D.

1972   Roll, Jordan, Roll: The World the Slaves Made. New York: Vintage.

Gilman, W., and J. Gilman

1811   Account of the Great Fire in Newburyport. Newburyport, MA: W & J Gilman.

Ginzburg, Carlo

1976   The Cheese and the Worms: The Cosmos of a Sixteenth-Century Miller. Harmondsworth, UK: Penguin Books.

1980a   The Cheese and the Worms: The Cosmos of a Sixteenth-Century Miller. Baltimore: Johns Hopkins University Press.

1980b   The Cheese and the Worms: The Cosmos of a Sixteenth-Century Miller. London: Routledge and Kegan Paul.

1982   The Cheese and the Worms: The Cosmos of a Sixteenth-Century Miller. London: Penguin Books.

1983   Night Battles: Witchcraft and Agrarian Cults in the Sixteenth and Seventeenth Centuries. Baltimore: Johns Hopkins University Press.

1989a   Clues, Myths, and the Historical Method. Baltimore: Johns Hopkins University Press.

1989b   Clues: Roots of an Evidential Paradigm. *In* Clues, Myths, and the Historical Method. Pp. 96–125. Baltimore: Johns Hopkins University Press.

1991   Ecstasies: Deciphering the Witches' Sabbath. New York: Pantheon.

1993   Microhistory: Two or Three Things That I Know about It. Critical Inquiry 20(1):10–35.

2000   The Enigma of Piero: Piero della Francesca. New York: Verso Books.

Ginzburg, Carlo, and Carlo Poni
1991   The Name of the Game: Unequal Exchange and the Historiographic Marketplace. *In* Microhistory and the Lost Peoples of Europe. Edward Muir and Guido Ruggiero, eds. Eren Branch, trans. Pp. 1–10. Baltimore: Johns Hopkins University Press.

Gleach, Fred
1997   Powhatan's World and Colonial Virginia: A Conflict of Cultures. Lincoln: University of Nebraska Press.

Goldberg, Vicki
1987   Margaret Bourke-White: A Biography. New York: Harper and Row.

Goldman, Robert, and Ann Tickamyer
1984   Status Attainment and the Commodity Form: Stratification in Historical Perspective. American Sociological Review 49:196–209.

Golovnin, Vasilii M.
1979   Around the World on the Kamchatka, 1817–1819. E. L. Wiswell, trans. Honolulu: Hawaiian Historical Society and University Press of Hawaii.

González, Luis
1974   San José de Gracia: Mexican Village in Transition. Austin: University of Texas Press.

Goodrich, Diana Sorensen
1998   Facundo and the Construction of Argentine Culture. Austin: University of Texas Press.

Goodwin, Jeff, James M. Jasper, and Francesca Polletta
2001   Why Emotions Matter. *In* Passionate Politics: Emotions and Social Movements. Jeff Goodwin, James M. Jasper, and Francesca Polletta, eds. Pp. 1–24. Chicago: University of Chicago Press.

Gordon, Linda
1994   Pitied but Not Entitled: Single Mothers and the History of Welfare. New York: Free Press.
1999   The Great Arizona Orphan Abduction. Cambridge, MA: Harvard University Press.
2006   Dorothea Lange: The Photographer as Agricultural Sociologist. Journal of American History 93(3):698–727.

Grady, Ann A.
1992   Spencer-Peirce-Little House Historic Structures Report. Boston: Society for the Preservation of New England Antiquities.

Graff, Harvey J.
1987   The Legacies of Literacy: Continuities and Contradictions in Western Culture and Society. Bloomington: Indiana University Press.

Graham, Frank Porter

1937   Address Delivered at Old Fort Raleigh, August, 18, 1937. North Carolina Collection, UNC–Chapel Hill.

Graves-Brown, Paul, Sian Jones, and Clive Gamble, eds.

1996   Cultural Identity and Archaeology: The Construction of European Communities. London: Routledge.

Gravlee, Clarence C., H. Russell Bernard, and William Leonard

2003   Boas's Changes in Bodily Form: The Immigrant Study, Cranial Plasticity, and Boas's Physical Anthropology. American Anthropologist 105:326–32.

Grendi, Edoardo

1977   Micro-analisi e storia sociale. Quaderni storici 35:506–20.

Gunther, Richard, Jose Ramon Montero, and Joan Botella

2004   Democracy in Modern Spain. New Haven, CT: Yale University Press.

Gupta, Akhil, and James Ferguson, eds.

1997   Anthropological Locations: Boundaries and Grounds of a Field Science. Berkeley: University of California Press.

Hagen, William W.

2002   Ordinary Prussians: Brandenberg Junkers and Villagers, 1599–1840. Cambridge: Cambridge University Press.

Hair, Paul Edward Hedley

1966   The Use of African Languages in Afro-European Contacts in Guinea: 1440–1560. Sierra Leone Language Review 5:5–26.

1994   The Founding of the Castelo de Sao Jorge da Mina: An Analysis of the Sources. Madison: African Studies Program, University of Wisconsin.

Hall, James

1974   Hall's Dictionary of Subjects and Symbols in Art. London: John Murray.

Hall, Stuart

1988   "The Toad in the Garden": Thatcherism among the Theorists. *In* Marxism and the Interpretation of Culture. Lawrence Grossberg and Cary Nelson, eds. Pp. 35–74. Urbana: University of Illinois Press.

Hall, Thomas D.

1998   The Rio de la Plata and the Greater Southwest: A View from World-System Theory. *In* Contested Ground: Comparative Frontiers on the Northern and Southern Edges of the Spanish Empire. Donna J. Guy and Thomas E. Sheridan, eds. Pp. 150–66. Tucson: University of Arizona Press.

Handler, Richard, and Eric Gable

1997   The New History in an Old Museum: Creating the Past at Colonial Williamsburg. Durham, NC: Duke University Press.

Handler, Richard, and William Saxton

1988   Dyssimulation: Reflexivity, Narrative, and the Quest for Authenticity in "Living History." Cultural Anthropology 3:242–60.

REFERENCES

Hannerz, Ulf
1996   Transnational Connections: Culture, People, Places. New York: Routledge.

Hariot, Thomas
[1590]   A Briefe and True Report of The New Found Land of Virginia. Paul Hulton,
1972   ed. New York: Dover.
[1590]   A Briefe and True Report of The New Found Land of Virginia. *In* The
1991   Roanoke Voyages, vol. 1. David Beers Quinn, ed. Pp. 317–87. New York: Dover.

Harkin, Michael
1988   History, Narrative, and Temporality: Examples from the Northwest Coast.
            Ethnohistory 35:99–130.

2004   Thirteen Ways of Looking at a Landscape. *In* Coming to Shore: New
            Perspectives on Northwest Coast Ethnology. Marie Mauzé, Michael E. Harkin,
            and Sergei Kan, eds. Pp. 385–406. Lincoln: University of Nebraska Press.

2005   "I'm an Old Cow Hand on the Banks of the Seine": Representations of Indians
            and Le Far West in Parisian Commercial Culture. *In* New Perspectives on
            Native North America: Cultures, Histories and Representations. Sergei Kan
            and Pauline Turner Strong, eds. Pp. 815–46. Lincoln: University of Nebraska
            Press.

2006   Towering Conflicts: Bear Lodge/Devils Tower and the Climbing Moratorium.
            International Journal of Environmental, Cultural, Economic and Social
            Sustainability 2(3):181–88.

2007   Performing Paradox: Narrativity and the Lost Colony of Roanoke. *In* Myth and
            Memory: Rethinking Stories of Indigenous-European Contact. John Lutz, ed.
            Pp. 103–17. Vancouver: University of British Columbia Press.

Harris, Jane
1978   Eighteenth-Century French Blue-Green Bottles from the Fortress of
            Louisbourg, Nova Scotia. History and Archaeology (Parks Canada) 29:83–149.

Helm, Richard
2004   Re-Evaluating Traditional Histories on the Coast of Kenya: An Archaeological
            Perspective. *In* African Historical Archaeologies. A. M. Reid and P. J. Lane,
            eds. Pp. 59–90. New York: Kluwer Academic/Plenum Publishers.

Henige, David P.
1973   The Problem of Feedback in Oral Tradition: Four Examples from the Fante
            Coastlands. Journal of African History 14(2):223–35.

1974   Kingship in Elmina before 1869: A Study in "Feedback" and the Traditional
            Idealization of the Past. Cahiers d'Etudes Africanes 14(3):499–520.

Herlihy, David, and Christiane Klapisch-Zuber
1981   Census and Property Survey of Florentine Domains in the Province of Tuscany,
            1427–1480. Machine readable data file. Madison: University of Wisconsin, Data
            and Program Library Service.

1985   Tuscans and Their Families: A Study of the Florentine Catasto of 1427. New
            Haven, CT: Yale University Press.

Hernández, José

1974 The Gaucho Martín Fierro. Frank G. Carrino, Alberto J. Carlos, and Norman Mangouni, trans. Albany, NY: SUNY Press.

Herz, Nat

1963 Dorothea Lange in Perspective: A Reappraisal of the FSA and an Interview. Infinity 12(4):5–11.

Herzfeld, Michael

1991 A Place in History: Social and Monumental Time in a Cretan Town. Princeton, NJ: Princeton University Press.

Hills, Patricia

1983 Social Concern and Urban Realism: American Painting of the 1930s. Boston: Boston University Art Gallery.

Hobsbawm, Eric, and George Rudé

1968 Captain Swing: A Social History of the Great English Agricultural Uprising of 1830. New York: Norton.

Holland, Dorothy, and Jean Lave, eds.

2001 History in Person: Enduring Struggles, Contentious Practice, Intimate Identities. Santa Fe, NM: School of American Research Press.

Hollinger, David A.

1987 The Knower and the Artificer. American Quarterly 39(1):37–55.

Howarth, Ken

1998 Oral History: A Handbook. Phoenix Mill, UK: Sutton Publishing Limited.

Hulbert, Laurance P.

1989 The Mexican Muralists in the United States. Albuquerque: University of New Mexico Press.

Hulton, Paul

1984 America, 1585: The Complete Drawings of John White. Chapel Hill: University of North Carolina Press; London: British Museum Publications.

Hurley, F. Jack

1972 Portrait of a Decade: Roy Stryker and the Development of Documentary Photography in the Thirties. Baton Rouge: Louisiana University Press.

Hyland, A. D. C.

1970 Documentation and Conservation. Occasional Report 13. Kumasi, Ghana: Faculty of Architecture, University of Science and Technology.

Istomin, Alexei A.

1992 The Indians at the Ross Settlement According to the Censuses by Kuskov, 1820–1821. Fort Ross, CA: Fort Ross Interpretive Association.

Jasper, James M.

2004 A Strategic Approach to Collective Action: Looking for Agency in Social Movement Choices. Mobilization 9(1):1–16.

REFERENCES

Jobson, Richard

[1623]   The Discovery of the River Gambra. David P. Gamble and P. E. H. Hair, eds.
1999   and trans. London: Hakluyt Society.

Johnson, Lyman L.

1998   The Frontier as an Arena of Social and Economic Change: Wealth Distribution
            in Nineteenth-Century Buenos Aires Province. *In* Contested Ground:
            Comparative Frontiers on the Northern and Southern Edges of the Spanish
            Empire. Donna J. Guy and Thomas E. Sheridan, eds. 167–81. Tucson:
            University of Arizona Press.

Jones, Adam

1985   Brandenburg Sources for West African History, 1680–1700. Studien zur
            Kulturkunde 77.

1987   Raw, Medium, Well Done: A Critical Review of Editorial and Quasi-Editorial
            Work on European Sources for Sub-Saharan Africa, 1960–1986. Madison:
            African Studies Program, University of Wisconsin.

1994   Drink Deep, or Taste Not: Thoughts on the Use of Early European Records in
            the Study of African Material Culture. History in Africa 21:349–70.

Jones, David

1976   Thomas Campbell Foster and the Rural Labourer: Incendiarism in East Anglia
            in the 1840s. Social History 1:5–43.

Jones, Kristine L.

1984   Conflict and Adaptation in the Argentine Pampas, 1750–1880. PhD disserta-
            tion, University of Chicago.

1986   Nineteenth-Century British Travel Accounts of Argentina. Ethnohistory
            33(2)195–211.

1994a   Comparative Ethnohistory and the Southern Cone. Latin American Research
            Review 29(1):107–18.

1994b   Indian-Creole Negotiations in the Southern Frontier. *In* Revolution and
            Restoration: The Rearrangement of Power in Argentina, 1776–1860. Mark D.
            Szuchman and Jonathan C. Brown, eds. Pp. 103–23. Lincoln: University of
            Nebraska Press.

1998   Comparative Raiding Economies: North and South. *In* Contested Ground:
            Comparative Frontiers on the Northern and Southern Edges of the Spanish
            Empire. Donna J. Guy and Thomas E. Sheridan, eds. Pp. 97–114. Tucson:
            University of Arizona Press.

Jones, Olive R.

1986   Cylindrical English Wine and Beer Bottles, 1735–1850. Studies in Archaeology,
            Architecture, and History. Ottawa, ON: Parks Canada, Environment Canada.

1993   Commercial Foods, 1740–1820. Historical Archaeology 27(2):25–41.

Jones, Olive R., and E. Ann Smith

1985   Glass of the British Military ca. 1755–1820. Studies in Archaeology,
            Architecture, and History. Ottawa, ON: Parks Canada, Environment Canada.

Jones, Sian S.

1997   The Archaeology of Ethnicity: Constructing Identities in the Past and the
        Present. New York: Routledge.

Joyce, Rosemary A.

2002   The Languages of Archaeology: Dialogue, Narrative, and Writing. Oxford:
        Blackwell.

2006   Writing Historical Archaeology. *In* The Cambridge Companion to Historical
        Archaeology. Dan Hicks and Mary C. Beaudry, eds. Pp. 48–65. Cambridge:
        Cambridge University Press.

Juan, Adelaida de

1985   Pintura y grabado coloniales cubanos. Havana: Editorial Pueblo y Educación.

Julía, Santos

2003   Memoria y amnistía en la transición. Claves de razón practica 129:14–25.

Karmin, Otto

1906   La legge del catasto fiorentino del 1427: Testo, introduzione e note. Florence:
        Bernardo Seeber.

Kea, Ray

1982   Settlements, Trade and Politics in the Seventeenth-Century Gold Coast.
        Baltimore: Johns Hopkins University Press.

Keller, Judith, ed.

2002   Dorothea Lange: Photographs from the J. Paul Getty Museum. Los Angeles: J.
        Paul Getty Museum.

Kelly, Michael

1996   Playing with Fire. New Yorker, July 15, 28–35.

Kelso, Gerald K.

1992   Pollen Analysis of Stairwell Fill under the Kitchen. *In* Beneath the Kitchen Floor.
        Mary C. Beaudry, ed. Not paginated. Archaeology of the Spencer-Peirce-Little
        Farm, Interim Report 3. Boston: Department of Archaeology, Boston University.

Khlebnikov, Kirill

1990   The Khlebnikov Archive: Unpublished Journal (1800–1837) and Travel Notes
        (1820, 1822, and 1824). J. Bisk, trans. Fairbanks: University of Alaska Press.

Kirshenblatt-Gimblett, Barbara

1998   Destination Culture: Tourism, Museums, and Heritage. Berkeley: University of
        California Press.

Knapp, Jeffrey

1993   Elizabethan Tobacco in the Discovery of Guiana. *In* New World Encounters.
        Stephen Greenblatt, ed. Pp. 273–312. Berkeley: University of California Press.

Kostromitinov, P.

1974   Notes on the Indians in Upper California. *In* Ethnographic Observations on
        the Coast Miwok and Pomo by Contre-Admiral F. P. Von Wrangell and P.
        Kostromitinov of the Russian Colony Ross, 1839. F. Stross and R. Heizer, eds.
        Pp. 7–18. Berkeley: Archaeological Research Facility, University of California.

REFERENCES

Kotzebue, Otto Von

1830   A New Voyage Round the World, in the Years 1823, 24, 25, and 26, vols. 1 and 2. London: Henry Colburn and Richard Bentley.

Kowalewski, Stephen A.

1997   A Spatial Method for Integrating Data of Different Types. Journal of Archaeological Method and Theory 4(3–4):287–306.

Kracauer, Siegfried

1969   History: The Last Things before the Last. Oxford: Oxford University Press.

Kristiansen, Kristian, and Michael Rowlands

1998   Social Transformations in Archaeology: Global and Local Perspectives. New York: Routledge.

Kulikoff, Allan

1992   The Agrarian Origins of American Capitalism. Charlottesville: University Press of Virginia.

Kupperman, Karen

1984   Roanoke: The Abandoned Colony. Totowa, NJ: Rowman and Allanheld.

Labaree, Benjamin W.

1975   Patriots and Partisans: The Merchants of Newburyport, 1764–1815. New York: Norton and Company.

Ladurie, Emmanuel Le Roy

1979   Carnival in Romans. Mary Feeney, trans. New York: George Braziller.

Landis, Michele

1999   Fate, Responsibility, and "Natural" Disaster Relief: Narrating the American Welfare State. Law and Society Review 33(2):257–318.

Landon, David B.

1991a   The Potential Applications of Tooth Cement Increment Analysis in Historical Archaeology. Northeast Historical Archaeology 17:85–99.

1991b   Zooarchaeology and Urban Foodways: A Case Study from Eastern Massachusetts. PhD dissertation, Boston University.

1992   Pigs' Feet and Pigeon Pie: Faunal Remains from the Spencer-Peirce-Little Farm Kitchen. In Beneath the Kitchen Floor. Mary C. Beaudry, ed. Not paginated. Archaeology of the Spencer-Peirce-Little Farm, Interim Report 3. Boston: Department of Archaeology, Boston University.

Lane, Ralph

[1589]   Ralph Lane's Discourse on the First Colony. In The Roanoke Voyages, vol. 1.
1991   David Beers Quinn, ed. Pp. 255–93. New York: Dover.

Lapique, Zoila

1974   Una tradición litográfica. Cuba Internaciónal 6(59):38–45.

Laplace, Cyrille

2006   Visit of Cyrille Pierre-Theodore Laplace to Fort Ross and Bodega Bay in

August 1839. Glens Farris, trans. and ann. Jenner, CA: Fort Ross Interpretive Association.

Laplante, Eduardo, and Justo Cantero

1857 Los ingenios: Colección de vistas de los principales ingenios de azúcar de la isla de Cuba. Havana: Litografía de L. Marquier.

Larson, Magali, and Silvia Sigal

2001 Does "The Public" Think Politically? A Search for "Deep Structures" in Everyday Political Thought. Qualitative Sociology 24:285–309.

LaViolette, Adria

2004 Swahili Archaeology and History of Pemba, Tanzania: A Critique and Case Study of the Use of Written and Oral Sources in Archaeology. *In* African Historical Archaeologies. A. M. Reid and P. J. Lane, eds. Pp. 125–62. New York: Kluwer Academic/Plenum Publishers.

Lawton, Harry W., Philip J. Wilke, Mary De Decker, and William Mason

1976 Agriculture among the Paiute of Owens Valley. Journal of California Anthropology 3:13–50.

Lee, Thomas Amory

1906 The Tracy Family of Newburyport. Essex Institute Historical Collections 52:57–74.

1916 Nathaniel Tracy, Harvard, 1769. Harvard Graduates Magazine, December, 193–97.

1917 The Lee Family of Marblehead. Reprinted from the Essex Institute Historical Collections. Salem, MA: Essex Institute.

Lepore, Jill

2001 Historians Who Love Too Much: Reflections on Microhistory and Biography. Journal of American History 88(1):129–44.

Levi, Giovanni

1988 Inheriting Power: The Story of an Exorcist. Lydia G. Cochrane, trans. Chicago: University of Chicago Press.

1991 On Microhistory. *In* New Perspectives in Historical Writing. Peter Burke, ed. Pp. 93–113. University Park: Pennsylvania State University Press.

2001 On Microhistory. *In* New Perspectives on Historical Writing. 2nd ed. Peter Burke, ed. Pp. 97–119. Cambridge: Polity Press.

Levin, Howard M., and Katherine Northrup

1980 Dorothea Lange: Farm Security Administration Photographs, 1935–39. Glencoe, IL: Text-Fiche Press.

Levine, Lawrence W.

1988 The Historian and the Icon: Photography and the History of the American People in the 1930s and 1940s. *In* Documenting America, 1935–1943. Carl Fleischhauer and Beverly W. Brannan, eds. Pp. 15–42. Berkeley: University of California Press.

REFERENCES

Lewis, Gordon K.
1983   Main Currents in Caribbean Thought: The Historical Evolution of Caribbean Society in Its Ideological Aspects. Baltimore: Johns Hopkins University Press.

Lewis, Philippa, and Gillian Darley
1986   Dictionary of Ornament. New York: Pantheon.

Lightfoot, Kent G.
1995   Culture Contact Studies: Redefining the Relationship between Prehistoric and Historical Archaeology. American Antiquity 60(2):199–217.

2005a   Archaeology and Indians: Thawing an Icy Relationship. News from Native California 19(1):37–39.

2005b   Indians, Missionaries, and Merchants: The Legacy of Colonial Encounters on the California Frontiers. Berkeley: University of California Press.

2006   California Colonial Histories: The Integration of Historical Data, Native Oral Traditions, and Archaeology. In Pedagogies of the Global: Knowledge in the Human Interest. A. Dirlik, ed. Pp. 255–71. Boulder, CO: Paradigm Publishers.

Lightfoot, Kent, Antoinette Martinez, and Ann Schiff
1998   Daily Practice and Material Culture in Pluralistic Social Settings: An Archaeological Study of Culture Change and Persistence from Fort Ross, California. American Antiquity 63(2):199–222.

Lightfoot, Kent G., Ann M. Schiff, and Thomas A. Wake
1997   The Archaeology and Ethnohistory of Fort Ross, California. Vol. 2: The Native Alaskan Neighborhood: A Multiethnic Community at Colony Ross. Berkeley: Archaeological Research Facility, University of California.

Lightfoot, Kent G., Thomas A. Wake, and Ann M. Schiff
1991   The Archaeology and Ethnohistory of Fort Ross, California, vol. 1. Berkeley: Archaeological Research Facility, University of California.

Little, Barbara, ed.
1992   Text-Aided Archeology. Boca Raton, FL: CRC Press.

Lopez, Juan Severino
1977   El rescate de las cautivas: Un episodio de la guerra y paz en las fronteras del desierto (1857–1858). Buenos Aires: Academia Nacional de la Historia.

Lowenthal, David
1985   The Past Is a Foreign Country. Cambridge: Cambridge University Press.

Lüdtke, Alf, ed.
1995   The History of Everyday Life: Reconstructing Social Experiences and Ways of Life. Princeton, NJ: Princeton University Press.

Lydon, Sandy
1985   Chinese Gold: The Chinese in the Monterey Bay Region. Capitola, CA: Capitola Book Company.

MacLeish, Archibald
1938   Land of the Free. New York: Harcourt, Brace.

Maddox, Richard

1993   El Castillo: The Politics of Tradition in an Andalusian Town. Urbana: University of Illinois Press.

1997   Bombs, Bikinis, and the Popes of Rock 'n' Roll: Reflections on Resistance, the Play of Subordinations, and Liberalism in Andalusia and Academia, 1983–1995. *In* Culture, Power, Place: Explorations in Critical Anthropology. James Ferguson and Akhil Gupta, eds. Pp. 275–90. Durham, NC: Duke University Press.

1998   Founding a Convent in Early Modern Spain: Cultural History, Hegemonic Processes, and the Plurality of the Historical Subject. Rethinking History 2(2):173–98.

2004   The Best of All Possible Islands: Seville's Universal Exposition, the New Spain, and the New Europe. Albany: State University of New York Press.

Magnússon, Sigurður Gylfi

2003   The Singularization of History: Social History and Microhistory within the Postmodern State of Knowledge. Journal of Social History 36(3):701–35.

Mahoney, James

2000   Path Dependence in Historical Sociology. Theory and Society 29:507–48.

Mallios, Seth

2006   The Deadly Politics of Giving: Exchange and Violence at Ajacan, Roanoke, and Jamestown. Tuscaloosa: University of Alabama Press.

Mancall, Peter C.

2007   Hakluyt's Promise: An Elizabethan's Obsession for an English America. New Haven, CT: Yale University Press.

Mandrini, Raul

1983   Argentina Indaigena: Los aboraigenes a la llegada de los españoles. Buenos Aires: Biblioteca del Docente.

Mansilla, Lucio V.

[1870] An Expedition to the Ranquel Indians. Mark McCaffrey, trans. Austin:
1997   University of Texas Press.

Martin, Ann Smart

1996   The Context for Choice in the Material World of Backcountry Consumerism. *In* Historical Archaeology and the Study of American Culture. Lu Ann De Cunzo and Bernard L. Herman, eds. Pp. 71–102. Winterthur, DE: Winterthur Museum.

Mason, Ronald J.

2000   Archaeology and Native American Oral Traditions. American Antiquity 65(2):239–66.

Mayo, Carlos, A.

1985   Fuentes para la historia de la frontera: Declaraciones de cautivos. Mar del Plata, Argentina: Universidad Nacional del Mara del Plata.

1995   Estancia y sociedad en la Pampa, 1740–1820. Buenos Aires: Editorial Biblos.

REFERENCES

McAdam, Doug

2001   Harmonizing the Voices: Thematic Continuity across the Chapters. *In* Silence and Voice in the Study of Contentious Politics. Ronald R. Aminzade, Jack A. Goldstone, Doug McAdam, Elizabeth J. Perry, William H. Sewell, Jr., Sidney Tarrow, and Charles Tilly, eds. Pp. 222-40. New York: Cambridge University Press.

2003   Beyond Structural Analysis: Toward a More Dynamic Understanding of Social Movements. *In* Social Movements and Networks: Relational Approaches to Collective Action. Mario Diani and Doug McAdam, eds. Pp. 281–98. New York: Oxford University Press.

McCracken, Grant

1990   Culture and Consumption: New Approaches to the Symbolic Character of Consumer Goods and Activities. Bloomington: Indiana University Press.

McKendrick, Neil

1982   The Consumer Revolution of Eighteenth-Century England. *In* The Birth of a Consumer Society: The Commercialization of Eighteenth-Century England. Neil McKendrick, John Brewer, and J. H. Plumb, eds. Pp. 9–33. Bloomington: Indiana University Press.

Melosh, Barbara

1991   Engendering Culture: Manhood and Womanhood in New Deal Public Art and Theater. Washington, DC: Smithsonian Institution Press.

Meyerowitz, Eva L. R.

1952a   Review of *Sao Jorge da Mina* by Sylvanus Wartemberg. Africa 22(2):179–80.

1952b   Akan Traditions of Origin. London: Faber and Faber.

Miller, George L.

2000   Telling Time for Archaeologists. With contributions by Patricia Samford, Ellen Shlasko, and Andrew Madsen. Northeast Historical Archaeology 29:1–22.

Miller, Naomi F.

1989   What Mean These Seeds? A Comparative Approach to Archaeological Seed Analysis. Historical Archaeology 23(2):50–59.

Mitchell, W. J. T., ed.

1994   Landscape and Power. Chicago: University of Chicago Press.

Molho, Anthony

1988   Deception and Marriage Strategy in Renaissance Florence: The Case of Women's Ages. Renaissance Quarterly 41(2):193–217.

Molotch, Harvey, William Freudenburg, and Krista E. Paulsen

2000   History Repeats Itself, but How? City Character, Urban Tradition, and the Accomplishment of Place. American Sociological Review 65:791–823.

Moore, Jason

2000   Sugar and the Expansion of the Modern World Economy: Commodity Frontiers, Ecological Transformation, and Industrialization. Review 23(3):409–33.

Moore, Margaret B.

1988 The Laudable Art of Gardening: The Contribution of Salem's George Heussler. Essex Institute Historical Collections 124(2):125–41.

Moratto, Michael J.

1984 California Archaeology. Orlando, FL: Academic Press, Inc.

Moreno Fraginals, Manuel

1976 The Sugarmill: The Socioeconomic Complex of Sugar in Cuba. New York: Monthly Review Press.

1978 El ingenio. 3 vols. Havana: Editorial de Ciencias Sociales.

Muir, Edward

1991 Introduction: Observing Trifles. *In* Microhistory and the Lost People of Europe. Edward Muir and Guido Ruggiero, eds. Eren Branch, trans. Pp. vii–xxviii. Baltimore: Johns Hopkins University Press.

Muir, Edward, and Guido Ruggiero, eds.

1991 Microhistory and the Lost Peoples of Europe. Eren Branch, trans. Baltimore: Johns Hopkins University Press.

Naipaul, V. S.

1969 The Loss of El Dorado. New York: Penguin Books.

Namias, June

1993 White Captives: Gender and Ethnicity on the American Frontier. Chapel Hill: University of North Carolina Press.

Natanson, Nicholas

1992 The Black Image in the New Deal: The Politics of FSA Photography. Knoxville: University of Tennessee Press.

Nylander, Jane

1993 Our Own Snug Fireside: Images of the New England Home, 1750–1860. New York: Charles Scribner's Sons.

Oberg, Michael Leroy

1999 Dominion and Civility: English Imperialism and Native America, 1585–1685. Ithaca, NY: Cornell University Press.

Obeyesekere, Gananath

1992 The Apotheosis of Captain Cook: European Mythmaking in the Pacific. Princeton, NJ: Princeton University Press; Honolulu: Bishop Museum Press.

O'Connor, Francis V.

1986 The Influence of Diego Rivera on the Art of the United States during the 1930s and After. *In* Diego Rivera: A Retrospective. Detroit Institute of the Arts, ed. Pp. 157–83. Detroit: Founders Society, Detroit Institute of the Arts.

Operé, Fernando

2001 Historias de la frontera: El cautiverio en la América hispánica. Buenos Aires: Fondo de Cultura Económica.

Osborn, Sannie Kenton
1997   Death in the Daily Life of the Ross Colony: Mortuary Behavior in Frontier
        Russian America. PhD dissertation, Department of Anthropology, University of
        Wisconsin, Milwaukee.

Oswalt, Robert L.
1964   Kashaya Texts. University of California Publications in Linguistics, vol. 36.
        Berkeley: University of California Press.

Oxford English Dictionary
1971   The Compact Edition of the Oxford English Dictionary, vol. 2. New York:
        Oxford University Press.

Pachter, Henry
1974   Defining and Event: Prolegomenon to Any Future Philosophy of History.
        Social Research 41:439–66.

Parks, Tim
2001   Borges and His Ghosts. New York Review of Books, April 26, 41–45.

Parramore, Thomas C.
2001   The "Lost Colony" Found: A Documentary Perspective. North Carolina
        Historical Review 78(1):67–83.

Pearce, Haywood
1938   New Light on the Roanoke Colony: A Preliminary Examination of a Stone
        Found in Chowan County, North Carolina. Journal of Southern History
        4(2):148–63.

Peeler, David P.
1987   Hope among Us Yet: Social Criticism and Social Solace in Depression America.
        Athens: University of Georgia Press.

Peltonen, Matti
2001   Clues, Margins, and Monads: The Micro-Macro Link in Historical Research.
        History and Theory 40:347–59.

Pendleton, Sally
1990   The Plant Remains from the Spencer-Peirce-Little Kitchen: An Historical
        Ethnobotanical Analysis. MA thesis, Department of Archaeology, Boston
        University.
1992   Plant Remains from the Kitchen Crawlspace. In Beneath the Kitchen Floor.
        Mary C. Beaudry, ed. Not paginated. Archaeology of the Spencer-Peirce-Little
        Farm, Interim Report 3. Boston: Department of Archaeology, Boston
        University.

Pereira Duarte, Pacheco
1967   Esmerado de situ orbis. George H. Kimble, trans. Nendeln, Liechtenstein:
        Kraus Reprint.

Petralia, Giuseppe
2000   Fiscality, Politics and Dominion in Florentine Tuscany at the End of the
        Middle Ages. In Florentine Tuscany: Structures and Practices of Power. William

J. Connell and Andrea Zorzi, eds. Pp. 65–89. Cambridge: Cambridge University Press.

Polletta, Francesca

2002   Freedom Is an Endless Meeting: Democracy in American Social Movements. Chicago: University of Chicago Press.

Polletta, Francesca, and Ed Amenta

2001   Second That Emotion? Lessons from Once-Novel Concepts in Social Movement Research. *In* Passionate Politics: Emotions and Social Movements. Jeff Goodwin, James M. Jasper, and Francesca Polletta, eds. Pp. 303–16. Chicago: University of Chicago Press.

Porter, Kenneth Wiggins

1937   The Jacksons and the Lees: Two Generations of Massachusetts Merchants, 1765–1844, vol. 1. Cambridge, MA: Harvard University Press.

Posnansky, Merrick

1987   Prelude to Akan Civilization. *In* The Golden Stool: Studies of the Asante Center and Periphery. E. Schildkrout, ed. Pp. 14–22. New York: American Museum of Natural History.

Praetzellis, Mary, and Adrian Praetzellis

1989   Archaeological Biography: A Method for Interpreting Women's History. Paper presented at the 22nd annual meeting of the Society for Historical Archaeology, Baltimore, Maryland.

Pred, Allan

1981   Production, Family, and Free-Time Projects: A Time-Geographic Perspective on the Individual and Societal Change in Nineteenth-Century U.S. Cities. Journal of Historical Geography 7:3–36.

1984   Place as Historically Contingent Process: Structuration and the Time-Geography of Becoming Places. Annals of the Association of American Geographers 74:279–97.

1985   Presidential Address: Interpenetrating Processes: Human Agency and the Becoming of Regional Spatial and Social Processes. Papers of the Regional Science Association 57:7–17.

Preston, Paul

1994   Franco. New York: Basic Books.

Purser, Margaret

1992   Oral History and Historical Archaeology. *In* Text-Aided Archaeology. B. J. Little, ed. Pp. 25–35. Boca Raton, FL: CRC Press.

Putnam, Oliver

1794–   Account Book of Oliver Putnam. Manuscript Collection, James Duncan Phillips
1800   Library, Peabody Essex Museum, Salem, Massachusetts.

Quinn, David Beers

1949   Raleigh and the British Empire. New York: Macmillan.

1984   The Lost Colonists: Their Fortune and Probable Fate. Raleigh, NC: Division of Archives and History, Department of Cultural Resources.

[1955]   The Roanoke Voyages. 2 vols. New York: Dover.
1991

Reid, Andrew M., and Paul J. Lane

2004   African Historical Archaeologies: An Introductory Consideration of Scope and Potential. *In* African Historical Archaeologies. A. M. Reid and P. J. Lane, eds. Pp. 1–32. New York: Kluwer Academic/Plenum Publishers.

Repetti, Emanuele

[1839]   Dizionario geografico fisico, storico della Toscana, contenente la descrizione
1969   di tutti i luoghi del Granducato, Ducato di Lucca, Garfagnana e Lunigiana, vol. 3. Rome: Multigrafica Editrice.

Restall, Matthew

1997   The Maya World: Yucatec Culture and Society, 1550–1850. Stanford, CA: Stanford University Press.

1998   Maya Conquistador. Boston: Beacon Press.

Revel, Jacques

1995   Microanalysis and the Construction of the Social. *In* Histories: French Constructions of the Past. Jacques Revel and Lynn Hunt, eds. Pp. 492–502. New York: New Press.

Revel, Jacques, ed.

1996   Jeux d'échelles: La micro-analyse à l'expérience. Paris: Gallimard.

Rhomberg, Christopher

2004   No There There: Race, Class, and Political Community in Oakland. Berkeley: University of California Press.

Ricoeur, Paul

1979   The Model of the Text: Meaningful Action Considered as a Text. *In* Interpretive Social Science: A Reader. Paul Rabinow and William M. Sullivan, eds. Pp. 73–101. Berkeley: University of California Press.

Riess, Suzanne

1968   Dorothea Lange: The Making of a Documentary Photographer. Transcript of interviews, Berkeley: University of California Regional Oral History Office.

Rigol, Jorge

1982   Apuntes sobre al pintura y el grabado en Cuba: De los origins à 1927. Havana: Editorial Letras Cubanas.

Roberts, Daniel G., and David Barrett

1984   Nightsoil Disposal Practices of the 19th Century and the Origin of Artifacts in Plowzone Proveniences. Historical Archaeology 18(1):108–15.

Rock, David

1985   Argentina, 1516–1987: From Spanish Colonization to Alfonsín. Berkeley: University of California Press.

Rodrigo, J.
2003   Los campos de concentración franquistas: Entre la historia y la memoria. Madrid: Siete Mares.

Rosenzweig, Roy, and Barbara Melosh
1990   Government and the Arts: Voices from the New Deal Era. Journal of American History 77(2):596–608.

Rountree, Helen C.
1990   Pocahontas's People: The Powhatan Indians of Virginia through Four Centuries. Norman: University of Oklahoma Press.

Rountree, Helen C., and E. Randolph Turner III
2002   Before and After Jamestown: Virginia's Powhatans and Their Predecessors. Gainesville: University Press of Florida.

Russell, Thomas J.
1982   A Long, Deep Furrow: Three Centuries of Farming in New England. Hanover, NH: University Press of New England.

Sabean, David Warren
1984   Power in the Blood: Popular Culture and Village Discourse in Early Modern Germany. Cambridge: Cambridge University Press.

Sahlins, Marshall
1981   Historical Metaphors and Mythical Realities: Structure in the Early History of the Sandwich Islands Kingdom. Ann Arbor: University of Michigan Press.
1985   Islands of History. Chicago: University of Chicago Press.
1995   How "Natives" Think: About Captain Cook, For Example. Chicago: University of Chicago Press.

Salem Registry of Probate
1813   Account Sales of Real and Personal Estate on Account of the Estate of Offin Boardman by John Porter Auctioneer on the 20th 22 & 23 April 1813 at Public Auction. Folios 27–29 of unnumbered bound volume in the collections of the Historical Society of Old Newbury, Newburyport, Massachusetts.

Sarmiento, Domingo F.
1998   Facundo: Or, Civilization and Barbarism. New York: Penguin Books.
[1868]

Saxton, Alexander
1971   The Indispensable Enemy: Labor and the Anti-Chinese Movement in California. Berkeley: University of California Press.

Scarlett, Timothy J.
1992   Through the Cracks: Artifacts from Three and One-Half Centuries under a Kitchen Floor. In Beneath the Kitchen Floor. Mary C. Beaudry, ed. Not paginated. Archaeology of the Spencer-Peirce-Little Farm, Interim Report 3. Boston: Department of Archaeology, Boston University.

REFERENCES

Schama, Simon
1995   Landscape and Memory. New York: A. A. Knopf.

Schmidt, Peter R.
2006   Historical Archaeology in Africa: Representation, Social Memory, and Oral Traditions. Lanham, MD: Rowman and Littlefield.

Schulte, Regina
1994   The Village in Court: Arson, Infanticide, and Poaching in the Court Records of Upper Bavaria, 1848–1910. New York: Cambridge University Press.

Scott, David
2004   Conscripts of Modernity: The Tragedy of Colonial Enlightenment. Durham, NC: Duke University Press.

Scott, James
1998   Seeing Like a State: How Certain Schemes to Improve the Human Condition Have Failed. New Haven, CT: Yale University Press.

Shackel, Paul A.
1993   Personal Discipline and Material Culture: An Archaeology of Annapolis, Maryland, 1695–1870. Knoxville: University of Tennessee Press.

Shapiro, David, ed.
1973   Social Realism: Art as Weapon. NY: Frederick Ungar.

Shennan, Stephen J., ed.
1989   Archaeological Approaches to Cultural Identity. London: Unwin Hyman.

Shipton, Clifford Kenyon
1975   Nathaniel Tracy. Sibley's Harvard Graduates Volume XVII: 1768–1771. Boston: Massachusetts Historical Commission.

Shumway, Nicholas
1991   The Invention of Argentina. Berkeley: University of California Press.

Simmons, William S.
1992   Of Large Things Remembered: Southern New England Indian Legends of Colonial Encounters. *In* The Art and Mystery of Historical Archaeology: Essays in Honor of James Deetz. A. E. Yentsch and M. C. Beaudry, eds. Pp. 317–29. Boca Raton, FL: CRC Press.

Slatta, Richard
1983   Gauchos and the Vanishing Frontier. Lincoln: University of Nebraska Press.

Smith, Gavin
1999   The Dialectics of History and Will: The Janus Face of Hegemonic Processes. *In* Confronting the Present: Towards a Politically Engaged Anthropology. Oxford: Oxford University Press.

Socolow, Susan Migden
1992   Spanish Captives in Indian Societies: Cultural Contact along the Argentine Frontier, 1600–1835. Hispanic American Historical Review 72(1):73–99.

1998   Women of the Buenos Aires Frontier (or the Gaucho Turned Upside Down). *In*
        Contested Ground: Comparative Frontiers on the Northern and Southern
        Edges of the Spanish Empire. Donna J. Guy and Thomas E. Sheridan, eds. Pp.
        67–82. Tucson: University of Arizona Press.

Sparks, Corey S., and Richard L. Jantz
2003   Changing Times, Changing Faces: Franz Boas's Immigrant Study in Modern
        Perspective. American Anthropologist 105:333–37.

**Stahle, David W., Malcolm K. Cleaveland, Dennis B. Blanton, Matthew D. Therrell,
and David A. Gay**
1998   The Lost Colony and Jamestown Droughts. Science 280:53–63.

Stange, Maren
1986   "Symbols of Ideal Life": Technology, Mass Media, and the FSA Photography
        Project. Prospects 11:81–104.
1989   Symbols of Ideal Life: Social Documentary Photography in America,
        1890–1950. Cambridge: Cambridge University Press.
1991   Mind's Eye, Mind's Truth: FSA Photography Reconsidered. Winterthur
        Portfolio 26(2–3):210–13.

Starr, Paul
1987   The Sociology of Official Statistics. *In* The Politics of Numbers. William Alonso
        and Paul Starr, eds. Pp. 7–57. New York: Russell Sage Foundation.

Stein, Sally
1994   Peculiar Grace: Dorothea Lange and the Testimony of the Body. *In* Dorothea
        Lange: A Visual Life. Elizabeth Partridge, ed. Pp. 57–89. Washington, DC:
        Smithsonian Institution Press.

Stein, Walter J.
1973   California and the Dust Bowl Migration. Westport, CT: Greenwood.

Stick, David
1983   Roanoke Island: The Beginnings of English America. Chapel Hill: University of
        North Carolina Press.

Stoler, Ann, ed.
2006   Haunted by Empire: Geographies of Intimacy in North American History.
        Durham, NC: Duke University Press.

Stoler, Ann, and Carole McGranahan, eds.
2007   Imperial Formations and Their Discontents. Santa Fe, NM: School of American
        Research Press.

Stone, Lawrence
1979   The Revival of Narrative: Reflections on a New Old History. Past and Present
        85:3–24.

Stott, William
1973   Documentary Expression and Thirties America. New York: Oxford University
        Press.

REFERENCES

Stryker, F. Roy

1936–42 Manuscripts, University of Louisville. Copy in Library of Congress, Washington, DC.

1973 In This Proud Land: America 1935–1943 as Seen in the FSA Photographs. Greenwich, CT: New York Graphic Society.

Sullivan, Paul

2004 Xuxub Must Die: The Lost Histories of a Murder on the Yucatán. Pittsburgh: University of Pittsburgh Press.

Thompson, E. P.

1966 The Making of the English Working Class. New York: Vintage.

1975a The Crime of Anonymity. *In* Albion's Fatal Tree: Crime and Society in Eighteenth-Century England. Douglas Hay, Peter Linebaugh, John G. Rule, E. P. Thompson, and Cal Winslow, eds. Pp. 255–309. London: Allen Lane.

1975b Whigs and Hunters: The Origin of the Black Act. New York: Pantheon.

Thompson, Paul

2000 The Voice of the Past: Oral History. Oxford: Oxford University Press.

Thornton, Tamara Plakins

1989 Cultivating Gentlemen: The Meaning of Country Life among the Boston Elite, 1785–1860. New Haven, CT: Yale University Press.

Tilly, Charles

1978 From Mobilization to Revolution. Reading, MA: Addison-Wesley.

1984 Big Structures, Large Processes, Huge Comparisons. New York: Russell Sage Foundation.

1988 Future History. Theory and Society 17:703–12.

Tinnemeyer, Andrea

2006 Identity Politics of the Captivity Narrative after 1848. Lincoln: University of Nebraska Press.

Tonkin, Boyd

1986 "Icons of the Dispossessed": Bert Hardy and the Documentary Photograph. History Workshop Journal 21(1):157–65.

Tracy, Nathaniel

1793 Letter from Nathaniel Tracy, Esq. respecting the Posterity of Daniel Gookin. Extract of a Letter from N. Tracy, Esq. Jan 21, 1793, to a Member of the Historical Society. Collections of the Massachusetts Historical Society for the Year 1793, vol. 2 (1st series):25.

Trouillot, Michel-Rolph

1995 Silencing the Past: Power and the Production of History. Boston: Beacon Press.

Tucker, Alice

1789–90 Journal of Alice Tucker. Historical Society of Old Newbury, Newburyport, Massachusetts.

U.S. Census Bureau

2006   Quick Facts: North Carolina. Electronic document, http://quickfacts.census. gov/qfd/states/37000.html, accessed September 5, 2007.

Van Dantzig, Albert

1980   Forts and Castles of Ghana. Accra, Ghana: Sedco Publishing Limited.

1990   The Akanists: A West African Hansa. *In* West African Economic and Social History. David Henige and T. C. McCaskie, eds. Pp. 205–16. Madison: African Studies Program, University of Wisconsin.

Vansina, Jan

1985   Oral Tradition as History. Madison: University of Wisconsin Press.

1990   Paths in the Rainforests: Toward a History of Political Tradition in Equatorial Africa. Madison: University of Wisconsin Press.

Venegas, Carlos

1966   El libro de los ingenios. *In* Agua, trabajo y azúcar Actas del VI Seminario Internacional de caña de azúcar. Antonio Malpica Cuello, ed. Pp. 87–99. Grenada, Spain: Diputación Provincial de Granada.

Vickers, Daniel

1990   Competency and Competition: Economic Culture in Early America. William and Mary Quarterly 48(3):3–29.

1994   Farmers and Fishermen: Two Centuries of Work in Essex County, Massachusetts, 1630–1850. Chapel Hill: University of North Carolina Press.

Villalobos, Sergio R.

1986   Comercio y contrabando en el Río de la Plata y Chile, 1700–1811. Buenos Aires: EUDEBA.

Villamarin, Juan A., and Judith E. Villamarin

1982   The Concept of Nobility in Colonial Santa Fe de Bogotá. *In* Essays in the Political, Economic and Social History of Colonial Latin America. Kenneth Ackerman, ed. Pp. 125–53. Occasional Papers and Monographs 3. Newark: Latin American Studies Program, University of Delaware.

Vogt, John

1979   Portuguese Rule on the Gold Coast, 1469–1682. Athens: University of Georgia Press.

Wallace, Anthony F. C.

1999   Jefferson and the Indians: The Tragic Fate of the First Americans. Cambridge, MA: Belknap Press of Harvard University Press.

Wallerstein, Immanuel

1974   The Modern World-System. New York: Academic Press.

Walther, Juan Carlos

1973   La conquista del desierto: Síntesis histórica de los principales sucesos ocurridos y operaciones militares realizados en la Pampa y Patagonia, contra los indios, años 1527–1885. Buenos Aires: Biblioteca del Oficial.

REFERENCES

Walton, John
1992   Western Times and Water Wars: State, Culture, and Rebellion in California. Berkeley: University of California Press.
2001   Storied Land: Community and Memory in Monterey. Berkeley: University of California Press.

Ward, W. E. F.
1958   A History of Ghana. London: Allen and Unwin.

Ware, Katherine C.
1991   Photographs of Mexico, 1940. *In* Paul Strand: Essays on His Life and Work. Maren Stange, ed. New York: Aperture.

Wartemberg, J. Sylvanus
1951   Sao Jorge d' El Mina, Premier West African European Settlement: Its Traditions and Customs. Ilfracombe, UK: Stockwell Ltd.

Weber, David J.
2005   Bárbaros: Spaniards and Their Savages in the Age of Enlightenment. New Haven, CT: Yale University Press.

Weber, Max
1978   Economy and Society. Guenther Roth and Claus Wittich, eds. Berkeley: University of California Press.

Wells, Allen
1985   Yucatán's Gilded Age: Haciendas, Henequen, and International Harvester, 1860–1915. Albuquerque: University of New Mexico Press.

Wells, Allen, and Gilbert M. Joseph
1996   Summer of Discontent, Seasons of Upheaval: Elite Politics and Rural Insurgency in Yucatán, 1876–1915. Stanford, CA: Stanford University Press.

White, Richard, and Patricia Nelson Limerick, eds.
1994   The Frontier in American Culture. Berkeley: University of California Press.

White, Robert W.
1991   A Witness for Eleanor Dare: The Final Chapter of a 400 Year Old Mystery. San Francisco: Lexikos.

Wilkie, Laurie A.
2006   Documentary Archaeology. *In* The Cambridge Companion to Historical Archaeology. Dan Hicks and Mary C. Beaudry, eds. Pp. 13–33. Cambridge: Cambridge University Press.

Wilks, Ivor
1962   A Medieval Trade-Route from the Niger to the Gulf of Guinea. Journal of African History 3(2):337–41.
1982   Wangara, Akan and the Portuguese in the Fifteenth and Sixteenth Centuries: The Struggle for Trade. Journal of African History 23(3):463–72.
1993   Forests of Gold: Essays on the Akan and the Kingdom of Asante. Athens: Ohio University Press.

Williams, Raymond

1977   Marxism and Literature. Oxford: Oxford University Press.

Winsor, Justin, ed.

1881   The Memorial History of Boston, Volume III, 1630–1880. Boston: Tichnor and Co.

Winthrop, Robert H.

1991   Dictionary of Concepts in Cultural Anthropology. New York: Greenwood Press.

Wolf, Eric

1966   Peasants. Englewood Cliffs, NJ: Prentice Hall.

Wrangell, F. P. Von

1974   Some Remarks on the Savages on the Northwest Coast of America. The Indians in Upper California. *In* Ethnographic Observations on the Coast Miwok and Pomo by Contre-Admiral F. P. Von Wrangell and P. Kostromitinov of the Russian Colony Ross, 1839. F. Stross and R. Heizer, eds. Pp. 1–6. Berkeley: Archaeological Research Facility, University of California.

Wylie, Alison

1999   Why Should Historical Archaeologists Study Capitalism? The Logic of Question and Answer and the Challenge of Systemic Analysis. *In* Historical Archaeologies of Capitalism. Mark P. Leone and Parker B. Potter Jr., eds. Pp. 23–50. New York: Kluwer Academic/Plenum.

Yarak, Larry

1990   Asante and the Dutch, 1744–1873. Oxford: Oxford University Press.

Zanetti, Oscar, and Alejandro García

1998   Sugar and Railroads: A Cuban History, 1837–1959. Chapel Hill: University of North Carolina Press.

Zuckerman, Michael

1987   Identity in British America: Unease in Eden. *In* Colonial Identity in the Atlantic World, 1500–1800. Nicholas Canny and Anthony Pagden, eds. Pp. 115–57. Princeton, NJ: Princeton University Press.

Zunz, Olivier, ed.

1985   Reliving the Past: The Worlds of Social History. Chapel Hill: University of North Carolina Press.

Index

School for Advanced Research Advanced Seminar Series

PUBLISHED BY SAR PRESS

PUBLISHED BY SAR PRESS

AMERICAN ARRIVALS: ANTHROPOLOGY
ENGAGES THE NEW IMMIGRATION
  Nancy Foner, ed.

VIOLENCE
  Neil L. Whitehead, ed.

LAW & EMPIRE IN THE PACIFIC:
FIJI AND HAWAI'I
  Sally Engle Merry & Donald Brenneis, eds.

ANTHROPOLOGY IN THE MARGINS
OF THE STATE
  Veena Das & Deborah Poole, eds.

PLURALIZING ETHNOGRAPHY: COMPARISON
AND REPRESENTATION IN MAYA CULTURES,
HISTORIES, AND IDENTITIES
  John M. Watanabe & Edward F. Fischer, eds.

THE ARCHAEOLOGY OF COLONIAL
ENCOUNTERS: COMPARATIVE PERSPECTIVES
  Gil J. Stein, ed.

GLOBALIZATION, WATER, & HEALTH:
RESOURCE MANAGEMENT IN TIMES OF
SCARCITY
  Linda Whiteford & Scott Whiteford, eds.

A CATALYST FOR IDEAS: ANTHROPOLOGICAL
ARCHAEOLOGY AND THE LEGACY OF
DOUGLAS W. SCHWARTZ
  Vernon L. Scarborough, ed.

THE ARCHAEOLOGY OF CHACO CANYON: AN
ELEVENTH-CENTURY PUEBLO REGIONAL
CENTER
  Stephen H. Lekson, ed.

COMMUNITY BUILDING IN THE TWENTY-
FIRST CENTURY
  Stanley E. Hyland, ed.

AFRO-ATLANTIC DIALOGUES:
ANTHROPOLOGY IN THE DIASPORA
  Kevin A. Yelvington, ed.

COPÁN: THE HISTORY OF AN ANCIENT MAYA
KINGDOM
  E. Wyllys Andrews & William L. Fash, eds.

THE SEDUCTIONS OF COMMUNITY:
EMANCIPATIONS, OPPRESSIONS, QUANDARIES
  Gerald W. Creed, ed.

THE EVOLUTION OF HUMAN LIFE HISTORY
  Kristen Hawkes & Richard R. Paine, eds.

IMPERIAL FORMATIONS
  *Ann Laura Stoler, Carole McGranahan,
  & Peter C. Perdue, eds.*

THE GENDER OF GLOBALIZATION: WOMEN
NAVIGATING CULTURAL AND ECONOMIC
MARGINALITIES
  Nandini Gunewardena & Ann Kingsolver, eds.

OPENING ARCHAEOLOGY: REPATRIATION'S
IMPACT ON CONTEMPORARY RESEARCH AND
PRACTICE
  Thomas W. Killion, ed.

NEW LANDSCAPES OF INEQUALITY:
NEOLIBERALISM AND THE EROSION OF
DEMOCRACY IN AMERICA
  *Jane L. Collins, Micaela di Leonardo,
  & Brett Williams, eds.*

PUBLISHED BY CAMBRIDGE UNIVERSITY PRESS

THE ANASAZI IN A CHANGING ENVIRONMENT
  George J. Gumerman, ed.

REGIONAL PERSPECTIVES ON THE OLMEC
  Robert J. Sharer & David C. Grove, eds.

THE CHEMISTRY OF PREHISTORIC HUMAN
BONE
  T. Douglas Price, ed.

THE EMERGENCE OF MODERN HUMANS:
BIOCULTURAL ADAPTATIONS IN THE LATER
PLEISTOCENE
  Erik Trinkaus, ed.

THE ANTHROPOLOGY OF WAR
  Jonathan Haas, ed.

THE EVOLUTION OF POLITICAL SYSTEMS
  Steadman Upham, ed.

CLASSIC MAYA POLITICAL HISTORY:
HIEROGLYPHIC AND ARCHAEOLOGICAL
EVIDENCE
  T. Patrick Culbert, ed.

TURKO-PERSIA IN HISTORICAL PERSPECTIVE
  Robert L. Canfield, ed.

CHIEFDOMS: POWER, ECONOMY, AND
IDEOLOGY
  Timothy Earle, ed.

RECONSTRUCTING PREHISTORIC PUEBLO
SOCIETIES
  William A. Longacre, ed.

Participants in the School for Advanced Research advanced seminar "Place, Event, and Narrative Craft: Method and Meaning in Microhistory," Santa Fe, New Mexico, July 6–7, 2004. From left: James Brooks, Richard Maddox, Paul Eiss, Rebecca Jean Emigh, Mary Beaudry, Chris DeCorse, Linda Gordon, Michael Harkin, Kathleen Blee, Dale Tomich, Kent Lightfoot. Not shown: John Walton.